OSAKA

OSAKA

The Merchants' Capital of Early Modern Japan

Edited by
James L. McClain
and Wakita Osamu

Cornell University Press

ITHACA AND LONDON

Copyright © 1999 by Cornell University

All rights reserved. Except for brief quotations in a review, this book, or parts thereof, must not be reproduced in any form without permission in writing from the publisher. For information, address Cornell University Press, Sage House, 512 East State Street, Ithaca, New York 14850.

First published 1999 by Cornell University Press

Printed in the United States of America

Library of Congress Cataloging-in-Publication Data

Osaka, the merchants' capital of early modern Japan / edited by James
  L. McClain and Wakita Osamu.
    p. cm.
  Includes indexes.
  ISBN 0-8014-3630-3 (cloth : alk. paper)
  1. Osaka Region (Japan)—History.   I. McClain, James L., 1944–
II. Wakita, Osamu, 1931– .
DS897.08140837   1999
952'.1834—DC21   98-45675

Cornell University Press strives to use environmentally responsible suppliers and materials to the fullest extent possible in the publishing of its books. Such materials include vegetable-based, low-VOC inks and acid-free papers that are recycled, totally chlorine-free, or partly composed of nonwood fibers. Books that bear the logo of the FSC (Forest Stewardship Council) use paper taken from forests that have been inspected and certified as meeting the highest standards for environmental and social responsibility. For further information, visit our website at www.cornellpress.cornell.edu.

Cloth printing   10 9 8 7 6 5 4 3 2 1

海原乃
由多気伎見都都
安之我知流
奈尓波尓等之之波
倍奴倍久於毛保由

Gazing out upon
The vast expansive sea,
I feel I might lose my heart
To this Naniwa of wind-blown reeds,
And pass here years upon years
Man'yōshū, XX, 4362

Contents

List of Maps and Illustrations	ix
List of Tables	xi
Editors' Preface	xiii
Chronology	xvii

1   *Osaka across the Ages* 1
    JAMES L. MCCLAIN AND WAKITA OSAMU

2   *Ports, Markets, and Medieval Urbanism in the Osaka Region* 22
    WAKITA HARUKO

3   *Space, Power, Wealth, and Status in Seventeenth-Century Osaka* 44
    JAMES L. MCCLAIN

4   *Protest and the Tactics of Direct Remonstration: Osaka's Merchants Make Their Voices Heard* 80
    UCHIDA KUSUO

5   *Takemoto Gidayū and the Individualistic Spirit of Osaka Theater* 104
    C. ANDREW GERSTLE

6   The Five Men of Naniwa: Gang Violence and
    Popular Culture in Genroku Osaka   125
    GARY P. LEUPP

7   Osaka's Brotherhood of Mendicant Monks   158
    YOSHIDA NOBUYUKI

8   Inari Worship in Early Modern Osaka   180
    NAKAGAWA SUGANE

9   Ambiguous Encounters: Ogata Kōan and Inter-
    national Studies in Late Tokugawa Osaka   213
    TETSUO NAJITA

10 Osaka as a Center of Regional Governance   243
    MURATA MICHIHITO

11 The Distinguishing Characteristics of Osaka's
    Early Modern Urbanism   261
    WAKITA OSAMU

Glossary   273
Contributors   281
Index   285

Maps and Illustrations

Maps

Japan in the early modern era	xxx
The Osaka region in the early modern era	xxxi
The Osaka region in the seventh century	4
Osaka under Toyotomi Hideyoshi	16
Watanabe Port in the medieval period	27
The Osaka region in the medieval period	35
Osaka under Matsudaira Tadaakira	47
Major waterways within Osaka	51
Osaka at the beginning of the eighteenth century	66
Office-residences of Osaka's merchant delegates in 1728	258

Illustrations

Naniwakyō	5
The West Gate at Shitennōji	9
"Ikutama no shōnai, Ōsaka to iu zaisho"	10
The Toyotomi citadel	14
The siege of Osaka Castle	19
An entertainer-prostitute on a riverboat	25
Sengan Turret	54
The office compound of the castle warden	55
The office-residence of a city magistrate	55
The fruit and vegetable market near Tenma Bridge	57
The fish market at Zakoba-chō	58

The rice market at Dōjima	59
A daimyo warehouse	63
Pressing oil from rapeseeds	69
Refining copper	70
The Mitsui (Echigoya) dry goods store	74
Shoppers at Junkei-machi	74
Osaka in 1657	76
Osaka in 1759	77
A prostitution district	78
Performers at Nanba Shinchi	78
The *jōruri* stage at the end of the seventeenth century	106
The *jōruri* stage in the eighteenth century	107
Kaga no Jō	110
Takemoto Gidayū	115
"Bunshichi and His Friends in Crested Outerwear," by Shunshō	149
"The Five Men of Karigane's Gang Strolling in the Licensed Quarter," by Koryūsai	149
Bakin's version of the "real" Five Men of Naniwa	151
The memorial to Bunshichi at the temple Kōzu Shōhōji	153
Bunshichi's confession	157
The Fox Deity at Fushimi Inari Grand Shrine	182
The *kagura* stage at Ikota Shrine	187
Torii marking the entry to the Inari chapel at Ikota Shrine	190
"The Fox Woman Leaving Her Child," by Yoshitoshi	201
Mischief-makers at the Sunamochi Festival	203
Ogata Kōan	214
The Tekijuku	215
The sword-slashed pillar at the Tekijuku	229

Tables

3.1	Canal construction in Osaka	52
3.2	Commodities shipped by Osaka wholesalers, 1714	62
3.3	Osaka's merchant and artisan population	75
4.1	Rice prices as set by Osaka city officials in 1735 and 1736	85
7.1	The exchange of gifts and letters between the Osaka association of mendicant monks and Daizōin in 1852	170
8.1	Veneration of Inari and other popular deities in the Osaka region	205
10.1	Regional levies imposed in Settsu, Kawachi, and Izumi Provinces during the seventeenth century	253
10.2	Regional levies imposed in Settsu, Kawachi, and Izumi Provinces after 1722	255

Editors' Preface

In January 1994, Wakita Osamu invited a group of scholars from Europe, Japan, and the United States to visit Osaka and share their knowledge and ideas about the history of that city. Inspired by the enthusiasm of the debates that took place, Wakita and James L. McClain decided to collaborate on a broader project to result in a collection of scholarly essays about the history of Osaka during the early modern period. A year after the initial roundtable discussions, they hosted a second meeting, in Honolulu, where the experts represented in this volume offered formal presentations of their research. To establish a focal point for that symposium, the organizers asked their fellow participants to direct their attention toward three principal concerns: to provide an overview of the dynamics that resulted in Osaka's emergence as one of Japan's leading cities during the early modern period; to expand our understanding about the distinctive nature of Osaka's urban experience, especially in contrast to Edo and Kyoto, the other conurbations making up Japan's Three Metropoles; and to explore the contributions that Osaka's residents made to political, social, and economic developments across Japan. The scholars who convened in Honolulu addressed those issues in depth, and we present their essays, revised and augmented, in this book.

From the beginning, the editors hoped to produce a volume that would be useful to a wide audience, ranging from persons who are just beginning their exploration of Japanese history to advanced specialists in that country's urban history. With that objective in mind, we asked the translators who rendered the Japanese essays into English to be faithful to the authors' meaning, but we departed from such a strictly literal approach during the editing process. In particular, we added introductory sections to certain chapters, rearranged material so as to present the sequence of evidence and conclusion in a manner that is congenial to non-Japanese readers, and added background information in those instances when an author seemed to be speaking exclusively to the expert reader. In the same spirit of rhetorical expediency, we scrutinized lengthy quotations, which are such a prominent feature of Japanese academic writing, and decided to prune some and paraphrase others. Throughout, our goal has been to advance fluency of expression; we hope that we have intervened as unobtrusively as possible and sacrificed nothing of significance.

We have made certain other adjustments to the text as well. As far as possible, we have supplied in the Index vital dates for all individuals who appear in the narratives. In addition, we generally have interjected brief definitions of persons and events upon their first occurrence, as well as of Japanese terms that do not appear in standard dictionaries such as *Merriam Webster's Collegiate Dictionary* and the *Concise Oxford Dictionary*. Entries in the Glossary provide additional explanation of Japanese terms. Wherever appropriate, we have followed the guidance of the *Kodansha Encyclopedia of Japan* in providing translations of Japanese terms and names. Other reference works that guided the definition of terms, the dating of events, and the reading of personal and place names include *Kokushi daijiten*, *Nihon-shi yōgo jiten*, *Nenpyō: Nihon rekishi* (Chikuma Shobō), and *Nihon rekishi chimei taikei* (Heibonsha).

We have adhered to the Japanese convention of placing surnames before personal names. Furthermore, events generally are dated according to the imperially proclaimed era year and the subsequent month and day of the lunar calendar, with a conversion of the era year to the nearest corresponding Western year. That is, an event occurring in the third lunar month of Genna 4 is cited as taking place in the Third Month of 1618. Since premodern Japanese lunar-based years were not exactly coterminous with Western solar-based years, however, events falling toward the end of a Japanese year might find their equivalent in the following Western year. For instance, the Notification of 1672, a government edict designed to regulate the activities of mendicant monks and cited in Yoshida Nobuyuki's chapter, was issued on the twenty-seventh day of the Eleventh Month, Kanbun 12, a date that converts to January 14, 1673, on the Gregorian calendar. Since Kanbun 12 most closely corresponds to 1672, however, the set of regulations is referred to here as the Notification of 1672.

During the course of this project, we have become vastly indebted to a great many individuals. Our colleagues Jurgis Elisonas, William B. Hauser, Imai Noriko, Imai Shūhei, Miyamoto Mataro, Nishizaka Yasushi, Sone Hiromi, Takaoka Hiroyuki, Tsukada Takashi, and Yokota Fuyuhiko attended one or both of the symposiums, and we are grateful to them for their generous advice and insightful contributions into those proceedings. Gary P. Leupp, Andrea Damon, Kikuko Yamashita, and Akio Yasuhara prepared draft translations of several chapters. It has been a genuine pleasure to work with Roger Haydon, acquisitions editor at Cornell University Press, and we have benefited enormously from his judicious professional advice and patient goodwill from the very beginning of this undertaking. Nancy J. Winemiller skillfully guided the manuscript through the editing process. Murata Michihito and Nakagawa Sugane unselfishly put aside their own work to help gather illustrations and provide guidance concerning the compilation of the Chronology and Glossary. The maps came from the computer of A Michelle. Thanks also are due to Karen Mota and Cherrie Guerzon of the History Department at Brown University for providing administrative support, and to Sharon Minichiello of the University of Hawaii, who graciously gave her time to help us make arrangements for our meeting in Honolulu. Andrew F. Bell, Lisa E. Hartmann, Kai-lin

Hsu, and Anne and Kathryn McClain assisted in preparing the manuscript for publication.

Finally, we are grateful to the Kaitokudō Tomo no Kai, the Kaitokudō Kinenkai, and the Faculty of Letters of Osaka University for the financial support that made possible the symposium in Osaka; we also acknowledge the further assistance of the Ōsaka-fu Kyōiku Iinkai, the Ōsaka-shi Kyōiku Iinkai, and the governments of Osaka city and Osaka Municipal Prefectural. Generous grants from the Japan Foundation and the National Endowment for the Humanities enabled us to meet again in Hawaii and to bring the project to completion.

To all the organizations and individuals who helped make this book possible, we doff our caps and offer our profound thanks.

JAMES L. MCCLAIN and WAKITA OSAMU

Providence and Kyoto

Chronology

Era Names during the Early Modern Period

Keichō	1596–1615	Genroku	1688–1704	Kansei	1789–1801
Genna	1615–1624	Hōei	1704–1711	Kyōwa	1801–1804
Kan'ei	1624–1644	Shōtoku	1711–1716	Bunka	1804–1818
Shōhō	1644–1648	Kyōhō	1716–1736	Bunsei	1818–1830
Keian	1648–1652	Genbun	1736–1741	Tenpō	1830–1844
Jōō	1652–1655	Kanpō	1741–1744	Kōka	1844–1848
Meireki	1655–1658	Enkyō	1744–1748	Kaei	1848–1854
Manji	1658–1661	Kan'en	1748–1751	Ansei	1854–1860
Kanbun	1661–1673	Hōreki	1751–1764	Man'en	1860–1861
Enpō	1673–1681	Meiwa	1764–1772	Bunkyū	1861–1864
Tenna	1681–1684	An'ei	1772–1781	Genji	1864–1865
Jōkyō	1684–1688	Tenmei	1781–1789	Keiō	1865–1868

663 BC (Jōmon epoch)
  According to an account in the *Nihon shoki*, the legendary founder of the imperial line, Jimmu, steps ashore at Nami-haya ("swift waves")

313 AD (First Year in the reign of Nintoku)
  Nintoku, head of the Yamato line, builds his famous Takatsu Palace (Takatsu no Miya) at Naniwa according to the *Nihon shiki*, although most scholars prefer to place the event at the turn of the fifth century—First Month, third day

512 (Sixth Year in the reign of Keitai)
  Envoys from the Korean kingdom of Kudara (Paekche) stop at Naniwa

593 (Second Year in the reign of Suiko)
  Shōtoku Taishi is said to have ordered the construction of the temple Shitennōji

608 (Seventeenth Year in the reign of Suiko)
  An official delegation from Sui China arrives at Naniwa and lodges in a new residence constructed especially for the visit

620 (Twenty-ninth Year in the reign of Suiko)
: The Yamato Court builds residences and meeting halls for the comfort of envoys traveling to Japan from Kudara, Shiragi (Silla), and Kōkuri (Koguryŏ)

645 (Taika 1)
: The Taika coup d'état occurs—Sixth Month, twelfth day
: The Taika era begins—Sixth Month, nineteenth day
: Emperor Kōtoku locates the new imperial capital at Naniwakyō—Twelfth Month, ninth day

694 (Eighth Year in the reign of Jitō)
: The capital is moved to Fujiwarakyō—Twelfth Month

744 (Tenpyō 16)
: Emperor Shōmu decides to reside at Naniwa—Second Month, twenty-sixth day

745 (Tenpyō 17)
: The capital is moved back to Nara from Naniwa—Fifth Month

785 (Enryaku 4)
: A riparian project opens the Mikuni (Kanzaki) River to shipping, providing a route to Kyoto that bypasses Naniwa

1031 (Chōgen 4)
: Jōtōmon'in, consort of Emperor Ichijō, makes a pilgrimage to the temple Shitennōji and Sumiyoshi Shrine, common destinations for aristocratic pilgrims by this date—Ninth Month

1274 (Bun'ei 11)
: The *Ippen Shōnin eden* pictures Ippen visiting the temple Shitennōji

1289 (Shōō 2)
: A toll station is in operation at Watanabe Port at least by this date

1294 (Einin 2)
: The priest Ninshō constructs two retreats at Shitennōji to minister to the needs of the poor and erects a stone torii at the approach to the West Gate

1467 (Ōnin 1)
: The Ōnin era begins—Third Month, fifth day
: Fighting breaks out in Kyoto between troops of the Eastern and Western alliances, marking the beginning of the Ōnin War—Fifth Month, twenty-sixth day
: Fighting spreads into the Naniwa region as the armies of Hosokawa Mochihisa confront those of Ōuchi Masahiro at Amagasaki—Eighth Month, twenty-third day

1472 (Bunmei 4)
A tax document indicates that merchants at the seaside market of Tennōji dealt in rice, saké, salt, textiles dyed in dark blue and indigo, straw matting, salted fish, paper, foreign merchandise, cast metal goods, bamboo, cloth woven in nearby Kimura village, and various woods

1476 (Bunmei 8)
The shogunate dispatches an embassy to China from Sakai, the first of four missions to be outfitted by merchants of that city

1484 (Bunmei 16)
A city council (*egōshū*) exists in Sakai by at least this date

1496 (Meiō 5)
A wholesaler-distributor at Tennōji receives rights to sell sedge hats in Kyoto and other parts of the Kinai region—Fourth Month, twenty-third day
Rennyo Kenju, eighth head abbot of the Honganji, establishes his retirement chapel "on Ikutama manor, at a place called Osaka"

1499 (Meiō 8)
An entry in the *Daijōin jisha zōjiki* dated the thirteenth day of the Ninth Month states that seven thousand households clustered around the entrance to Shitennōji

1531 (Kyōroku 4)
Hosokawa Harumoto and Miyoshi Motonaga attack Hosokawa Takakuni at Tennōji—Sixth Month, fourth day

1532 (Tenbun 1)
Tenbun era begins—Seventh Month, twenty-ninth day
Rokkaku Sadayori and Nichiren adherents destroy Honganji's temple at Yamashina, and Ishiyama Honganji subsequently becomes the sect's headquarters—Eighth Month, twenty-fourth day

1538 (Tenbun 7)
Ishiyama Honganji negotiates immunity from debt moratoriums and from entry by military governors for its adjacent merchant community and receives the right to levy and apportion land taxes—Seventh Month

1554 (Tenbun 23)
Kennyo Kōsa becomes the Honganji's eleventh abbot—Eighth Month

1562 (Eiroku 5)
Fire destroys two thousand homes in the merchant community at Ishiyama Honganji—First Month, twenty-third day

1564 (Eiroku 7)
: Fire destroys nine hundred homes in the merchant community at Ishiyama Honganji and damages several temple buildings—Twelfth Month, twenty-sixth day

1570 (Genki 1)
: Genki era begins—Fourth Month, twenty-third day
: Fighting breaks out between Oda Nobunaga and the adherents of the True Pure Land sect at Ishiyama Honganji—Ninth Month

1580 (Tenshō 8)
: Oda Nobunaga has an imperial Letter of Advice sent to Ishiyama Honganji urging peace—Third Month, seventeenth day
: Leaders at Ishiyama Honganji agree to lay down their arms and turn over their temple-fortress to Nobunaga—intercalary Third Month, seventh day
: Kyōnyo Kōju surrenders Ishiyama Honganji, which burns to the ground, apparently upon his orders—Eighth Month, second day

1582 (Tenshō 10)
: Oda Nobunaga commits suicide after being attacked by his retainer Akechi Mitsuhide at the temple Honnōji in Kyoto—Sixth Month, second day
: Hideyoshi overcomes Akechi Mitsuhide's forces at the Battle of Yamazaki, assumes the mantle as Nobunaga's successor—Sixth Month, thirteenth day

1583 (Tenshō 11)
: Hideyoshi begins construction of Osaka Castle—Eighth Month, twenty-eighth day (Ninth Month, first day, according to some sources)

1584 (Tenshō 12)
: Hideyoshi formally takes up residence at Osaka Castle—Eighth Month, eighth day

1585 (Tenshō 13)
: Hideyoshi gives land to Honganji so that it may reestablish itself at Osaka—Fifth Month, fourth day

1594 (Bunroku 3)
: Completion of the outer moats, a portion of which later became commonly known as the Higashi Yoko Canal, around Osaka Castle

1597 (Keichō 2)
: A fish market opens at Utsubo-chō, near the northern approach to Kyō Bridge

1598 (Keichō 3)
: Toyotomi Hideyoshi dies—Eighth Month, eighteenth day

1600 (Keichō 5)
  Tokugawa Ieyasu triumphs at the Battle of Sekigahara—Ninth Month, fourteenth and fifteenth days
  Hideyori is reduced to daimyo status with a 657,000-*koku* domain located in Settsu, Kawachi, and Izumi Provinces—Tenth Month, first day

1603 (Keichō 8)
  Ieyasu is appointed as shogun—Second Month, twelfth day
  Sen Hime, the five-year-old granddaughter of Ieyasu, is sent to Osaka to be a consort to Hideyori—Seventh Month, twenty-eighth day

1605 (Keichō 10)
  Hidetada is appointed as shogun, and Ieyasu receives the title of *ōgosho*, retired shogun—Fourth Month, sixteenth day

1614 (Keichō 19)
  The armies of Tokugawa Ieyasu and Hidetada begin the Winter Campaign against Osaka Castle—Eleventh Month, fifteenth day

1615 (Genna 1)
  Tokugawa armies begin the final assault of the Summer Campaign against Osaka Castle—Fifth Month, fifth day
  Tokugawa forces enter Osaka Castle—Fifth Month, seventh day
  Hideyori and his birth mother, Yodogimi (the Lady Asai), commit suicide as Osaka Castle is consumed by fire—Fifth Month, eighth day
  Ieyasu and Hidetada withdraw to Kyoto—Fifth Month, eighth day
  Ieyasu transfers his grandson Matsudaira Tadaakira from his 50,000-*koku* domain in Ise Province to a new 100,000-*koku* domain centered at Osaka—Sixth Month, eighth day
  Hidetada summons various daimyo to Fushimi Castle and issues the thirteen-clause Regulations concerning Military Households (*Buke shohatto*)—Seventh Month, seventh day
  Genna era begins—Seventh Month, thirteenth day
  Ieyasu invites the aristocrats to Nijō Castle and issues the Regulations concerning the Imperial Household and the Aristocracy (*Kinchū narabi ni kuge shohatto*)—Seventh Month, seventeenth day
  Matsudaira authorizes completion of Dōton Canal—Ninth Month, nineteenth day
  The fish market reopens on orders from Matsudaira Tadaakira

1616 (Genna 2)
  Tokugawa Ieyasu dies—Fourth Month, seventeenth day
  A fruit and vegetable market opens on the residential estate of Yodoya Koan

1617 (Genna 3)
  Kikyōya Goroēmon and Kinokuniya Tōzaemon finance construction of Edo Canal

1618 (Genna 4)
- The fish market moves to Kami Uoya-machi

1619 (Genna 5)
- Hidetada arrives at Fushimi Castle, the first stop on his tour of western Japan—Fifth Month, twenty-seventh day
- The shogunate transfers Matsudaira Tadaakira from Osaka to a new domain in Yamato Province—Seventh Month, twenty-second day
- The shogunate removes its garrison from Fushimi Castle, announces that it will directly administer Osaka, and appoints Naitō Nobumasa as the castle warden at Osaka—Eighth Month
- Hidetada visits Osaka, finalizes plans to rebuild the castle—Ninth Month, seventh and eighth days
- The residential quarters for merchants and artisans are divided into the Northern and Southern Precincts, and Hisakai Masatoshi and Shimada Naotoki are appointed as the first Osaka city magistrates—Ninth Month, tenth day
- The shogunate grants monopoly rights to specific shippers to operate *uwani* and tea boats (*chabune*) on the rivers around Osaka—Ninth Month, twenty-sixth day
- Hidetada returns to Edo—Tenth Month, sixth day

1620 (Genna 6)
- Reconstruction of Osaka Castle commences—First Month, eighteenth day
- Hidetada's daughter Kazuko enters the imperial household—Sixth Month, eighteenth day

1622 (Genna 8)
- Wholesalers of salted and dried fish move their operations to the northern fringe of the city

1623 (Genna 9)
- Hidetada departs Edo (Fifth Month, twelfth day) and arrives at Nijō Castle in Kyoto—Sixth Month, eighth day
- Hidetada inspects the progress of construction work on Osaka Castle—Seventh Month, sixth to thirteenth days
- Iemitsu departs Edo (Sixth Month, twenty-eighth day) and arrives at Fushimi Castle—Seventh Month, thirteenth day
- Hidetada retires and Iemitsu is appointed as shogun—Seventh Month, twenty-seventh day
- Iemitsu makes his first visit to Osaka Castle—Eighth Month, nineteenth to twenty-third days
- Iemitsu arrives back in Edo—intercalary Eighth Month, twenty-fourth day
- Hidetada arrives back in Edo—Ninth Month, seventh day
- Hidetada authorizes the rebuilding of Shitennōji
- The shogunate makes first assignment of regular guards (*jōban*)

1626 (Kan'ei 3)
   Yasui Kuhei successfully petitions to open theaters and houses of prostitution on the southern bank of Dōton Canal

1629 (Kan'ei 6)
   Daughter of Kazuko and Go-Mizunoo ascends the throne as Empress Meishō—Eleventh Month, eighth day

1632 (Kan'ei 9)
   Hidetada dies—First Month, twenty-fourth day

1634 (Kan'ei 11)
   Iemitsu makes a grand procession to Kyoto and Osaka—Sixth Month, twentieth day to Eighth Month, twentieth day
   Iemitsu announces exemptions from land taxes for residents of Osaka—Seventh Month, twenty-sixth day
   Residential neighborhoods north of the Ō River are incorporated into Osaka as the Tenma Precinct (Tenmagumi)

1635 (Kan'ei 12)
   Iemitsu augments and reissues the Regulations concerning Military Households—Sixth Month, twenty-first day
   Shogunate announces that the system of alternate attendance and residence (*sankin kōtai*) is to be enforced for all "outside lords" (*tozama daimyō*)—Sixth Month, thirtieth day

1636 (Kan'ei 13)
   The Izumiya (Sumitomo) family opens a copper refinery at Unagidani

1641 (Kan'ei 18)
   The shogunate orders the Dutch trading station transferred from Hirado to the man-made island of Dejima in Nagasaki Harbor, thus completing the so-called national seclusion policy—Fifth Month, ninth day

1642 (Kan'ei 19)
   Shogunate instructs "allied lords" (*fudai daimyō*) to comply with the requirements of the alternate attendance system—Fifth Month, ninth day

1653 (Jōō 2)
   The city's fruit and vegetable market is moved to the northern approach to Tenma Bridge—Seventh Month, thirtieth day

1665 (Kanbun 5)
   The shogunate issues the *Shoshū jiin hatto* (Ordinances regarding the Temples of the Various Sects) to impose greater controls over religious institutions and to prohibit "new interpretations" and "strange doctrines"—Seventh Month, eleventh day

1670 (Kanbun 10)
   The shogunate authorizes ten money changers to form a privileged association to conduct the shogunate's business and oversee the operations of other money changers in Osaka

1672 (Kanbun 12)
   A dispute among the members of the association of mendicant monks results in the promulgation of a seventeen-clause code of behavior—Eleventh Month, twenty-seventh day
   Kawamura Zuiken completes development of coastal shipping routes around Japan

1678 (Enpō 6)
   Kaga no Jō publishes *Takenoko-shū* (A Collection of Bamboo Shoots)

1679 (Enpō 7)
   All wholesalers of fresh fish relocate at Zakoba-chō

1684 (Jōkyō 1)
   Takemoto Gidayū opens his puppet theater on the banks of Dōton Canal—Second Month, first day
   Jōkyō era begins—Second Month, twenty-first day

1685 (Jōkyō 2)
   Kaga no Jō opens a theater in Osaka and publishes *Kotake-shū* (The Little Bamboo Collection), with a preface by Ihara Saikaku

1687 (Jōkyō 4)
   Takemoto Gidayū publishes *Gidayū danmono-shū* (Collection of Jōruri Scenes) outlining his artistic philosophy

1688 (Genroku 1)
   Genroku era begins—Ninth Month, thirtieth day
   Officials open up Dōjima Shinchi for settlement, and in the next decade rice merchants begin to transfer their facilities to the area

1701 (Genroku 14)
   Members of Karigane Bunshichi's gang are involved in a stabbing incident—Sixth Month, sixth day

1702 (Genroku 15)
   Authorities execute Bunshichi and four members of his gang—Eighth Month, twenty-sixth day
   The puppet play *Karigane Bunshichi aki no shimo* (Karigane Bunshichi: Dew of Autumn) debuts at the Okamoto Theater—Ninth Month, ninth day

1703 (Genroku 16)
   Chikamatsu's *Sonezaki shinjū* (The Love Suicides at Sonezaki) debuts at the Takemoto Theater—Fifth Month, seventh day
   Toyotake Wakatayū opens his puppet theater on the banks of Dōton Canal—Seventh Month

1705 (Hōei 2)
The shogunate confiscates the estate and property of the Yodoya family —Fifth Month

1716 (Kyōhō 1)
The Kyōhō era begins on Sixth Month, twenty-sixth day
Yoshimune is appointed shogun and soon launches what become known as the Kyōhō reforms—Eighth Month, thirteenth day

1722 (Kyōhō 7)
The shogunate authorizes 124 shops in Doshō-machi to form a protective association with monopoly rights over imported medicines—Seventh Month, twenty-seventh day
The Osaka city magistrates assume responsibility for administering villages in Settsu, Kawachi, Izumi, and Harima Provinces—Ninth Month, twenty-fourth day

1724 (Kyōhō 9)
Five merchants contribute funds to open the Kaitokudō—Eleventh Month

1733 (Kyōhō 18)
Edo's commoners riot for the first time—First Month, twentieth-sixth day

1735 (Kyōhō 20)
The crisis concerning obligatory rice purchases in Osaka begins as the city magistrates issue a decree setting a floor price for superior-grade rice—Tenth Month, fifth day
As the crisis worsens, the city magistrates order the rice dealers at Dōjima and money changers involved in financing the rice trade to purchase an aggregate total of 130,000 *koku* of rice—Twelfth Month, fifteenth day
The city magistrates direct four individual merchants to lend 3,200 *kanme* of silver to the government—Twelfth Month, nineteenth and twenty-first days

1736 (Genbun 1)
The city magistrates order Osaka's merchant community to purchase, within ninety days, approximately 140,000 *koku* of rice from daimyo warehouses and the shogunate's granaries—Third Month
In response to appeals from Osaka's merchant community, officials agree to reduce the mandated prices for the forthcoming compulsory purchases and to defer payments until the twentieth and twenty-eighth days of the Sixth Month and the eleventh day of the Seventh Month—Fourth Month, third day
Neighborhood elders petition for further reductions in the mandated prices for compulsory purchases—Fourth Month
Genbun era begins—Fourth Month, twenty-eighth day
The city elders announce that they will not accept any further petitions—Sixth Month, sixth day

The crisis of 1736 reaches its climax as more than one thousand representatives from Osaka's merchant community mass in front of the offices of the city magistrates to make direct remonstrations to delay the payments due for the compulsory rice purchases—Sixth Month, eighth day

The crisis recedes as Osaka city officials promise to postpone payments for the compulsory purchases for an additional thirty days—Sixth Month, twentieth-eighth day

1742 (Kanpō 2)
Otokodate itsutsu no Karigane by Takeda Izumo II opens at the Takemoto Theater—Ninth Month

1759 (Hōreki 9)
The residents of a residential quarter on the banks of the Itachi Canal capture a fox and the event becomes the talk of the town

1761 (Hōreki 11)
Fifteen (later twenty-eight) Inari shrines in Osaka become a popular pilgrimage circuit

1765 (Meiwa 2)
Osaka's artisan and merchant population reaches a premodern peak of 423,453 persons

1776 (An'ei 5)
The character of Karigane Bunshichi is given a second persona as Soga no Gorō in the kabuki play *Maki kaesu mikari Soga*, which opens at the Morita Theater in Edo

1789 (Kansei 1)
The Kansei era begins—First Month, twentieth-fifth day
The Sunamochi Festival held at Tamatsukuri Inari Shrine becomes a popular event celebrated by the entire city

1791 (Kansei 3)
An Inari devotional confraternity is active in Ikeda by this year

1801 (Kyōwa 1)
The Kyōwa era begins—Second Month, fifth day
The Inari devotional confraternity active in Ikeda begins to sponsor a local Hatsuuma Festival during the Kyōwa period

1803 (Kyōwa 3)
Takizawa Bakin publishes *Chōsakudō isseki-banashi*, a factual account of Bunshichi and his gang

1805 (Bunka 2)
Uemura Bunrakuken probably opens his playhouse

1809 (Bunka 6)
Officials at Ikota Shrine in Ikeda authorize the construction of an Inari chapel

1811 (Bunka 8)
The Osaka city magistrates issue prohibitions against shamans who preside over "descents of Inari" and engage in other occult practices

1817 (Bunka 14)
The carpenter Mohei conducts a midnight seance at the Inari chapel at Ikota Shrine

1827 (Bunsei 10)
Ōshio Heihachirō begins to investigate Toyoda Mitsugi and other shamans in the Osaka region—First Month

1829 (Bunsei 12)
The shogunate orders investigations of Christian cults
The Christian Incident leads to the conviction of Toyoda Mitsugi and fellow shamans—Twelfth Month

1837 (Tenpō 8)
Ōshio Heihachirō calls on the poor to rise up against the shogunate, and nearly one-quarter of Osaka is destroyed by fire after two days of fighting—Second Month, nineteenth day

1838 (Tenpō 9)
Ogata Kōan opens the Tekijuku

1842 (Tenpō 13)
Ogata Kōan completes portions of his translation of Hufeland's *Enchiridion Medicum* under the title *Fushi keiken ikun* (Practical Instructions of Mr. Fu)

1845 (Kōka 2)
Osaka city magistrates promulgate an ordinance designed to enhance their regulatory powers over "diviners, evangelists, vergers, sisters of Buddha, and begging monks"

1849 (Kaei 2)
Ogata Kōan opens a smallpox vaccination station in Osaka—Eleventh Month

1851 (Kaei 4)
Because of famine conditions, the association of mendicant monks in Osaka has difficulty raising funds through customary mendicancies and asks the patriarchs at Daizōin to reschedule their offerings

1853 (Kaei 6)
Osaka's mendicant monks settle their differences with *yamabushi* concerning the right to undertake surrogate pilgrimages to Konpira Shrine—Fifth Month

1864 (Genji 1)
  Genki period begins—Second Month, twentieth day
  The Tekijuku closes its doors—Eighth Month

1868 (Meiji 1)
  Tokugawa Yoshinobu and his troops retreat from Osaka to Edo by ship—First Month, eighth day
  The Kaitokudō closes its doors
  The Meiji government includes Osaka within the newly created Osaka Municipal Prefecture (Ōsaka-fu)—Fifth Month, second day
  Meiji era begins—Ninth Month, eighth day

OSAKA

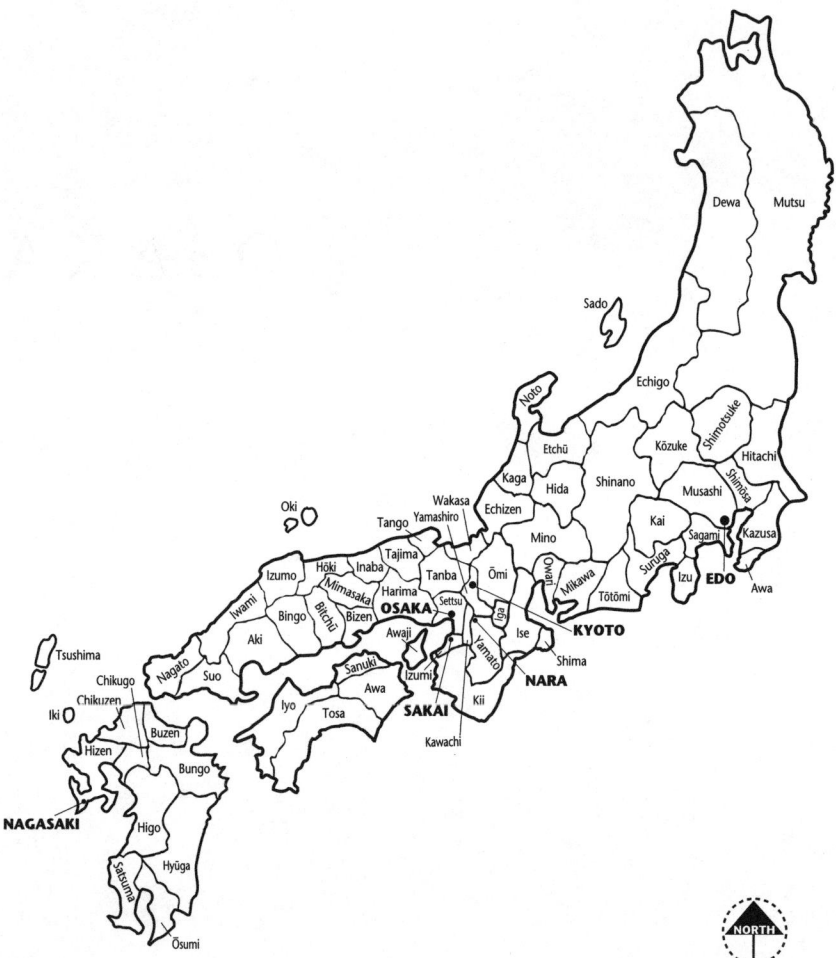

Map 1. Japan in the early modern era

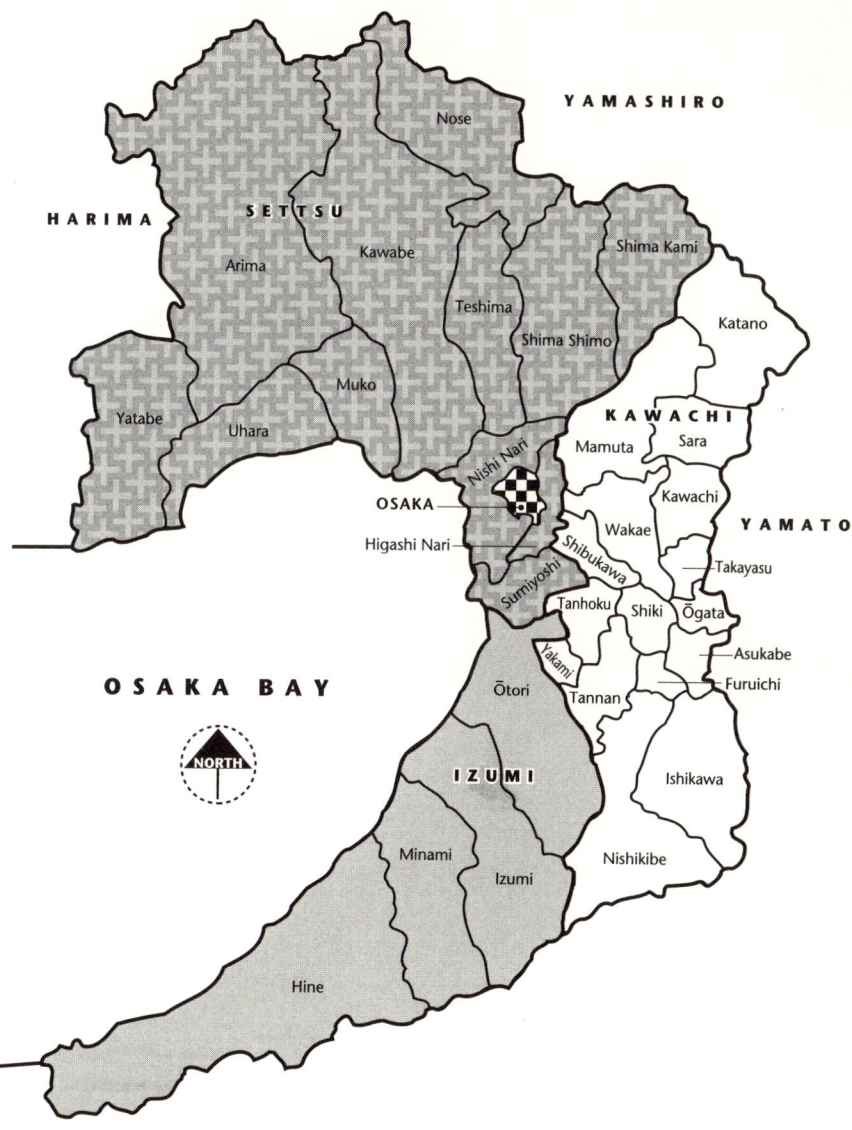

Map 2. The Osaka region in the early modern era

CHAPTER ONE

Osaka across the Ages

— James L. McClain and Wakita Osamu

The first written mention of the Osaka region appears in the *Nihon shoki*, Japan's oldest historical chronicle and conventionally dated to 720 A.D. As set forth in that account, the legendary Jimmu, great-great-grandson of the Sun Goddess Amaterasu Ōmikami, in the seventh century B.C. left his home in Kyūshū on an expedition to bring the Japanese islands under his family's dominion, gradually fought his way up the Inland Sea, and eventually sailed into what later would be named as Osaka Bay, landing his forces on the estuary formed by the Yodo River.[1] The site where Jimmu stepped ashore was known as "swift waves," Nami-haya, a name later rendered as Naniwa and written with a pair of ideographs whose meaning connoted "dangerous waves." Following some initial military setbacks in the Naniwa area, the compilers of the *Nihon shoki* continued, Jimmu called upon divine assistance to help him and his Yamato clan defeat rival local chieftains. Three years later, in 660 B.C. according to the mythology, Jimmu established his headquarters at nearby Kashiwabara, where he was crowned as Japan's first "emperor," and in subsequent years the Yamato Court extended its hegemony over central Japan.

Archeological evidence details a more complicated sequence of events as leading to the Yamato conquest. The recent unearthing of tools, home sites, and skeletal remains indicates that tribal communities inhabited the Osaka area from the most remote eons of the Jōmon era (ca. 10,000–ca. 300 B.C.). The material record further suggests that several waves of migrants from the Asian mainland reached Japan and the Osaka region between 300 B.C. and 250 A.D. and that elites among the newcomers and indigenous Japanese formed themselves into lineage groups (*uji*) which vied for power in central Japan between the late third and fifth centuries A.D. The Yamato line was among those contenders. Scholars debate the clan's origins—some see them as emerging first in central Japan whereas others assign them an ancestral home in Kyūshū or

---

1. *Kokushi taikei*, vol. 1, *Nihon shoki* (Tokyo: Keizai Zasshisha, 1906), *kan* 3, p. 78; for an English translation, see *Nihongi: Chronicles of Japan from the Earliest Times to A.D. 697*, trans. W. G. Aston (Rutland, Vt.: Charles E. Tuttle, 1972), vol. 1, bk. 3, pp. 112–13.

even on the Korean peninsula—but most agree that the family began its final assent to power only in the early sixth century. Using persuasion, intimidation, and military force, the Yamato line at that time asserted its supremacy over the lineage groups of central and western Japan, achieving a status approximating that of *primus inter pares* by the early seventh century.

During its rise to power, the Yamato lineage established no permanent capital or seat of government for itself, perhaps because of strategic concerns, divisive jealousies within the extended clan, or a preference to relocate every generation in order to escape the debilitating pollution associated with death. Indeed, conventional histories relate that between approximately 400 and 645 A.D. some twenty-three successive Yamato chieftains directed clan affairs from thirty-one different settlements. Despite that sort of geographic mobility, the Yamato line went to considerable effort to maintain an ongoing presence at Naniwa during those centuries. According to the *Nihon shoki*, Nintoku reigned from 313 to 399 A.D. and in the spring of the first year of his tenure established his headquarters at Naniwa, where he built his famous Takatsu Palace (Takatsu no Miya).[2]

Scholars view the dates set forth in the *Nihon shoki* with considerable skepticism, and most are inclined to locate Nintoku and his palace-building endeavors at the turn of the fifth century. Whatever the exact chronology, however, Japan's earliest poets venerated the new community at Naniwa:

> Once in the long-gone age,
> So has it ever been told to this day,
> The emperor Nintoku ruled the under-heaven
> From his court in the land of wave-bright Naniwa.
> . . . .
>
> O the imperial palace of Naniwa!
> Hither from all the provinces of the realm
> The tribute ships come,
> A noisy throng like a flight of teal,
> Piloted through the canal,
> Bending their oars upstream
> In the calm of the morning,
> Or plying their poles downstream
> On the evening's flood tide.
> Out beyond the beach are seen
> The fishermen's boats, dotting the sea-plain
> Amid the white waves breaking one upon another.
> They are fishing to provide for the august table.
> O how spacious the view!
> How free and open!
> Well was here established the imperial abode
> From the ages of the gods.

2. *Nihon shoki*, kan 11, p. 194; *Nihongi*, vol. 1, bk. 11, p. 277.

Envoys

The cherry trees are in full bloom
Now, while at the palace by the sea
Of wave-bright Naniwa
Reigns our gracious Empress.

Gazing out upon
The vast expansive sea,
I feel I might lose my heart
To this Naniwa of wind-blown reeds,
And pass here years upon years.[3]

As the poem suggests, the Yamato Court became attracted to Naniwa chiefly because of its prominence as a harbor. Situated at the inner recesses of a magnificent bay and at the terminus of a major river, Naniwa could serve as a convenient port for seaborne and inland waterway traffic. There is no way of knowing the number and size of boats that dropped anchor at Naniwa, but it is likely that the ability of the Yamato lineage to extend the boundaries of its dominance in central Japan owed much to the transport of soldiers and goods through the port.[4] Of equal significance, Naniwa was strategically located to facilitate communication with the Asian mainland. Ancient records suggest, for instance, that envoys from the Korean kingdom of Kudara (Paekche) stopped at Naniwa in 512. Similarly, in 608 an official delegation from Sui China arrived at Naniwa and lodged in a new residence constructed especially for the visit. Some twenty-one years later, in 620, the Yamato Court went to the expense of building residences and meeting halls for the comfort of envoys traveling to Japan from Kudara, Shiragi (Silla), and Kōkuri (Koguryŏ) on the Korean peninsula.

In the middle of the seventh century, the port of Naniwa became Naniwakyō, Japan's first imperial capital. By that time, a leading faction within the Yamato Court had become determined to convert the family head from a chieftain who presided, often precariously, over a loose hierarchy of clans into a true national sovereign who ruled directly over all the people and land of Japan. On the twelfth day of the Sixth Month, 645, the intriguers carried out a bold coup d'état, slew their leading opponents, and on New Year's Day of 646 proclaimed the Taika Reform edict. As elaborated and implemented over the subsequent decades, the Taika Reforms promoted the chief of the Yamato lineage to the position of heavenly sovereign (*tennō*), the term usually translated into

---

3. Kojima Noriyuki, Kinoshita Masatoshi, and Satake Akihiro, comps., *Nihon koten bungaku zenshū*, vol. 5, *Man'yōshū* (Tokyo: Shōgakukan, 1975), pp. 393–95. The poem is dated the thirteenth day of the Second Month, 755. The version presented here is based on *The Man'yōshū*, Nippon Gakujutsu Shinkōkai translation (New York: Columbia University Press, 1965), pp. 174–75.

4. Delmer M. Brown, "The Yamato Kingdom," in John W. Hall et al., gen. eds., *The Cambridge History of Japan*, vol. 1, *Ancient Japan*, ed. Brown (Cambridge: Cambridge University Press, 1993), p. 130.

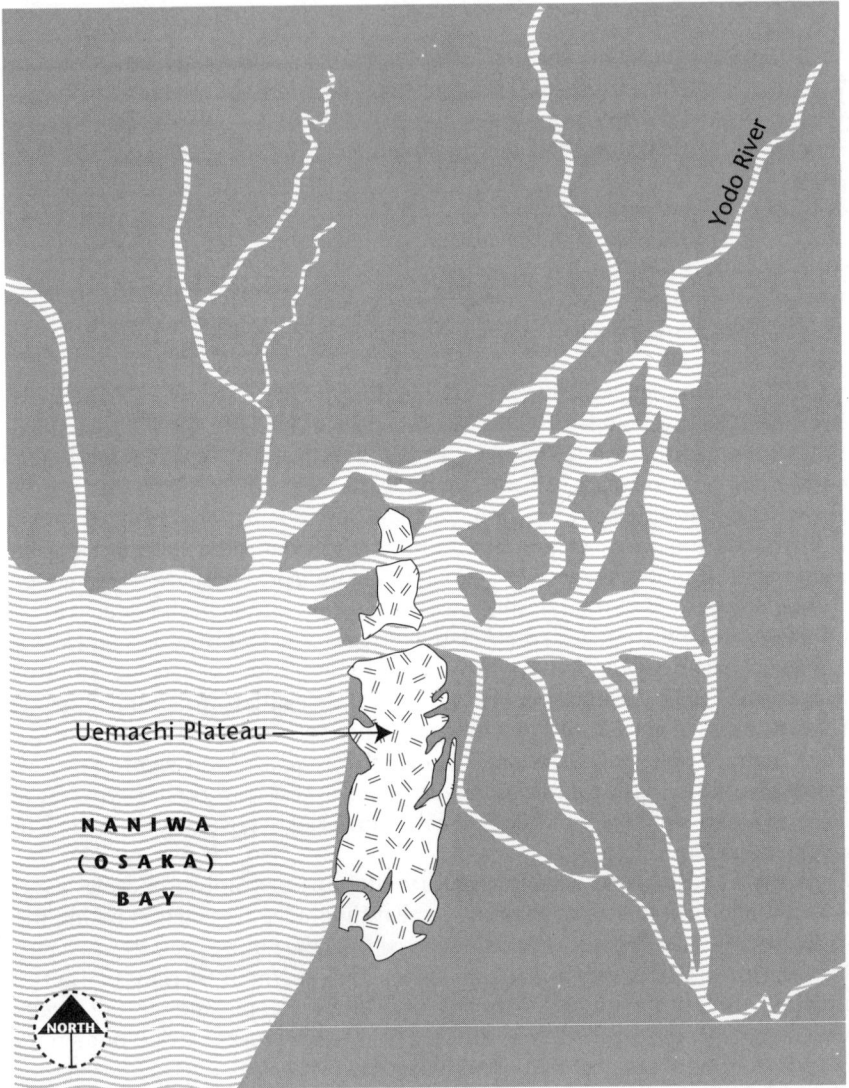

Map 3. The Osaka region in the seventh century

English as emperor; declared that all rice-producing lands belonged to the imperial institution; outlined a complex system for periodically redistributing such lands to peasant families who then became responsible for paying taxes to the sovereign; wrote new civil and criminal codes; called for the establishment of a conscript army; created elaborate central and provincial bureaucracies to serve the imperial will; abolished the old *uji* lineage groups and refashioned loyal supporters into an aristocracy to staff the emperor's bureaucracy; and de-

Naniwakyō. Reprinted from Kikan Ōbayashi 31, *by permission of Ōbayashi Corporation.*

creed the founding an imperial city to house the new emperor and his government and to make manifest the power, prestige, and permanency of the new imperial regime.

As he readied the reform edict for promulgation, Emperor Kōtoku (r. 645–54) designated Naniwa as the seat of imperial government, thus earning the settlement the suffix of *kyō*, or capital. The precise site of the new city was on the Uemachi Plateau, a rise of land adjacent to the Yodo River estuary. Building continued for several years; when completed, Naniwakyō was an imposing settlement, and probably the first community in Japan to be laid out in accordance with Chinese precedents of orthogonal urban design. By the time of Emperor Tenmu (r. 672–86), Naniwakyō consisted of a walled government compound and nearly two hundred "blocks" set aside for the residences of the new aristocracy and for the shops and homes of the merchants, artisans, and service personnel who attended to their needs. In all, the new, rectangular imperial city probably measured some three kilometers by four in extent.

The governing compound at Naniwakyō was arranged along a north-south axis, as was the case with the Chinese prototypes known to the Japanese. Upon completion, admission into the complex was through a series of twelve gateways, whose lacquered red pillars and gabled roofs sat atop impressive raised stone platforms. Eventually, the bureaucrats and officials arrived at the inner Chōdōin, the spacious Office Compound where a great deal of routine government business was conducted, and then, after passing through another gate, entered the Daigokuden, the Great Hall of State where the sovereign presided over state councils. Beyond that was the Dairi, the secluded inner palace containing the emperor's lodgings and the shrines where the "heavenly sovereign," or his official delegate, performed the religious rituals that were such an inherent part of governing. The residential community spread out to the south of the official government compound. It took the shape of a grid, with sixteen broad blocks running north to south and twelve from east to west.

For reasons that are not entirely clear, Empress Jitō (r. 686–97), successor to her late husband Tenmu, decided to relocate the government and its attendant aristocracy at Fujiwarakyō in 694, and Empress Genmei (r. 707–15) moved once again, to Heijōkyō (Nara) in 710. Although built to a larger scale, both of the new capitals followed the design principles that guided the construction of Naniwakyō. The successive emergence of the two new capitals sapped Naniwakyō of much of its vitality, but the settlement remained an important urban center for most of the eighth century. Indeed, in 744 the government even proclaimed that Naniwa once again would become the headquarters of imperial rule. A great deal of building activity ensued, until the crown suddenly canceled the plans and returned the court to Nara in the Eighth Month of the following year. Finally, the government buildings at Naniwakyō fell into ruin at the end of the century when the emperor and his aristocracy settled permanently in Heiankyō (Kyoto).

Despite the decline of Naniwakyō, a port located close to the site of the former imperial capital and two nearby communities emerged as important centers of commerce, trade, and religion during the Heian (794–1185) and Kamakura (1185–1333) periods. As Wakita Haruko explains in the following chapter, the Watanabe warrior clan settled on the Uemachi Plateau not far from the remains of the old imperial city, became the leading figures at a port that went by the name of *Watanabe no tsu*, and dominated ocean shipping and river transportation in the surrounding region (see the map "The Osaka region in the medieval period" in Chapter 2). To the south of that settlement, one *monzen machi*, or a "town in front of the gate," grew up at the approach to Sumiyoshi Shrine and another at the temple complex of Shitennōji, each drawing settlers who catered to the needs of the permanent religious community and visiting pilgrims.

Like Naniwa itself, the Sumiyoshi Shrine faced the sea and sat very close to the shore at the time of its founding. Linkages between the shrine and the Yamato line were especially intimate: Izanagi and Izanami, who counted Amaterasu Ōmikami among their offspring, were credited with giving birth to the main Sumiyoshi deities. Those divinities, in turn, were said to have bestowed "gold and silver lands beyond the sea" to Ōjin, Nintoku's predecessor, while he was still in his mother's womb, and the shrine itself supposedly was constructed on its present site during the reign of Nintoku. Once they were enshrined at Sumiyoshi, the four principal gods were believed to offer security and prosperity to mariners and were deemed capable of insuring the success of any overseas military adventure, thus providing a natural affinity of protection and patronage between the shrine and the Yamato Court, which at the time was struggling to extend its dominance over territories located along the

Inland Sea and which needed to maintain open lines of communication with the Korean peninsula.

Shitennōji's pedigree is scarcely less distinguished. The temple's own documents claim that it was founded by Shōtoku Taishi, the Yamato prince who labored to advance his family's fortunes and introduced Buddhism into Japan. According to the *Nihon shoki*, in 593 (a date that recent archeological discoveries tend to confirm), Shōtoku built the temple to honor the Shitennō, the Four Heavenly Kings, after they helped him achieve victory over his anti-Buddhist foes.[5] Originally, the Four Heavenly Kings were figures within the Hindu pantheon; later they became incorporated into the Buddhist tradition, endowed with unique powers to protect the state according to the sutra *Prajñā pāramitā* (Transcendent Wisdom). In Japan, a tenth-century treatise on the life of Shōtoku Taishi asserts that the statues of the four kings at Shitennōji were installed facing to the west so that they could aid in subjugating foreign enemies, a somewhat ironical embellishment since the exemplar for Shitennōji seems to have been the temple Kunsurisa in Paekche.

By the middle of the Heian period, the temple Shitennōji and Sumiyoshi Shrine had become home to a sizable number of priests and other ecclesiastics and had emerged as important destinations for a growing number of pilgrims. In particular, as Heian's nobility increasingly were drawn to the eschatological concept of *mappō*, the "final days of the Buddhist law," courtiers and members of the imperial family regularly began to visit important religious institutions in central Japan, offering prayers and making supplications in hopes of receiving both divine favors during what might remain of this lifetime and the wonderful promise of rebirth in the Buddhist paradise. At the beginning of the eleventh century such luminaries as Higashi Sanjōin (consort to Emperor En'yū, r. 969–84), Fujiwara no Michinaga, Jōtōmon'in (Michinaga's daughter and the official wife of Emperor Ichijō, r. 986–1011), and Fujiwara no Yorimichi boated down the Yodo River to the port of Watanabe, where they rested at special inns before boarding oxcarts and palanquins for the short trip to Shitennōji and Sumiyoshi.

At Shitennōji the pilgrims held memorial services and recited the Lotus Sutra in the great Main Hall, bowed in reverence to a nearby statue of Shōtoku Taishi, and strolled the grounds chanting *nenbutsu* prayer formulas. Pilgrimage had another side to it, however, for the visitors to Shitennōji also feasted at evening banquets and enjoyed performances by musicians and masked dancers. At Sumiyoshi, the aristocrats continued to mix recreation with pious activities. They paid their respects to the enshrined gods and then adjourned to the pleasure of communal poetry sessions and dinner parties. Many of the pilgrims reverently offered their *waka* poems to the deities at Sumiyoshi, whose new reputations as the patron saints of verse, interestingly enough, had come to supersede their former role as the protectors of mariners and warring seafarers.

---

5. *Nihon shoki*, kan 22, p. 373; *Nihongi*, vol. 2, bk. 22, p. 123.

The growing popularity of Shitennōji and Sumiyoshi drew other visitors as well. In particular, the great variety of religious subgroups who placed their faith in the saving grace of the Amida Buddha tended to congregate around the West Gate to Shitennōji. This entryway was reputed to be an especially propitious place to recite *nenbutsu* prayer formulas in Amida's name since it afforded a fine view of the setting sun across an inlet of Naniwa (Osaka) Bay and thus promoted thoughts about the glory of the Western Paradise. Prominent among the many persons seeking salvation and blessings at the West Gate were the poor, the ill, and the outcast—those who felt most keenly the distress engendered by the upheavals of the late Heian and Kamakura periods. Toward the end of the thirteenth century, the priest Eizon, who already had earned acclaim for his efforts to popularize Buddhist moral precepts, arrived at the West Gate to minister to the needs of the destitute. The priest Ninshō carried out a similar mission, constructing two retreats at Shitennōji in 1294 and erecting what became a well-known stone torii at the approach to the West Gate.

The hustle and bustle of the late Heian and early medieval periods gave rise at Shitennōji and Sumiyoshi to *monzen machi*, commercial settlements at the approaches to the religious precincts where clerics and pilgrims could find the artisans and shopkeepers who made and sold religious paraphernalia and the food, drink, and clothing necessary to daily survival. The first pictorial evidence of a *monzen machi* in the Osaka area can be found in the *Ippen Shōnin eden*, a scroll thought to date to 1274. That work of art illustrates Ippen's journeys across Japan, when the founder of the Timely sect (Jishū) of Pure Land Buddhism preached the importance of reciting the name of the Amida Buddha and instructed his followers on the finer points of the "dancing *nenbutsu*" as a means of expressing the joy of an assured salvation. The *Ippen Shōnin eden* shows Ippen holding forth at the West Gate at Shitennōji, surrounded by a crowd of nuns, aristocratic looking men, and ordinary people. Off to one side linger some beggars, and one can identify clerics, minstrels, carpenters, and stonemasons among the persons making their way to and from the temple grounds.

Written records flesh out that picture. By the fifteenth century a permanent seaside market had affixed itself to the existing *monzen machi*, and the community became known as Tennōji. At that time, the merchants at the Tennōji market sold goods produced locally and in villages along the Inland Sea and also arranged to transship that merchandise to population centers inland. A tax document dated 1472 indicates the merchants at Tennōji dealt in rice, saké, salt, dyed textiles, straw matting, salted fish, paper, cast metal goods, bamboo, and various woods.[6] There are few references to the populations of the settlements at Sumiyoshi and Shitennōji, but an entry dated the thirteenth day of the Ninth Month of 1499 in the *Daijōin jisha zōjiki*, a collection of priestly diaries and temple records, states that seven thousand households clustered around the entrance to Shitennōji.[7]

6. Wakita Osamu, *Kinsei Ōsaka no machi to hito* (Kyoto: Jinbun Shoin, 1986), pp. 16–17.
7. Tsuji Zennosuke, ed., *Daijōin jisha zōjiki*, vol. 12 (Tokyo: Sankyō Shoin, 1964), p. 366.

The West Gate at Shitennōji. Reprinted from Ippen Shōnin eden, *by permission of Chūō Kōronsha.*

Toward the end of the medieval epoch, the Uemachi Plateau became the principal base of operations for the True Pure Land sect (Jōdo Shinshū), a militant, far-flung religious monarchy. In 1496, three years before the compilers of the *Daijōin jisha zōjiki* set down their estimation of the population of Tennōji, Rennyo Kenju established a retirement chapel for himself on a sweeping bend of the Yodo River. As the eighth head abbot of the Honganji, a major branch of the True Pure Land denomination, Rennyo was a religious leader of considerable prestige. It was under his determined leadership that the Honganji, then headquartered at Yamashina outside of Kyoto, took its place as the sect's main center of worship. At the same time, True Pure Land adherents, commonly referred to as constituting the "single-minded" (Ikkō) sect, took over control of extensive portions of the Hokuriku region and emerged as one of the largest and most powerful religious organizations of the late medieval period.

Rennyo established his chapel, according to a contemporary account, "on Ikutama manor, at a place called Osaka" (*Ikutama no shōnai, Ōsaka to iu zaisho*), the first documented use of Osaka as a place name.[8] Recent archeological discoveries suggest that the precise location was on the site of the old imperial city of Naniwakyō, which, because of a changed topography, could then

---

8. "Rennyo Shōnin gobunshō," located in the archives of the Osaka Castle Museum (Ōsaka-jō Tenshukaku).

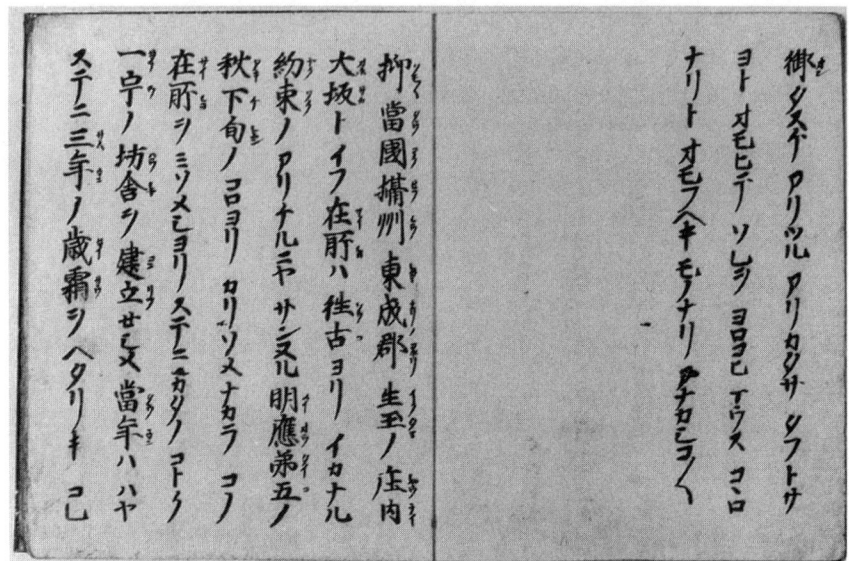

"Ikutama no shōnai, Ōsaka to iu zaisho." From "Rennyo Shōnin gobunshō," by permission of the Osaka Castle Museum (Ōsaka-jō Tenshukaku).

be found just to the south of the confluence of the Yodo and Yamato rivers. Even in retirement, Rennyo commanded a loyal following and considerable resources, and the Ishiyama Chapel soon came to include great prayer halls, spacious residences for monks, and extensive gardens, all surrounded by moats and walls. Tradesmen quickly moved in to serve the needs of the clerics, and by the late 1520s at least six residential neighborhoods had grown up around the religious complex.

Under the leadership of its tenth abbot, Shōnyo Kōkyō, the Honganji sect continued to attract more adherents during the opening decades of the sixteenth century. As centralized political authority collapsed following the onset of the Ōnin War (1467–77), the sect fortified the temple compound at Yamashina and emerged as a mighty religious confederation wielding considerable secular power. Despite Honganji's growing strength, however, in 1532 forces of the warlord Rokkaku Sadayori and militant Nichiren adherents from Kyoto sacked the temple-fortress, and Shōnyo escaped to Ishiyama, which thereupon became the national headquarters for the sect. Quite naturally, the surrounding merchant community experienced a growth spurt: several new residential quarters sprang up during the 1530s; and Kennyo Kōsa, who became Honganji's eleventh abbot in the Eighth Month of 1554, sponsored another round of urban expansion, with carpenters, dyers, woodworkers, and so forth living in specified neighborhoods.

In 1538, not long after Shōnyo arrived at Ishiyama, the prelates negotiated a settlement with the court and the local military governor that made the surrounding merchant community into a *jinaichō*, a "temple town" with immunity from debt moratoriums and from entry by outside military forces. At the same time, the commercial settlement was deemed to be within the official precincts of Ishiyama Honganji, which claimed the right to levy land taxes and to exercise police and judicial affairs within the community. That symbiotic relationship between church and town certainly contributed to the growing prosperity of the merchant quarters, just as the activities of the tradesmen made Ishiyama Honganji a stronger and more self-confident denomination. Unfortunately, there are no extant documents that permit a satisfactory assessment of the population or wealth of the merchant neighborhoods, but as an indication of the affluence of Ishiyama Honganji and the temple town, it is worth noting that rebuilding commenced immediately after a fire destroyed two thousand homes in the First Month of 1562 and again after another conflagration consumed nine hundred residences and some temple buildings in the Twelfth Month of Eiroku 7 (1564).

By the middle of the sixteenth century, more than a dozen similar temple towns, most associated with the Ikkō sect, dotted the countryside in the surrounding provinces of Settsu, Kawachi, and Izumi, generally taken as making up what most historians refer to as the Osaka region. Those religious and commercial redoubts—and none were stronger than the fortified Ishiyama Honganji and its attached merchant community—stood as major obstacles to Oda Nobunaga, the brilliant general who aspired to reunite the fragmented realm and all its wealth under his control. In the First Month of 1570, Nobunaga demanded that Kennyo and his followers abandon Ishiyama Honganji. The prelate turned a cold shoulder to the warlord, and in the Ninth Month Nobunaga launched an offensive against the temple-fortress. The monk-soldiers at Ishiyama Honganji repulsed that attack, but Nobunaga would continue a campaign of attrition for the next several years. In the spring of 1576 Nobunaga's forces pressed their attack against Ishiyama Honganji with renewed urgency and began to overrun outlying communities and religious institutions that were supplying food and munitions to the besieged temple. Fearful that his entire congregation might be massacred, in the spring of 1580 Kennyo agreed to allow Nobunaga's armies to enter Ishiyama Honganji. On the ninth day of the Fourth Month, Kennyo transferred the temple's headquarters to Saginomori in Kii Province and left his son Kyōnyo Kōju to prepare for the surrender. Kyōnyo put off Nobunaga until the fall, finally abandoning Ishiyama Honganji on the second day of the Eighth Month. That evening a fire broke out, apparently set on Kyōnyo's orders, and the conflagration destroyed the entire temple complex and merchant community before burning itself out three days later.

His successful campaign against the Ishiyama Honganji constituted one of Oda Nobunaga's greatest victories, consummated in full soon thereafter when his forces overcame the remaining strongholds of the Ikkō sect in the Hokuriku region. Yet less than two years later, the first of Japan's great unifiers lay dead, ambushed at Kyoto's Honnōji temple by one of his own followers, Akechi Mitsuhide, whose motives never have been fully explicated. By the time of Nobunaga's death in the Sixth Month of 1582, he had extended his sway over more than one-third of Japan's provinces, located mostly in the crucial central heartland, and stood poised to invade daimyo domains in Shikoku and western Japan.

The task of unifying Japan militarily would be completed by Toyotomi Hideyoshi, who had risen through the ranks to became one of Nobunaga's leading generals. At the time of the Honnōji Incident, Hideyoshi was in western Japan, pressing the attack against the Mōri family of daimyo and its allies; quickly he pulled his troops off the line, wheeled toward Kyoto, and eleven days later caught up with Akechi, who ignominiously fell victim to marauding peasants as he tried to escape Hideyoshi's revenge. With Nobunaga's mantle now secure around his shoulders, Hideyoshi subdued his old foe Shibata Katsuie and claimed uncontested dominion over the Hokuriku provinces, drove his armies into Shikoku in 1585, and by 1587 had defeated or secured the submission of all the daimyo on Kyūshū. In 1590–91 Hideyoshi pursued his campaign into eastern Japan, crushing the Go-Hōjō at Odawara in the Seventh Month of 1590 and overcoming all resistance north of the Kantō region the following year. The military reunification of Japan then was complete; all territory either belonged directly to Hideyoshi, who had buttressed his claims to civil authority in 1585 by receiving the title of regent (*kanpaku*) from the emperor, or to daimyo who had sworn fidelity to him.

Caught up in the swirl of nearly continuous warfare, Nobunaga and Hideyoshi inaugurated an era of building grand castles. First at Azuchi and then at Osaka, the two erected enormous, impregnable defensive bastions that served as the administrative headquarters and economic nucleus of their territorial holdings. Nobunaga began construction of Azuchi Castle in 1576; when finished three years later, the stronghold spread across a mountainside and featured a magnificent seven-storied donjon. Sensitive to the rituals and symbols as well as the substance of power, Nobunaga enunciated at Azuchi another tenet of the new castle architecture: a fortress should dazzle with its opulence and aesthetics as well as with its might. Castles were to be built large not just for defensive purposes, but to display the wealth and prestige of the lord and to impress upon his vassals and the general population the hegemon's ability to harness the material and human resources of his realm. They also were to embody refined luxury. At Azuchi, Nobunaga could escort his guests to spacious and richly decorated living quarters and then guide them through the donjon where Kanō Eitoku, one of the leading artists of the day, had lavishly decorated walls, petitions, and sliding papered doors with paintings—landscapes, rocks and trees, birds and flowers, animals real and imagined—that spelled out a different representation of Nobunaga's political aspirations on each of the tower's seven stories.

Some sense of the splendor of Azuchi Castle can be gleaned from the reaction of the Jesuit missionary Luis Frois. "On top of the hill in the middle of the city Nobunaga built his palace and castle, which as regards architecture, strength, wealth, and grandeur may well be compared with the greatest buildings of Europe," Frois wrote. "Inside the walls," he continued, "there are many beautiful and exquisite houses, all of them decorated with gold and so neat and well fashioned that they seem to reach the acme of human elegance. In the middle there is a donjon decorated with designs richly painted in gold and different colors. In a word the whole edifice is beautiful, excellent and brilliant."[9]

Hideyoshi was quick to grasp the utility of Nobunaga's precedents. In 1583 Hideyoshi claimed the Osaka region from the daimyo Ikeda Nobuteru, who had held the territory in fief after the fall of Ishiyama Honganji, and immediately summoned the most famous master builders of the era to his side. Construction of Osaka Castle began at the end of the Eighth Month, 1583, and when completed several years later, it was the greatest and strongest fortress-palace in Japan. The castle measured nearly twelve kilometers in circumference, and it included residences for the most trusted retainers, office compounds, wells for drinking water, and warehouses for food and military provisions, all distributed among several enceintes, each protected by its own internal walls and fortified gates. The enceintes were laid out in maze-like fashion, designed to confuse enemy troops who might penetrate the outer defenses and to shepherd them into confined passageways where hidden defenders could pepper them with musket fire and rain arrows, spears, and boulders upon them. Surrounding the complex were sturdy stone walls, soaring white watchtowers, and broad, meandering moats. The Jesuit Frois, perhaps having exhausted his vocabulary during his earlier visit to Azuchi Castle, contented himself with noting that the new buildings of Osaka Castle "are incomparably finer than those of Azuchi in which Nobunaga displayed his power and magnificence."[10]

Hideyoshi apparently was equally pleased with the grand conception and brilliant execution of his new palatial Osaka Castle. After he formally took up residence on the eighth day of the Eighth Month, 1584, for instance, Hideyoshi personally escorted around the grounds and buildings such powerful lords as Kobayakawa Takakage and Chōsokabe Motochika, who wrote that the grandiose donjon in the main enceinte that served as Hideyoshi's residence "soared upwards for nine stories, nearly reaching the heavens."[11] For Hideyoshi, who relished lavish entertainments and the pretensions of power as much as he did military conquests, the pièce de résistance within his opulent home surely was

---

9. Michael Cooper, ed., *They Came to Japan: An Anthology of European Reports on Japan, 1543–1640* (Berkeley: University of California Press, 1965), p. 134 (quotation modified).

10. Ibid., p. 135 (quotation modified).

11. Fujimoto Atsushi, *Ōsaka-fu no rekishi*, Kenshi shiriizu 27 (Tokyo: Yamakawa Shuppansha, 1969), p. 134. Other reports, notably that by the Shinto priest Yoshida Kanemi in his *Kanemi Kyō ki* (Historiographic Institute, University of Tokyo; Tōkyō Daigaku, Shiryō Hensanjo), claim that the donjon was eight stories high, whereas the screen painting that depicts the Summer Campaign of 1615 (*Ōsaka Natsu no Jin zu-byōbu*) shows a five-storied donjon. The modern reconstruction has five exterior tiers and eight interior floors.

The Toyotomi citadel. From Ōsaka Natsu no Jin zu-byōbu, *by permission of the Osaka Castle Museum.*

his radiant tea room, gilded completely with gold leaf, where Sen no Rikyū, arms merchant and tea master to the overlords, presided over parties meant to awe the daimyo guests who often received, as a treasured memento of the occasion, a selection of the utensils, all crafted from pure gold.

For the great hegemons who presided over the reunification of Japan, castles served as the germination beds for an era of unprecedented urban growth. At Osaka, Hideyoshi encouraged warriors, clerics, merchants, and artisans to move into the area around his citadel; provided each group with a separate residential district, a tactic of social engineering that mirrored his growing preoccupation with creating a society of discrete social estates defined by clear correlates between wealth, prestige, power and status; and encouraged the flowering of commerce and crafts. Across Japan, daimyo did likewise. From Hirosaki to Kanazawa and south to Kagoshima, more than two hundred castle towns emerged between the 1580s and the 1620s, communities that enhanced the lord's authority by symbolizing his ability to project his power and magnificence, control the economy, bend organized religion to his will, and dictate the direction of social change. In that sense, just as Naniwakyō had done for imperial cities nearly a millennium earlier, Osaka represented the prototype for what became an entire category of urban settlement, the castle town.

Of the warriors who gravitated to Osaka, some did so because of Hideyoshi's prodding; others came on their own volition. Hideyoshi's direct vassals were among those who had little choice in the matter, and they tended to be settled within the castle compound or in the immediate shadows of the southern and western ramparts, where they could stand guard against potential invaders. Many daimyo flocked to Osaka in hopes of taking part in the great events that were unfolding at century's end. Important, too, were opportunities for leading warriors to demonstrate their unconditional allegiance to Japan's unifier through ritualized acts of homage and joint participation in tea parties and other social rituals. Consequently, many built palatial residential estates, where they lived during their periodic visits to Osaka and where they voluntarily left consorts and heirs as symbolic hostages testifying to their loyalty to the House of Toyotomi. Thus, before his death in 1584 Tsutsui Junkei had taken up residence in Senba, to the west of the castle, and by the mid-1590s, the powerful Hosokawa, Ukita, Maeda, Nabeshima, Asano, and Hachisuka daimyo families had constructed estates at Tamatsukuri, an important approach to the southeast flank of Osaka Castle; the Date had built just west of Shitennōji and the Kuroda to the north of the confluence of the Yodo and Yamato rivers; and the Ishida and Mōri families could be found nearer to the ocean, downstream on the banks of the Yodo River.

As Hideyoshi settled into Osaka Castle in the 1580s, he also encouraged many of Kyoto's leading Buddhist institutions to transfer their headquarters to Osaka, or at least to establish major branch temples there. To that end, Hideyoshi set aside specific temple districts (*teramachi*). As shown in the map "Osaka under Toyotomi Hideyoshi," one cluster of temple districts was to the north of the confluence of the Yodo and Yamato rivers, in an area known then as Nakajima, and a second cluster occupied Hatchōme, a stretch of land between the southern ramparts of the castle and the temple Shitennōji. Hideyoshi even went so far as to invite Honganji to reestablish itself in Osaka, and in 1585 the prelates moved into new quarters, apparently located between the Nakajima temple district and the Yodo River. Hideyoshi never was entirely successful in making Osaka into Japan's preeminent Buddhist center, but he did establish a similar *teramachi* at Kyoto in 1591, and temple districts could be found in most of Japan's early modern castle towns.

By the time of Hideyoshi's death in 1598, a steady migration of merchants and artisans made Osaka into an exceptionally large city, perhaps second only to Kyoto in all of Japan. Some of those tradesmen, surely including many families who had fled Ishiyama Honganji at the time of its destruction, arrived even before Hideyoshi began construction on Osaka Castle. Frois estimated that some 2,500 merchants had opened up shop by the end of the Eighth Month, 1583, and another contemporary observer, Yoshida Kanemi, noted that mer-

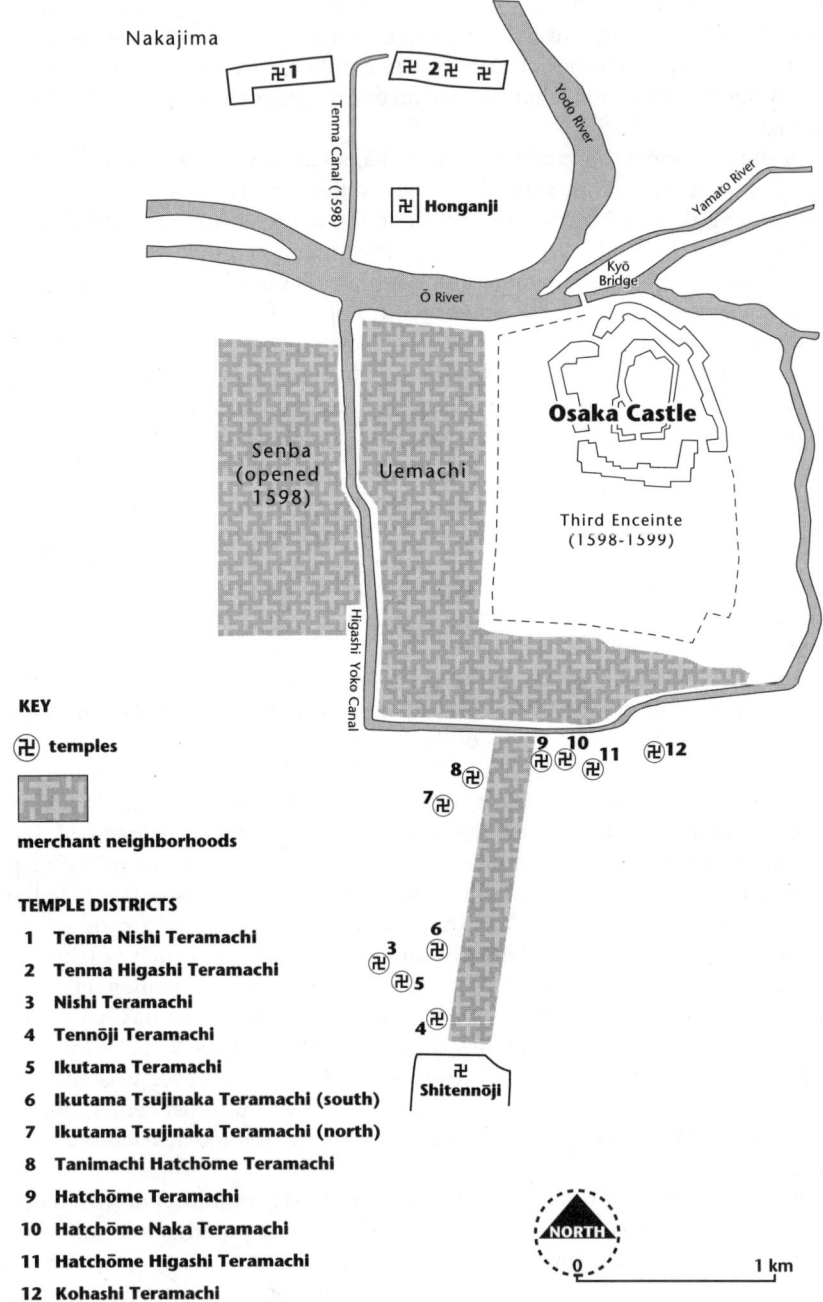

Map 4. Osaka under Toyotomi Hideyoshi

chant housing seemed to stretch from the castle site all the way to the temple Shitennōji.[12] The lure of a growing number of clerical and warrior customers drew many other merchants and artisans into Osaka during the late 1580s and 1590s. Like many other warlords, Hideyoshi intended to capture for his own purposes the vitality and profits of the commercial revolution that was sweeping across Japan, and he provided incentives to encourage additional merchant families to migrate to Osaka through such measures as freeing urban trade from the restrictions enforced through the old medieval guilds and by improving the navigability of the Yodo River. Giving in to his coercive impulses, Hideyoshi even went so far as to compel the members of several residential quarters to move to Osaka en masse from Sakai and Fushimi after a devastating earthquake rocked those two communities in 1596.

A dearth of documentation makes it impossible to know Osaka's exact population in 1598, or even the names of most of its residential quarters. Records do indicate, however, that living in the city were wholesalers who handled goods shipped in from Awa and Tosa Provinces, physicians who dealt in medicines imported from Korea and China, fish retailers who lined the northern approach to Kyō Bridge, and carpenters and laborers who clustered together in their own neighborhoods—men and women, that is, who purveyed the full range of goods and services that one might expect to find in a city of Osaka's size and vitality. Most of those merchant and artisan families lived to the south and east of the castle, although a few had begun to spill over into the Senba area. Hideyoshi dug the Higashi Yoko Canal as a protective moat for the castle in 1594 and, just before his death, announced his intention to add a third enceinte to the castle. In conjunction with those projects, Hideyoshi ordered merchant families to abandon the area set aside for castle expansion. According to some accounts, nearly seventeen thousand merchant households relocated to Senba at that time, a figure that would suggest that Osaka's population at the end of the sixteenth century numbered in the several tens of thousands.

Hideyoshi's death on the eighteenth day of the Eighth Month, 1598, portended the demise of the House of Toyotomi and, ultimately, even the destruction of the merchant community at Osaka. Within months, pretenders to Hideyoshi's incumbency began to indulge their ambitions to compete for national hegemony, and in the autumn of 1600 armies commanded by Tokugawa Ieyasu, last in the line of great unifiers, routed his foes at the Battle of Sekigahara in Mino Province. Shortly thereafter, on the twelfth day of the Second Month of 1603, Ieyasu accepted the title of shogun from the emperor, an acknowledgment of his authority to rule Japan in the name of the sovereign. As Ieyasu maneuvered to consolidate Tokugawa power, he reduced Hideyoshi's son and heir, Hideyori, to the status of a mere daimyo, lord of a domain made up of scattered holdings in Settsu, Kawachi, and Izumi Provinces.

Despite his diminished stature, Hideyori remained a considerable threat to the House of Tokugawa. The young man had at his disposal the resources of a 657,000-*koku* domain, one of the largest in the country; he was entrenched

---

12. Tsuda Hideo, *Ōsaka-fu no rekishi* (Tokyo: Kawade Shobō, 1990), p. 176.

at the greatest fortresses in western Japan; and he stood as a potential rallying point for those who still opposed or remained suspicious of the Tokugawa shogunate. In response, Ieyasu garrisoned nearby Fushimi Castle, stationed a military governor in Kyoto at newly built Nijō Castle, and sent his granddaughter Sen Hime to Osaka to be a consort to Hideyori. Such measures came to naught, however, as thousands of *rōnin*, masterless samurai who had been set adrift after their lords had fallen to Ieyasu, poured into Osaka, an increasingly powerful magnet for those who harbored anti-Tokugawa sentiments. Tension mounted further in the early 1610s as Yodogimi, Hideyori's mother and favorite consort of Hideyoshi, called upon her late husband's allies to help preserve the integrity of the Toyotomi family against the Tokugawa affronts.

For Ieyasu and his son Hidetada, who had succeeded to the position of shogun in 1605, an excuse to move forcefully against Hideyori and Yodogimi appeared in the form of the Shōmei Incident of 1614. Just as Hideyori finished rebuilding a temple in Kyoto in his father's honor that year, Ieyasu's advisors interpreted an inscription on a bell cast especially for the dedication ceremonies as an invocation to overthrow the Tokugawa shogunate. Seizing upon that pretext, Ieyasu and Hidetada marched an army of nearly two hundred thousand troops into Osaka, where they confronted a force of about half that size marshaled at Osaka Castle. Tokugawa forces besieged the fortress beginning on the fifteenth day of the Eleventh Month, and the Winter Campaign ended some forty days later, when Ieyasu negotiated a truce that allowed him to fill in a portion of the moats. That agreement was Hideyori's undoing; Ieyasu launched his Summer Campaign on the fifth day of the Fifth Month, 1615, and overran the citadel after three days of intense fighting. On the afternoon of the eighth, Hideyori and Yodogimi committed suicide in the smoldering ruins of Osaka Castle.

The merchant community of Osaka suffered horribly in the fighting of 1614–15. As he prepared his defenses in 1614, Hideyori torched several residential quarters to create open zones for the benefit of his archers and musket bearers, and soldiers turned the city streets into a bloody battlefield in the summer of 1615. By the time Hideyori ended his life, most merchant and artisan families had fled the city, their homes and shops in total ruin. A generation after the devastation of Ishiyama Honganji, Osaka once again lay in ashes.

During the seventeenth and eighteenth centuries, Osaka rose from those ashes to become one of Japan's, and one of the world's, great cities. Given the strategic and economic importance of the Osaka region, it is not surprising that the Tokugawa family would erect its own castle on the site of the fallen Toyotomi edifice. Osaka's rich urban heritage—its long history as a port, imperial capital, marketing community, religious center, and military citadel—inclined merchant and artisan families to resettle the city and rebuild their shops, homes, and lives. By the 1630s Osaka had reemerged as an important castle town under Tokugawa patronage, and over the next century it would blossom into one of Japan's Three Metropoles. As it did so, the men and women who populated Osaka created a new identity for the city as the country's leading

The siege of Osaka Castle. From Ōsaka Natsu no Jin zu-byōbu, *by permission of the Osaka Castle Museum.*

center of commerce and production, the "merchants' capital" that shared equal standing at the apex of Japan's urban hierarchy with Kyoto, the seat of the imperial court, and with Edo, headquarters for the nation's administrative officialdom.

The individual authors writing in this volume examine various aspects of the history of Osaka during the early modern era. At the center of our collective endeavor is a desire to understand more completely what kind of city Osaka became during the seventeenth, eighteenth, and early nineteenth centuries. Osaka's rebirth owed an obvious debt to the nation's political leadership, which needed a military bastion and administrative outpost in western Japan, and many of the chapters examine how the desires of the Tokugawa shogunate and the efforts of its samurai governors stationed in the city influenced the direction of Osaka's development and the conditions of life within the city. The scholars who have contributed their thoughts to this volume are equally aware, however, that Osaka was populated almost entirely by nonsamurai and that the merchants and artisans, clerics and outcasts, artists and scholars—the entire, dazzling assemblage of men and women, rich and poor, young and old who lived in the city—organized themselves economically, socially, and culturally so as to cope, and sometimes even to prosper, in an environment that did not always treat them well. They, too, shaped the history of the city.

Another hope inspired this attempt to present a mosaic of Osaka life. As scholars, we sensed a need to advance our appreciation of the distinctiveness of Osaka's early modern urbanism. Osaka was one of the Three Metropoles, but it was not Kyoto and it was not Edo. As communities that the shogunate administered directly and as communities that orbited in relatively close proximity to one another within a common cultural universe, the three cities obviously shared certain attributes. But it is important to bear in mind that each conurbation had its own history, its own evolutionary dynamic, and its own population mix. One central purpose of this volume, then, is to call attention to the richness and diversity of urban life in the early modern period by trying to understand better what made Osaka Osaka.

To argue that Japan's Three Metropoles flourished in a shared environment yet matured in disparate ways during the early modern era is to suggest another proposition: that the inhabitants of Osaka forged new economic organizations, cultural ideals, religious habits, and intellectual modes of thought that influenced the lives of people in the surrounding provinces and, indeed, in other communities across Japan. Put somewhat more starkly, to label the years from 1590 to 1868 the "Edo Period," as so often is done, tips the scales of historical attention too much in the favor of that one city and does a disservice to the complexities and nuances of Japan's urban experience. In that regard, most of the chapters in this volume touch on life outside the city as a means of assessing how people elsewhere received the creative energies generated in the urban vortex of Osaka.

As a means of understanding Osaka's transformation into a leading urban center, as well as of comprehending its distinctiveness and contributions to life in Japan, each author represented in this volume takes up a particular theme and relates that topic to broader historiographic issues. Thus, Wakita Haruko begins our inquiry by dealing with the relationship between economic growth and urbanization, analyzing how the emergence of the Osaka region as a significant commercial and marketing center in the medieval era made explicable the city's rapid resurgence in the decades following the catastrophic warfare of 1614–15. James L. McClain and Uchida Kusuo next examine some of the ways in which the merchant community exerted its influence upon the course of Osaka's development and helped to make the city their own during the seventeenth and early eighteenth centuries: McClain by tracing how the relationships among wealth, power, and status etched themselves into Osaka's geography; Uchida by investigating how the merchants used protest and remonstration to advance their political and economic interests.

Later chapters move us into the world of culture, religion, and scholarship. C. Andrew Gerstle and Gary P. Leupp direct our attention to Osaka's performers and artists. Gerstle shows how *jōruri* chanters created new performance ideals and modes of training that contrasted with the world of Edo theater and contributed to the shaping of a particular kind of "Osaka personality," whereas Leupp presents an intriguing look at how a variety of playwrights and print artists converted a gang of mean-spirited thugs and hoodlums into cultural heroes adored by the merchants and artisans of Osaka as well as by common people in other cities throughout the country. Yoshida Nobuyuki offers the first of two chapters on popular religion in Osaka as he tells the story of a small band of mendicant monks who performed as street entertainers even while they ministered to the religious needs of Osaka's merchant families. Another aspect of the urban religious scene comes to life in Nakagawa Sugane's detailed recounting of the activities of a group of shamans and diviners who emerged from the economically marginalized classes at the end of the eighteenth century and beginning of the nineteenth. Tetsuo Najita extends our portrait of life in Osaka in yet another direction as he discusses how Ogata Kōan and the students at his academy, the Tekijuku, helped to advance the study of Western medicine and science in Japan. Murata Michihito's chapter returns us to one of the volume's central themes as he explains how some of Osaka's leading merchants played a role in regional governance, thus providing a new context for assessing the relationship between the rulers and the ruled.

No single volume can hope to explore all dimensions of Osaka's urban experience. The intention of these chapters is to sketch in a few of the missing segments in the incredibly rich mosaic of that city's history, and to do so in a thematic fashion that explores the roles of political elites and ordinary people, elaborates upon the particular qualities that defined the nature of Osaka's urbanism, and spells out some of the ways in which the activities of Osaka's merchants, scholars, puppeteers and priests influenced the beliefs and lives of people in other parts of Japan. To that end, Wakita Osamu brings the volume to a close with an appraisal of the distinctive features of urban life found in Osaka during the early modern era.

CHAPTER TWO

Ports, Markets, and Medieval Urbanism in the Osaka Region

— *Wakita Haruko*

TRANSLATED BY GARY P. LEUPP AND JAMES L. MCCLAIN

Discussions of Osaka's early history typically center either on the ancient imperial capital of Naniwa or on the early modern city which grew up around the castles founded successively by the House of Toyotomi and the Tokugawa shogunate. As a consequence, our knowledge of Osaka during the medieval period is incomplete, our attitude toward those centuries indifferent. Yet, considerably more urban growth took place during the thirteenth through sixteenth centuries than is generally assumed, and several important ports, marketing centers, and commercial towns sprang up in the Osaka region. The appearance of those thriving hubs of production and trade contributed to the burgeoning importance of the Kinai region and gave rise as well to new economic and political relationships between the common people and governing authorities. As merchants and craftspeople settled into the marketing centers and towns of the Osaka region, they formed cooperative organizations, first to manage their commercial endeavors more effectively and rationally, and second to bargain with outside authorities for more autonomous control over the internal affairs of their own communities. The growth of that sort of medieval urbanism and the increasing economic significance of the region are historically important phenomena, and they suggest that Osaka's emergence in the seventeenth century as one of the world's greatest cities was linked intimately to the urban vitality of the middle ages.

NANIWA ŌTSU

As James L. McClain and Wakita Osamu write in their introductory chapter to this volume, the ancient capital of Naniwa was an impressive city. The whitewashed walls that encircled the community, the massive gateways that provided entry into the city proper, and the gridlike pattern of streets and avenues immediately reminded all visitors that this was a planned city, designed to serve the aspirations of imperial government. The inner compound, surrounded by its own handsome walls, contained expansive halls of state and the emperor's personal residence; spread across several dozen acres of the Uemachi Plateau, it was scarcely less inspiring than similar constructions at what would become the more famous capitals of Heijō (Nara) and Heian (Kyoto). Indeed, had Japanese history taken only a few slightly different geographical twists and turns, it is possible to imagine that today's tourist, eager to recapture a vision of Japan's imperial and aristocratic heritage, might well wish to beat a path to Naniwa-Osaka rather than to Heijō-Nara or Heian-Kyoto.

Naniwa's fleeting brilliance as an imperial capital, however, should not be allowed to overshadow completely its significance as a center of commerce and shipping. Several anchorages ringed the shore of Naniwa (later, Osaka) Bay, just a short distance away, and after authorities dug a channel to the sea, Naniwa emerged as a port of national significance. That waterway ran along the course of what later would be known as the Ō River, and its busiest landing, Ōtsu, literally Big Port, is thought to have been close to the site of the Kōrai Bridge in the early modern period, a location that was much closer to the sea in the seventh century than it was in the seventeenth. There, at Ōtsu, stood the storehouses of court officials, alongside those belonging to aristocrats and temples, as well as facilities for the reception of distinguished envoys from the continent. From that royal and commercial hub, the residential quarters for the people who lived and worked in the court city of Naniwa spread southward, reaching toward the temple and shrine complex at Shitennōji.[1]

The port facilities at Naniwa Ōtsu did not diminish in significance during the eighth century, even after Emperor Shōmu (r. 724–49) abandoned the city in 745 so that he could reconsolidate his court at Nara. One reason was that Naniwa Ōtsu constituted an important transshipment center for a variety of commodities bound for the great temple of Tōdaiji at Nara. In 741 Shōmu decreed that the Kegon sect, with financial support from the throne and leading aristocratic houses, build in each province a monastery and convent where priests and nuns could dedicate themselves to praying for the well-being of the state and the atonement of sin. Tōdaiji was to serve as the headquarters for the nationwide network of Kegon temples, and Shōmu spared no expense in demonstrating his patronage for Buddhism. According to Tōdaiji records, between the years 745 and 752 more than 50,000 carpenters, 370,000 metal workers, and 2,000,000 laborers leveled the side of a mountain; forged a colossal

---

1. For additional details, see Yoshida Akira, *Kodai no Naniwa* (Tokyo: Kyōikusha, 1982).

bronze statue of Birushana (Sanskrit: Vairocana), the cosmic form of Buddha; constructed the world's largest wooden building to house the statue; and put up a belfry, sutra repository, two seven-storied pagodas, several impressive entry gates, and spacious monks' quarters. The completion of Tōdaiji made Nara into a major religious center, and priests journeyed from all parts of the Buddhist world to attend its consecration ceremonies.

So that it might maintain its buildings and support the resident monks, the emperor granted to Tōdaiji proprietary rights to several estates (shōen) in the two regions commonly referred to as San'yō (the provinces bordering the Seto Inland Sea from modern-day Hiroshima to the western tip of Honshū) and Nankai (Kii, Awaji, and the four Shikoku provinces). In the latter half of the eighth century, Tōdaiji also acquired Shiragie no Shō, a property located in the Higashi Nari District, along the northern bank of the channel that connected Naniwa Ōtsu with the sea. Agents working on behalf of Tōdaiji collected various goods as annual rent from the temple's holdings in the San'yō and Nankai regions and shipped them through the Inland Sea to Naniwa Ōtsu. Records dated to 783 indicate that several wooden storehouses stood on the Shiragie estate, perhaps as a place to hold those commodities until they, and the levies collected from the peasants on Shiragie no Shō, could be forwarded to Tōdaiji's headquarters at Nara.[2]

Early in the Heian period (794–1185), the city of Naniwa and the landing at Ōtsu began to lose some of their economic vitality, despite the fact that the court acquired part of the Shiragie estate and established a post station there in 783, complete with overnight lodgings and boats and horses for the use of couriers and shippers. However, the waterway that connected Naniwa Ōtsu with the outer harbor gradually silted up with sand and debris deposited by the Yodo River. Moreover, in 785 an ambitious riparian project linked the Yodo and Mikuni (modern Kanzaki) rivers. Consequently, boats arriving from the Inland Sea could enter the Kanzaki River at Kawajiri, easily and safely navigate their way to Eguchi, and then sail up the Yodo River directly to the new capital of Kyoto. As maritime transport between the western provinces and central Japan made increasing use of the Kanzaki-Yodo route, economic activity shifted away from Naniwa toward Eguchi and Kawajiri, as indicated in the records of the prosperous brothels located in those and other riverside towns and in travel diaries such as *Sarashina nikki* (As I Crossed a Bridge of Dreams), whose author was entranced by the eerie appearance of an entertainer-prostitute one evening as her riverboat lay anchored at Takahama, upstream from Eguchi.[3]

    2. Nishioka Toranosuke, *Shōen-shi no kenkyū*, vol. 1 (Tokyo: Iwanami Shoten, 1978), pp. 189–90.
    3. Takeuchi Rizō, ed., *Heian ibun*, vol. 1 (Tokyo: Tōkyōdō, 1964), p. 1; Kawane Yoshiyasu, "Chūsei Watanabe no tsu no keisei katei—Heian jidai no Naniwa," in Naoki Kōjirō Sensei Koki Kinen, ed., *Kodai-shi ronshū*, vol. 2 (Tokyo: Hanawa Shoten, 1989), p. 350; and *Sarashina nikki* in Fujioka Tadaharu et al., comps., *Nihon koten bungaku zenshū*, vol. 18 (Tokyo: Shōgakukan, 1979), p. 354. See also *As I Crossed a Bridge of Dreams: Recollections of a Woman in Eleventh-Century Japan*, trans. Ivan Morris (New York: Dial, 1971), p. 115, for the scene at Takahama.

An entertainer-prostitute on a riverboat. From Hōnen Shōnin eden, *by permission of the Osaka Castle Museum.*

The Emergence of *Watanabe no tsu* in the Heian Period

The shifting economic center of gravity did not leave the Uemachi Plateau a desolate wilderness, since persons who made a living by fishing or by working in some aspect of ocean and river transport continued to live in the region.[4] The emperor's government in Kyoto designated the area around Naniwa, as well as most imperial holdings in Kawachi and Settsu Provinces, as bestowal lands (*mikuriya*), meaning that the people residing there fell under the dominion of the Bureau of Palace Storehouses (*uchitsukura no tsukasa*). That office, as its name implies, was charged with safeguarding government and imperial property, and it collected levies, or "bestowals," of rice, other foodstuffs, and specialty products from persons living within its jurisdiction, whom it also subjected to labor requisitions.

As the authority of the imperial government began to wane in the middle and late Heian period, powerful local families increasingly asserted their own private control over territories that were neither included in the bestowal system nor attached to the proprietary estates claimed by court aristocrats and re-

---

4. Kawane, "Chūsei Watanabe no tsu no keisei katei," p. 361.

ligious institutions.[5] In the area around the former capital at Naniwa, the so-called Watanabe clan, an alliance of several families linked by real and fictive kinship ties, came to wield considerable influence over such lands. Some of the Watanabe leaders originally may have come to the region as estate managers for courtiers or temples. Once those families settled permanently in the Naniwa area, however, they apparently began to shed their identity as agents of Kyoto-based proprietors, drifted away from their assigned duties, and used their positions of local influence to take private possession of land holdings and to gain considerable sway over the supervision of marine transportation.[6]

The Watanabe clan could secure its claims to territory because of its ability to mobilize considerable armed might. For instance, the man honored as the alliance's founder, Watanabe no Tsuna, was hailed as one of Minamoto no Yorimitsu's "Four Heavenly Deities" when that warrior and his younger brother led the Seiwa Genji branch of the Minamoto family to fame and fortune during the latter half of the tenth century and the opening decades of the eleventh by serving as the "claws and teeth" of the powerful imperial regent Fujiwara no Michinaga. Watanabe warriors could also be found fighting with Minamoto no Yorimasa on the side of Emperor Go-Shirakawa in the Hōgen Disturbance of 1156. A generation later, in 1185, the Watanabe clan contributed five ships to the Minamoto cause, and the fifty mounted warriors they conveyed into battle proved to be a decisive factor as Minamoto no Yoshitsune routed the rival Taira family at the Battle of Yashima.[7] Even the famous warrior-turned-priest Mongaku—who in the *Heike monogatari* (The Tale of the Heike) is depicted as securing the edict from Retired Emperor Go-Shirakawa, which enabled Minamoto no Yoritomo to take up arms against the Taira—was a kinsman of the Watanabe clan.[8]

The base of operations for the Watanabe alliance, the "samurai of the sea" as they also were known, was *Watanabe no tsu*, or Watanabe Port, a landing thought to be in the vicinity of the former Naniwa Ōtsu and not far from the locally famous Ikasuri Shrine.[9] From their home anchorage, the Watanabe familial union completely dominated shipping in central Japan. So far-reaching did their operations become that they maintained ties with provincial officials in Settsu and Kawachi, with representatives of Tōdaiji's Tamai no Shō in Yamashiro, and even with local managers on privately held estates as far away as northern Kyūshū.

5. Wakita Haruko, *Nihon chūsei shōgyō hattatsu-shi no kenkyū*, rev. ed. (Tokyo: Ochanomizu Shobō, 1977), pp. 86–126.

6. Kawane, "Chūsei Watanabe no tsu no keisei katei," pp. 361–62; Miura Keiichi, *Chūsei minshū seikatsu-shi no kenkyū* (Kyoto: Shibunkaku Shuppan, 1981), pp. 3–33.

7. See the chapters "Sakaro" and "Katsuura tsuketari Ōzaki goe" from *Heike monogatari*, in Ichiko Teiji, comp., *Nihon koten bungaku zenshū*, vol. 30 (Tokyo: Shōgakukan, 1979), pp. 351–63. For an English translation, see *The Tale of Heike*, trans. Helen Craig McCullough (Stanford: Stanford University Press, 1988), pp. 358–63.

8. "Fukuhara inzen," in *Heike monogatari*, pp. 391–95; *Tale of Heike*, pp. 183–84.

9. For a weighing of the evidence about the location of Watanabe Port, see Shinshū Ōsaka Shishi Hensan Iinkai, ed., *Shinshū: Ōsaka shishi*, vol. 2 (Osaka: Ōsaka-shi, 1988), pp. 8–26, 238–39, 590–91, and Kawane, "Chūsei Watanabe no tsu no keisei katei," pp. 363–67.

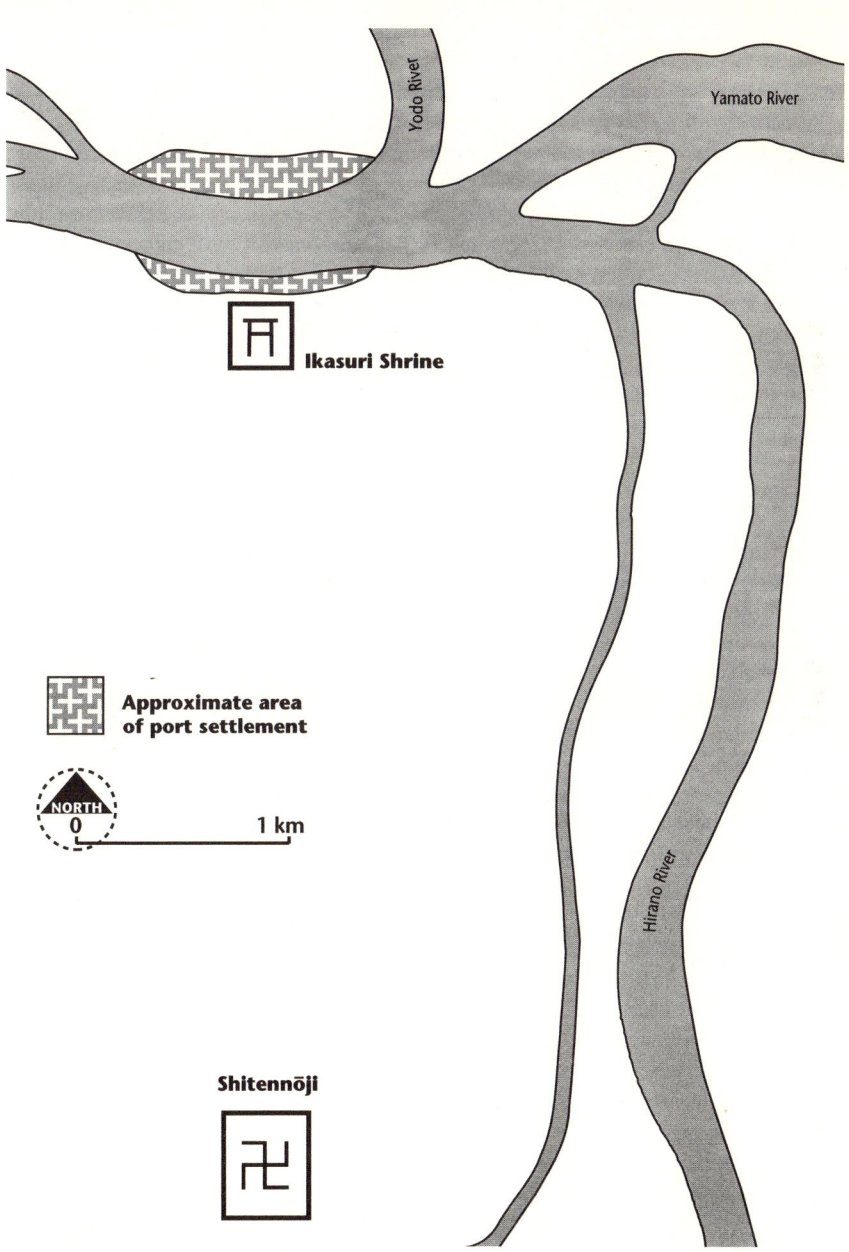

Map 5. Watanabe Port in the medieval period

The Watanabe families enjoyed especially close ties with the temple officials of Tōdaiji, a symbiotic relationship that nurtured economic activity in and around Watanabe Port. After many of Tōdaiji's buildings and its huge statue of Birushana suffered extensive damage during the Genpei Wars (1180–85), the abbot Shunjō Chōgen decided to raise funds to reconstruct Tōdaiji's structures in the style of religious architecture that the monk had observed during a visit to China. This was an enormous project that, like the original construction of Tōdaiji, stretched over several years and involved the procurement of special lumber and building materials from several provinces throughout central and western Japan. During the course of the monk's endeavors, Tōdaiji built at Watanabe Port a sizable two-storied warehouse, some sixteen meters in length along each side, and used it to store lumber delivered from Suō and other provinces before forwarding the timbers and planking to the construction site at Nara.[10]

Extant documents yield little additional information about Chōgen's lumber storehouse at Watanabe landing, or about the property upon which it was sited. We do know, however, that by the late Heian period boats sailing up the Inland Sea with lumber bound for Nara and Kyoto first touched shore somewhat downstream from the anchorage at Watanabe Port, at the mouth of the Kizu River (written, tellingly enough, with the ideographs for lumber and port). Some seventeen lumber storehouses, as well as other properties of high-ranking aristocrats, crowded the banks around the estuary of the Kizu River.[11] In addition, the temples of Tōdaiji and Kōfukuji each owned four *chō* of land there (approximately twelve acres), while Yakushiji and Daianji temples had two *chō* each.[12]

Given the number and density of warehouses at the mouth of the Kizu River, it seems reasonable to conclude that the imperial government, aristocratic families who held estate proprietorships, and major shrines and temples such as Tōdaiji also maintained numerous facilities, perhaps on the scale of two or three *chō* each, along the banks of the channel at Watanabe Port. As the rows of lumber storehouses belonging to influential families and powerful institutions expanded, the Watanabe clan, which itself functioned collectively as a local proprietor with its own landed estates, supervised the many workers engaged in various maritime occupations in the region's harbors. Consequently, in 1235 the Kamakura shogunate assigned the families within the Watanabe alliance the responsibility of overseeing large shipments of tax and tribute goods due the shogunate from the provinces of western and central Japan.[13]

---

10. Kobayashi Takeshi, ed., *Shunjōbō Chōgen shiryō shūsei* (Nara: Nara Kokuritsu Bunkazai Kenkyūjo, 1965), pp. 366–67, 439–40; Tōkyō Teikoku Daigaku, ed. and pub., *Dai Nihon shiryō*, 4–7 (Tokyo, 1908), pp. 140–41; and *Shinshū: Ōsaka shishi*, 2:238–39.

11. *Heian ibun*, vol. 5 (1964), pp. 1800–1803.

12. Wakita Haruko, *Nihon chūsei toshi-ron* (Tokyo: Tōkyō Daigaku Shuppankai, 1981), pp. 74–76, 84–86.

13. Kawane Yoshiyasu, "Kamakura jidai no Settsu kuni Watanabe no tsu," *Jinbun kenkyū* 39:11 (November 1987), pp. 44–45.

Watanabe and the Emergence of Medieval Urbanism

The port at Watanabe underwent a major transformation during the late Heian and Kamakura (1185–1333) periods, evolving from a warehousing and transshipment center into a larger and more densely settled community that offered a wider variety of urban amenities and shipping facilities. Certainly, that sort of transition characterized developments at other ports in central Japan as well. In the Heian period, as noted above, the settlement at the mouth of the Kizu River consisted principally of docking areas, lumberyards, and storehouses belonging to influential families and religious institutions, and it served as the point of arrival for building materials and other goods brought into Yamato Province. Later in the Heian and early Kamakura periods, however, more elaborate facilities capable of supporting a greater volume of shipping already had been brought together on the holdings of the temple Kōfukuji, and in time a more full-fledged urban community would appear at Kizu.[14]

Once again, we can see at work the hand of Tōdaiji's abbot, Shunjō Chōgen. Beginning in 1196, Chōgen directed the development of a better port, protected by stone levees and piers, for oceangoing cargo vessels at Uozumi Harbor in Harima Province. Presumably Chōgen's main purpose was to provide safe anchorages for the boats transporting materials for the reconstruction and future maintenance of Tōdaiji, but he financed the facilities by charging a slight fee to any ship that wished to put in at Uozumi, such as those carrying grain and commodity levies from *shōen* estates in the San'yō and Nankai regions to their proprietors in the capital. Chōgen constructed a similar anchorage at Ōwada in Settsu Province, and provided for signal fires and other aids so that cargo boats could more safely navigate the rocky coast along Settsu Province. Later, in 1230, other shippers even created an artificial island at Kanegamisaki in Chikuzen Province and provided facilities to rescue boats adrift at sea.[15] Those sorts of projects stimulated the construction and improvement of other anchorages and led to the growth of sizable towns not just at Uozumi and Ōwada, but also up and down the coast, at places like Hyōgo and Kanzaki, as well as Kizu.

The lumber storehouses and other facilities established at Watanabe by Chōgen probably did not function as a public harbor in the same manner as the anchorage at Uozumi. That is, the lumberyards and docks at Watanabe Port were not routinely available to all comers; rather, they were located on the grounds of Watanabe (Nagara) Bessho, a branch temple of Tōdaiji. In that sense, the installation at Watanabe existed for the private use of an individual religious institution, and the other landings and storage yards constructed later by functionaries of the imperial government and by powerful aristocratic pro-

---

14. Wakita, *Nihon chūsei toshi-ron*, pp. 74–76, 84–86.
15. Kobayashi, *Shunjōbō Chōgen shiryō shūsei*, pp. 439–40; Takeuchi Rizō, ed., *Kamakura ibun*, vol. 2 (Tokyo: Tōkyōdō, 1972), pp. 188–89, and vol. 6 (1974), p. 211; and Wakita Haruko, "Chūsei no kōtsū • un'yu," in Amakasu Ken et al., eds., *Kōza Nihon gijutsu no shakai-shi*, vol. 8, *Kōtsū • Un'yu* (Tokyo: Nihon Hyōronsha, 1985), p. 110.

prietors at Watanabe Port almost certainly had a similar purpose and character. The closed, exclusive nature of the services provided at Watanabe acted as a natural brake on the settlement's potential growth, and Watanabe, like other river ports, could not evolve into a more fully urbanized entrepôt community until it began to permit more unencumbered usage of its landings, warehouses, and storage yards.

An examination of the collection of fees at toll stations (*sekisho*) can help determine when Watanabe first became an open, public port, charging mooring fees and servicing a large if unspecified number of boats. The earliest documentary evidence of a toll station comes in the year 1289, when Emperor Fushimi (r. 1287–98), usually remembered more for his talents as a calligrapher and poet than for his acts as the sovereign, issued a decree commanding that 1 percent of the fees collected at toll stations at the anchorages of Muro, Amagasaki (formerly Kawajiri), and Watanabe be used to repair the facilities at Uozumi.[16] Such tolls provided a source of income for the imperial court and often were levied for the shared purpose of underwriting renovations at major shrines and temples. Consequently, authorities established barriers at transportation nodes along well-traveled major roads and shipping routes where carriers made such handsome profits that they came to have an almost inexhaustible patience for paying tolls.[17] That was especially the case during the Muromachi period (1333–1568), when contemporary expressions such as "the six hundred toll stations of Kawachi Province" and the "six hundred barriers of Yodogawa Kawakami" indicate how extreme matters had become.

The purely mercenary aspect of toll collection cannot be denied. But it is important to remember that when many toll stations originally were opened, as at Muro and Amagasaki, the chief purpose was to collect users' fees from travelers and shippers in order to be able to properly maintain harbors, levees, docks, moorings, roadbeds, and so forth.[18] In time, the function of many toll stations tended to change, and authorities began arbitrarily to assess fees that had little or nothing to do with the maintenance of transportation facilities. The fact that the fees being collected at Watanabe were used to repair and improve port facilities, at least when the toll station was first established in the thirteenth century, indicates that ships elected to dock at the port, in spite of the fees, because the facilities were of high quality. This suggests, in turn, that during the thirteenth century Watanabe Port was becoming something of a public entrepôt community in the style of Kizu and Uozumi.

The transformations that were taking place at Watanabe and other ports were historically significant because they heralded the arrival of the medieval urban community. The new urbanism was defined by the presence of concentrated, nonfarming populations; the performance of economic activities that revolved around the distribution of commodities supplied by peasant and

16. *Kamakura ibun*, vol. 22 (1982), p. 310.
17. Wakita, "Chūsei no kōtsū • un'yu," pp. 115–17.
18. Ibid., pp. 118–24.

artisan producers; and a decline in the influence and power of the traditional proprietary lords, as urban residents themselves claimed more authority to manage their businesses and govern their communities. Viewed from that perspective, Kyoto, Nara, and Kamakura could be labeled as medieval cities, but the new urbanism was associated particularly with entrepôt communities.[19] A nonfarming population consisting of lumbermen, stevedores, dockworkers, raftsmen, temple servants, and warehousemen clearly lived at Watanabe, and the appearance of the toll station indicates the port's growing importance as a nodal point in the transshipment and distribution of a wide range of commercial goods. Considerably more difficult to document is the emergence of patterns of communal self-governance, but events at Watanabe probably paralleled developments in other entrepôts that also had toll stations.

The anchorage at Fuku in Harima Province offers a vivid example of the complicated political and administrative transformations that attended entrepôt urbanization. In 1302 Andō Rensei, the shogun's deputy military governor (*shugodai*) for Izumi Province, laid out a considerable sum, an amount equivalent to several tens of thousands of *ryō* of gold, to acquire huge stones and construct walls and levees that enclosed a secure harbor nearly six acres (two *chō*) in size.[20] Although the construction of the harbor was Andō's brainchild, a certain Gyōen Shōnin, who was the priest in charge of fundraising at the temple Kumedadera in Izumi from at least 1293, supervised all aspects of the project.[21] Interestingly enough, one document indicates that Rensei's son contributed to Kumedadera an annual land rent of thirty *kanmon* of copper coins during one particular two-year period, suggesting that the religious authorities were more interested in receiving income than in directly managing affairs at the facility.[22]

In addition to the documents that bear witness to the activities of the Andō family, other sources mention a toll station at Fuku. According to those records, Nara's Kasuga Shrine claimed ultimate proprietary rights over the toll station. The religious institution appointed local managers to collect fees from boats, although those officials proceeded to try to compel all vessels to enter Fuku harbor and pay the levy, even those ships which were bound for Hyōgo and which had no intention of stopping at Fuku. Not surprisingly, such behavior led to trouble with Kasuga's religious neighbor, Tōdaiji, which maintained its own toll station at Hyōgo.[23] The functionaries at Fuku acted aggressively

---

19. Wakita Haruko, "Cities in Medieval Japan," *Acta Asiatica* 44 (1983), pp. 28–52; Wakita with Susan B. Hanley, "Dimensions of Development: Cities in Fifteenth- and Sixteenth-Century Japan," in John W. Hall, Nagahara Keiji, and Kozo Yamamura, eds., *Japan before Tokugawa: Political Consolidation and Economic Growth, 1500–1650* (Princeton: Princeton University Press, 1981), pp. 295–326.

20. Hanawa Hokiichi, ed., *Zoku: Gunsho ruijū*, vol. 28, rev. Ōta Tōshirō (Tokyo: Zoku Gunsho Ruijū Kanseikai, 1926), p. 247.

21. "Kamenaka Kyō ki shihai monjo," located at the Historiographic Institute, University of Tokyo (Tōkyō Daigaku, Shiryō Hensanjo).

22. "Kumadadera Ryūchiin yuishogaki," Historiographic Institute, University of Tokyo.

23. *Kamakura ibun*, vol. 38 (1989), pp. 257–58.

because they were not members of Kasuga's religious community, but, rather, worked for the shrine on a kind of tax-farming or contract basis. That is, the functionaries levied the fees under the authority afforded to them by Kasuga Shrine, passed the proprietor's share to the religious institution, and then used any remaining balance to cover their own expenses and salaries. In time, the managers came to consider their rights to be a private possession that they might sell or bequeath to others. At one point, for instance, some sold their position to monks of the Ritsu sect, headquartered at Nara's great temple of Tōshōdaiji, and later the proceeds even were used to cover the expenses incurred in compiling Kōfukuji's *Issaikyō* (The Complete Scriptures).[24]

The complicated chronology of events at Fuku suggests that the function of the fund-raising cleric Gyōen Shōin was to plan the construction project, win the backing of an influential religious institution by promising it a source of funds to use for the maintenance of shrine and temple buildings, and then, with the mediacy of the religious organization, obtain official approval to establish a toll station from appropriate authorities at court or within the shogunate. As construction got underway, the actual builders, men such as Andō and the fiscally astute priest, presumably intended to assume control over the land rents and lower-level rights usually exercised by the managers. The very complex petitioning of the multiple layers of rights and responsibilities discernible at Fuku meant that no single party exercised complete jurisdiction over the entrepôt. The major religious patrons collected rents and dues, but were on their way to becoming absentee proprietors who were little concerned with day-to-day affairs within the community in the way that Tōdaiji and the abbot Chōgen originally had been at Watanabe. Concurrently, at Fuku, builders and local officials were assuming more personal responsibility for managing the collection and payment of the rents and dues, an indication that the people of the community were beginning to extract themselves from the control of outside proprietors and to exercise a measure of self-governance.

It is not clear how far self-governance developed at Fuku during the fourteenth century. Fuller documentation is available, however, for Ōyamazaki, which provides an example of how residents in one entrepôt community acquired rather extensive power to manage their own affairs.[25] Located to the southwest of Kyoto on alluvial flatland where three rivers converge, that community was an important transportation center from early times. By the medieval period Iwashimazu Hachiman Shrine, situated just a short distance away, served as the proprietor-patron of Ōyamazaki, much as Kasuga Shrine stood in relationship to Fuku. As the proprietor, Iwashimazu Hachiman Shrine was entitled to receive land rents, but the sources indicate that a self-governing group of residents (*sōchū*) collected those on a contract basis and passed them along to the religious institution, just as the managers at Fuku served as tax farmers. In addition to gaining a degree of independence con-

---

24. Aida Nirō, *Chūsei no sekisho* (Tokyo: Bōbō Shoten, 1943), p. 97.
25. Wakita, *Nihon chūsei toshi-ron*, pp. 181–248; Wakita, "Cities in Medieval Japan," pp. 35–39.

cerning decisions about how much each individual member of the community should contribute to the overall rent bill, the self-governing body at Ōyamazaki also won a degree of control over the administration of local justice when shrine authorities successfully negotiated with the imperial government to limit visits to the entrepôt by police agents. Ironically, later in the fifteenth century, after Iwashimazu Hachiman Shrine had helped free the community from intrusion by the state's police officials, Ōyamazaki extricated itself from the control of the shrine, thus achieving near total autonomy as a self-governing community.

The paucity of historical documentation about the port at Watanabe is unfortunate, but the analogous cases of Fuku and Ōyamazaki do permit us to advance some speculative suggestions about what happened at Watanabe in the medieval period. The establishment of a toll station at Watanabe in the Kamakura era paralleled the development of a similar facility at Fuku, and thus it is not unlikely that port facilities were created and tolls collected in a similar manner at both locales. Moreover, the construction of docks, moorings, and so forth at both ports must have involved land reclamation and, thus, probably entailed a considerable amount of negotiation between local property owners and outside proprietors concerning the use of land and the collection and disbursement of rents. Against that background, it is tempting to imagine that self-governing organizations materialized at both Fuku and Watanabe, just as a group of residents with firm authority over local matters appeared at Ōyamazaki. A look at Tennōji and Sakai, two other growing centers of trade and commerce, can yield additional insights into the evolutionary patterns of medieval urbanism and suggest how pervasive self-governance became in the Osaka area during the middle ages.

Tennōji: Seaside Market and Commercial Town

According to a document dated the twenty-third day of the Fourth Month, 1496, a wholesaler residing in the community of Tennōji acquired a monopsony right to purchase and distribute all sedge hats produced in Fukae village in Settsu Province.[26] Sedge hats were an important commodity in the medieval period, and those crafted in the Naniwa region enjoyed an especially fine reputation, even to the point that they receive favorable mention in *Ashikari* (The Reed Cutter), the noh play written in the early Muromachi period and usually attributed to Zeami.[27] That drama, of course, is a work of fiction—the

---

26. "Kazunaga Kyō ki," entry for Meiō 5 (1496), Fourth Month, twenty-third day, in the manuscript collection of the Cabinet Library (Naikaku Bunko).

27. For an English translation of the play, see "The Reed Cutter," trans. James A. O'Brien, in Donald Keene, with the assistance of Royall Tyler, ed., *Twenty Plays of the Nō Theatre* (New York: Columbia University Press, 1970), pp. 147–64.

poignant recounting of the reunion of a husband and wife who had parted after falling upon hard times—but the playwright's statement about how much the people of Kyoto "appreciated" the hats made in Naniwa suggests that they were sold widely throughout the Kinai area.

In acting to secure monopoly rights over the wholesaling of sedge hats, the Tennōji merchant effectively absorbed the functions and responsibilities of two existing guilds (*za*). The first of those was the "original guild" (*hon za*), which paid an officially sanctioned levy (*kuji*) to the distinguished Konoe family, whose head served as the imperial regent in 1496; the second was the "new guild" (*shin za*), which paid a similar fee to the Nijō house, another of Kyoto's noble families that also claimed the regency from time to time. As the patrons of the guilds, the aristocrats protected the right of guild members to market their goods in the capital on an exclusive basis, a privilege that passed to the Tennōji merchant in 1496. At roughly the same time, the Tennōji wholesaler-distributor secured monopoly rights to sales in Sakai, Nara, and his hometown of Tennōji by paying fees to proprietors with holdings in those locales.[28]

The example of the activities of the Tennōji wholesaler-distributor is filled with significance. For one thing, it exemplifies how the early decades of the Muromachi period witnessed a spurt in the production and exchange of commodities, as well as the formation of an integrated marketing network in the Kinai provinces. That "capital marketing sphere" served the large-scale urban consumption centers of Kyoto and Nara, whose residents needed all sorts of goods, such as the sedge hats, that were being produced in ever greater quantities in the hinterland villages of the Kinai.[29] Linking the rural producers to the urban consumers were the distributors and wholesalers who resided in marketing and commercial towns such as Tennōji, Sakai, and Hiranogō, which were situated at strategic points throughout the capital marketing sphere. Tennōji, for instance, fortuitously sat between Osaka Bay and the temple Shitennōji, a location that naturally gave rise to a thriving "seaside market" (*hamaichi*) where shoppers could find goods from western Japan as well as crops and other commodities grown and produced locally. That site also made it convenient for wholesalers to transship such merchandise to customers in Kyoto and Nara.

The second point to emerge from the Tennōji example has to do with the ability of producers and merchants in local marketing and commercial towns to regulate themselves and their business practices. The existence of both original and new guilds indicates that an important transition was underway at Tennōji. We know from an abundance of other documentation that members of original guilds typically were compelled to perform personal service for their patrons or the proprietors of the estates upon which they lived, whereas the new guilds tended to be more cohesively organized as business enterprises and usually paid a fee to the patron in exchange for the right to carry on their

---

28. Tsuji Zennosuke, ed., *Daijōin jisha zōjiki*, vol. 12 (Tokyo: Sankyō Shoin, 1964), pp. 58–59.

29. Wakita, *Nihon chūsei shōgyō*, pp. 405–17.

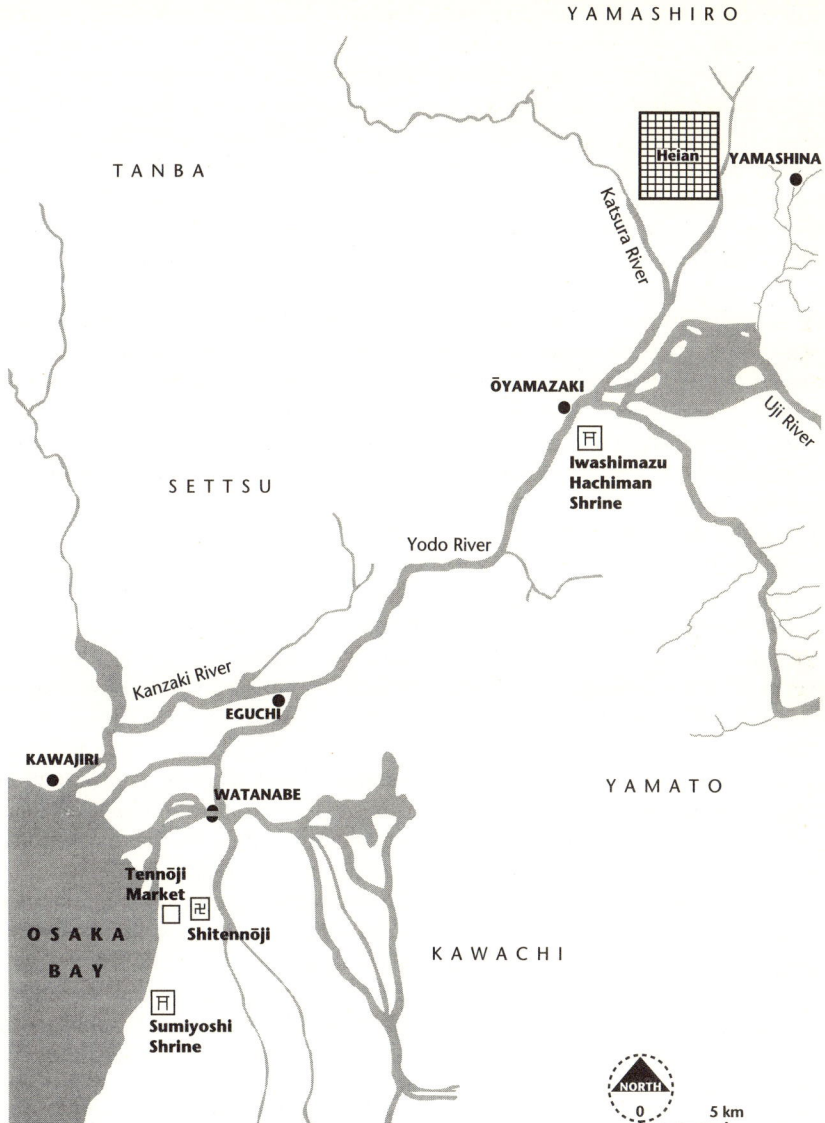

Map 6. The Osaka region in the medieval period

activities. In the case of sedge hat production, by 1496 even the original guild submitted a cash payment to its benefactor, implying that it had removed itself from personal-service obligations. That the Tennōji-based wholesaler now compensated the Kyoto patrons on behalf of the producers suggests that the guilds had further extracted themselves from some of the traditional constraints that constituted an unavoidable part of any direct association with a patron.

It would not do, of course, to overemphasize the degree of autonomy afforded the producers, since the wholesaler himself exercised oligarchic powers that permitted him to dictate many aspects of trade in sedge hats. Still, it seems reasonable to conclude that the appearance of the Tennōji wholesaler at an intermediate level between the guilds and the patrons meant that all persons involved in the production and distribution of sedge hats enjoyed an unprecedented degree of business autonomy at the end of the fifteenth century. Moreover, the merchant's agility in negotiating additional sales rights outside of Kyoto, in Sakai and Nara and elsewhere, demonstrates how the old geographical restrictions on trade were increasingly ineffectual in the face of a determined effort by wholesalers and guilds to expand trade and commerce and to free themselves from the burdensome shackles of proprietary control. In short, what is revealed at Tennōji is an example of producers and merchants mitigating the traditional limitations on trade and expanding the scope of their operations.

Other sources confirm the inferences drawn from the guild-wholesaler's example. Extremely useful is the "Tennōji shigyō mandokoro hikitsuke" (An Extract from Offices Conducting Affairs at Tennōji), which most scholars believe was compiled sometime at the end of the fifteenth century or beginning of the sixteenth.[30] Among other things, the document lists religious observances, the annual round of festivals and celebrations in the community, the kinds of commodities dispatched from Tennōji to aristocratic and military proprietors in Kyoto, and the amount of fees and taxes collected from wholesalers and others who participated in the local seaside market. Most important, the "Tennōji shigyō mandokoro hikitsuke" inventories the kinds of goods which reached that popular marketplace, located near the famous stone torii that marked entry onto sacred soil at the western approach to the temple Shitennōji.

It is not possible to know if the seaside market was permanent or whether it convened periodically, such as on the fifth, fifteenth, and twenty-fifth days of each month. For certain products, dealers apparently came to Tennōji on a regular basis each month. The wholesaler who monopolized the distribution of sedge hats produced at Fukae village in Settsu Province, for instance, paid a tax to sell the headgear at the Tennōji market, which he also peddled throughout the Kinai region, suggesting that he followed a fixed circuit of periodic markets. Other persons from villages surrounding Tennōji paid a similar fee to sell their goods at the market, including those who dealt in textiles dyed in dark blue and indigo, straw matting, salted fish, paper, foreign merchandise, cast metal goods, bamboo, cloth woven in nearby Kimura village, rice, and various woods. The straw matting was especially prized, so we can further conjecture that a guild-wholesaler system functioned for it in much the same

---

30. The original is in the possession of the temple Shitennōji; a photocopy is available at the Historiographic Institute, University of Tokyo.

way as for Fukae's sedge hats, and it is likely that the farmer-producers of Kimura cloth probably paid a fee for a permanent place at the market.[31]

As was the case with sedge hats, one or two dominant wholesalers controlled the marketing of each of the commodities transported into Tennōji, and they probably supervised the distribution of those goods throughout the entire capital marketing sphere. Few historical documents bear testimony to this, but we do know something about another oligopsony, the distribution of free-standing screens woven from various plants and grasses by the families of Otogi village in Yamato Province. By the middle of the fifteenth century those blinds had become a popular household item, useful as sunscreens and as temporary partitions, and persons as far away as Kyoto annually purchased several horse loads for use during that city's Hollyhock Festival, held in the Fifth Month. Two wholesalers in Nara oversaw all production and marketing operations, even making advance payments to the forty to fifty weavers in Otogi and then buying up their entire output, thus insuring prosperity for all.[32]

Increasingly, however, the tendency was for a larger number of wholesalers to became involved jointly in marketing a particular product. One example of that new type of arrangement is embodied in the example of the Tennōji ramie wholesalers' guild. One document mentions that the "ramie wholesalers' guild pays one hundred *mon* per room" at Tennōji, indicating the presence of multiple dealers at the market. The *Sanetaka Kō ki* (The Diary of Sanjōnishi Sanetaka) also informs us that the Tennōji group purchased raw, unprocessed plants in Echizen, a famous growing area, and wholesaled them to ramie merchants in Kyoto.[33] Accordingly, we know that guild members used Tennōji as their headquarters, traveled back and forth to Echizen, and sold ramie at markets located in several provinces.

Furthermore, the ramie wholesalers made decisions in a corporate, egalitarian fashion. That is to say, the members apportioned annual dues among themselves, distributed profits according to each individual's contribution to the health of the common enterprise, exercised an equal vote in electing the group's representatives and officials, decided business guidelines and guild regulations, and determined what sanctions to impose against anyone who violated the rules. In that sense, the wholesalers' guild constituted a *kyōdōtai*, a term that Japanese scholars commonly use to refer to social and economic organizations that people created in premodern communities in order to promote their individual survival through joint, cooperative effort. To the extent that the ramie dealers and other wholesalers at Tennōji increasingly were coming together in such corporate associations, they were able to advance their own autonomous control over the conduct of their businesses and enterprises.

In addition to the persons who traveled from the surrounding region to

---

31. In general, merchants in agricultural villages could hold "seats" at particular markets; for several examples of quarrels over such rights in Ōmi and Yamato Provinces see Wakita, *Nihon chūsei shōgyō*, pp. 419–87.
32. *Daijōin jisha zōjiki*, vol. 10 (1964), pp. 428–29; Wakita, *Nihon chūsei shōgyō*, pp. 514–15.
33. Wakita, *Nihon chūsei shōgyō*, pp. 371–85.

trade at Tennōji, the market also seems to have become home to permanent shops. The "Tennōji shigyō mandokoro hikitsuke," for instance, draws our attention to shops at the Tennōji market that specialized in chestnuts and persimmons, flax and ramie, sundry goods, long swords, saké, lacquer ware, costume jewelry, long-bladed hoes, salt, and the malted rice used to make miso. Thanks to its bustling market, alive with permanent shops and visiting merchants, Tennōji had emerged by the beginning of the sixteenth century as one of the most important transshipment centers and commercial towns in the capital marketing sphere. Reportedly, the community boasted more than seven thousand households, suggesting a total population that numbered several tens of thousands of residents.[34] Those persons made their livelihoods at commerce and trade, and Tennōji owed its prosperity as an urban center to the rows of permanent shops that lined the approaches to the Shitennōji religious complex as well as to the seaside market that attracted producers and wholesalers from the surrounding hinterland. The traders and merchants at Tennōji also enjoyed a burgeoning degree of independence to fix the terms of their commercial existence, a distinguishing feature of Japan's new medieval urbanism that would reach a fuller flowering at nearby Sakai.

The Jeweled Market of Sakai

Historians are not entirely certain about the origins of Sakai, which lies at the eastern end of the Seto Inland Sea, comfortably within what today is Osaka Municipal Prefecture. Its location made Sakai a natural center for the transshipment of estate rents from western Japan to proprietors in the capital and a convenient way station for pilgrims bound for the shrines and temples at Nara and Kyoto. Sakai also owed something to its association with Sumiyoshi Shrine. Once each year shrine officials carried Sumiyoshi's deities around the parish on sacred *mikoshi* palanquins and, as was customary, left them for a few days at a temporary abode, the *tabisho*, so that worshippers could come and pay their respects. Persons with goods to sell also tended to congregate around the *tabisho* and constituted the festival's so-called Jeweled Market (*takara no ichi*). Even today the shrine reenacts the ritual of the Jeweled Market each October 17, and it is possible to suggest that the community of Sakai originally took shape when that early market became a permanent settlement.[35]

Whatever its precise origins, Sakai emerged into full view as an urbanized community, functionally distinct from the surrounding rural countryside, during the fourteenth century when it served both as an entrepôt for the estate rents destined for the aristocratic families and religious establishments of Ky-

---

34. *Daijōin jisha zōjiki*, 12:366.
35. *Dai Nihon shiryō*, 6–23 (reprint; Tokyo: Tōkyō Daigaku Shuppankai, 1983), pp. 276–77, couples the Jeweled Market with Sumiyoshi Shrine and associates the site of the *tabisho* with the location of Sakai.

oto and as a supply port for the Southern Court during the schism that divided rival factions of the imperial house from 1337 until 1392.[36] What eventually distinguished Sakai from other ports along the Inland Sea, however, was the role it played as a transshipment center after the shogunate decided to cultivate relations with Ming China during the latter part of the fifteenth century. The shogunate dispatched three embassies to China from Sakai in 1476, 1483, and 1493, and a fourth sailed from Sumiyoshi no Ura, immediately to the north of Sakai, in 1506. Favored merchants in Sakai acted as the outfitters for each of the embassies, earning an enormous amount of wealth and helping to transform Sakai into a city numbering at least thirty to forty thousand residents. Concurrently, Sakai was becoming an important center of production. The city's craftsmen first became famous for their ironwork, and by the sixteenth century, when most of Japan's guns were manufactured there, Sakai's handicraft industries included printing, brewing, and the production of damask and bleached cotton.

The merchants of Sakai began to exercise certain prerogatives of self-government during the fifteenth century, at the same time that merchant groups in places like Tennōji, Fuku, and Ōyamazaki were beginning to assume responsibility for the internal management of their own commercial affairs and business organizations. In Sakai, that trend went even further as an autonomous council of elders known as the *egōshū* ruled over the community. The council is first mentioned in a document that dates to 1484, and most sources state that ten men served on the board. All councilors, apparently, were wealthy merchants, and most came from the families that were involved in the trade with Ming China. The existence of the city council should not be taken to signify that Sakai was totally independent from outside authority; several different warlords occupied the city at various times in the middle of the sixteenth century, for instance, and some demanded the payment of tribute. Nevertheless, as a corporate group, the *egōshū* was empowered to negotiate those imposts and to apportion them among the city's residents. Moreover, the *egōshū* maintained law and order in Sakai, oversaw the conduct of local shrine festivals and religious celebrations, and at times may even have decided what punishments to mete out to wrongdoers who violated the community's legal codes.

Self-governing councils appeared in other communities in the capital marketing sphere late in the medieval period; Uji, Yamada, and Ōminato, which lay outside Ise Shrine, all had bodies similar to the *egōshū*, and the northern

---

36. The history of Sakai in the medieval period is covered in Toyoda Takeshi, *Sakai* (Tokyo: Shibundō, 1957), and Kobata Atsushi, *Chūsei Nishi tsūkō bōeki-shi no kenkyū* (Tokyo: Tōkō Shoin, 1941), pp. 81–203. In English see two articles by V. Dixon Morris: "Sakai: From Shōen to Port City," in John W. Hall and Toyoda Takeshi, eds., *Japan in the Muromachi Age* (Berkeley: University of California Press, 1977), pp. 145–58, and "The City of Sakai and Urban Autonomy," in George Elison [Jurgis Elisonas] and Bardwell L. Smith, eds., *Warlords, Artists, and Commoners: Japan in the Sixteenth Century* (Honolulu: University Press of Hawaii, 1981), pp. 23–54.

and southern sections of Kyoto each contributed ten representatives to a joint city council.[37] Those merchant boards carried out the same sorts of functions as their counterpart in Sakai, and some even attempted to provide for the security of their cities by hiring mercenaries and erecting walls around the community. Sakai, too, would surround itself with defensive walls and moats as nearly continuous warfare swept across Japan during the sixteenth century, but such ramparts could do little to protect the merchants of Sakai and preserve their prerogatives of self-governance against the onslaught of the new, powerful military lords who imposed their hegemony over Japan in the final decades of that century.

Ishiyama Honganji and the Collapse of the Medieval World

The Ōnin War, as McClain and Wakita Osamu observe, destroyed the foundations of the medieval polity. The emperor and shogun were debilitated, increasingly unable to project their authority very far beyond the city of Kyoto, and ceaseless strife engulfed Japan as warlords battled among themselves to carve out powerful domains and claim control over the vestiges of prestige and power that remained in the imperial capital. Fighting was introduced to the Naniwa region in the Eighth Month of 1467 when Hosokawa Mochihisa, the military governor of Nishi Nari District and uncle to Hosokawa Katsumoto, leader of the Eastern Alliance in the dispute over which Ashikaga claimant should be named as the heir to the shogunal house, drew up his armies at Amagasaki to confront the warriors being carried up the Inland Sea in five hundred ships commanded by Ōuchi Masahiro, lord of several provinces at the southwestern tip of Honshū and a supporter of Yamana Sōzen's Western Alliance. Peace was a rare commodity in Naniwa for the next several decades, and especially devastating battles took place in the summer of 1531 at Tennōji, where the battalions of Hosokawa Takakuni clashed with the combined armies of Hosokawa Harumoto, Takakuni's nephew and rival for control of the family, and Miyoshi Motonaga, Harumoto's chief lieutenant.[38]

Soldiers were not the only newcomers to the Naniwa region. Rennyo Kenju, the eighth head abbot of the temple Honganji, often sailed down the Yodo River from Kyoto to Watanabe and then continued to Sakai and other communities on horseback.[39] Rennyo came in search of converts to augment the ranks of his growing True Pure Land sect, and in 1496 he built a chapel on a rise of land near the anchorage at Watanabe. The monks and believers who gathered around the temple, known as Ishiyama Honganji, often had to fight

---

37. Toyoda Takeshi, *Nihon no hōken toshi* (Tokyo: Iwanami Shoten, 1952), pp. 69–73; in English, see Toyoda Takeshi and Sugiyama Hiroshi, with V. Dixon Morris, "The Growth of Commerce and the Trades," in Hall and Toyoda, *Japan in the Muromachi Age*, pp. 140–41.

38. Those wishing further details about the battles and family treacheries of the era should consult *Shinshū: Ōsaka shishi*, 2:567–616.

39. Honganji-shi Hensanjo, ed. and pub., *Honganji-shi*, vol. 1 (Kyoto, 1961), pp. 356–57.

in order to survive the chaos of the Sengoku period, as Japan literally became a Country at War. In 1532, for instance, less than a year after Hosokawa Harumoto and Miyoshi Motonaga had joined forces to defeat their common foe, the two suffered a falling-out, and Harumoto called upon the armed adherents at Ishiyama Honganji to help him destroy his former ally. The religious community did so, only to have to war with the aggressive, belligerent Harumoto when he suddenly turned against them.

It was also in 1532 that the warlord Rokkaku Sadayori torched the sect's main temple at Yamashina, immediately east of Kyoto, and the next year, amid the melee of treacheries being committed by the Hosokawa and Miyoshi warrior families, Shōnyo Kōkyō, Honganji's tenth abbot, transferred the denomination's most sacred icons to Ishiyama Honganji, thus converting the temple-fortress into the headquarters of the far-flung religious monarchy. The introductory chapter to this volume describes how Ishiyama Honganji, together with the residential and artisan neighborhoods that sprang up on its precincts and became known as Osaka, prospered and grew into an important center of religion, commerce, and culture. All that remains to add to that story is mention of how the community also constituted one the most eloquent, and final, examples of medieval urban self-governance.

Officials at Ishiyama Honganji maintained cordial relations with the court and aristocrats who remained in Kyoto. In 1528, for instance, Shōnyo was adopted into the family of the former imperial regent Kujō Naotsune, and in 1536 the priests at Honganji graciously paid all expenses for the enthronement ceremonies for Emperor Go-Nara. The new emperor may not have enjoyed the authority his ancestors once exercised, but Shōnyo's cultivation of the court bore fruit when the throne named him an imperial archbishop, designated Ishiyama Honganji as an official prayer temple, and granted its merchant quarters exemptions from imperial corvée and service levies, immunity from entry by military governors, and exemptions from debt moratoriums.[40] That last prerogative was especially significant. During the middle ages the Ashikaga shogunate and local lords frequently granted debt amnesties, canceling obligations owed by one individual to another within their jurisdiction, so as to relieve economic distress and head off possible peasant unrest. Since farmers typically owed a portion of their outstanding loans to urban merchants, the city dwellers labored to obtain immunities from such debt remissions. In 1520 the merchants at Ōyamazaki were the first group to acquire such an exemption, and after that date other self-governing communities sought the same entitlement. By the 1530s immunity from debt cancellations, which confirmed the merchants' rights to private property acquired through commercial transactions, had became the most important measure of a city's prestige, the sine qua non of its existence, and the privileges won by the merchant community at Ishiyama Honganji defined it as an exemplar of medieval urbanism.

Shōnyo settled Honganji's differences with Hosokawa in 1535, agreeing to

---

40. Uematsu Torazō, ed., *Ishiyama Honganji nikki* (Osaka: Zaishoku Nijūgo-nen Kinenkai, 1984), pp. 70, 121–22, 248.

collect property taxes (*jishi zeni*) from merchants in the temple town and disburse them to the warlord, who then redirected his attention toward other foes.[41] It is worth noting that the collection of taxes based on property frontages further distinguished Ishiyama Honganji–Osaka as an urban community, in contrast to agricultural villages which typically paid a proportion of the crop to outside authorities, just as it further signified that the merchants and priests were not truly independent from outside authority, anymore than were their neighbors at Sakai. Still, satisfied with an arrangement that filled his coffers with tax receipts, Hosokawa did honor the self-governing privileges granted to Ishiyama Honganji–Osaka by the throne. Left free to manage their own internal affairs and business enterprises, the priests and merchants achieved new levels of urban prosperity.[42] Osaka never did subsume the port settlement of Watanabe, which interestingly enough seems to have retained its own autonomous identity, but the number of merchant quarters in the temple town rapidly expanded from six to seventeen, which the residents surrounded with elaborate moats and earthworks. As the pace of commercial activities quickened, Osaka became a new and important part of the capital marketing sphere. Concurrently it became the esteemed ideal for a dozen or more other temple towns, which also sought from outside authorities a package of self-governing privileges "just like Osaka's" (*Ōsaka nami*).

Osaka's growing prestige and defensive ramparts could not protect the community against the onslaught unleashed upon it by Oda Nobunaga. By the end of the 1560s, that warlord had seized control of an extensive set of holdings in central Japan, marched into Kyoto and compelled the shogun to recognize his primacy in matters of state, and articulated the goal of *tenka fubu*, of reuniting Japan by bringing the entire realm under a single authority. Throughout the 1570s Nobunaga waged war against the other warlords who dared stand in his way, and his armies carried out a gruesome campaign against the strongholds of the True Pure Land sect in the provinces of Kaga, Noto, Ise, and Kii, as well as at Ishiyama Honganji. By early 1580, Nobunaga had isolated the temple-citadel and its merchant community. With his forces exhausted by ten years of nearly constant fighting and with the merchant community of Osaka already in ruins, the abbot Kyōnyo Kōju reluctantly surrendered his fortress on the second day of the Eighth Month. That same day, the temple burned to the ground, apparently on his orders.

None of the self-governing communities of the middle ages survived the wars of reunification intact. Sakai capitulated to Nobunaga even before he began his attack on the community at Ishiyama Honganji; Watanabe fell in 1570; and the remaining self-governing temple towns had to bow before the armed might of Oda Nobunaga or that of his successors, Toyotomi Hideyoshi and Tokugawa Ieyasu. But the vitality of the urban experience in the medieval period provided an important legacy for early modern Japan. It was no acci-

41. *Honganji-shi*, 1:421.
42. Wakita Haruko, "Sengoku-ki ni okeru tennō ken'i no ukiage (1)," *Nihon-shi kenkyū* 340 (December 1990), pp. 23–24.

dent that Hideyoshi built an immense fortress on the Uemachi Plateau, that the House of Tokugawa erected its own imposing castle there, or that Japan's greatest commercial city during the seventeenth century grew up on the remains of the temple town of Osaka. As McClain will show in the next chapter, the Tokugawa shoguns understood the importance of commercial wealth and the symbiotic centrality of the warrior-merchant relationship. Ieyasu and his successors fully recognized that their regime could share the benefits to be gained from trade and production, and consequently their shogunate would be willing to permit the merchants and artisans of Osaka to manage many aspects of the city's internal affairs, even as it simultaneously subjected them to the stern dictates of the new polity.

CHAPTER THREE

Space, Power, Wealth, and Status in Seventeenth-Century Osaka

— James L. McClain

On the seventh and eighth days of the Ninth Month, 1619, the second Tokugawa shogun, Hidetada, toured the ruins of Osaka Castle. Four years earlier, in 1615, armies commanded by Hidetada and his father Ieyasu had laid waste to the citadel during the great Summer Campaign against Toyotomi Hideyori and his followers. That victory seemed to insure the hegemony of the Tokugawa family, but Ieyasu's death the subsequent spring raised new questions about Hidetada's claims to act in his own name as shogun, and his journey in the autumn of 1619 was part of a determined quest to ensure that former rivals from western Japan would never rise up to contest his suzerainty. In Osaka, Hidetada met with engineers and designers to finalize plans to rebuild the citadel. To oversee the project, the Tokugawa overlord chose Tōdō Takatora, the daimyo of a substantial domain in the provinces of Ise and Iga. Ironically, Tōdō had helped to construct the Toyotomi stronghold before he threw his support behind the Tokugawa cause; now Hidetada commissioned him to oversee the erection of a new fortress designed to challenge the grandeur of the former Toyotomi edifice. Under the patronage of Hidetada and his successors as shogun, Osaka Castle and the surrounding community would arise anew, emerging as a city of samurai and power, an anchor of strength that would guarantee Tokugawa military supremacy in western Japan for the next two centuries.

Hidetada also visited Kyoto in the autumn of 1619, ostensibly to pay official respects to the reigning emperor, Go-Mizunoo (r. 1611–29). Behind the ritualized aspects of that elaborate ceremonial, however, lurked a more practical purpose, to confirm the lines of political legitimacy that ran from emperor to shogun, leading from Kyoto, seat of traditional imperial sovereignty, to Osaka and then on to Edo, the nation's new administrative capital. Ieyasu had advanced the process of subordinating the imperial will to the military overlord's political needs by donating funds to rebuild palaces and aristocratic residences, by stationing a deputy shogun at the massive Nijō Castle in Kyoto, and by issuing in 1615 the "Regulations concerning the Imperial Household and the Aristocracy" (Kinchū narabi ni kuge shohatto), which restricted the emperor and nobility to traditional arts and ceremonials. Hidetada's touch was more subtle. Less than a year after he returned to Edo in the Tenth Month of 1619, Hidetada wed his daughter Kazuko to Go-Mizunoo. In 1629 an offspring of that particular union of camp and court ascended the throne as Empress Meishō. The first woman to reign since the eighth century, Meishō represented the Tokugawa family's climb to the top of the samurai and aristocratic hierarchies, just as Hidetada's possession of the Three Metropoles—Edo, Kyoto, and Osaka—symbolized his domination of Japan administratively, politically, and militarily.

In the summer of 1634, fifteen years after Hidetada ordained the reconstruction of Osaka Castle, Tokugawa Iemitsu, son of Hidetada and third in the line of Tokugawa shoguns, departed Edo at the head of a grand processional of nearly forty thousand persons, who with great pomp and circumstance swept into Kyoto late in the Sixth Month. It was a sojourn of considerable moment. With no pretense to subtlety, Iemitsu basked in the image of shogunal legitimacy that Meishō's ascension had wrought, made lavish displays of his power and wealth, and seized every chance to remind the emperor and daimyo that the nation's destiny could not stand separate from the fate of the Tokugawa family itself. In that sense 1634 marked the beginning point of another journey, one that led toward the final consolidation of Tokugawa power, for in subsequent years Iemitsu secured the foundations of rule that his father and grandfather had prepared by augmenting and reissuing the "Regulations concerning Warrior Households" (Buke shohatto), first promulgated in 1615, by compelling all outside lords to participate in the system of alternate attendance and residence (sankin kōtai), by enforcing a policy of national seclusion, and by initiating economic policies designed to encourage commercial growth and bring prosperity to the nation.

As most would have deemed appropriate, Iemitsu's first stop in 1634 was Kyoto, city of sovereignty, where he arrived on the eleventh day of the Seventh Month. Toward the end of the month, on the twenty-fifth, Iemitsu moved on to Osaka, city of power, where he inspected the new castle's military defenses. Early the next morning Iemitsu, who seldom missed an opportunity for a dramatic gesture, ordered subordinates to unfurl an enormous golden banner from one of the citadel's main turrets. Inscribed upon that banner was a tiding welcomed by the merchants and artisans of Osaka—henceforth their lord graciously would exempt them from paying land taxes. Implicit in Iemitsu's grand concession was a second message—he intended to encourage urban and commercial growth. A flourishing economy would buttress the foundations of national strength and security, just as a more prosperous country would constitute a new symbol of shogunal authority and prestige. Osaka, the city of samurai and power, was about to become as well a city of merchants and wealth.

The City of Samurai and Power

The awesomely destructive assaults of 1614–15 left Osaka Castle in virtual ruin and reduced nearly half of the surrounding merchant quarters to ashes—contemporary accounts described the havoc caused by savage firestorms and likened the ravaged community to a desolate village in some forgotten, far-off hinterland.[1] Shortly after Ieyasu retired from the battlefield in the Fifth Month of 1615, he entrusted future affairs in the war-wasted Osaka region to Matsudaira Tadaakira. That daimyo previously had ruled a 50,000-*koku* domain in Ise Province, and he had requited himself with honor in the siege of Osaka Castle. More significantly perhaps, Matsudaira came from good stock. He was the son of Ieyasu's eldest daughter and the veteran campaigner Okudaira Nobumasa, and Matsudaira's appointment as the lord of a new 100,000-*koku* domain headquartered at Osaka signified the importance that Ieyasu attached to the possession of that region. No matter how devastated the fortress and its merchant community might be, Osaka was still strategically located at a vital military crossroads within the economic heartland of Japan.

Upon his arrival, Matsudaira turned his attention to bolstering the settlement's outer defenses, relocating nearly all of Osaka's temples and shrines to new sites ringing the perimeter of the city. Exempted were temples affiliated with the Ikkō sect, but most other religious institutions found themselves concentrated at the three nearby villages of Kōzu, Obase, and Tenma.[2] Similarly, Matsudaira instructed that all graveyards be transferred to five new locations on the circumference of the city, at Obase, Hama, Sennichi Mae, Umeda, and Yoshihara villages, with two new sites added later at Noda and Tobita villages. Matsudaira acted out of military concerns; he could garrison the temple and shrine buildings in case of attack, and the graveyards opened up spaces that an advancing army could cross only at risk. Within Osaka, Matsudaira dismantled what was left of the old Third Enceinte, covered the rubble and ashes in the Main and Second Enceintes with a thick layer of earth, and carried out modest repairs to the parapets. But Matsudaira did little else to bring the old fortress back to respectability, perhaps as some historians have suggested because he could not afford to do so, or perhaps because he suspected that

---

1. Firsthand accounts are available in Ōsaka Shiritsu Chūō Toshokan, ed. and pub., *Ōsaka hennen-shi*, vols. 3 and 4 (Osaka, 1967, 1968).
2. Some documentary evidence suggests that the transfer of some temples and shrines may have taken place after Matsudaira's tenure as castle master; see Shinshū Ōsaka Shishi Hensan Iinkai, ed., *Shinshū: Ōsaka shishi*, vol. 3 (Osaka: Ōsaka-shi, 1991), p. 335, and Nakabe Yoshiko, "Kinsei toshi Ōsaka no kakuritsu," in Toyoda Takeshi, Harada Tomohiko, and Yamori Kazuhiko, eds., *Kōza Nihon no hōken toshi*, vol. 3, *Chiiki-teki tenkai* (Tokyo: Bun'ichi Sōgō Shuppan, 1981), p. 101.

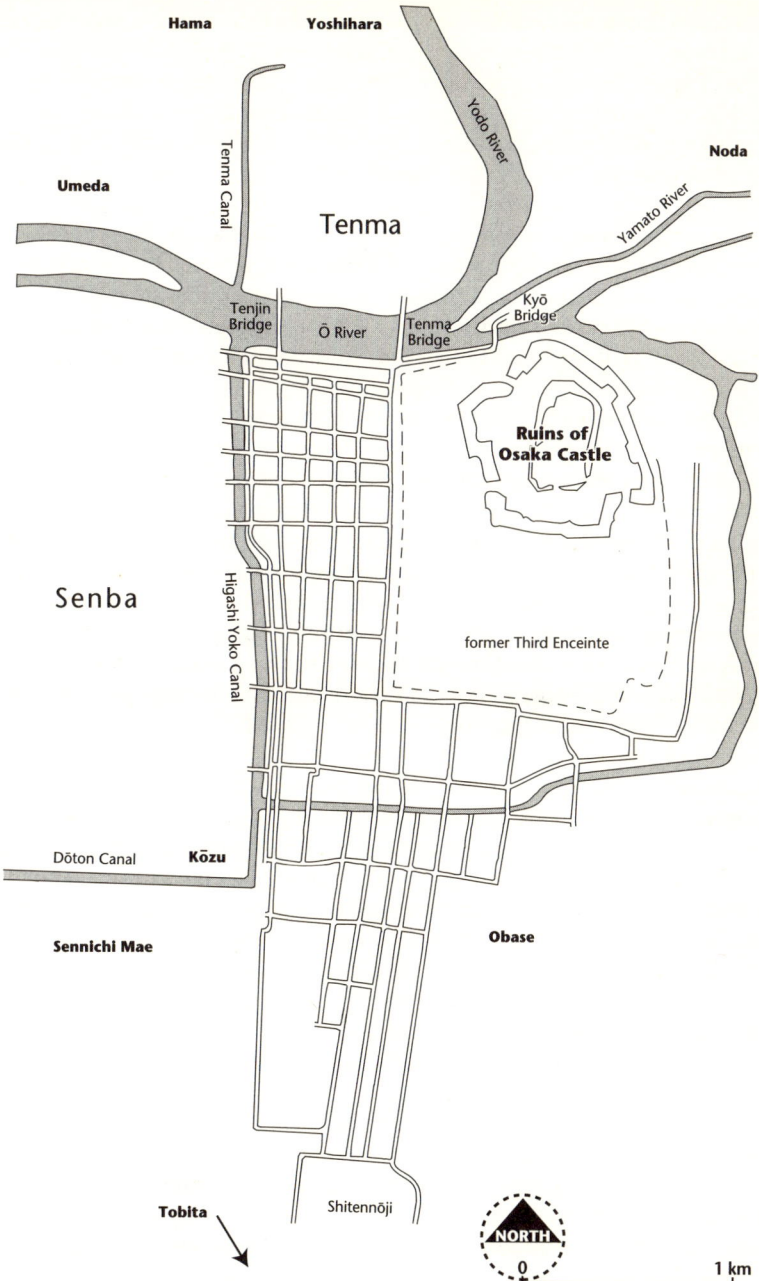

Map 7. Osaka under Matsudaira Tadaakira

his tenure in Osaka would be too brief to justify major investments in castle construction.[3]

Indeed, in 1619 the shogunate decided that Osaka was potentially too important to be left in the hands of a junior vassal, no matter who his mother and grandfather had been. On the twenty-second day of the Seventh Month, Hidetada transferred Matsudaira to a domain in Yamato Province. The following month the shogun withdrew his garrison from Fushimi Castle, the other chief Tokugawa stronghold in western Japan; announced that the shogunate would assume direct control and administration of Osaka, where it henceforth would marshal the bulk of its forces billeted in western Japan; and named Naitō Nobumasa as the castle warden there. The subsequent month Hidetada arrived in Osaka with his ambitious plans to raise high a great new castle that would fulfill his military and strategic ambitions.

The rebuilding of Osaka Castle was one of the grandest projects in an epoch of architectural indulgence. Intent upon expressing their political ambitions in physical form, the early Tokugawa shoguns erected castles at Edo, Sunpu, and Nagoya, financed the restoration of major temples such as Chion'in and Nanzenji in Kyoto, and constructed ornate mausolea at Nikkō and in the Shiba district of Edo. As one of the more magnificent examples of the shogun's architectural pretensions, Osaka Castle was designed to house representatives of the new political order, enhance the overlord's authority, and advertise the inevitability of continued rule by the House of Tokugawa. For reasons of practicality as well as prestige, Hidetada chose to build his fortress on the site of the former Toyotomi stronghold, at the highest elevation on the Uemachi Plateau where the Yodo and Yamato Rivers ran together before flowing west to the sea. The lord's project proceeded in three distinct phases.[4] Beginning in the spring of 1620 construction crews, laboring from dawn to dusk nearly every day for almost three years, put up great stone walls along the north, east, and west sides of the Second Enceinte. After an inspection tour by Hidetada in the Seventh Month of 1623, engineers early the next year turned their efforts to ringing the innermost Main and Yamazato Enceintes with walls and moats. During that second phase of the project, they also erected the towering, five-storied donjon and finished walling the Second Enceinte. Phase three, which began in the spring of 1628 and continued into the next year, saw the completion of all walls and gateways, as well as the digging of an outer moat that in places stretched nearly 120 meters wide.

Hidetada made manifest his claims to political authority not just by building on a monumental scale, but also by requiring that the daimyo of western Japan, many of whom formerly had been rivals and enemies, pay for it. When Hidetada arrived in Osaka in 1619 to finalize construction plans with Tōdō, he brought with him a document bearing the seals of his inner circle of advisors

---

3. *Shinshū: Ōsaka shishi*, 3:204.

4. There is some debate concerning dating and the specific projects completed during each of the three phases; for details, see *Shinshū: Ōsaka shishi*, 3:215–30, and Uchida Kusuo, "Tokugawa-ki Ōsaka-jō saichiku kōji no keika ni tsuite," in Okamoto Ryōichi, ed., *Ōsaka-jō no shokenkyū* (Tokyo: Meicho Shuppan, 1982), pp. 339–81.

and specifying the contributions expected from individual daimyo. In all, the shogun compelled requisitions of men and material from more than sixty different lords who ruled domains located in some thirty provinces in western Japan.[5] According to extant maps prepared by the master builders, Tōdō assigned each lord to a particular project and held individual daimyo responsible for erecting specified portions of the walls.[6] Experts directed the daimyo's work crews: the experienced builders Tominaga Masayoshi and Yokichi Yoshitsugu oversaw the fabrication of storehouses and armories; the noted archer Yoshida Motosada supervised the erection of turrets and gates; and Kobori Enshū—tea master, poet, pottery connoisseur, garden designer, and architect—supposedly gave his own individual touch to the design of the central keep and the shogun's personal residence inside it.

The levies imposed upon the daimyo were enormous, as indicated in the surviving records of daimyo houses. The experience of Kuroda Nagamasa was not untypical.[7] Lord of a large domain in Kyūshū assessed at approximately 520,000 *koku*, Kuroda bore particular responsibility for erecting a portion of the walls that extended about four hundred meters in length. To accomplish that task, he dispatched workers from his domain to hack out huge boulders from the slopes of Mount Rokkō in Harima Province and transport the massive rocks by barge across Osaka Bay and upriver to the Uemachi Plateau, where they were off-loaded, moved overland to the castle site, and finally cut to shape and lifted into place. Kuroda mobilized seventeen thousand workers to quarry and transport the fifty-two stones he needed for the first stage of construction between 1620 and 1623, and in 1620 alone Kuroda paid out twenty-one thousand man-days of wages for just one of the four work crews that he employed in Osaka. Each year for a decade, Kuroda's outlays for material, for the living expenses and stipends paid to the hundreds of officials, servants, and workers brought from the home domain, and for wages to hire thousands of day laborers in Osaka amounted to approximately 20 percent of the annual income that Kuroda derived from the taxes he extracted from the peasants of his domain.

When finished, Osaka Castle represented, for all to see, the full measure of shogunal wealth and power, an eloquent revelation of the overlord's ability to mobilize the personnel and command the resources of his realm. The grounds were immense, even though the Tokugawa shoguns did not choose to rebuild

---

5. Details about the levies may be found in Watanabe Takeru, "Ōsaka-jō no saiken," in Okamoto Ryōichi et al., *Ōsaka-jō yonhyakunen* (Osaka: Ōsaka Shoseki, 1982), pp. 205–7, and in William B. Hauser, "Osaka Castle and Tokugawa Authority in Western Japan," in Jeffrey P. Mass and Hauser, eds., *The Bakufu in Japanese History* (Stanford: Stanford University Press, 1985), pp. 162–63.

6. Maps of Osaka Castle illustrating the assignments made to individual daimyo are located at the National Diet Library (Kokuritsu Kokkai Toshokan) and the Ōsaka Furitsu Naka no Shima Toshokan; one such map is reproduced in Ōsaka-jō Tenshukaku (Ōsaka-shi Keizai Kyoku), ed., *Tokubetsu-hen: Jōkamachi Ōsaka—Chichū yori ima yomigaeru gekidō no rekishi* (Osaka: Ōsaka Tenshukaku Tokubetsu Jigyō Iinkai, 1993), p. 39.

7. Wakita Osamu, *Nihon kinsei toshi-shi no kenkyū* (Tokyo: Tōkyō Daigaku Shuppankai, 1994), pp. 231–33.

the former Third Enceinte. The new citadel sprawled over nearly 175 acres. Surrounding the main enceintes were walls that extended for almost nine thousand meters in length and that in places soared more than twenty meters above the level of the surrounding moats. Whitewashed storehouses and armories filled the complex, and elegant gates and turrets perched gracefully atop the stone walls, enhancing the castle militarily and aesthetically. Most luxurious of all was the shogun's personal quarters, located within the southern portion of the Main Enceinte. When visiting, Japan's hegemon could take his ease in any of sixty-six rooms, most adorned with hand-carved beams, ceilings decorated with gold leaf, and sliding papered partitions (*fusuma*) graced with paintings by artists of the Kanō school.

Surprisingly, for all the glory cast by the donjon at Osaka Castle, and despite all of the nation's treasure devoured by its construction, the Tokugawa shoguns never fully garrisoned the fortress. The commanding officer was the castle warden (*jōdai*), appointed from among allied daimyo (*fudai daimyō*) who possessed domains assessed in the range of fifty to sixty thousand *koku*. The warden could call on the services of the regular guards (*jōban*) and four units of great guards (*ōban*), as well as several squads of constables (*yoriki*) and patrolmen (*dōshin*) attached to the guards. In total, the combined rosters of all the samurai stationed in Osaka enumerated just slightly more than one thousand men. The projection of Tokugawa power in western Japan rested on that small number of warriors.

The largest rock used in the construction of Osaka Castle was the so-called Octopus Stone, located in the courtyard at Sakura Gate and named for the squiggly image that sometimes seemed to appear on its face. More than five meters high and eleven meters in length, the giant stone has an exposed face of nearly sixty square meters and an estimated weight of 130 tons. Imposing in its dimensions and appearance, situated at a major point of entry so that it might awe all who pass by it, the Octopus Stone is not even one meter thick; it is a thin shell that could fulfill successfully its intended function only because it is held up by the combined strength of a vast number of smaller rocks, hidden from view. So it was with the castle warden and his auxiliary warriors; they constituted a lean, highly symbolic line of defense whose might was proportionally much greater because they were lodged in one of the most impressive castles in the realm and were supported by powerful shogunal forces and allied daimyo marshaled out of sight in central and eastern Japan.

Even while the castle warden was standing vigilant against potentially troublesome daimyo, the shogunate also expected him to project the hegemon's power inward, providing the ultimate policing authority over the city of merchants and artisans that was growing up around the base of Osaka Castle. Matsudaira began the reurbanization of Osaka by enticing commoners who had fled during the battles of 1614–15 to come back to the city. To win their favor, he permitted returnees to settle portions of the former Third Enceinte, and he initiated what became a regular government policy of cooperating with wealthy merchant families to dredge out a network of canals and waterways to transport goods conveniently and cheaply into and around the community.

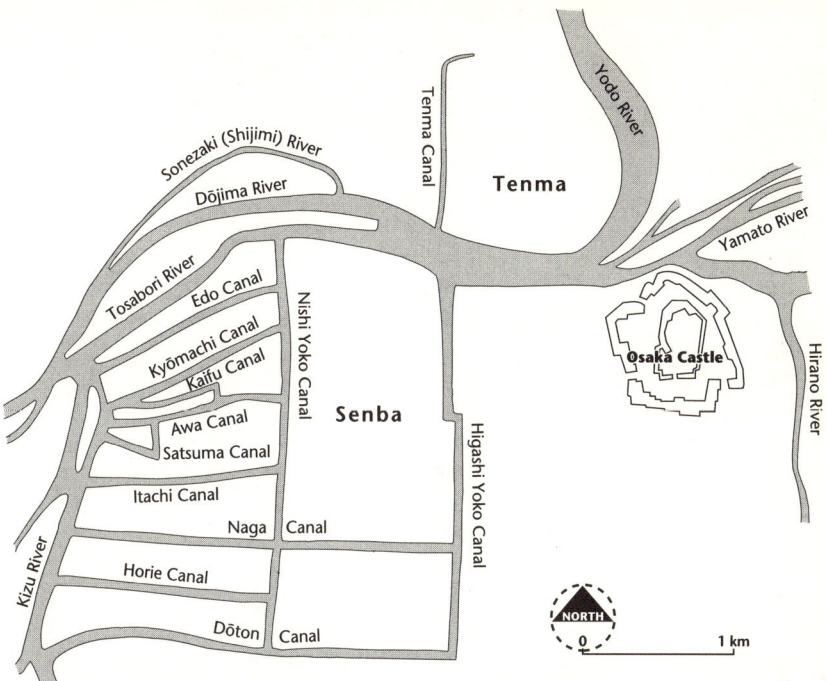

Map 8. Major waterways within Osaka

In the autumn of 1615, for instance, Matsudaira authorized Hirano Tōjirō and Yasui Kuhei to complete the Minami Horikawa, later renamed Dōton Canal in honor of the merchant Yasui Dōton (alternatively, Nariyasu Dōton), who had begun its construction during the Toyotomi era before meeting his untimely death in the defense of Osaka Castle. Two years later, the merchants Kikyōya Gorōemon and Kinokuniya Tōzaemon financed the construction of Edo Canal; the following decade Shishikuiya Jirōemon sponsored efforts to develop the Itachi Canal; and toward the end of the 1620s Satsumaya Jinbei underwrote the costs of the Satsuma Canal, dug in order to better accommodate goods shipped to Osaka from that domain in Kyūshū. In all, leading members of the merchant community financed more than half a dozen important canals between 1615 and 1630, each elaborating upon the existing transportation network while simultaneously draining marshy land on the flanks of Uemachi Plateau that could then be platted for use as residential neighborhoods for merchants and artisans.

About the time that the Kyōmachi and Naga Canals were being dug, the joint migration of more than one hundred neighborhoods of merchants and artisans from Fushimi further revitalized Osaka. The details of that movement of several thousand persons are not entirely clear, but an early seventeenth-century document, the "Fushimi Sakai-chō ikken," states that Hidetada or-

Table 3.1. Canal construction in Osaka

Name	Date completed
Higashi Yoko Canal	1594
Tenma Canal	1598
Awa Canal (Awaza Canal)	1600
Nishi Yoko Canal	One portion opened in 1600, completed in 1620
Dōton Canal	Begun in 1612, completed in 1615
Edo Canal	1617
Kyōmachi Canal	1619–20
Naga Canal	1619–22
Itachi Canal	1620–26
Kaifu Canal	1624
Satsuma Canal	1628–30
Horie Canal	1698

Source: Adapted from Tsuda Hideo, Ōsaka-fu no rekishi (Tokyo: Kawade Shobō Shinsha, 1990), p. 230.

dered the transfer of nearly one hundred residential quarters to Osaka in 1619, after he had decided to rebuild the castle.[8] Upon their arrival, many of the more prosperous merchants apparently settled along the Naga and Kyōmachi Canals, while the artisans who found employment working on the castle—carpenters, plasterers, sawyers, and so forth—moved into lodgings around Tamatsukuri, one of the main approaches to the castle.

The migration of Fushimi residents was only one part of a massive influx of merchants, artisans, and laborers who poured into Osaka during the 1620s expecting to find work in the construction trades. According to the calculations of Wakita Osamu, during the decade of the 1620s the shogunate and the various daimyo annually expended in Osaka, on average, a sum equivalent to at least four hundred thousand *koku* of rice.[9] If we accept the common proposition that the yearly living expenses of an ordinary person amounted to the equivalent of approximately two *koku* of rice, then the outlays for the castle project alone would have supported a population of nearly two hundred thousand persons. Most of the newcomers to Osaka built homes or moved into apartment-style dwellings located to the west of the castle, filling up the area familiarly known as Senba, originally opened to settlement in 1598, before

---

8. Uchida Kusuo, "Ōsaka sangō no seiritsu: Shigaichi no keisei o chūshin to shite," in Ōsaka Shishi Hensanjo, ed. and pub., *Ōsaka no rekishi* (Osaka, 1982), pp. 40–47; *Shinshū: Ōsaka shishi*, 3:195, 205. Other scholars have relied on the "Shohatsu gonjō sōrō chōmen utsushi," a history of the naming of residential quarters in Osaka compiled in 1753, to conclude that merchants and artisans from eighty neighborhoods in Fushimi moved to Osaka between 1615 and 1619 upon the invitation of Matsudaira Tadaakira; see, for instance, Inoue Kaoru, *Ōsaka no rekishi* (Osaka: Sōgensha, 1979), pp. 250–51.

9. Wakita Osamu, *Kinsei Ōsaka no machi to hito* (Kyoto: Jinbun Shoin, 1986), p. 67.

pushing westward toward the recently constructed Nishi Yoko Canal. On the basis of that geographic expansion, and in consideration of the economic stimulus that the construction projects of the 1620s must have imparted to the urban economy, it is possible to place some credence in estimates that the community's total population may have exceeded four hundred thousand in the 1620s, making Osaka one of the world's largest cities.

The shogunate acted quickly to develop procedures to govern and police the growing urban population of merchants, artisans, and laborers, whose neighborhoods after 1619 were divided into two clusters for administrative purposes. The Northern Precinct (Kitagumi) included the five Hon-machi neighborhoods, which formed an east-west axis across the city, and all residential quarters northward to the Dōjima and Ō Rivers, while the Southern Precinct (Minamigumi) consisted of the merchant and artisan neighborhoods located between Hon-machi and the Dōton Canal.[10] Whereas the castle warden retained jurisdiction over the samurai stationed at Osaka and thus loomed as a figure of enormous authority, the city magistrates (*machi bugyō*) managed the day-to-day affairs of the merchants and artisans who lived within the city. Appointed on a regular basis from 1619, the two city magistrates issued legal codes, dispensed justice, collected taxes, oversaw the maintenance of roads and waterways, regulated commercial activities and artisan organizations, and exhorted commoners to exhibit appropriate social behavior. Assisting the magistrates were several dozen constables and patrolmen, as well as a variety of functionaries appointed from among leading merchant families, such as the city elders (*sōdoshiyori*) and neighborhood elders (*machidoshiyori*). In the tradition of medieval urbanism as described by Wakita Haruko, both sets of elders helped to supervise civil affairs in merchant and artisan neighborhoods, although they did so under the close supervision of their samurai masters and within the framework of law as established by the shogunate.

The authority of the castle warden emanated from his residential-office compound located just inside the western walls of Osaka Castle. Perched high above the moat and situated next to the imposing Sengan Turret, the compound must have exuded authority and exerted an awesome effect upon both the samurai and the ordinary people of the city, perhaps all the more so since the massive stone walls blocked a clear view of the office buildings from below, thus suggesting a concealed power made more ominous by its lofty, veiled existence. The presence of other officials and samurai outside the castle walls gave concrete expression to the cloistered authority. The city magistrates had their office-residences within Baba Kado, as the area adjacent to the western walls between Tenma Bridge and Hon-machi was then known, while the constables and patrolmen assigned to the magistrates, as well as units of archers and musket bearers, could be found just a short distance away,

---

10. The neighborhoods formed by the families that migrated from Fushimi were known as the Fushimigumi until that group was abolished and its quarters distributed between the Northern and Southern Precincts, probably in the Shōhō period (1644–48).

Sengan Turret. Photograph by Murata Michihito.

to the east and south of the castle. Each city magistrate had a spacious compound nearly as large as that of the castle warden himself, while the twenty-five constables assigned to the magistrates received residential plots of about 1,600 square meters each, and the patrolmen lived on lots measuring some six hundred meters square. Situated on the periphery of the merchant and artisan quarters of the city, those properties stood as sentinels of official authority, representations of Osaka as a city of samurai and power.

The City of Merchants and Commerce

Near the end of the early modern epoch, the highly respected Osaka city magistrate Kusumi Sukeyoshi wrote that "Naniwa lies at the intersection of the great sea routes of the country and is congested with goods and traffic. Thus, people commonly say that Osaka is the 'country's kitchen,' a storehouse of provisions for all of Japan. Indeed, the eaves of the affluent and of wealthy merchant families line the streets of the city, and ships from many provinces always lie at anchor in the harbor. Canals and waterways for smaller boats

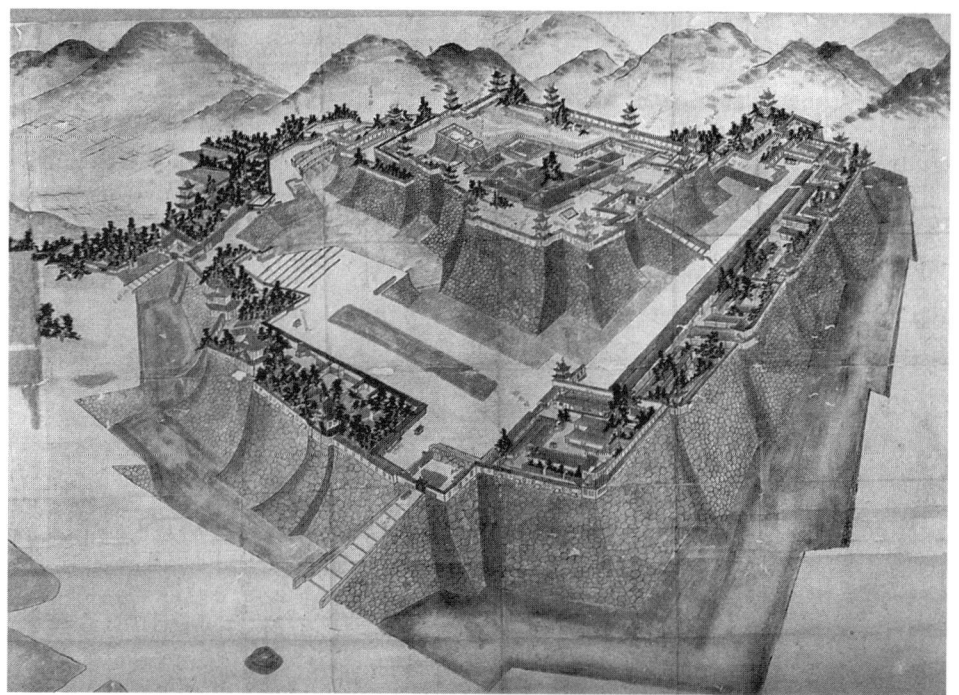

The office compound of the castle warden. From "Naniwa-jō zenzu," by permission of the Osaka Castle Museum.

The office-residence of a city magistrate. Reprinted from Ōsaka shishi, vol. 2. Courtesy of Murata Michihito.

slice through the city right and left, leading off in every direction. Rice, the necessities of daily life, even goods from abroad; all are brought to this place and put on sale. The people lack nothing."[11]

Osaka became the "country's kitchen" because it was a major consumption center, a city of perhaps four hundred thousand persons in the 1620s and 1630s, and was located at the primary nodal point conjoining the rivers and coastal shipping routes that had constituted the arteries of commerce in the economically advanced Kinai region from the medieval period, as Wakita Haruko explains in the previous chapter. The Seto Inland Sea sheltered ships arriving from western Japan, while the Yodo and Yamato Rivers linked Osaka with the towns and villages of the Kinai region and with Kyoto, the nation's leading center of production, trade, and finance during the opening decades of the seventeenth century. By the late 1610s more than two hundred river boats and barges carried goods to the edge of Osaka, where they were off-loaded onto more maneuverable "tea boats" (*chabune*) and so-called *uwani*, vessels that could more easily navigate the inner-city waterways. In 1619, the Osaka city magistrates licensed 1,031 tea boats, each capable of carrying ten *koku* of cargo, and another 1,592 *uwani*, twice as large and piloted by two helmsmen, as Osaka quite literally was becoming a *mizu no toshi*, a "city on water." The newly commissioned *uwani* and tea boats also plied the Yodo and Yamato rivers, supplying the residents of Osaka with vast quantities of finished goods turned out by the artisans of Kyoto and with agricultural produce grown in the villages of the Kinai region—daikon, carrots, and squash from the two nearby Nari districts, melons, persimmons, and mountain peaches from the more distant Teshima and Shima shimo Districts, even bounty from as far away as Kii and Ōmi Provinces.[12]

The establishment within Osaka of the Three Great Markets provided physical evidence of the city's emergence as the leading urban consumption center in western Japan. The first of those thriving outlets was a market for fruits and vegetables, originally founded during the Toyotomi years at the southern approach to Kyō Bridge, close to the castle. The fighting of 1614–15 doomed that facility, but as peace returned the wealthy merchant Yodoya Koan set aside a portion of one of his many properties, located near the original market, to use as a central marketplace. In time, the market expanded, and in 1653 it was relocated adjacent to the northern approach to Tenma Bridge, where fruit and vegetable dealers could more conveniently receive cargoes and serve the city's merchant and artisan populations.

In similar fashion, a central fish market also grew up near the castle, at Utsubo-chō near the northern approach to Kyō Bridge, where some eighteen wholesalers operated during the Toyotomi era. Destroyed in the Winter and

---

11. Kusumi Sukeyoshi, *Naniwa no kaze*, as quoted in Fujimoto Atsushi, *Ōsaka-fu no rekishi*, Kenshi shiriizu 27 (Tokyo: Yamakawa Shuppansha, 1969), p. 168.
12. For a detailed study of the economic relationships between Osaka and its hinterland, see Wakita Osamu, "Kinsei Ōsaka chiiki no toshi to nōson," in Wakita, ed., *Kinsei Ōsaka chiiki no shiteki bunseki* (Tokyo: Ochanomizu Shobō, 1980), pp. 295–320.

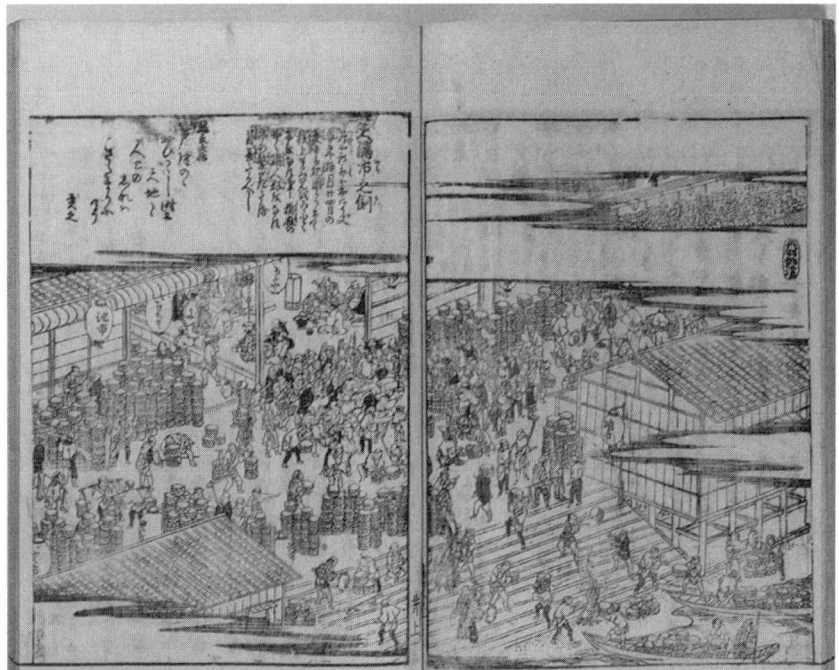

The fruit and vegetable market near Tenma Bridge. From Settsu meisho zue. *Courtesy of the Japanese History Research Office, Faculty of Letters, Osaka University (Ōsaka Daigaku Bungakubu, Nihon-shi Kenkyū Shitsu).*

Summer Campaigns, the market reopened in 1615 upon the orders of Matsudaira Tadaakira, who wished to ensure a steady supply of fish for his samurai retainers. In 1618 the dealers moved to Kami Uoya-machi, near the intersection of Hon-machi and Higashi Yoko Canal and in the heart of the expanding residential quarters for commoners. Four years later those wholesalers who handled salted and dried fish, as well as sardines used by farmers as fertilizer, split off and opened new businesses on the northern fringe of the city, an area being settled by merchant and artisan families. Meanwhile, the fresh-fish dealers at Kami Uoya-machi established a secondary market at Sagishima, downstream on the Kizu River between the Edo and Kyōmachi Canals and closer to the wharves where fishermen delivered their cargoes. For several decades the Sagishima market operated from the Third Month until the twenty-fifth day of the Tenth Month, with transactions taking place at Kami Uoya-machi during the balance of the year. Finally, in 1679, nearly all of the fresh-fish dealers relocated at Sagishima, which became known as Zakoba-chō. There, customers had their choice of catches from provinces along the Seto Inland Sea—Harima, Bizen, Bitchū, Bingo, Aki, Izumi, and Awaji—and even from as far away as Kyūshū and Shikoku.

The fish market at Zakoba-chō. From Settsu meisho zue. *Courtesy of the Japanese History Research Office, Faculty of Letters, Osaka University.*

Osaka also emerged as the principal marketing outlet for rice from nearly every province of western Japan. Pressed with a need for cash in order to purchase weapons and other goods which they could not produce within their home domains, some daimyo had begun to sell tax rice in Osaka during the Toyotomi years, and the Maeda lords of Kaga and the Asano house of Akō resumed the practice in the 1620s. Yodoya Koan, responsible for helping to establish the fruit and vegetable market, offered the use of his principal residential estate as a trading center for Japan's chief grain, and he even constructed a bridge across the Tosabori River so that merchants could have easier access to the facility. Cramped for space, however, some rice merchants began to move their operations north of the Dōjima River in the decade after city officials platted the area referred to as Dōjima Shinchi for settlement in 1688, and others followed after 1705, when the shogunate confiscated the Yodoya family's estate, supposedly because the household head, Saburōemon (Hiromasa), had made too many ostentatious displays of wealth that were inappropriate, in the shogun's mind, for a person of merchant status. Even after establishing themselves at Dōjima, however, rice merchants annually commemorated the origins of Osaka's rice market by holding the first trading session of each New Year season at the southern approach to Yodoya Bridge.[13]

13. *Shinshū: Ōsaka shishi*, 3:456–60, 692–99.

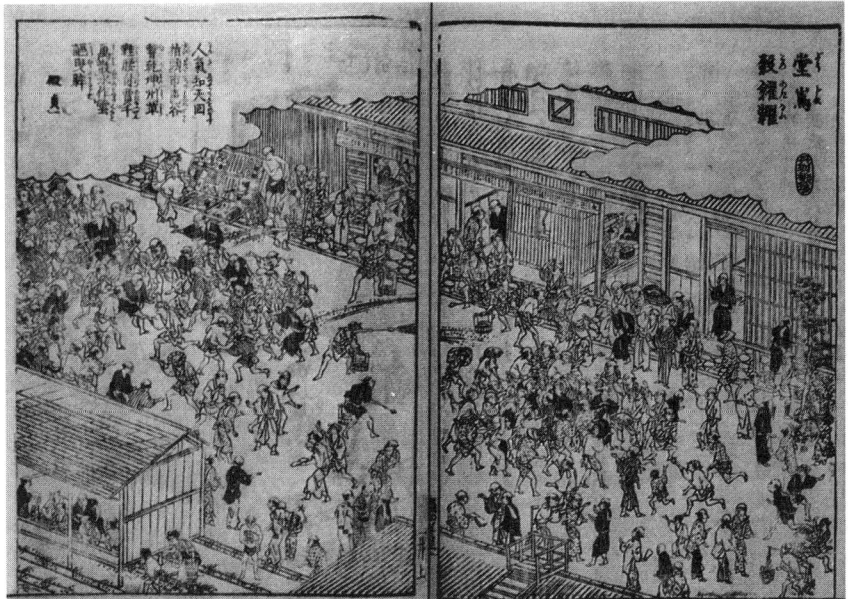

The rice market at Dōjima. From Settsu meisho zue. *Courtesy of the Japanese History Research Office, Faculty of Letters, Osaka University.*

Osaka's reputation as the "country's kitchen," it must be stressed, did not rest solely upon the city's importance as a consumption center with an economic hinterland that included all of the vast Kinai region and extended as far afield as Kyūshū and Shikoku. It derived, as well, from the exceptional role that Osaka came to play in the regional and national marketing systems that emerged during the seventeenth century. As Edo grew into Japan's and then the world's largest city, a great metropolis of more than one million persons, the residents of the shogun's capital began to rely on villages and towns in every section of the country for farm products and processed goods. Villagers living in the Kantō region and in the domains of nearby northern Japan supplied Edoites with significant amounts of perishable foods, firewood, charcoal, and salt. But the people of Edo also depended on the villages and handicraft centers of western Japan for crucial supplies of tea, oil, saké, vinegar, soy sauce, flat- and hollowware, household furnishings, cotton and silk textiles, and a seemingly endless list of other commodities used in the course of daily living.

Located at the gateway to the production centers of the Kinai region and astride Japan's main shipping lanes, Osaka became a primary transshipment node for many such goods, and thousands upon thousands of wholesalers, distributors, jobbers, and forwarding agents made the city home. Such occupations sprang up in great profusion, and in bewildering variety, during the latter half of the seventeenth century—there were *ongoku-doiya*, purchasing agents who dealt with products from the far-off provinces of Kyūshū and Shikoku, and *kingoku-doiya,* who handled cotton, cloth, saké, oil, and so forth from areas nearer the city; there were purchasing agents who specialized in certain goods produced in multiple locales, while others bought up all manner of things, but only from a particular, geographically bounded region; there were receiving agents (*niuke-doiya*) who acquired goods from purchasing agents and sold them, on commission, to distributors (*nakagai*); and there were distributors who used their own cash to buy goods on speculation, while still others took consignment of items only after receiving an order from a third party, who might be a retailer in Osaka or a merchant in Edo or some other city in eastern Japan.

Those middlemen first began to appear in Osaka even as Matsudaira Tadaakira still was trying to put right the disorder wrought by warfare. As early as 1616, for instance, cotton wholesalers in Osaka set to work soliciting orders from retailers in Edo and other settlements in eastern Japan. Those merchants purchased cotton grown in villages surrounding Osaka and then arranged for it to be ginned and willowed, spun into thread and woven into cloth, and bleached and dyed before shipping it to their customers. As the cotton trade became more routinized, merchants established a permanent market for raw and ginned cotton at Aioi-chō Nishi-no-machi, located at the northern approach to Kyō Bridge and close to the original fresh-fish market. After that, trade grew rapidly, chiefly because commoners in the cities of northern Japan prized cotton for its warmth and affordable price, compared to clothes woven from ramie and flax. Although documentation is sketchy, it is likely that most of the cotton cloth retailed in Edo during the seventeenth century moved through Osaka, and by century's end more than three hundred Osaka middlemen were involved in the cotton business.[14]

As important as the merchandising of cotton became, those middlemen represented just a small fraction of the persons who eventually settled in Osaka and engaged in some aspect or another of the complicated wholesale trade. The expansion of Osaka's internal network of canals and waterways in the 1620s, later riparian works that made the Yamato and Yodo Rivers safer to navigate, and the completion of the eastern and western ocean-shipping circuits in the early 1670s enhanced Osaka's attractiveness as a wholesaling and transshipment center. The western shipping circuit, an especially significant development, was engineered by the famous entrepreneur Kawamura Zuiken, who also oversaw the Yodo River projects. Commissioned by the shogunate to develop shipping routes that would remove existing dangers to coastal vessels, Kawamura charted dangerous waters, erected beacons and lighthouses, and provided lifesaving and rescue facilities along the entire coastline from Osaka through the Seto Inland Sea, around the Straits of Shimonoseki, and up the northwest coastline of the Sea of Japan. He then did the same for the Pacific

---

14. William B. Hauser, *Economic Institutional Change in Tokugawa Japan: Osaka and the Kinai Cotton Trade* (London: Cambridge University Press, 1974), pp. 23, 59–64.

coast between Osaka and Edo.[15] The Osaka economy immediately felt the stimulus. A 1679 survey, for instance, revealed that nearly four hundred shops functioned as purchasing agents (*toiya*), and by the 1710s more than 5,500 persons listed their principal activity as purchasing agent and another 8,756 shop owners called themselves distributors.[16]

Those middlemen moved an astonishing variety and volume of goods into and out of Osaka. Table 3.2, which summarizes information available in the 1714 document "Shōtoku yonen Ōsaka ishutsu shōhin hyō," illustrates the immense range of wholesaling operations. Many of the goods listed in that document as shipments from Osaka were destined for Edo, as Osaka middlemen supplied the million or more residents of that eastern city with nearly all the cotton cloth, lamp oil, tatami-mat facing, lacquer-ware, face powder, footwear, umbrellas, kitchenware, pharmaceuticals, paper, tobacco, and dried bonito that they consumed during the latter decades of the seventeenth century.

Another indicator of Osaka's growing national importance was the appearance of daimyo warehouses, known as *kura yashiki*. The oldest extant map of Osaka, executed in 1657, shows twenty-five such repositories within the city. That number later increased; a map dated Genroku 3 (1690) reveals the locations of ninety-five warehouses, and another map drawn in the Tenpō period (1830–44) indicates that some 125 were in operation by that date. The daimyo shipped their tax rice to those Osaka warehouses and then sold it through the city's rice market, located initially at the Yodoya family's estate and then at Dōjima Shinchi. Unfortunately, a paucity of reliable documents frustrates any attempt to reconstruct the details of the Osaka rice trade during the seventeenth century, but historians have pieced together records from individual daimyo domains, thus providing a sense of the general dimensions of trading activity.[17] The Mōri lords of Chōshū, for instance, sent 18,887 *koku* of rice to Osaka in 1643 and 49,630 *koku* a decade later; Akō domain began to market rice in Osaka in 1620 and by mid-century shipped nearly all of its tax rice to the city; and the Maeda daimyo of Kaga sold nearly seventy thousand *koku* of rice through his Osaka facility in 1682. Overall, calculations indicate that nearly 1.4 million *koku* of rice reached the Osaka warehouses annually during the Genroku period (1688–1704). As daimyo domains began to promote local specialty products in the eighteenth century, they also shipped those commodities to Osaka—sugar from Satsuma, indigo plants from Awa, tatami-mat facing from Bingo, candle wax from Higo and Iyo, salt from Harima and Suō, and paper from Tosa, Nagato, and Iwami.

15. For a further discussion of the shipping circuits and Osaka's economic development, see Nakai Nobuhiko and James L. McClain, "Commercial Change and Urban Growth in Early Modern Japan," in John W. Hall et al., gen. eds., *The Cambridge History of Japan*, vol. 4, *Early Modern Japan*, ed. Hall with McClain (Cambridge: Cambridge University Press, 1991), pp. 547–54, 558–64.

16. Yasuoka Shigeaki, "Edo chūki no Ōsaka ni okeru torihiki soshiki," in Miyamoto Mataji, ed., *Ōsaka no kenkyū*, vol. 2 (Osaka: Seibundō Shuppan, 1968), pp. 196, 202.

17. *Shinshū: Ōsaka shishi*, 3:356–57; Miyamoto Mataji, "Kinsei shoki no Ōsaka ni okeru beikoku ryūtsū," in Miyamoto, *Ōsaka no kenkyū*, vol. 4 (1970), pp. 1–46.

Table 3.2. Commodities shipped by Osaka wholesalers, 1714

Shipments into Osaka				Shipments from Osaka			
Item	Quantity		Value	Item	Quantity		Value
rice	282,792	koku	40,814	rapeseed oil	33,233	koku	26,005
rapeseed	151,226	koku	28,049	striped cotton cloth	698,747	tan	7,066
lumber			25,751	export copper	5,000,000	kin	6,588
dried sardines			17,760	bleached cotton cloth	739,938	tan	6,265
bleached cotton cloth	2,061,473	tan	15,750	cottonseed oil	7,900	koku	6,116
paper	148,464	rolls	14,464	used articles	409,838		6,045
iron	1,878,168	kan	11,804	ginned cotton	108,640	kan	4,299
firewood	31,092,394	kan	9,125	soy sauce	32,207	koku	3,899
copper	5,429,220	kan	7,171	iron implements			3,750
raw cotton	1,722,781	kin	6,705	oil cakes	1,596,560	kan	3,267
tobacco	3,631,562	kin	6,496	lacquered implements			2,840
sugar	1,992,197	kin	5,614	personal accessories			2,838
soy beans	49,931	koku	5,320	sesame oil	2,055	koku	2,089
salt	358,435	koku	5,230	ceramic ware			1,574
wheat	39,977	koku	4,586	saké	5,910	koku	1,200
salted fish			4,156	leather sandals	597,480	pairs	1,174
sesame oil	17,143	koku	4,129	copper	250,429		966
cottonseeds	2,187,438	kan	3,920	umbrellas	234,250		650
fresh fish			3,475	kitchenware			569
cotton thread	116,647	kan	3,430	kettles	124,222		536
ramie & flax cloth	310,558	tan	3,401	leather-soled tabi	59,544	pairs	507
silk	35,573	hiki	3,013	raw cotton	192,580	kin	502
ceramic ware			2,876	wooden cabinets			496
tatami-mat facing	1,102,907		2,866	oars	19,602	sets	479
striped cotton cloth	236,923	tan	2,832	bean seed oil	495	koku	430
flax	145,874	kan	2,815	miscellaneous export goods			400
imported medicines			2,788	doors	52,928		317
charcoal	767,814	bags	2,504	leather haori jackets	3,189		312
dried bonito			2,178	wax			309
Kyoto silk textiles			2,066	confectionery			308
vegetable wax	42,785	kan	1,915	sōmen wheat noodles			211
mochi rice cakes	12,294	koku	1,829	folding fans	1,761,646		210
straw mats	1,485,460		1,729	copper implements			207
used articles	135,744		1,717	dolls			197
Yūki thread	17,485,464	coils	1,606	side swords	8,648		177
indigo	320,460	kan	1,466	sesame-flavored candy	31,475	kan	172
green tea	1,478,010	kin	1,460	silk-floss veils			166
imported textiles			1,293	paint	3,855	kan	161
dried fish			1,244	glue plants	33,687	kan	159
domestic lacquer	27,626	kin	1,164	cotton tabi footwear	77,002	pairs	152
Nara bleached ramie	22,821	hiki	1,087	festival altars			151
lacquered bowls & nestled boxes	96,383		1,064	iron anchors	460		139

(continues)

Table 3.2. Continued

	Shipments into Osaka			Shipments from Osaka		
Item	Quantity	Value	Item	Quantity	Value
lead	556,170 kin	881	processed shark skin and shark parts	10,877	137
used lumber	392,198 kin	827	hair oil		136
silk floss	2,455 kan	806	incense sticks	2,814,830	135
bamboo	1,188,980 poles	805	face powder		118
bean seeds	5,085	775	shoji sliding doors	25,592	103
domestic medicines		698	vinegar	1,858 koku	99
imported lacquer	20,129 kin	687	books and manuscripts		98
fruit		686	bellows	1,522 sets	74
sixty-nine additional commodities			forty-five additional commodities		
Total		286,561	Total		95,800

Source: Adapted from Wakita Osamu, *Kinsei hōken shakai no keizai kōzō*, rev. ed. (Tokyo: Ochanomizu Shobō, 1978), chart 83, and Shinshū Ōsaka Shishi Hensan Iinkai, ed., *Shinshū Ōsaka shishi*, vol. 3 (Osaka: Ōsaka-shi, 1991), pp. 506–7.

Note: All values are in *kanme* of silver. One *kin* equals approximately 600 grams. One *kan* equals approximately 3.75 kilograms. One *tan* equals a standard bolt of cloth, usually measuring about 12.7 by .73 meters. One *hiki* equals 2 *tan*.

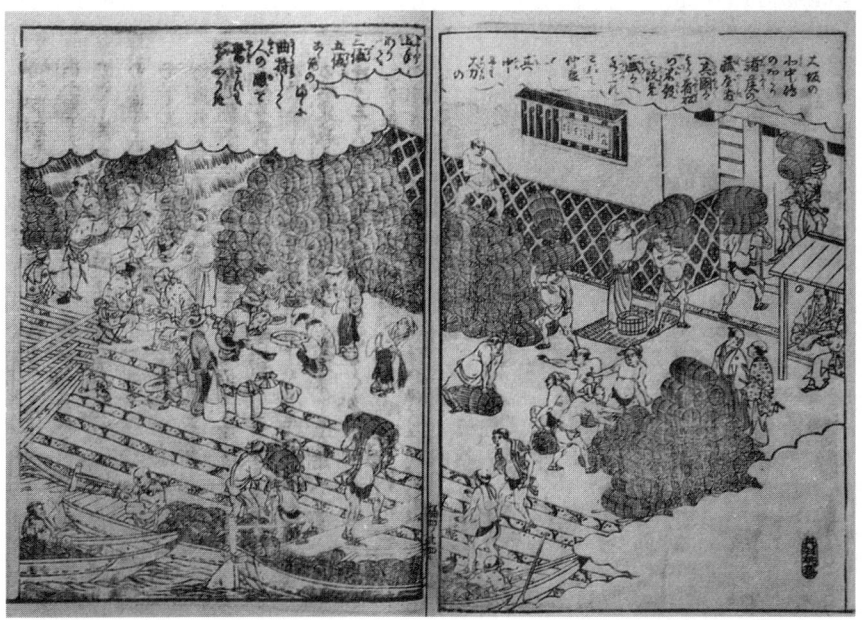

A daimyo warehouse. From Settsu meisho zue. *Courtesy of the Japanese History Research Office, Faculty of Letters, Osaka University.*

The scarcity of documentation makes it difficult to write with confidence about the final destination of the daimyo's rice and specialty goods. Quite obviously, Osaka's burgeoning population consumed a considerable proportion of the rice and bought significant amounts of processed goods. But one million *koku* of rice was more than sufficient to feed Osaka's residents, and much grain found its way to the villages surrounding the city, where many farmers had abandoned rice cultivation in order to concentrate on growing commercial crops, especially cotton, that could be sold to Osaka middlemen. Moreover, substantial quantities of daimyo tax rice found their way to Edo and the Kantō region. In many years, for instance, as much as 8–10 percent of the rice consumed by Edoites passed through the Dōjima market, although that figure fluctuated widely since the distribution networks for certain commodities, and for rice in particular, were elastic and capable of adjusting rapidly to changing conditions of supply and demand.[18]

The decision of Japan's daimyo to market their products through Osaka gave employment, and in some cases brought almost unimaginable wealth, to many merchant families. In the early seventeenth century, daimyo dispatched their own retainers to Osaka to manage the warehouses, but during the latter half of the century most lords hired Osaka merchants, more savvy to local conditions and the subtleties of the marketplace, to conduct business on their behalf. The two key posts were that of the warehouse manager (*kuramoto*), who arranged for the transportation of goods to Osaka and for their subsequent sale, and the controller (*kakeya*), who tended the accounts and arranged for the transfer of funds back to the home domain after transactions were consummated. Among the more prominent managers were the successive heads of the Yodoya house; Masuya Heiemon and his descendants, noted retailers of textiles who faithfully served the Date daimyo of Sendai for generations; and the Kōnoike family, which added to its fame and fortune by serving as joint manager-controllers for Kaga, Hiroshima, Okayama, and Awaji domains.[19]

Osaka financiers proved themselves to be indispensable to the growth of the wholesale commodity trade. Gold, silver, and copper coins of varying degrees of purity circulated in the early modern period, and money changers (*ryōgae*) handled the complex business of assessing the value of coins and helping merchants complete their transactions. In 1670 the shogunate authorized ten money changers, including Kōnoike Zen'emon, to form a privileged association to conduct the shogunate's business and to oversee the operations of other money changers, who by century's end numbered more than one thousand persons organized into some twenty-two groups according to special-

---

18. For additional details of the Osaka-Edo commodity trade in the early eighteenth century, see Hayashi Reiko, "Provisioning Edo in the Early Eighteenth Century: The Pricing Policies of the Shogunate and the Crisis of 1733," in James L. McClain, John M. Merriman, and Ugawa Kaoru, eds., *Edo and Paris: Urban Life and the State in the Early Modern Era* (Ithaca: Cornell University Press, 1994), pp. 217–20.

19. Miyamoto Mataji, "Ōsaka no kura yashiki to kura yakunin," in Miyamoto, *Ōsaka no kenkyū*, vol. 3 (1969), pp. 393–430; idem, "Ōsaka no kura yashiki to kuramoto oyobi kakeya" and "Ōsaka no kura yashiki to myōdai," ibid., 4:47–84, 85–105.

ization. As the money lenders increased in number, they began to perform generalized commercial services akin to those offered by modern banks. Financiers such as the Kōnoike, for instance, bought and sold stocks of coins, accepted deposits from other merchants, and issued letters of credit, promissory notes, and bills of exchange.[20]

Many money changers also engaged in usury. Some, for example, advanced loans to lacquer wholesalers in Osaka, who insured themselves of a steady supply of that commodity by reloaning the funds to farmers in exchange for the right to purchase guaranteed amounts of the sap harvested from lacquer bushes. Similarly, as demand increased for fertilizers made from dried sardines, Osaka importers took out loans from the city's money changers in order to finance the operations of fishermen in villages in the Kantō region. Other money changers, especially those who also served as controllers at daimyo warehouses, advanced loans to those lords. The Kōnoike again stand as a prominent example. The founder of that house, Shinroku, made his original stake as a saké brewer in the village of Kōnoike in Settsu Province and then in 1619 moved his business to the residential quarter of Kyūhōji in Osaka. Not long thereafter, Shinroku became an agent for sales of daimyo rice, and in 1637 he began to advance loans to various daimyo. Shinroku's son, Zen'emon, opened the money-changing shop, which became the chief source of profits for the family for nearly two generations and generated additional capital for loans to the regional lords. So lucrative did usury become that by 1704 daimyo loans accounted for nearly three-quarters of the Kōnoike family's total house capital.

Osaka merchants also played a key role in the conduct of Japan's foreign trade during the Tokugawa period. Some forty to sixty merchant houses—including, as might be expected, the ubiquitous Yodoya family—received authorization from the shogunate to participate in the raw silk trade with China. Together with designated merchants in Nagasaki, Sakai, Kyoto, and Edo, those men imported Chinese raw silk through Nagasaki, Japan's only open port after the 1640s, and arranged for its distribution and sale nationwide. Early the next century, Osaka's Doshō-machi became the country's central distribution point for all imported medicines. In 1722 the shogunate authorized 124 shops located in that residential quarter to form a protective association (*kabu nakama*), with monopoly rights over the sales of all pharmaceuticals imported from the Asian continent. In practice, those shops imported medicines and assessed their content once they arrived in Osaka. They then negotiated prices with a group of shippers, who in turn packaged the medicines and sold them to retail shops in Osaka and to druggists throughout Japan.[21]

The growth of the varied commercial enterprises changed the geography of Osaka. During the second half of the seventeenth century, the city continued to push westward, following the contours of the canal network that carried the

---

20. Wakita Osamu, *Kinsei Ōsaka no keizai to bunka* (Kyoto: Jinbun Shoin, 1994), pp. 44–52.
21. Imai Shūhei, "Edo chūki ni okeru Tō-yakushu no ryūtsū kōzō," *Nihon-shi kenkyū* 169 (September 1976), pp. 1–29.

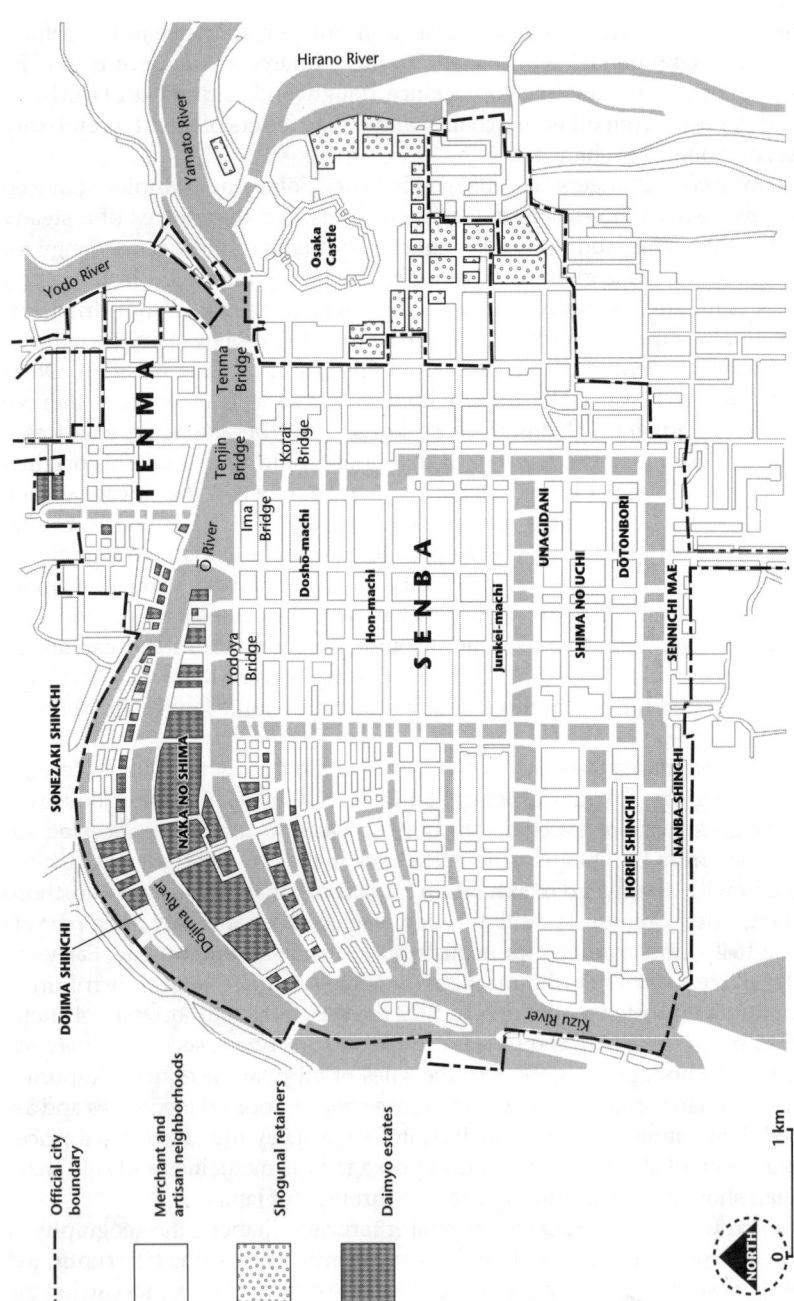

Map 9. Osaka at the beginning of the eighteenth century

city's commerce. Many purchasing agents who shipped commodities from the Kinai provinces into Osaka via the Yodo and Yamato Rivers, for instance, clustered together along the waterways that defined the Senba area, lining the banks of the Higashi Yoko, Naga, and Nishi Yoko Canals and the Ō River. In contrast, the purchasing agents who delivered goods from more distant provinces to Osaka markets tended to set up shop farther to the west, in the neighborhoods bounded by the Edo and Dōton Canals on the north and south, and by the Nishi Yoko Canal and the Kizu River on the east and west. There, in an area ribboned by waterways leading to the wharves where coastal vessels offloaded cargoes, could be found the so-called Satsuma purchasing agents, who imported sugar, camphor, and shiitake mushrooms from southern Kyūshū, and the Tosa agents, who delivered paper, lumber, charcoal, and dried bonito from Shikoku to the Osaka market.[22]

The growing density of money changers and daimyo warehouses added their weight to the westward tilt of the city. Many of the most important money changers, those who handled transactions on behalf on the shogunate, located themselves relatively close to the castle, their shops lining the streets on the western bank of Higashi Yoko Canal between the Kōrai and Ima Bridges. The dozens of smaller money changing businesses, however, found it more convenient to be closer to their merchant customers, and they tended to bunch together along the banks of the Ō River and in Shima no Uchi, the common appellation for the residential quarters encircled by the Naga, Higashi Yoko, Dōton, and Nishi Yoko Canals. The daimyo, for their part, preferred to acquire land for their warehouses on Naka no Shima and along the banks of the Tosabori River and Edo Canal. The 1657 map of Osaka, for instance, shows several warehouses on Naka no Shima, and toward the end of the Tokugawa period more than thirty daimyo repositories sprawled over nearly the entirety of the river island.[23]

The City of Artisans and Production

Osaka's emerging reputation as Japan's kitchen and as the nation's leading city of commerce and finance impressed itself on the maps of the early modern period, obscuring to a considerable degree the city's prominence as an energetic center of production and manufacture. Yet even a cursory examination of the statistics from the year 1714 contained in Table 3.2 quickly reveals that a significant proportion of the commodities flowing into the city consisted of raw materials—rapeseed, dried sardines, copper ore, raw cotton—that Osaka's artisans squeezed, pounded, refined, and fashioned into finished goods that merchants then sold to residents of the city, to families in the commercialized

22. For additional examples and a discussion about the mapping of Osaka in the early modern period, see Harada Tomohiko, Yamori Kazuhiko, and Yanai Akira, *Ōsaka kochizu monogatari* (Tokyo: Asahi Shinbunsha, 1980), pp. 63–85.
23. Yanai Akira, "Kinsei Ōsaka no keikan fukugen e no kokoromi—sono rekishi-chiriteki shomondai," in Toyoda, Harada, and Yamori, *Kōza Nihon no hōken toshi*, 3:138–39.

villages of the Kinai region, to the samurai and commoners of Edo and eastern Japan, and even to foreign customers. Indeed, Osaka's ten leading exports in the early eighteenth century—from rapeseed oil to cotton cloth and the oil cakes used as agricultural fertilizer—were all items produced (or in the case of used articles, refurbished) by the city's rapidly multiplying artisan population, and it is easy to concur with one assessment which claims that processing industries formed the basis of the urban economy in Osaka.[24]

Certain of the processing enterprises stand out for the distinctive traits that they imparted to Osaka's artisanal character. In the medieval period, for example, the sole available clean-burning lamp fuel was perilla oil. Only limited amounts were produced, however, in part because of a scarcity of nutlets borne by the plants and in part because dealers at Ōyamazaki, on the outskirts of Kyoto, monopolized the production and distribution processes, releasing only regulated amounts to the market. As a consequence, few beyond the well-heeled aristocrats and religious institutions of the imperial city could afford the luxury of oil lamps. Those circumstances changed during the Genna period (1615–24), when two Osaka merchants—Matsuya Yasōemon, who lived in Yamato-chō on the southern bank of the Dōton Canal, and Kizuya San'emon of Owarisaka-chō, near the Higashi Yoko Canal—discovered a technique for extracting oil from cottonseed, and not long thereafter others learned how to press oil from rapeseed.[25]

Farmers in the villages surrounding Osaka found that they could grow those two crops quite easily; indeed, so many rural families planted rape as a second crop on rice paddy that in the early spring fields seemed to be dyed a brilliant yellow. Abundant supplies of raw seeds spelled lower production costs, and persons of all economic levels throughout the country quickly realized that they could enjoy the comfort provided by oil lamps, whose light reassured and enchanted even as it enhanced security by discouraging thieves and robbers. Soaring consumer demand stimulated further production, and Osaka became Japan's primary source of "water oil" and "white oil," the common designations for rapeseed and cottonseed fuels. By the end of the seventeenth century, nearly three hundred producers had opened up shops along the Awa, Nishi Yoko, and Higashi Yoko Canals and to the north of the Ō River in the new neighborhoods that were taking shape in the Tenma region, an area incorporated into the growing conurbation in 1634 as Tenmagumi, the third residential precinct that officially made up the city of Osaka. In all, lamp oil represented about one-third of the value of all commodities shipped from Osaka in 1714, and records from the 1720s show that the residents of Edo purchased at least three-quarters of their oil from Osaka dealers.[26]

Osaka artisans also smelted and refined great quantities of copper. As early as the 1620s Ōsakaya Kuzaemon and Marudōya Jirōbei opened workshops at

---

24. Wakita, *Kinsei Ōsaka no machi to hito*, pp. 112–17.
25. *Shinshū: Ōsaka shishi*, vol. 4 (1990), pp. 236–38, 355; Nakabe, "Kinsei toshi Ōsaka no kakuritsu," p. 112.
26. Hayashi, "Provisioning Edo," p. 219.

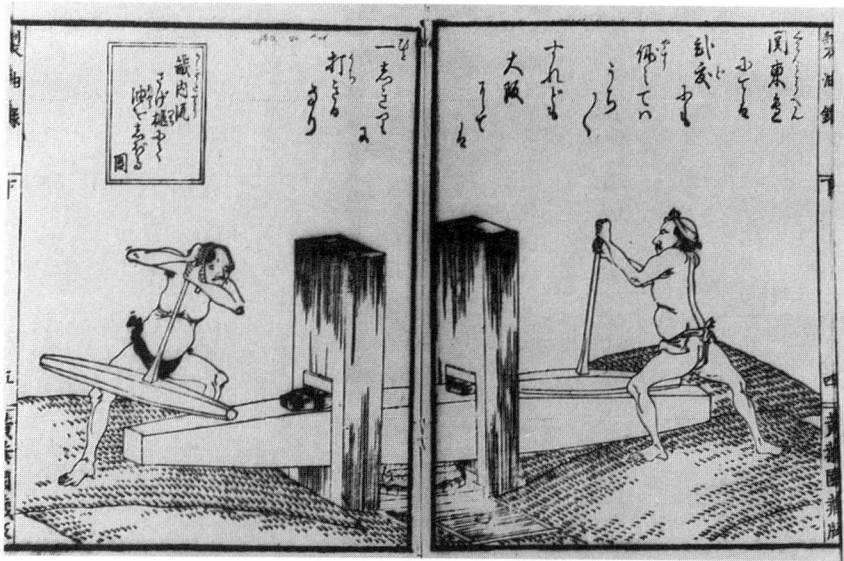

Pressing oil from rapeseeds. From "Seiyu roku," by permission of Ōsaka Furitsu Naka no Shima Toshokan.

Sumiya-machi, on the banks of Nishi Yoko Canal, and later maps and documents show several other smelting businesses along the Naga and Dōton Canals.[27] Among those enterprises, Osaka's most famous copper-refining business belonged to the Izumiya (Sumitomo) family. The man honored as the founder of that lineage was Monjuin Masatomo, a Buddhist priest in the Nehan sect. When the shogunate ordered that his congregation be absorbed into the Tendai sect, which the shoguns patronized, Masatomo left the priesthood, began to call himself Fujiya, and opened a bookstore and pharmacy in Kyoto. Somewhat later, Masatomo adopted the son of his elder sister and arranged for the young man, named Tomomochi, to marry his daughter. Although he had become Masatomo's heir, Tomomochi took with him his natal family's shop name, Izumiya, when he decided to move to Osaka in 1623 (or perhaps 1624), just as the city was beginning to recover from the battles of 1614–15. From his own father Tomomochi had learned how to refine silver and copper ore, and so perhaps quite naturally he opened a workshop in 1636 at Unagidani, on the southern banks of Naga Canal, where he employed numerous artisans.

Thanks to the initiatives of men such as Izumiya and Ōsakaya, the refining industry prospered. During the first half of the seventeenth century, gold and silver represented Japan's principal exports to foreign countries, but as the shogunate restricted the outflow of those precious metals in order to preserve the integrity of its currency, copper climbed to the top of the nation's export

27. *Shinshū: Ōsaka shishi*, 3:818–22; Wakita, *Kinsei Ōsaka no machi to hito*, pp. 126–30, 190–94; and Harada, Yamori, and Yanai, *Ōsaka kochizu monogatari*, pp. 165–66.

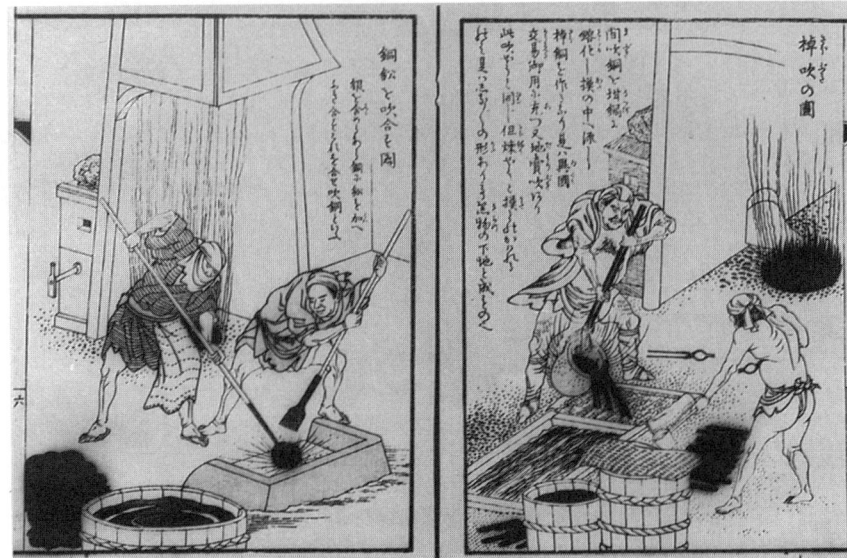

Refining copper. From "Kodō zuroku," by permission of Ōsaka Furitsu Naka no Shima Toshokan.

list. From the latter half of the seventeenth century, the shogunate authorized the export of five million *kin* (about 3,300 tons) of refined copper through Nagasaki each year, and it bestowed upon a group of leading smelting houses in Osaka the exclusive right to refine all export copper. In addition, Osaka smelters produced a metal that was fashioned into tools and fittings for sale to consumers in Osaka and, as Table 3.2 indicates, in many other cities and villages throughout Japan. In all, according to records dating to 1685, Osaka smelters handled five to nine million *kin* of copper annually. The Izumiya were the largest producers, turning out 1.1 million *kin* of copper in 1680 and an average of almost 2.3 million *kin* each year for most of the initial decade of the eighteenth century.

As the volume of trade swelled, so too did the number of persons employed by industry leaders such as Izumiya and Ōsakaya. Indeed, some documents suggest that by the end of the seventeenth century as many as ten thousand persons found employment in the copper trade. That figure may be somewhat exaggerated, but not by much. Izumiya household records indicate that in 1721—not a particularly robust year for copper refineries—the family employed 119 artisans as smelters at its workshop, which extended over more than two thousand square meters on the banks of the Naga Canal. If the Izumiya family kept that many on its payroll in a poor year, then in more normal times as many as five to seven hundred skilled smelters might well have been at work in all the city's workshops. If one adds to that core number all of the smiths, charcoal dealers, jobbers, and shippers whose business success was tied directly to the prosperity of the refineries, then surely several thousand persons relied on the copper trade for their livelihoods. Moreover, many of those families enjoyed a decent standard of living; master smelters, for instance, earned a daily wage roughly on par with that commanded by well-paid master carpenters.

Near the opposite end of the economic scale clustered many of the leather workers of Osaka. Those families had origins as outcasts (*eta*) in the medieval period, when they apparently resided in five villages scattered along the northern banks of the Ō River, near the sites of the later Tenma and Tenjin Bridges, living and working under the jurisdiction of a shrine for which they performed miscellaneous services. As the population of Osaka began to expand in response to the efforts of the Tokugawa shoguns to revive the city in the 1620s, officials opened up space for merchant and artisan families who wished to move into the community by compelling the residents of the five outcast villages to resettle at Watanabe, beyond the official southern boundary of the city. That location was significant, for it illuminated the ambiguities surrounding the outcasts' existence. On the one hand, the families of Watanabe suffered social discrimination as officials sought to segregate them physically from the other residents of Osaka; on the other hand, the government valued the services that the outcasts of Watanabe performed, and so it placed them under the jurisdiction of the city magistrates, thus incorporating the people of Watanabe into the city in an administrative sense.[28]

Since the outcasts were subject to the authority of Osaka's city magistrates, officials included the leather goods produced by the families of Watanabe in the statistics they compiled listing commodities shipped into and out of the city. Indeed, during the seventeenth century, Watanabe emerged as the hub of the nationwide trade in hides and leather. The craftsmen of Watanabe purchased large numbers of pelts from various parts of Japan and even imported through Nagasaki deer and shark skins by the tens of thousands from southeast Asia. They cured and tanned the hides, processing them into a variety of useful products: armor and sword fittings for samurai; bellows for smiths; and leather footwear, coats, and headgear for ordinary persons. As Table 3.2 indicates, Osaka wholesalers in 1714 shipped more than one-half million pairs of leather sandals, sixty thousand pairs of leather-soled *tabi* footwear, three thousand leather jackets, and one thousand sets of bellows. Aggregated, the total value of those leather products exceeded the value of the saké, ceramic ware, or sesame oil dispatched by Osaka middlemen to consumers around Japan.

During the course of the Tokugawa period, Watanabe grew into the largest outcast settlement in the country; its population numbered 2,341 inhabitants in 1713 and peaked at slightly more than five thousand persons in the early 1830s. The community included a handful of extremely wealthy, elite families —Taikoya Matabei allegedly amassed a fortune of some seven hundred thousand *ryō* in the eighteenth century—and a far greater number of persons whose

---

28. Wakita, *Kinsei Ōsaka no machi to hito*, pp. 136–41; *Shinshū: Ōsaka shishi*, 3:824–46.

lifestyles were more modest, such as the craftsmen who fashioned leather footwear. Perhaps the most humble existence was endured by those outcasts whom the government charged with certain official duties, such as cleaning the prison and disposing of the corpses of amorous couples who committed double suicide and of unfortunate travelers who died on the road. The life experiences of those residents of Watanabe was not far removed from that of the even more socially despised *hinin*, the "nonpersons" who assisted the police with the apprehension and punishment of criminals. Those outcasts also lived on the periphery of the city—in segregated settlements on the far northern edge of Tenma, near Dōton Canal, around the Shitennōji temple complex, and close to the graveyard at Tobita.

The families who pressed oil, refined copper, and tanned hides were only a small part of Osaka's growing artisan community. During the course of the seventeenth century, Osaka also became well known for the cotton cloth finished by its dyers, who formed production groups based on the color of the cloth they turned out; the combs, barrettes, toupees, tobacco pouches, bags, and myriad other personal accessories that were sold in great quantities in Edo; the soy sauce that flooded the markets of eastern Japan; the saké fermented by more than six hundred local brewers; and a thousand and one other products that people used in their daily lives—engraved signature seals, lacquerware, gold leaf, umbrellas, shamisen strings, carved whalebone, pictorial votive offerings, folding screens, storage chests, sliding doors, raincoats, carpenters' tools, mirrors, lanterns, and so forth.

The artisan families lived along the streets and byways of the city, fleshing out the sinews and tendons formed by the canals and rivers that defined Osaka as a city of commerce and overflowing into the neighborhoods of the Tenma Precinct. By the end of the seventeenth century, for example, the seal engravers had settled in Hirano-machi near the Kōrai and Tenjin Bridges, where families who ground powders and dyes into facial makeup also had their lodgings. Those who crafted dolls, pictorial votive offerings, and footwear favored Midōmae-chō. The workshops of some lacquerers lined the streets between Kita Kyūtarō-machi and Andōji-chō, while other lacquerware craftsmen lived in Nanba Shinchi, where abacus makers also clustered together. Tamatsukuri Ise-chō, meanwhile, had become home to whalebone carvers, Minami Kyūhōji-machi to raincoat makers, Kita Kyūtarō-machi to those who pounded and shaped gold leaf, and Saburōemon-chō to craftsmen who put together sliding *fusuma* partitions. Variegated and ceaselessly involved in productive creation, the artisan population of Osaka contributed to a complicated and constantly changing urban geography whose center of gravity seemed constantly to be moving west and north, away from the castle, during the seventeenth century.

Adding to the kaleidoscopic intricacy of Osaka's geographical patterns was the fact that most neighborhoods were home to a mix of artisans and merchants. In many instances, of course, business logic dictated that artisans involved in the production of the same commodity live in proximity to one another so that wholesalers and jobbers could conveniently call on many workshops in a single visit. Despite that, by the end of the seventeenth century few residential quarters in Osaka were the domain of a single occupational group. As noted above, families that made dolls, votive offerings, and footwear lived cheek by jowl in Midōmae-chō, and the complexion of most neighborhoods usually was even more complicated than that. According to a land register compiled in 1700, many of the fifty-five residential quarters that made up Shima no Uchi, for example, numbered artisans, money changers, jobbers, and wholesalers among their residents. The story was the same across town at Hirano-machi, home to saké brewers as well as seal engravers, and at Kita Kyūtarō-machi and Minami Kyūhōji-machi, where lacquerware producers and raincoat makers shared their neighborhoods with shop owners who sold textiles and personal accessories imported from the continent.[29]

Small-scale retailers, such as those found at Kita Kyūtarō-machi and Minami Kyūhōji-machi, added another measure of complexity to the rich flavor of Osaka's evolving geography. Again, there was no simple pattern: shop owners who purveyed ordinary foodstuffs and other essentials of daily life populated nearly every artisan neighborhood, large retail outlets that drew customers from across the city established themselves at more central locations, and special shopping districts sprouted up at many points on the urban landscape. The great Echigoya (Mitsui) and Masuya (Iwaki) dry goods stores, to take a pair of examples, spread themselves out along the western approach to Kōrai Bridge, from Shiken-chō all the way to Mamenoha-chō. Across town one of the more lively shopping districts, which served a cluster of residential quarters in the southern portion of the city, filled the streets of Junkei-machi, which ran on an east-west axis just north of Naga Canal. According to one document, "merchants from dusk hung out colored lanterns . . . and shops stretched out along all sides of the streets." The prosperity of the district, added the later *Settsu meisho zue*, "was beyond compare. The merchants lack nothing that one might desire; there are shops that specialize in cotton cloth and clothing, household furnishings, bags, and pouches."[30] Other offerings included flatware and metal tools, straw raincoats and umbrellas, footwear and stockings—nearly the entire cornucopia of goods produced in the city's workshops and sold across the breadth of Japan as well as in Osaka.

As the merchants, artisans, retailers, and their families settled in, transforming Osaka into a center of commerce and production, the community emerged as western Japan's most populous city. Extant statistics indicate that the population of Osaka reached a seventeenth-century high of 404,929 persons in 1634 and then plunged by a third over the next three decades, to just 268,760 persons in 1665. As dramatic as that decline might seem, it is not implausible, since many of the workers who had labored on the castle probably left the city in the 1630s. However, as Osaka came into its own as a focal point of merchant

---

29. See specific entries in such geographic dictionaries as *Nihon rekishi chimei taikei*, vol. 28, *Ōsaka-fu no chimei* (Tokyo: Heibonsha, 1986), and *Kadokawa Nihon chimei dai jiten*, vol. 27, *Ōsaka-fu* (Tokyo: Kadokawa Shoten, 1991), which make extensive use of the document "Ōsaka <Kitagumi • Minamigumi • Tenmagumi> mizu-chō machikazu iekazu yakukazu yose-chō," located at Ōsaka Furitsu Naka no Shima Toshokan.

30. Harada, Yamori, and Yanai, *Ōsaka kochizu monogatari*, p. 156.

The Mitsui (Echigoya) dry goods store. From Settsu meisho zue. *Courtesy of the Japanese History Research Office, Faculty of Letters, Osaka University.*

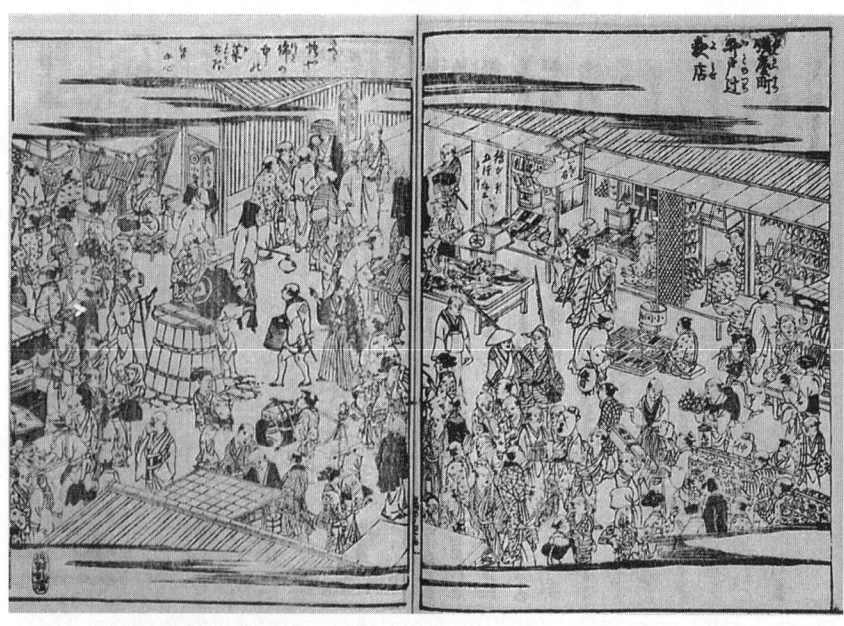

Shoppers at Junkei-machi. From Settsu meisho zue. *Courtesy of the Japanese History Research Office, Faculty of Letters, Osaka University.*

Table 3.3. Osaka's merchant and artisan population

Year	Number of persons	Year	Number of persons
1634	404,929	1765	423,453
1665	268,760	1769	412,997
1669	279,610	1779	408,717
1679	287,891	1789	381,529
1689	330,244	1799	384,866
1699	364,154	1809	385,746
1709	381,626	1819	377,079
1719	374,498	1829	379,590
1729	385,431	1839	331,759
1739	403,724	1849	338,261
1749	404,146	1859	312,986
1759	417,099		

Source: Adapted from Shinshū Ōsaka Shishi Hensan Iinkai, ed., *Shinshū Ōsaka shishi*, vol. 4 (Osaka: Ōsaka-shi, 1990), p. 199.

and artisanal activity during the middle of the century, its population began to rise once again, peaking at approximately 425,000 in the middle of the eighteenth century, as indicated in Table 3.3.

Even the mapping of the city changed as Osaka's importance as a city of commerce and production rivaled and then eclipsed its significance as a military headquarters for samurai. The oldest extant map of the city, dated 1657, is oriented to place the castle at top-center, with the merchant quarters spread out humbly below the castle. Moreover, the cartographer drew the castle compound with considerable care, attending even to details about the individual buildings within the ramparts. A century later, however, in 1759, a different mapmaker placed the merchant and artisan quarters at the center of his rendition of the city. He also relegated the castle to the far edge of the map and did not trouble himself even to sketch in the principal buildings within its walls, preferring instead to give more attention and detail to the commercial heart of the city.[31]

The metamorphosis from military redoubt to a bastion of commercial vitality and artisanal production represented just one of many transformations that Osaka experienced during the early modern period. In a manner undreamed by the first three shoguns, the city in time would emerge as a stage for theatrical and artistic inventiveness, a center of religious devotion, a hub of intellectual creativity, and the locus of regional governance. Osaka's changing urban geography mirrored those great transitions. By the early eighteenth century, Nanba Shinchi, on the southern periphery of the city, had taken its place as a vibrant locale of popular culture; neighboring Sennichi Mae appeared on

---

31. For depictions of Osaka, see Tamaki Toyojirō, ed., *Ōsaka kensetsu-shi yawa* (Osaka: Ōsaka Toshi Kyōkai, 1980).

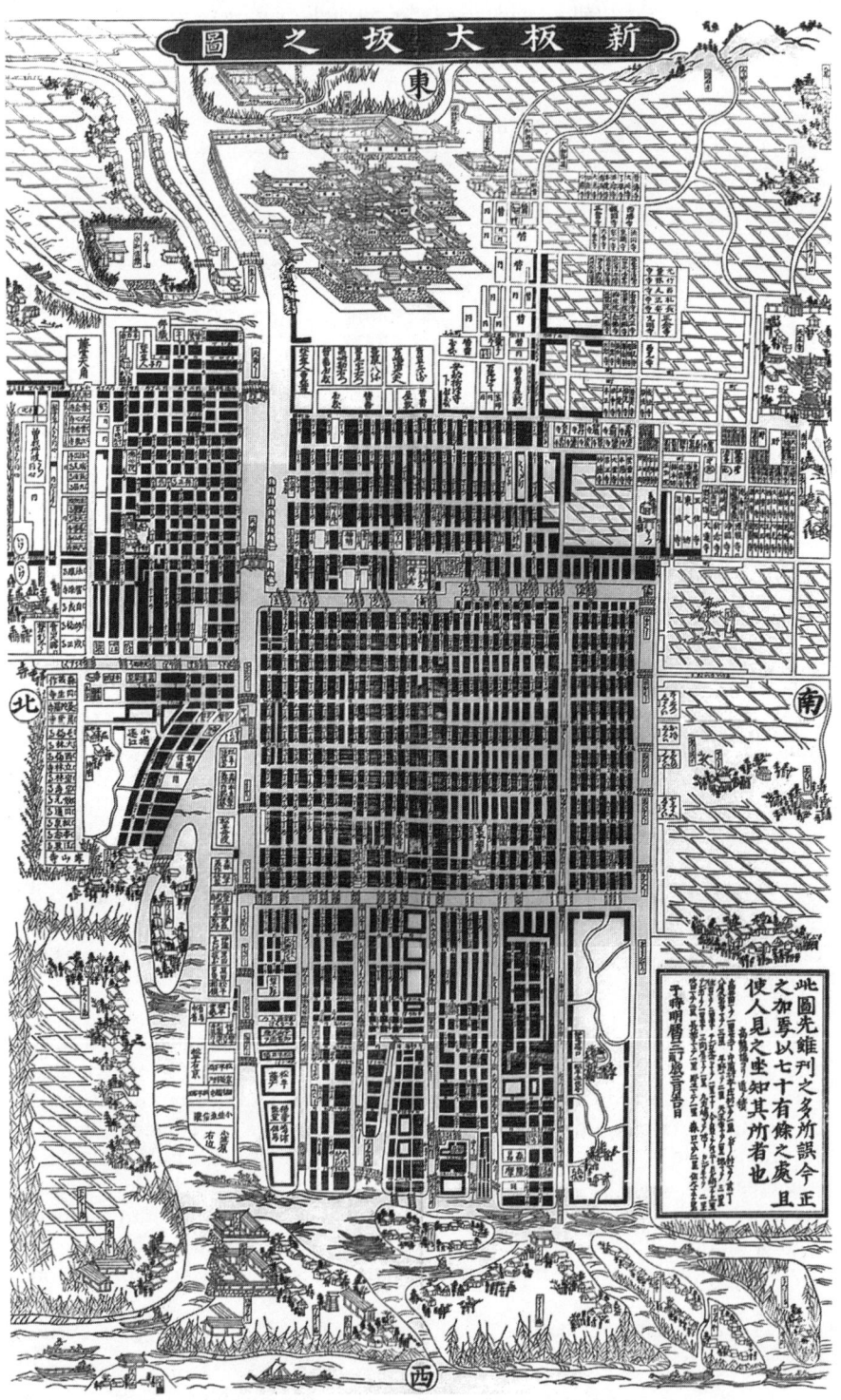

Osaka in 1657. Courtesy of Ōsaka Toshi Kyōkai.

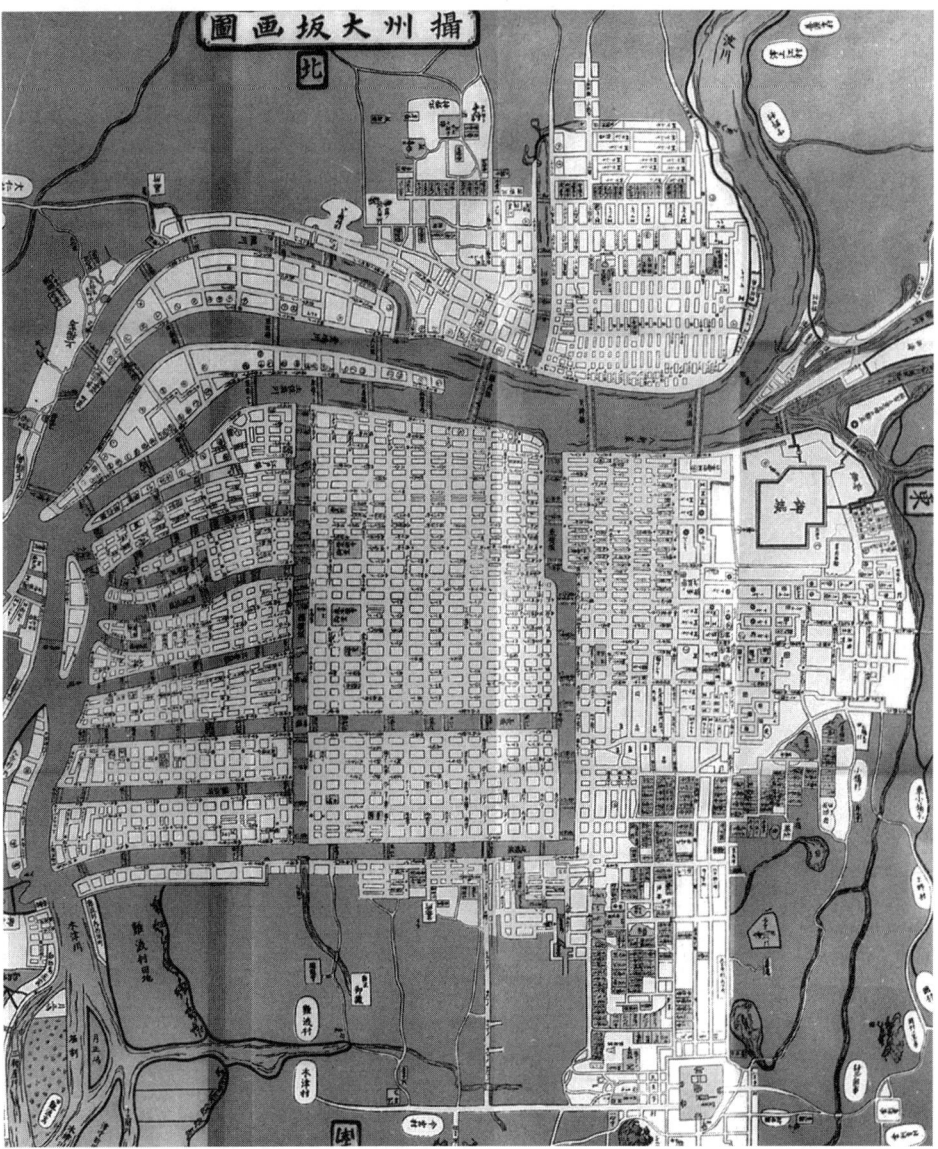

Osaka in 1759. Courtesy of Ōsaka Toshi Kyōkai.

maps as an official execution ground for criminals, while representing in the popular mind the birthplace of legends about petty thugs turned folk heroes; nearby, Dōtonbori stood out as a leading theater district where spellbound patrons thrilled to fictionalized accounts of romantic tragedies that involved their merchant neighbors and the glamorous prostitutes of Shinmachi and Sonezaki Shinchi, situated diagonally across town; and everywhere wandering monks

A prostitution district. From "Naniwa kagami." Courtesy of the Japanese History Research Office, Faculty of Letters, Osaka University.

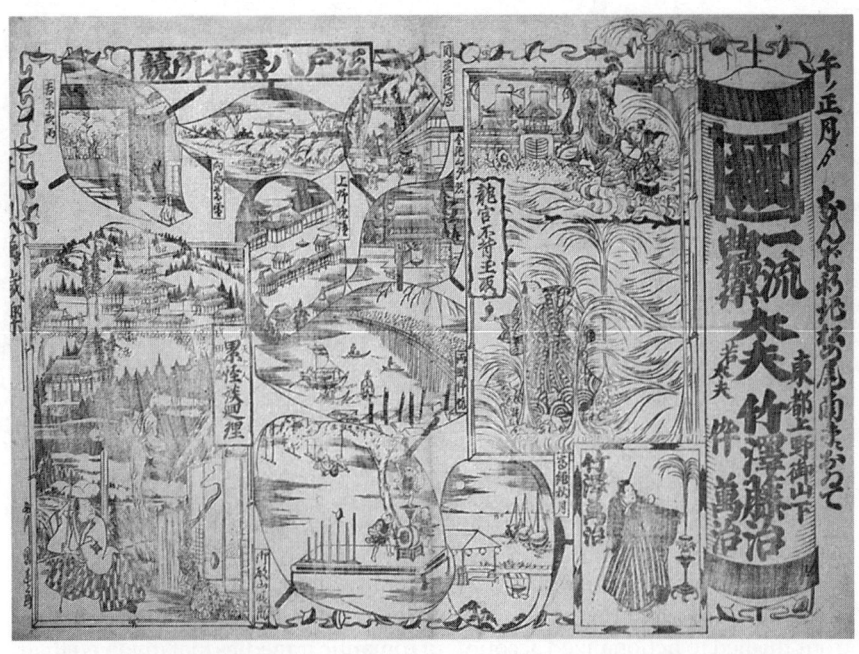

Performers at Nanba Shinchi. From "Banzuke-chō." Courtesy of the Japanese History Research Office, Faculty of Letters, Osaka University.

and charismatic shamans claimed the city's streets for their mendicancies and religious supplications.

As Osaka grew in size and changed its shape and physical appearance, it affirmed its place as one of the three jewels nestled at the apex of Japan's urban hierarchy. In common with all great world cities, however, Osaka's silhouette did not represent a mere tracing of the broad economic, social, and political trends of the times; rather, what happened within the city helped to define and breathe life into the great historical impulses that were reshaping society in general. Throughout the early modern epoch, Osaka's merchant and artisan families moved to the vanguard of a samurai-created world, and in doing so they brought together powerful concentrations of wealth and creativity that unleashed changes felt across the country. Osaka's craftspeople and entrepreneurs improved processing techniques, discovered new products, and reinvented old ones, and its wholesalers and jobbers crafted distribution systems that carried those goods to the far corners of the country, advancing standards of living throughout Japan. Subsequent chapters will elaborate upon Osaka's importance, showing how the city's playwrights, artists, intellectuals, and clerics enriched the nation by creating new genres of literary and dramatic production and by imagining new ways for the people of Japan to conceive of themselves, their relationship with the gods, their cultural past, and even their place in the world of the future. The activities of all those persons shaped the contours of Osaka's ceaselessly evolving urban geography and simultaneously placed the city at the very heart of the social and economic revolution that remade Japan during the early modern era.

CHAPTER FOUR

Protest and the Tactics of Direct Remonstration: Osaka's Merchants Make Their Voices Heard

— *Uchida Kusuo*
TRANSLATED BY JAMES L. MCCLAIN

The 1720s and 1730s were not easy times for merchant and artisan families in Osaka, or more generally for much of the commoner population throughout Japan. To an unprecedented degree, collective violence and organized dissidence scarred those two decades, providing an index of growing popular antipathy with the shogunate and regional daimyo governments. Flames of discontent flared up in every quadrant of the rural countryside, from Kyūshū to Tōhoku, and residents of Japan's major cities were equally restive. In Edo, the poor and angry employed violence as a tactic of protest for the first time in that city's history in 1733, when they attacked the shop of a rice dealer who was closely identified with the shogunate. Just three years later, thousands of merchants in Osaka gathered to express their unambiguous dissatisfaction with economic conditions and with shogunal policies that threatened to jeopardize their well-being.

Sparking the disquiet of the early eighteenth century in Osaka were complicated problems that resulted from the imposition of new taxes in the surrounding countryside, an upward ratcheting of urban rice prices, and fresh initiatives by the shogunate to intervene in the marketplace to advance its own fiscal interests at the expense of merchant and artisan families. Those events provoked a debate, carried on through legal petitions on some occasions and through acts of dissidence at others, about how much tax rice the state was entitled to collect and how much governing officials might be permitted to manipulate retail grain prices in urban areas in order to optimize revenues garnered from the sales of that rice. In the process of remonstrating against the actions of shogunal authorities, the commoners of Osaka allied themselves in new organizational groupings that both permitted them to articulate their political voice more forcefully and served them well in future contests with the state. In terms of this volume, the events of 1736 in Osaka assume an added importance, since they suggest new ways to appreciate how policies crafted by political elites in Edo and Osaka affected the lives of the residents of Japan's leading commercial metropolis, just as they help to explain how protest from below represented one aspect of Osaka's transformation into the people's city.

The Tumult of the Kyōhō Era

Setting tax rates was no easy matter. From the inception of Tokugawa rule at the beginning of the seventeenth century, the shogunate and the regional daimyo regimes had depended for their existence on revenues collected from villagers in rice, a circumstance that produced a delicate calculus of taxation and provisioning. On the one hand, the national regime and regional overlords were tempted to extract as much as they possibly could from the peasantry. On the other hand, Neo-Confucianism constituted the touchstone for a prevailing political ethos that compelled the shogunate and daimyo to demonstrate the legitimacy of their authority by moderating their coercive instincts, exhibiting benevolence, and nurturing the well-being of the people of Japan. Practical considerations underscored the efficacy of the more temperate approach; leaving adequate grain supplies in the hands of farm families could create a healthier economic environment and thus help to secure long-term political stability.

Laying claim to an appropriate amount of tax rice, however, represented for Japan's political elites only the entry point into a subtle labyrinth of problems. Once officials collected the grain, they also had to sell it, or arrange for it to be sold, and that raised another dilemma. The overarching umbrella of Neo-Confucian benevolence also sheltered the country's merchants and artisans by holding the shogunate and daimyo responsible for warranting that Japan's cities be provisioned with the necessities of daily life. That dictate did not mean that government itself had to feed the urban population, but it did obligate the shogun and daimyo to make certain that the merchant and artisan families had enough to eat. The surest way to accomplish that, at least in the minds of most urban commoners, was to maintain a relatively low price for rice, the grain of life. Set against that consideration was a second reality that loomed large in official thinking: the higher the price of rice, the greater the revenues of the Tokugawa shogunate and daimyo governments. Moreover, since the shogun and regional lords paid their samurai in grain, higher rice prices would benefit their retainers, the warriors who enjoyed a monopoly on the bearing of arms and served as the military and police arm of government.

For a considerable stretch of the seventeenth century, the shogunate and most daimyo domains kept tax revenues, commodity prices, and government expenditures in an astutely balanced equilibrium; abundant harvests and budgetary prudence permitted the overlords to collect sufficient amounts of tax rice and to market it at prices high enough to cover the expenses of governing, yet low enough to satisfy the diets of Japan's urban residents. But matters took a turn for the worse during the Kyōhō period (1716–36) when a general decline in rice prices eroded the tax base of the Tokugawa state, just as the expenditure side of shogunal and domain ledgers began to fill up with new demands: increased expenses associated with participation in the alternate attendance and residence system (*sankin kōtai*), moneys for castle repair and road maintenance, and funds to underwrite a multitude of other obligations. The natural response was to try to squeeze more taxes from the rural villagers. Consequently, soon after coming to power in 1716, the eighth shogun, Yoshimune, launched the famous Kyōhō reforms, which included various measures designed to encourage the development of new paddies and to increase the annual imposts collected from villagers. When many daimyo followed suit within their own domains, peasants protested by banding together in several hundred different locales, initiating the violence that colored the late 1720s and 1730s.

Despite such widespread rural discontent, the state's revenue enhancement policies proved successful. Nationwide, tax collections reached new heights, and rice flowed into Japan's cities. Abundant supplies, however, depressed the market value of the grain. Ironically, Yoshimune's triumphs had the unanticipated consequence of jeopardizing the financial underpinnings of the shogunate, the daimyo, and the entire samurai estate. Soon, government officials began to craft countermeasures to offset the adverse effects of "cheap rice, expensive commodities." In the Second Month of 1724, for instance, the city elders (*machidoshiyori*) in Edo issued a proclamation to the merchants and artisans of that city. "The price of rice has declined since last year," the elders began, even though "the prices of other commodities have stayed high."[1] The officials then went on to declare that producers of those other commodities, items ranging from personal clothing to household furnishings, "have an ethical obligation to sell at a low price. . . . We will conduct an investigation of prices, to be completed by the first day of the Third Month. Everyone must obey our instructions. All the details are to be announced in every province, in every place; and if prices are not reduced at the place of production, complaints should be brought against the producers."

Not content merely to jawbone against expensive commodity prices, the shogunate also moved during the Kyōhō period to implement policies in urban areas that would privilege the government and samurai by keeping the

---

1. Hayashi Reiko, "Provisioning Edo in the Early Eighteenth Century: The Pricing Policies of the Shogunate and the Crisis of 1733," in James L. McClain, John M. Merriman, and Ugawa Kaoru, eds., *Edo and Paris: Urban Life and the State in the Early Modern Era* (Ithaca: Cornell University Press, 1994), pp. 223–25.

value of rice as high as possible. One of government's more heavy-handed measures was simply to order well-to-do merchants to buy up surplus inventories of grain. In the Eleventh Month of 1725, for instance, the shogun's minions obliged three Edo merchants (Kinokuniya Genbei, Ōsakaya Riemon, and Nomuraya Jinbei) to dig into their own pockets and purchase rice from distributors and wholesalers in Edo and Osaka. The officials further directed the men to put the grain in storage and to sell it later, "at their own discretion," presumably after the price had risen. Besides decreeing compulsory purchases, the shogunate scouted out ways to intervene on the supply side of the provisioning equation. One favorite stratagem was to keep some tax rice off-market. Such was the case in 1725 when the shogunate placed temporary restrictions on the amount of grain that daimyo from northern Japan annually shipped into Edo and Osaka, and in the Seventh Month of 1730 the shogunate itself decided to suspend the scheduled transfer into Edo of some 600,000 *koku* of tax rice harvested on its own direct holdings. Later, in the Tenth Month of 1735, policymakers ventured into new territory: declaring that low rice prices were causing "suffering among samurai and peasants alike," officials set minimum prices for rice bought by wholesalers and distributors.

The government's pricing policies sometimes provoked a sharp reaction from merchant and artisan families, who found themselves paying more for a basic foodstuff than they considered justified. That happened in Edo in 1733. The previous year, the shogunate had embargoed the transfer of daimyo and commercial rice into the city in order to preserve its price, and that same fall an infestation of locusts severely damaged the rice crop in western Japan, bringing on widespread misery and starvation. In response to the dearth, the shogunate began to purchase large quantities of rice in Edo and Osaka for shipment to the famine area. As a consequence, rice prices surged in major urban centers during the autumn and early winter of 1732. In Edo, merchant and artisan families urged their neighborhood elders (*nanushi*) to send petitions to higher authorities. Many did so, calling attention to the suffering of the urban poor caused by the price spike and asking the shogun's officials to undertake corrective measures: to make certain that wealthy rice merchants did not hoard grain, to distribute relief supplies from shogunal granaries, and to authorize ships with rice from daimyo in the Hokuriku area to dock at Edo and unload their cargoes. Edo's city magistrates (*machi bugyō*) seemingly had little sympathy with the city's commoner population, however. Keeping the price of rice high, they responded at one point, was being done "out of consideration for the warriors who must sell their stipends in order to live. The more comfortable life becomes for the warriors, the more they will be able to buy from you. Commerce will flourish, and this should not make life difficult for the commoners. . . . We do not understand what your problem is."[2] Angered by such official arrogance and apparent lack of interest in their plight, on the twenty-sixth day of the First Month, 1733, the ordinary people of Edo rioted,

---

2. Anne Walthall, "Edo Riots," in McClain, Merriman, and Ugawa, *Edo and Paris*, p. 411.

attacking the shop of Takama Denbei, a wealthy rice dealer who marketed tax rice for the shogunate.

THE CRISIS MOVES TO OSAKA

After the violence of 1733, conditions nationwide improved and people enjoyed a succession of plentiful harvests. As ample supplies of grain moved through the marketing pipeline, however, urban rice prices began to fall, and the shogunate once again had to confront the problem of how to maintain a floor under grain prices for the benefit of the daimyo and its own retainers. Consequently, in the fall of 1735 (Kyōhō 20) the government intervened decisively in the Osaka rice market, just as it was doing in Edo. On the fifth day of the Tenth Month, the Osaka city magistrates issued an ordinance stipulating that superior-grade rice had to be traded at the rate of at least forty-two *monme* per *koku*, beginning on the fifteenth day of that month. Any transaction completed below that price would be subject to a surcharge of ten *monme* per *koku*, payable to the government. Subsequently, in the middle of the next month authorities set the price of low-grade rice at thirty-nine *monme* per *koku*, and on the sixth day of the Twelfth Month, they raised the minimum price of superior rice to forty-three *monme* five *fun* per *koku* and pegged the price for low-grade rice at forty *monme* per *koku*.[3] Yet another decree, made public on the final day of the year, jacked up prices one more time, as shown in Table 4.1.

The initial decisions about minimum prices paved the way for the government's dramatic announcement of a *kawasemai*, or mandatory rice purchase. On the fifteenth day of the Twelfth Month, Osaka's city magistrates decreed that the rice dealers at Dōjima and a group of money changers involved in financing the rice trade would be held responsible for purchasing an aggregate total of 130,000 *koku* of rice.[4] Specifically, Osaka's political leaders ordered the rice dealers to buy 100,000 *koku* of rice and the money changers to acquire the remaining 30,000 *koku*. Moreover, the city magistrates told the merchants to complete the purchases promptly, by the First Month of the subsequent year, and further instructed them to keep their own inventories of grain off-market until the supplies acquired from the daimyo warehouses were entirely liquidated. To put the burden of the mandatory purchase in perspective, it is useful to recall that the cash equivalent of 130,000 *koku* of rice would keep nearly one-fifth of Osaka's population in food, shelter, and clothing for an entire year.

The government soon announced another bold measure: on the nineteenth and twenty-first days of the Twelfth Month, the shogun's officials called on four Osaka merchants—Yamatoya Saburōzaemon, Izumiya Kichiemon, Hiranoya Gohei, and Tatsumiya Kyūzaemon—to loan the government a total of 3,200 *kanme* of silver, pledging as collateral specified inventories of rice stored

---

3. Ōsaka-shi, ed., *Ōsaka shishi*, vol. 3 (Osaka: Sanjikai, 1911), pp. 355–56, 363, 365, 368.
4. *Ōsaka shishi*, vol. 1 (1913), pp. 706–20.

Table 4.1. Rice prices as set by Osaka city officials in 1735 and 1736

Date	Grade			
	Superior	Middle	Low	Inferior
Kyōhō 20 (1735)				
Tenth Month, fifth day	42.0			
Eleventh Month, fifteenth day	42.0		39.0	
Twelfth Month, sixth day	43.5		40.0	
Twelfth Month, thirtieth day	48.0	45.0	42.3	
Genbun 1 (1736)				
Third Month, sixteenth day	48.0	43.0	38.5	33.0

Note: Prices are in *monme* of silver per *koku* of rice.

in daimyo warehouses in Osaka.[5] The government intended to funnel the moneys to needy daimyo, expecting repayment from the lords only after prices later rose and made the sale of warehouse rice more profitable. At the officially pegged price, the required sum of 3,200 *kanme* of silver could cover the cost of nearly eighty thousand *koku* of low-grade rice. In other words, the combination of mandatory purchases and cash loans meant that during the Twelfth Month of Kyōhō 20 alone city officials had enjoined Osaka's merchant community to take responsibility for the ultimate disposal of approximately 210,000 *koku* of rice.

In the new year, government officials stepped up their efforts to manipulate rice prices. One thrust aimed to postpone the marketing of new rice stocks so as to promote the sales of existing inventories. Thus, on the twenty-first day of the First Month, the shogunate announced that rice shipments from domains in the northern provinces of Mutsu and Dewa, which normally arrived at daimyo warehouses in Osaka in the Fourth Month, would have to be delayed and that such cargoes could not be off-loaded until the Sixth Month.[6] Subsequently, in the Second Month of 1736, officials resorted to mandating more compulsory purchases, this time tapping the purses of more than fifty farmers and rural merchants from certain villages in Izumi Province—men who could discharge this civic responsibility, the government claimed, because they enjoyed an abundance of "food and money" and personified "virtue."[7]

Another round of mandatory purchase orders went out to the merchants of Osaka's residential quarters in the Third Month, 1736.[8] Like the previous decree directed at farmers, local authorities announced the new requisitions, but the authorizing documents bore the seals of Hosoda Tanba no Kami and Ōoka Echizen no Kami, respectively the commissioner of finance and the Edo city magistrate, who had emerged as the chief architects of the shogunate's Kyōhō

5. "Koki-roku," ms collection, Cabinet Library (Naikaku Bunko). This assemblage of documents was compiled in Genbun 1 (1736).
6. *Ōsaka shishi*, 3:368–69.
7. "Koki-roku." The particular entry is dated the sixth day, Third Month, 1736; it does not state how much rice those men were required to purchase, either individually or in total.
8. *Ōsaka shishi*, 1:708.

reforms. According to the new directive, Osaka's merchant community had to buy some 139,696 *koku* of what was described as "the lord's rice" and "daimyo tax rice." In actuality, all the grain belonged to the shogunate. The "lord's rice" referred to the emergency reserves customarily stored in the shogunate's Naniwa and Tamatsukuri granaries, and the "daimyo tax rice" represented the amounts of grain that a particular group of daimyo, those lords who had received special loans from the shogunate during the famine of 1732, were slated to repay the Tokugawa regime.

Of the nearly 140,000 *koku* of rice set aside for compulsory purchase, Osaka's city officials directed a certain Matsuyasu Shōemon to market 50,944 *koku* of rice that was labeled as being "fouled," "half-spoiled," or "slightly putrescent."[9] Authorities then held individual residential quarters corporately responsible for buying specified allotments of the remaining grain: the landowners in the neighborhoods comprising Osaka's Northern Precinct (Kitagumi) were to pool their funds and acquire approximately 43,000 *koku* of warehouse rice; the families in the quarters making up the Southern Precinct (Minamigumi) jointly had to purchase 39,000 *koku*; and those of the Tenma Precinct (Tenmagumi) the balance of several thousand *koku*. The government also expected prompt action, for Matsuyasu was to begin sales almost immediately.

The exact date when officials in Osaka issued the purchase announcement to the people of the city is not clear.[10] It seems likely, however, that Hosoda and Ōoka drafted the document before the middle of the Third Month. The date is important because on the sixteenth of that month the Osaka city magistrates circulated a proclamation setting a new official price for commercial rice sold by the city's rice dealers to ordinary customers. However, when the Hosoda-Ōoka letter arrived in Osaka, presumably a few days later, it unilaterally established a different price for the compulsory purchases imposed on Osaka's merchants. As might be imagined, the disparity caused considerable confusion and consternation.

The new prices authorized by the Osaka city magistrates on the sixteenth set a price of 38.5 *monme* per *koku* for low-grade rice and thirty-three *monme* for inferior grain, as indicated in Table 4.1. The Hosoda-Ōoka memorandum, however, dictated a price of forty *monme* per *koku* for the compulsory purchases. To many in Osaka's merchant and artisan community, the consequences of the price differentials were obvious, and horrifying. According to most accounts, the rice stored in the warehouses and earmarked for compulsory sale was "three or four years old." The merchants knew that such rice had little market value, and they would have no choice but to categorize it as being of low or inferior quality. That meant, by the beads on anyone's abacus, that the merchant quarters would have to pay 1.5 *monme* more for each *koku* of low-grade rice than they could hope to sell it for, and a whopping seven *monme* more for rice graded as inferior. Cries of alarm could be heard in every corner of the city.

---

9. "Koki-roku."
10. As referenced in the *Ōsaka shishi*, 3:369, the document bears only the date of the Third Month, 1736.

The Beginnings of Protest

The experiences of Matsuyasu Shōemon, tapped to arrange the sale of some fifty thousand *koku* of the fouled, "slightly putrescent" rice, did nothing to comfort his neighbors. When Matsuyasu put the grain to auction in the Third Month, he received bids offering, on average, twenty-four *monme* per *koku*, or barely 60 percent of the price he originally paid for the rice.[11] Already alarmed about the amounts that they were slated to pay to complete their purchases, many members of Osaka's merchant community decided that the time had arrived to make their voices heard about the shogunate's pricing policies.

The initial round of appeals followed the standard procedures as decreed by Tokugawa law. As James L. McClain points out in the preceding chapter, the shogunate entrusted the Osaka city magistrates with day-to-day responsibility for managing the city. Three city elders (*sōdoshiyori*), appointed from the merchant estate, assisted the magistrates and performed such duties as transmitting laws, ordinances, decrees, and proclamations to the merchant and artisan population of the city; overseeing the collection of corvée levies and business taxes; mediating nonviolent quarrels among commoners; investigating and attesting to the facts raised in petitions submitted by commoners; and helping to arbitrate and settle all disputes and lawsuits involving merchants and artisans. The city elders also supervised Osaka's neighborhood elders (*machidoshiyori*). Named from among merchants and artisans of property, each neighborhood elder looked after the affairs of approximately six to ten residential quarters—exhorting their commoner neighbors to obey the law, conducting investigations as instructed by the city magistrates and city elders, resolving neighborhood disputes, auditing funds collected annually within each quarter to finance the operation of city government, supervising festivals, and so forth.

The urban administrative structure dictated that any appeal from below follow the same route—from neighborhood elder to city elder to city magistrate—with the neighborhood elders verifying the facts and certifying the appropriateness of any petition before passing it to the city elders, who would either settle the matter or forward it to the city magistrates for resolution. When the people of Osaka objected to the compulsory requisitions decreed in the Third Month of 1736, they persuaded numerous neighborhood elders to submit appeals asking Osaka's city officials to reduce the mandated purchase prices, set earlier at forty *monme* per *koku*, and to extend deadlines for submitting payments.

The requests traveled up the administrative ladder, but the issue of rice prices was so sensitive that the Osaka city magistrates needed to consult with policymakers in Edo, specifically, with Hosoda Tanba no Kami and Ōoka Echizen no Kami, who vigilantly followed developments in western Japan. Between the second day of the Third Month and the twentieth day of the Sixth Month, Hosoda and Ōoka sent to the Osaka city magistrates some twenty-

11. "Koki-roku."

seven letters concerning the sale of rice stored in the shogunate's granaries and daimyo warehouses.[12] Most of the missives demanded information about conditions in Osaka or else set forth instructions about what the Osaka authorities were expected to do, often enough in reply to worried inquiries from Osaka about acceptable courses of action. For example, a letter from Hosoda and Ōoka dated the twenty-fifth day of the Third Month requested a complete report about how much ordinary and how much old, contaminated rice the residential quarters purchased, as per earlier instructions; the amounts of rice marketed by Matsuyasu Shōemon (and the price he received); details about the quantities and condition of older rice stored in daimyo warehouses and the shogunate's granaries; and predictions about future rice shipments to the granaries. As can be seen, the shogun's ministers in Edo were the central figures who dictated policy, and the Osaka city magistrates played only a secondary role by supplying information, suggesting policy alternatives, and implementing specific directives.

Ultimately, the authorities in Edo agreed with the view of the people of Osaka that the price tendered during Matsuyasu's auction was extremely low, while at the same time concurring that the bids probably reflected rather accurately the market value of old, half-spoiled rice during a period of good harvests. In the end, Hosoda and Ōoka did not dispute the suggestion that the scheduled price for the forthcoming mandatory purchases would pose an unreasonable hardship on Osaka's merchants, for after some negotiations between shogunal officials in Edo and Osaka, the Osaka city magistrates issued a proclamation on the third day of the Fourth Month reducing the price for compulsory rice purchases to thirty-eight *monme* five *fun* per *koku* for low-grade rice. In addition to lowering the contract price, officials extended easier terms, deferring immediate payment and allowing merchants to pay in installments due on the twentieth and twenty-eighth days of the Sixth Month and the eleventh day of the Seventh Month.

The Escalation of Dissidence

Despite the concessions sanctioned by Hosoda and Ōoka in Edo, many merchants in Osaka remained dissatisfied with the terms decreed for the obligatory rice purchases. Resentful, and increasingly apprehensive about what the future might hold, they groped for ways to press the regime to lower the mandated prices even further. Eventually, the escalation of dissidence brought together thousands of Osakans who forged new organizational structures of protest, authored numerous petitions that set forth their disagreements with ruling authorities, and ultimately secured for themselves a new mode of communicating directly with the leading government officials in Osaka.

Within days of learning about the notification issued on the third day of the Fourth Month, merchants and artisans across the city began to meet. They re-

12. Ibid.

viewed the new terms, discussed their plight, and agreed to attempt to negotiate further concessions. In particular, they wished to be able to purchase at least some of the rice for thirty-three *monme* per *koku*, the price for inferior-grade commercial rice bought and sold in the city's markets as established by the official decree issued on the sixteenth day of the Third Month. During the course of the Fourth Month, the dissatisfied members of Osaka's merchant community showered upon city officials a blizzard of petitions, many of which repeated almost verbatim a document prepared by thirty-one neighborhood elders from Kita Senba, a collection of residential quarters within the Northern Precinct.[13]

> With due reverence, we submit the following letter:
> Item: We have received your instructions, directed to the various residential quarters, concerning the sale of the shogun's rice, and we certainly will purchase the specific allotments that have been assigned to each of our residential quarters. Moreover, we are grateful for your compassion that permits our quarters to purchase the ordinary rice at the price of thirty-eight *monme* five *fun* per *koku* of rice.
>
> Item: At this time, however, the people of the city are suffering through a period of profound distress and poverty. Moreover, there is old, half-spoiled rice included in the allotments, and this causes trouble for us. Consequently, we humbly request a further reduction in the purchase price, to the same level that authorities earlier established for inferior-grade rice [that is, thirty-three *monme* per *koku*]. Although we are reluctant to approach you with this supplication, matters are as we state them above. We shall be extremely grateful to receive the blessing of your gracious benevolence.
> [Date:] Kyōhō 21 [1736], Fourth Month
> [Signed] Enamiya Gohei, neighborhood elder, Kami Naka no Shima
>   [twenty-nine other neighborhood elders]
>   Wataya Ichiemon, neighborhood elder, Hama-machi

A memorandum of specification attached to the petition indicates that the thirty-one neighborhood chiefs met on the tenth day of the Fourth Month to discuss a possible appeal about the burden imposed upon the people of their quarters by the compulsory rice purchases. Each delegate then took a draft of the petition back to his home quarter for additional discussion and possible revision. As there were no suggestions for changing the phrasing or otherwise amending the letter, the neighborhood elders then put their seals to the

---

13. The petition is part of an untitled collection of materials compiled by the neighborhood leaders of Doshō-machi 3-chōme, the residential quarter where so many purveyors of imported medicines had their homes and shops, and stored in the archives of the Ōsaka Furitsu Naka no Shima Toshokan. For the most part, the documents record daily events in that neighborhood, suggesting that "Chōdai nisshi" might constitute a reasonable appellation for citation purposes.

document. In those few cases when a neighborhood elder happened to be away from the city, his quarter's officially authorized delegate for that month, the *gatsu gyōji*, affixed his seal to the appeal. With all preparations in place, the group of neighborhood elders sent the letter to their superiors, the city elders, who, as the highest-ranking merchant officials, liaised with the city magistrates, the target of the appeal.

Apart from the specifics of their grievances, one question that immediately arises is why those thirty-one specific residential quarters banded together in a collective act of protest. The answer seems to come from the fact that those neighborhoods jointly bore the responsibility for providing personnel and equipment for the Wa Fire-Fighting Company (Wagumi).[14] As in the other cities it administered, the Tokugawa shogunate held commoners in Osaka responsible for providing their own fire-fighting defenses, and it divided the city's residential quarters into districts responsible for maintaining equipment and providing volunteer squads that would turn out whenever a fire threatened their corner of the metropolis. Apparently, the requirement that the neighborhood elders within each district cooperate to provide fire-fighting services generated a sense of common purpose and identity that served as a basis of organization for other endeavors that might prove mutually beneficial for the residents of their quarters. Another petition written in the summer of 1736 lends credence to such an interpretation. On the twenty-eighth day of the Fifth Month, neighborhood elders from a different set of twenty-three residential quarters in Kita Senba submitted a document to the city elders concerning rice prices. Tellingly, those twenty-three residential quarters constituted a district that supported their own fire-defense squad, the Wo Fire-Fighting Company.[15]

The thirty-one neighborhood elders who signed the document asking for a further cut in mandated prices in the Fourth Month may have hoped that a united action would underscore their determination and awaken officialdom to the gravity of the situation confronting the ordinary people of Osaka. The city elders, however, did not look upon the joint protest activities with favor, and they signaled their rejection of the appeal by returning the document to its framers. Rebuffed, the residents of the merchant quarters either had to abandon their protest against the compulsory purchases or else map out a new tactical campaign that would somehow ameliorate the economic consequences of the government's demands.

After some discussion, the neighborhood chiefs and the residents of their quarters relinquished any hope of obtaining an outright reduction in the mandated price of the obligatory purchases and, instead, refocused their efforts on persuading the government to stretch out the required payments over a longer period of time. Consequently, in a subsequent document the protesters stated

---

14. The 1751 "Kōshi yōran," which appears in *Ōsaka machi bugyō kannai yōran* (Osaka: Ōsaka Shishi Hensanjo, 1984), identifies the thirty-one residential quarters that constituted the district supporting the Wa Fire-Fighting Company, *wa* being a syllabary element used in a manner equivalent to "A" Company in English.

15. *Ōsaka shishi*, 3:375–76; "Kōshi yōran."

their acquiescence to the decision of the city elders not to transmit the earlier appeal for a price reduction to higher authorities. Having acknowledged their acceptance of the dictates of higher authority, the neighborhood chiefs then went on to request that the city officials "please agree to accept payment in three separate installments, to be scheduled between the final day of the Tenth Month of this year [1736] and the last day of the Tenth Month of the Year of the Horse [1738]."[16]

Interestingly, the group of neighborhood elders did not submit their second petition directly to their superiors, the city elders, but, rather, worked through a different channel provided by the network of the so-called ten religious elders. As part of its effort to eradicate Christianity in the decades that accompanied its consolidation of power, the Tokugawa shogunate required all Japanese to become parishioners of a Buddhist temple, thus demonstrating their rejection of the foreign creed. Officials then ordered the compilation of registers that attested to each family's religious affiliation. In Osaka during the Kanbun period (1661–73), political authorities divided the city into religious districts (*shūshi kumiai*), each composed of a half-dozen or more residential quarters, that were supposed to maintain the registers and certify that no Christians disgraced their neighborhoods. Although the documentation is not entirely clear, it appears that by the eighteenth century functionaries known as *jūnin toshiyori* oversaw such reporting and surveillance functions within each of Osaka's three administrative precincts. Those delegates did not preside over communal religious services, but, given the duties entrusted to them, it is perhaps appropriate to designate the *jūnin toshiyori* as the "ten religious elders."

The tacit support of the religious elders—especially those from the Northern Precinct, home to the Wa Fire-Fighting Company—did nothing to change the minds of the city elders, who rebuffed the new petitions. Moreover, on the sixth day of the Sixth Month, the city elders summoned all the religious elders from the Northern, Southern, and Tenma Precincts to a meeting at the city offices located in the Southern Precinct. The residents of the merchant quarters could continue to draft as many petitions as they pleased, the city elders explained, but they should expect that any such future efforts would meet the same unhappy fate as the earlier appeals. The strong, uncompromising stand suggests that the city elders feared that the various assemblages of religious elders might emerge as agents capable of orchestrating the energies of residential quarters across the city, which already were mobilizing themselves in clusters that corresponded to the districts held responsible for supporting particular fire-fighting companies.

Ironically, however, the city elders' actions diminished their own credibility and blunted their capacity to influence future events. The officials' announcement that the ordinary people of Osaka "could continue to draft as many petitions as they pleased" was taken as an invitation to do exactly that, and since the city elders would not deign to accept such documents of protest,

16. *Ōsaka shishi*, 3:375–76.

the merchant representatives finally decided simply to step outside prescribed guidelines and to submit their petitions directly to the city magistrates.

Opening a New Route of Appeal

It was more than simple frustration with the city elders that drove the merchant community of Osaka to consider the unprecedented action of mobilizing themselves to dare a direct approach to the city magistrates. At other places in Japan and at other times in the early modern era, such behavior earned harsh punishments for those who circumvented legal procedures. In the summer of 1736, however, Osaka's commoners faced new and potentially devastating economic realities that turned up the temperature on an already flammable situation. Late in the Fifth Month, rumors that the shogunate planned to remint the silver coins that circulated in western Japan reached the ears of Osaka's merchants. Such a move would make eminent sense to Hosoda and Ōoka, since devaluating the purity of the official coinage would help to offset the regime's persistent budget deficits. But Osaka's merchants dreaded the inflationary consequences of reminting and believed that the conversion would throw trade and commerce into confusion and perhaps even lead to economic paralysis in Osaka and the entire Kinai area.

Events during the early days of the Sixth Month caused Osaka's commoners to become even more distressed. For one thing, the city elders' tough talk made it clear that the governing authorities had absolutely no intention of reducing the mandated purchase price for the old, "slightly putrescent" grain that had practically no commercial value. Moreover, on the twenty-fourth day of the Fifth Month, Hosoda and Ōoka notified the Osaka city magistrates that they intended to abolish price supports for ordinary commercial rice in Edo, effective the first day of the Sixth Month. Authorities in Osaka were to follow an identical course of action, Hosoda and Ōoka declared, although news about the policy shift was to be held in strictest confidence until the very day of its implementation. In addition, as officials lifted the restrictions on rice shipments into Osaka from northern Japan, new supplies of grain began to arrive in the city. That confluence of events—the determination of officials to maintain a high fixed price for the compulsory purchases even while an influx of new supplies of grain and a loosening of price controls depressed the proceeds that the merchant community could hope to get for old, "fouled" rice when they resold it on the commercial market—sent fear across the city.

Consequently, following the disheartening meeting with the city elders on the sixth day of the Sixth Month, the religious elders from the Northern Precinct convened a gathering of neighborhood leaders at the temple Senryūji, located in Awaji-machi on the eastern side of the Higashi Yoko Canal. At that convocation, the religious elders discussed what had transpired at the city offices and urged caution, but the meeting ultimately confirmed a decision to press for further action. Since everyone expected the city elders to honor their word and reject any new petitions, the conspirators alerted leaders from the residential quarters in other precincts to stand ready to respond to future events. Just two days later, the people of Osaka circumvented the city elders' obstinacy by presenting petitions directly to the city magistrates. One such "direct remonstration" (*jikiso*) read as follows.[17]

> With due reverence, we submit the following appeal:
> Item: Earlier, each residential quarter was instructed to purchase a specified amount of rice being held in the shogun's granaries and daimyo warehouses. At that time, the propertied merchants and artisans addressed an appeal to the city elders requesting an extension of the due date for the submission of the appropriate payments. The city elders, however, refused to acknowledge that request and returned the documents to the petitioners. For that reason, we are addressing you directly at this time, with deep respect and trepidation. Because the date for submitting payments for the rice purchases has not been extended and because it is not easy at this time to raise money, the merchants and artisans of our quarter are perplexed and in a quandary about what to do. For those reasons, we, in our capacities as a neighborhood elder and monthly delegate, today are submitting this letter to you, with all due respect. We would be extremely grateful if you graciously defer the payments temporarily.
> [Date:] Genbun 1 [1736], Sixth Month, eighth day
> [From:] Neighborhood elder, Doshō-machi 1-chōme
> Monthly delegate, Doshō-machi 1-chōme
> [To:] The honorable city magistrates

One striking feature of the petition submitted on the eighth day of the Sixth Month was that it dropped the earlier, more specific request to divide the payments for the compulsory purchases into three installments due "between the final day of the Tenth Month of this year [1736] and the last day of the Tenth Month of the Year of the Horse [1738]." Instead, the merchants simply asked the city magistrates to "defer the payments temporarily," probably a conscious attenuation of language that measured their anxiety about disregarding established procedures and approaching the magistrates directly after the lower-level city elders had vetoed their earlier requests.

The mild language of the document also suggests a certain timidity on the part of the neighborhood leaders. Reality, however, was different, for local representatives from across the city had written similar documents and had readied themselves to present all the petitions directly to the city magistrates in a single mass action. As one source puts it, when dawn rose on the eighth day, "representatives from all the residential quarters within the city converged on the offices of the city magistrates, beginning in the Fifth Hour of

---

17. "Chōdai nisshi."

the morning and continuing until the Fourth Hour [that is, from 8:00 until 10:00 A.M.], and presented to the authorities a mass of petitions."[18] If all of the neighborhood elders and monthly delegates in Osaka were in fact present, that would mean that more than 1,200 men surrounded the city offices on the eighth day of the Sixth Month to voice their unambiguous dissent to the terms of the mandated rice purchases.

In the Northern Precinct at least, the religious elders played a facilitating role in drafting and framing a model for the petitions that the neighborhood elders submitted to the city magistrates on the eighth day of the Sixth Month. In the case of Doshō-machi 1-chōme, the neighborhood elders and monthly delegates from fifteen residential quarters that made up three adjoining religious districts composed their protest documents in a joint meeting held on the seventh day of the Sixth Month. That is, the petition movement in the Northern Precinct was structured around religious districts, with each cluster of residential quarters drafting a petition, based on a common template, that the individual neighborhood elders and monthly delegates then submitted to the city magistrates in a single mass action.

At first, it appeared to many that the mass demonstration and joint submission of petitions would have little effect on Osaka's governing authorities, for the city magistrates stubbornly told the neighborhood elders and monthly delegates assembled in front of their offices to redirect their documents to the city elders. By that time, however, at least one of those city elders, Sumiyoshi Sōzaemon, seemed to be reassessing his view of matters, impressed perhaps by the new volatility of the Sixth Month. When he first caught wind of the possibility of a mass demonstration, for example, Sumiyoshi paid a visit on the seventh day of the Sixth Month to the merchant Nunoya Ihachi, who was probably a leading member of the group that met at Doshō-machi 1-chōme. The neighborhood elder from Doshō-machi 3-chōme and a certain Kizuya Shirōbei also appeared at that gathering, and the local leaders offered their version of current events and recounted their fears and apprehensions about the economic future. In response, Sumiyoshi advised the neighborhood elders and delegates to cease submitting petitions to the magistrates, and he promised that the city elders would frame a response to their demands.

The merchant community proceeded with its joint action the next day, despite Sumiyoshi's admonition, and, in the end, that demonstration apparently persuaded the city magistrates finally to conclude, as had Sumiyoshi, that closure to the crisis of 1736 was necessary. Consequently, within twenty-four hours of the mass protest at their doorsteps, the city magistrates summoned representatives from the religious districts to hear an important announcement. There was "no precedent for postponing the payment of taxes due to the government," the city magistrates explained to the community leaders who gathered on the ninth day. Nevertheless, the authorities continued, they understood that unhappy economic circumstances prevailed in the city, and they would accede to the request to "defer the payments temporarily," particularly

18. Ibid.

since the shogunate's prospective reminting program already seemed to be generating economic difficulties. However, they added, the merchants needed to amend the inappropriate language used to write the petition. The city elders then supplied the merchants with the following draft of an acceptable document.[19]

> With humble deference, we submit the following appeal:
> Item: Earlier, you informed us that the residential quarters could postpone for ninety days the payments due for the mandatory purchases of rice held in the shogun's granaries and daimyo warehouses. We are thankful for your instructions and will obey them respectfully. However, although we understand that we must not fall into arrears in our payments since our obligations have not changed, it is nearly impossible for us to obtain the requisite amounts of appropriate currency, perhaps, we suspect, because of the reminting of coins that is now taking place. Inevitably, our businesses have suffered due to confusion in the money markets. These circumstances have made it extraordinarily difficult for us to raise the money with which to make the mandatory purchases. With all due and great respect, we would be grateful if you have compassion for us, favor us with your benevolence, and grant us a temporary extension for submitting the required payments.
> [Date:] Genbun 1 [1736], Sixth Month
> [To:] The honorable city magistrates

The redrafted letter asks for an extension of the ninety-day deferment previously granted. The "obligations" that "have not changed" referred to the mandatory purchases, and the phrasing suggests that the city magistrates and city elders considered the mandated purchases to be a civic responsibility that merchants ought to discharge without complaint. Having received the model of an acceptable petition, the neighborhood elders, using the organizational network provided by the groupings of religious districts, submitted new documents asking to postpone the purchases.

Negotiating a Settlement

Despite the emerging consensus about the need to modify the payment schedule, Osaka's urban authorities and the city's merchant community still had to define specifically what each side meant by a "temporary" postponement. Any major deviation from what had been decreed earlier, moreover, would need the consent of the Edo policymakers Hosoda and Ōoka, whose own priorities would place constraints around initiatives that the Osaka city magistrates might put into motion. Indeed, Edo's continued, unrelenting demands for information about conditions in western Japan reveal just how little autonomy Osaka's city magistrates had. Throughout the Fourth and Fifth Months, for in-

19. Ibid.

stance, Hosoda and Ōoka called for reports about prices; instructed the Osaka city magistrates to dispatch express messengers to Edo carrying forecasts about projected sales of rice from the daimyo warehouses, both in the summer and after the autumn harvest; asked bluntly why it was so difficult to liquidate existing rice inventories in Osaka; hounded the Osaka city magistrates with queries about what plans they had formulated to facilitate the sale of daimyo rice; demanded to know how the mandatory purchases were to be apportioned among the residential quarters; and sent couriers scurrying down the Tōkaidō Highway bearing long lists of other questions about the "fouled" rice in the shogunate's granaries, sales of old rice from the warehouse maintained by Kaga domain, and loans that daimyo had contracted with Osaka's merchant community using future rice harvests as collateral.[20]

Hosoda and Ōoka had good reason to stay so closely attuned to affairs in Osaka; the two were putting the final touches on their program for reminting the shogunate's silver currency. For Osakans, those plans became reality shortly after the fourteenth day of the Sixth Month, when the two policymakers in Edo penned a letter instructing the Osaka city magistrates to collect somewhat more than two thousand *kan* of silver coins and send them to the mint in Kyoto for recasting.[21] Of that amount, the city magistrates were to set aside sixty-two *kan* from their own current year's operating budget and provide an additional 1,018 *kan* acquired through the compulsory purchases of rice from the shogunate's Naniwa and Tamatsukuri granaries slated for that month, with the balance coming from other sources.

Somewhere along the Tōkaidō Highway, the injunction to acquire silver for reminting, dated the fourteenth of the month, apparently crossed paths with a message from the Osaka city magistrates to Hosoda and Ōoka, dated the eleventh, that requested Edo's endorsement of the magistrates' promise to Osaka's merchants, made two days earlier on the ninth, to "temporarily" extend the payment dates for the mandated rice sales. The magistrates' letter of the eleventh is no longer extant, but a reply made by Hosoda and Ōoka on the seventeenth refers to its contents. It was their understanding, the two powerful figures began, that the merchants of Osaka "some time ago," late in the Third Month, had submitted petitions to the magistrates requesting a "rescheduling" of the mandated rice purchases. Accordingly, on the third day of the Fourth Month, the magistrates notified the merchants that "they could make their payments in three installments," due on the twentieth and twenty-eighth days of this, the Sixth Month, and on the eleventh day of the Seventh Month. Despite that concession, the summation continued, the magistrates now report that the merchants have requested yet an "additional delay" in making the payments for the mandated purchases, because of deteriorating economic conditions that allegedly resulted from the shogunate's plans to remint currency. Moreover, Hosoda and Ōoka added, the magistrates seemed to feel it "appropriate" to grant the extension.

20. "Koki-roku."
21. *Ōsaka shishi*, 3:375.

Hosoda and Ōoka had decidedly other thoughts about the matter, however. The merchant community of Osaka, they hastened to remind the city magistrates, was responsible for concluding the purchase of 2,083 *kanme* worth of rice by the twentieth day of the Sixth Month.[22] Moreover, plans concerning the issuance of new coinage called for the Osaka city magistrates to send to the mint in Kyoto 1,018 *kanme* of silver raised through that month's initial round of compulsory sales. To grant a further delay in consummating the compulsory purchases would compromise the reminting plans. Hosoda and Ōoka did concede there might be some merit to another suggestion from the magistrates, a proposal to reduce the amount of compulsory sales to a level that would net just the amount of silver coinage slated for transfer to the Kyoto mint. But in such a case, the two officials wrote, they would need to know immediately a revised schedule for the proposed compulsory sales, and, they warned, the Osaka city magistrates would have to dip into their own operating budgets as far as was necessary, should they not be able to come up with the required amounts in a timely fashion.

In other words, for Hosoda and Ōoka the highest priority was to forge ahead with reminting the currency, and they considered it absolutely essential for the Osaka city magistrates to complete compulsory purchases that would net at least 1,018 *kanme* of silver, which then could be shipped to Kyoto for recasting. Moreover, later in their letter of the seventeenth, Hosoda and Ōoka directed the Osaka city magistrates to make certain that an additional one thousand *kanme* would be raised through mandatory purchases slated for the twenty-eighth day of the Sixth Month, and they announced that they would dispatch inspectors from Edo to oversee matters until the entire sum had been delivered to Kyoto. In brief, the leading officials within the Tokugawa shogunate feared that any additional concessions to Osaka's merchants would complicate, and perhaps even seriously damage, their reminting strategy, and their promise to hold the Osaka city magistrates' budget hostage to any shortfalls suggests a ploy to head off any further delays in the mandated purchases.

Moving toward Closure

The letter from Hosoda and Ōoka announcing the details of the reminting plans and dated the fourteenth day of the Sixth Month put considerable pressure on the city magistrates to adhere to the schedule, agreed to on the third

22. The mathematics are rather complicated. Earlier injunctions had specified that Osaka's merchants were obligated to purchase a total of 6,249 *kanme* worth of rice, and thus 2,083 *kanme* equaled the first third of the compulsory purchases. Of the grand total of 6,249 *kanme*, nearly 1,222 *kanme* was raised when Matsuyasu Shōemon sold some 50,944 *koku* of half-spoiled rice at the price of 24 *monme* per *koku*. The families of Osaka's residential quarters corporately were being required to purchase a total of 88,752 *koku* of rice, which would yield 3,416 *kanme* at the mandated price of 38.5 *monme* per *koku*. The purchase by individual merchants and wealthy peasants of some 91,944 *koku* of rice, also at the officially determined price of 38.5 *monme* per *koku*, would net the balance of approximately 1,611 *kanme* of silver.

day of the Fourth Month, that called for consummating the obligatory purchases on the twentieth and twenty-eighth days of the Sixth Month and the eleventh day of the Seventh Month. To the magistrates' consternation, however, many people throughout the city were urging their neighbors to formulate another "direct remonstration" to the city magistrates concerning prices and the dates for submitting payments. Afraid that the bubbling ferment from below might erupt in violence, as had happened in Edo just three years earlier, yet hemmed in by the inflexible dictates of the shogunate's chief policymakers, the Osaka city magistrates sought to resolve the crisis in their city by appearing to be stern while simultaneously holding out the possibility of new concessions.

Not long after they received the letter of the fourteenth, the city magistrates had the city elders summon representatives of the religious districts to a meeting held at the city offices in the Northern Precinct. There, the city elders delivered what was described as "a special admonition," presumably against any threat to organize another mass protest and direct appeal. With almost the next breath, however, the city elders softened their tone as they explained the possibility of putting together what they termed a "one-half of one-third" scheme; that is, the city magistrates would compromise by requiring the residential quarters to submit only one-half of the amount due on the twentieth, the first of the three scheduled payments. Moreover, the city elders asked the religious elders to "Please call together the leaders of the residential quarters and inform them of this decision," phrasing their message in the form of a request rather than an order.

The movement toward conciliation can be read as an indication of how very concerned the city magistrates and city elders were about the sentiments of the people who resided in Osaka's merchant and artisan quarters. Yet the magistrates also had a line to toe; they needed to raise a specified amount of silver to send to the mint in Kyoto. The collection of "one-half of one-third" would allow them to assemble the requisite amount of metal. At the same time, the city elders intended the use of the expression "a special admonition" to convey an important message to the merchant community: the "one-half of one-third" plan was the final offer that the authorities would advance and no further compromise was possible. Perhaps because the city magistrates and their subordinates, the city elders, had revealed both a willingness to listen to the voice of the people and a toughness in defining a limit to concessions, all residential quarters in the city completed the necessary purchases on the twentieth.

On the twentieth-eighth day of the Sixth Month, the city elders summoned representatives from the religious districts to another meeting, this time held at the city offices in the Southern Precinct, for another taste of the carrot and rap with the stick. The residential quarters, the city elders intoned, must pay the balance of the initial installment by the first day of the Seventh Month. The funds from that installment were destined for the shogun's coffers, the officials explained, and so there was no room for negotiation. At the same time, the city elders pledged that the Osaka city magistrates would lobby with policymakers in Edo to arrange to postpone the payment of the two remaining installments.

An undated letter indicates that officials in Edo thereupon did agree to a plan proposed by the Osaka city magistrates to grant an additional thirty-day delay in the submission of the second and third installments. Furthermore, the city magistrates subsequently exhibited their "gracious benevolence" by permitting the two payments, rescheduled for the twenty-eighth day of the Seventh Month and the eleventh day of the Eight Month, to be submitted in one lump sum on the latter date. Suddenly, the crisis was resolved, and everyone felt relieved. The compilers of the "Chōdai nisshi" praised the efforts of the neighborhood elders and religious elders, applauded their perseverance throughout the long, hot Osaka summer, extolled the merchant community's accomplishment of raising all the required funds, and suggested that it was now possible to look forward to an auspicious conclusion to the year.

THE TROUBLED AFTERMATH

The smug, self-satisfied expressions in local records such as the "Chōdai nisshi" notwithstanding, harmony did not reign in Osaka as the year 1736 drew to a close. Rather, like the vibrations trailing behind a major earthquake, new tremors rippled across the city, threatening to topple the amicable resolution to the crisis of 1736 and again straining relations between the people of Osaka and the shogun's officials. Tensions first reappeared in the residential quarters of the Tenma Precinct during the Seventh Month and then spread into the Southern Precinct by the end of the Ninth Month. At the epicenter of the new aftershocks were troublesome questions about the proper functions of the city elders and their responsibility, when appropriate, to step forward as advocates for the merchant and artisan families of Osaka.

When the shogunate created the office of city elder in the seventeenth century, it endowed the appointees with several conceptually distinct roles: to serve as assistants to the city magistrates, with the concomitant obligation to implement policies initiated by those samurai-level officials; to constitute a distinct bureaucratic organ responsible for carrying out certain duties, such as overseeing fire-fighting preparations, that helped to make Osaka a safer and better place to live; and to act as "the voice of the people" (*machi sōdai*) by relaying the hopes, aspirations, and dissatisfactions of artisan and merchant families to higher officials. By the 1730s, however, the shogunate had come to expect the city elders to serve first and foremost as loyal aides to the city magistrates, even at the expense of their other responsibilities.[23] Consequently, in the crisis of 1736, the three city elders on the sixth day of the Sixth Month acted

23. Nishizawa Yasushi, "Ōsaka no hikeshi kumiai ni yoru tsūtatsu to sokan undō," *Shigaku zasshi* 94:8 (August 1985), pp. 1–40.

as agents of the city magistrates' will when they declined to receive petitions pleading for further reductions in mandated prices and thus closed off the normal path by which people made their grievances known to superior officials.

Even before the problems associated with the obligatory grain purchases peaked in the summer of 1736, many merchants and artisans already had become discontent with the new emphasis on the city elders' obligation to impose the dictates of higher authority upon them. In the Seventh Month of 1735, for instance, the city magistrates authorized a fund-raising campaign on behalf of the temple Daifukuin and told the city elders to specify an amount that each residential quarter within their respective jurisdictions would have to contribute. In response, the city elder responsible for the Northern Precinct set a levy of eight hundred *mon* of copper coins for each neighborhood under his jurisdiction, whereas the residential quarters in the Southern Precinct each had to pay two *kanmon* of copper, more than twice as much.

The second-wave protest movement that shattered the autumn calm in the Tenma and Southern Precincts in 1736 took aim at the city elders. In particular, the families of those two precincts complained about the levies they had to pay in order to support the activities overseen by the city elders, which included both regular taxes to support fire fighting, street repair, the maintenance of bridges and canals, and so forth, as well as such extraordinary exactions as the contribution to Daifukuin. One way to reduce the expenses associated with the office of the city elders, the protesters concluded, was to abolish the post of religious elder. After all, the city magistrates never had officially authorized the creation of that position, and it could not be found on the city's formal table of administrative organization. Indeed, the dissenters continued, the city elders had begun to appoint religious elders in the previous century merely to suit their own convenience and, over time, had come to depend on them to help impose official policies upon the general populace.

Interestingly enough, the attitudes of the residents of the Northern Precinct did not align exactly with those of their neighbors. Perhaps one reason that the people in the Northern Precinct did not choose to participate in the protest against the city elders and their surrogates, the religious elders, was because their particular city elder had not required an excessively burdensome contribution to Daifukuin's coffers. Moreover, the families in that precinct were counted among the most affluent in Osaka.[24] In addition, in 1736 the religious elders of the Northern Precinct had supported, more so than their counterparts elsewhere, the effort to reduce the mandated prices and to defer the payment dates for the compulsory rice purchases, and that too must have carried some weight with the people in that part of the city. No matter how ambivalent the people of the Northern Precinct may have been, however, in the end the city magistrates decided that enough contention had stalked Osaka's streets: they listened to the voices from below, from the Tenma and Southern Precincts, and abolished the post of religious elder.

24. Inui Hiromi, "Kinsei Ōsaka ni okeru chōsei sasshin undō," *Ōsaku-fu no rekishi* 6 (1975), pp. 25–61.

But matters did not rest there. Slightly more than a year later, in the First Month of 1738, local notables from the neighborhoods in the Northern Precinct that supported the Wa Fire-Fighting Company began to stir up another controversy. At last, they too had become agitated about the levies they had to pay to underwrite the activities of the city elder responsible for their portion of the city. Officials in the Tenma and Southern Precincts, they complained, had pruned budgets, and so the households in those areas now enjoyed lower tax rates than did the families in the northern part of Osaka. As calls for "an equable assessment" mounted, the disaffected residential quarters decided to entrust the fashioning of a solution to a delegation of representatives drawn from the neighborhoods that constituted the Wa Fire-Fighting district, and the neighborhood elders from those quarters put their seals to a letter conferring all decision-making powers to that committee.[25]

Clearly, the merchants and artisans of the Northern Precinct were striving to create an organizational structure that would enable them to express more effectively their concerns about how they were governed. Single neighborhoods had feeble voices, but collections of neighborhoods could shout out their demands with greater force. During the protest movement against obligatory rice purchases in 1736, both religious leaders and the representatives of fire-fighting districts had served as agents of protest in the Northern Precinct. The former had helped to draft model petitions in the Sixth Month, and the latter had played an even more crucial role by mobilizing blocs of neighborhoods earlier that year. The demise of the religious elders, a consequence of the campaign against the high operating budgets of the city elders, threatened to cripple the people's ability to communicate effectually with higher officialdom, and the emergence of the fire-fighting districts as the voice of the community can be seen as an attempt to restructure a basis for mass action.

In the estimation of many Osakan families, the decision of the shogun's policymakers, arrived at in closed session in Edo, to compel the Osaka merchant community to purchase, at prices far above fair market value, rice that had sat around daimyo and government granaries for several years amounted to nothing more than an undisguised expropriation of money from their pockets. Resentment toward the shogunate's fiscal policies, then, was the basic reason that propertied merchants and artisans across the entire city rose up in protest in 1736.

For all of their anger, however, Osaka's merchants and artisans did not contest the shogunate's legitimacy, nor did they controvert the regime's right to order them to make compulsory purchases of grain. The demands of Osaka's commoners were more modest: first, they wanted officials to reduce the level of the exactions, and second, they wished to make their payments for the rice in three installments spaced out over a two-year period, beginning in the Tenth Month of 1736 and ending in the corresponding month of 1738. Throughout the crisis, the attitude of the city magistrates and city elders remained adamant

25. "Chōdai nisshi."

—the merchants ought to make the compulsory purchases as ordered, without uttering any complaint—and that is why officials sometimes referred to the purchases as "tax levies" and declared that there was "no precedent for postponing the payment of taxes due to the government" in the documents they wrote for public consumption. In that regard, the merchants and artisans apparently shared common conceptual ground with the city magistrates and city elders, for the commoners never protested the purchase orders themselves, but, rather, focused their efforts on negotiating the terms of the injunctions.

That is not to suggest that the protests of 1736 lacked important political dimensions. For one thing, the actions of the merchant community raised questions about how much revenue the regime might legitimately, and morally, expect to lift from the purses of the merchant and artisan estates. In addition, the merchants' decision to make direct remonstrations to the city magistrates challenged the accepted procedures by which the lord's subjects might address his representatives. Furthermore, the very decision to appeal the mandated prices and payment dates threatened to derail the shogunate's plans to remint its currency, even though it may not have been the merchants' conscious intention to do so. Certainly, high-ranking officials were aware of the political implications of protest bubbling up in Osaka, as seen in the "special admonition" that the city elders gave to the merchants' representatives and as attested by the strenuous efforts the elders made to explain that shogunal officials in Edo would tolerate no further delays in collecting required levies.

When all was said and written, the protest movement did not result in any major concessions on the part of the government. The merchants never did persuade officials to lower the mandated price below the level of 38.5 *monme* per *koku*, as set in the Fourth Month, and the request to arrange a two-year payment schedule produced only a ninety-day postponement, later extended by an additional thirty days. Still, no sense of defeat colors the pages of local records such as the "Chōdai nisshi." On the contrary, the unfolding of events almost seems to have given birth to a sense of self-satisfaction among the merchant estate for having articulated a community view of how matters ought to go forward, for having stood up against the arbitrary and, for some, despotic expropriation of commoner wealth, and for having won at least some concessions concerning the timing of the payments. As the authors of the "Chōdai nisshi" noted, it was now possible to look forward to an auspicious conclusion to the year.

Perhaps an even more significant consequence of the protest movement of 1736 was that Osaka's merchants acquired the undisputed right to submit petitions directly to the city magistrates, and in the future they did not hesitate to do so. Between the Kyōhō period and the collapse of the Tokugawa regime in 1868, Osaka's merchant community organized a total of twenty-six joint petition movements.[26] As might be expected from what occurred during the aftermath of the crisis of 1736, delegates from the fire-fighting districts emerged as spokespersons for Osaka's commoners during times of trouble, styled them-

---

26. Nishizawa, "Ōsaka no hikeshi kumiai."

selves "the voice" of the merchant community, and stood at the head of twenty of those protests.

The tactic of direct remonstration to the city magistrates via joint petitions often worked out favorably for the merchants in those contests with state authority. In the Eighth Month of 1737, for example, directly after the city elders had refused to accept documents submitted by thirty-one neighborhood chiefs in Kita Senba, Osaka's merchant community petitioned the city magistrates concerning the purity of gold and silver coins in circulation.[27] Interestingly, the protesters entitled their petition "An Honorable Legal Action" rather than "A Humble Request," the traditional heading, a clear signal that Osaka's merchants had developed new attitudes about appealing to higher authorities. Significantly, as experience accumulated and taught its hard lessons, authorities sometimes altered their policies when confronted with the mere possibility of a unified petition drive. In 1744, when the government again resorted to a compulsory purchase order to tide it over another crisis, it did not require Osaka's residential quarters to participate en masse, but, rather, instructed individual wealthy merchants and members of protective associations (*nakama*) to buy specified amounts of grain.[28] Surely the reason for that was to avoid another mass protest movement directed at the city elders, as had happened eight years earlier in 1736.

There can be no doubt, as many contributors to this volume point out, that Osaka became a merchants' and artisans' city during the Tokugawa period. The vitality of the people changed the city's geography, created new art forms and popular heroes, and spawned new religious rituals and practices. Sometimes a symbiosis of interests between government and the people opened up ways for Osaka to become the "people's city"; but in the case of the direct petition movement of 1736, it was pressure from below protesting policies from above that provided the dynamic by which people engineered a new way to make their voices heard about matters that affected them the most.

27. "Chōdai nisshi." In his "Ōsaka no hikeshi kumiai," Nishizawa states that the events of 1737 led to the first instance of a direct remonstration, but, clearly, the petitioners of 1736 had established a precedent.
28. For details see Imai Shūhei, "Kaimei seisaku to chōnin shihai," in Nakabe Yoshiko, ed., *Ōsaka to shūhen shotoshi no kenkyū* (Osaka: Seibundō, 1994), pp. 151–82.

CHAPTER FIVE

Takemoto Gidayū and the Individualistic Spirit of Osaka Theater

— C. Andrew Gerstle

Ariyoshi Sawako's novella *Ningyō jōruri* (The Bunraku Puppet Theater), published in 1958, depicts in fiction a very real crisis that occurred in 1949 when one of Japan's most famous theatrical troupes, already weakened by the depredations of the war, split into two rival camps. The contention that racked the world of bunraku puppetry during the postwar years seemed rooted in contemporary conditions, as the economic dislocations that accompanied defeat added themselves to the miseries of the war years, and as the opposing groups articulated solutions that relied on the rhetoric of a newly democratic Japan. Despite the apparent modernity of the conflict, however, at the heart of the dispute lay fundamental beliefs and patterns of behavior that were nearly as old and venerable as the puppet theater itself.

The economic difficulties that beset the puppeteers in the late 1940s were only too real. In the wake of defeat, the people of Osaka had precious little time or money to spare for such traditional entertainments as the puppet theater and, as a consequence, ticket receipts were simply insufficient for the troupe's sponsor, the Shōchiku Company, to cover the salaries of everyone in the organization. Still, the senior star performers remained relatively well-off—they commanded much of the takings and drew extra income from their patrons and amateur disciples. The junior performers, in sharp contrast, were not earning enough to survive, and some suggested that the troupe share out its proceeds so as to allow the young to eat, even if they did not perform. The argument was set within the "new democracy" ideology of the postwar epoch, and the veterans castigated the junior rebels for having "communist leanings" when the younger generation proposed to use a performers' union to pressure the company to accede to the profit-sharing scheme. The older performers' severe views held that survival in the world of bunraku depended on skill and hard work, and that only through perseverance in the face of poverty would talent proliferate, as always had been the case.

The troupe did not mend its rift until nearly two decades later, only after the founding of the Bunraku Association in 1963 and the opening of the National Theater in Tokyo in 1966 provided an organizational and financial structure capable of sustaining a reinvigorated bunraku. Though only a footnote in the history of Occupation Japan, the prolonged discord within the bunraku troupe is significant for what it revealed about the nature of the puppet theater in particular and, it can be suggested, about Osaka culture in general. The idea that a troupe of performers should cooperate with one another to maintain the continuity of their artistic tradition was an unlikely brainchild of newly democratic postwar Japan, and could scarcely be labeled a communist or unionist conspiracy. On the contrary, the anomaly, in terms of Japanese traditional performing arts, is that the senior performers cared little whether the younger members stayed or not. Ultimately the older generation did not consider it possible to continue a tradition if it had to be nursed along artificially. An individualistic, self-reliant spirit is the radical element here, and it paid no heed to preserving any family or communal traditions. That ideological judgment reflected precisely an essential element in bunraku—a fierce, individual competitiveness that Takemoto Gidayū first articulated at the end of the seventeenth century and that carved out a distinctive place for the Osaka puppet theater in Japanese cultural history.

Bunraku and the Culture of Japan's Artistic World

Bunraku is the modern name for *jōruri* puppet theater (*ningyō jōruri*), which itself evolved out of earlier dramatic forms. The term *jōruri* has an extremely intriguing, if somewhat convoluted, history. It derives from "The Tale of Princess Jōruri" (*Jōruri Gozen monogatari*), a medieval oral narrative concerning Minamoto no Yoshitsune's fleeting love affair with a young woman who, later in the story, rescues the warrior after he falls ill, revealing in the process her second identity as an incarnation of Yakushi Nyorai, the Buddha of Healing. By the late fifteenth century wandering minstrels had made "The Tale of Princess Jōruri" a popular part of their repertoire, chanting it and other pieces to the accompaniment of the *biwa* lute, and when the shamisen replaced the lute as the minstrels' instrument of preference in the sixteenth century, *jōruri* became the common appellation for that style of dramatic, chanted performance. In the early seventeenth century, the story of Princess Jōruri and other well-known tales from the past made their way onto the stages of Japan's new puppet theaters, thus uniting narrative storytelling with a separate puppet tradition. Subsequently, the word *jōruri* became transformed into the standard terminology for various kinds of narrative and dramatic music that featured the shamisen, including presentations done on the kabuki stage.

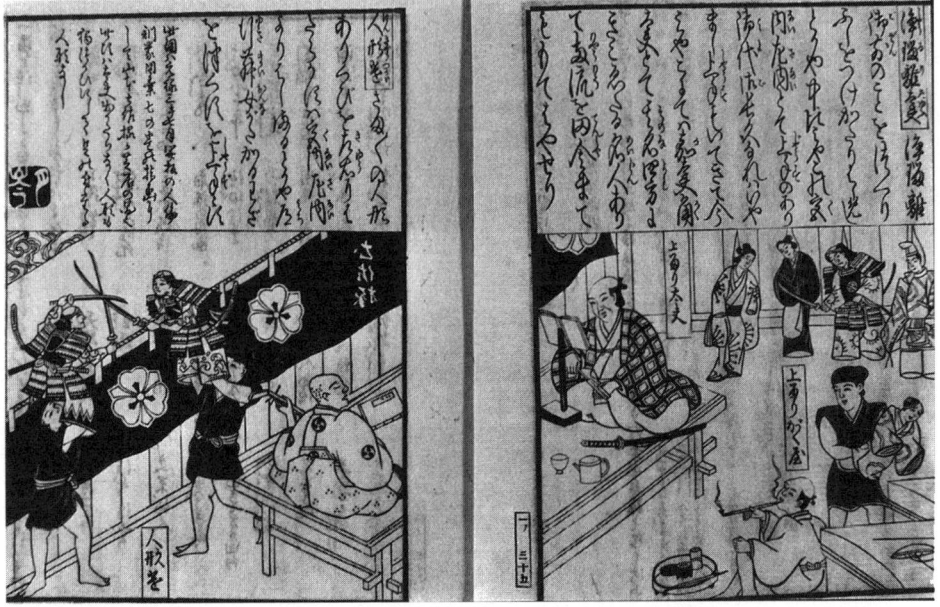

The jōruri *stage at the end of the seventeenth century. From "Jinrin kinmō zui," by permission of the Tsubouchi Memorial Theatre Museum, Waseda University, Tokyo.*

The puppet theater reached new heights of popularity in the late seventeenth century and early eighteenth, when Chikamatsu Monzaemon wrote about one hundred *jōruri* plays for Takemoto Gidayū and his troupe in Osaka. So dominant a figure was Takemoto that his name lent itself as the generic term *gidayū* (or more formally, *gidayū-bushi*) for the specific type of narrative chanting and music that he originated, and altogether well over one thousand plays came to be included in the Gidayū lineage of the *jōruri* puppet theater. As the puppets won an enduring place for themselves in the hearts of Japan's urban dwellers, especially in the Kyoto-Osaka region, dozens of theaters hung out their banners. Of all the troupes established in the Tokugawa period, however, only the lineage of Uemura Bunrakuken, who opened a playhouse in Osaka in the initial decade of the nineteenth century, survived commercially into the postwar era, and gradually the term "bunraku" became synonymous with the concept of an Osaka-based professional puppet theater.

In summary form, then, *jōruri* is a large category of narrative chanting and singing accompanied by the shamisen; *gidayū* is a genre of *jōruri* narrative music specific to the puppet theater; and today's bunraku chanters, shamisen players, and puppeteers constitute the only troupe left performing in the *gidayū* theatrical tradition, although a distinct and separate style of teaching and performing *gidayū* chanting to shamisen accompaniment but without the puppets flourished from the late seventeenth century until the end of World War II and remains alive today. Scholars tend to use the term *jōruri* in histori-

The jōruri *stage in the eighteenth century. From "Tōsei shibai katagi," by permission of the Tsubouchi Memorial Theatre Museum, Waseda University, Tokyo.*

cal discussions of the bunraku tradition, and this chapter follows that practice. In that context, it is important to bear in mind that *jōruri* was in the mainstream of Japan's national popular culture in the early modern period. Narrative chanting and singing to the accompaniment of the shamisen constituted the backbone not just of the puppet theater but of kabuki as well, and by the end of the eighteenth century merchant and artisan families had made the recitation of *jōruri* texts a popular hobby in virtually every major city and castle town of Japan.

Although *jōruri* is undeniably a major cultural form, it is distinguished, to my mind, by a fierce competitiveness among both professional and amateur performers alike. That unyielding, tough-minded individualism constitutes an alternative to the common and even scholarly view that Japanese performing arts function entirely within the *iemoto* (family or headmaster) system. Whether we consider the ancient *gagaku* music of the imperial court, classical *waka* poetry, noh drama, ink and landscape painting, the tea ceremony, or kabuki, the idea that there is an official household lineage presided over by an all-powerful headmaster is fundamental to our image of Japanese art. According to that conceptualization, each single school engaged in any particular category of artistic endeavor (such as the tea ceremony) has a current head who is related by blood or adoption to his (or, occasionally, her) predecessor and who inherits the lineage's secret teachings and artistic treasures. Each successive headmaster can claim the unassailable right to act as the sole arbiter regarding the school's orthodox practices, to set artistic standards, and to name his own successor. Open, public competition is anathema to the *iemoto* system.

The modern *iemoto* system is to a large degree an eighteenth-century development, although antecedents certainly exist from previous cultural epochs. The Japanese have been more successful than other highly industrial societies in keeping alive their many cultural arts because of the strong tradition of family-style lineages, based either on bloodline or adoption. This practice has insured authority through a clear sense of tradition over many generations and has promoted the creation of communities of dedicated amateur disciples and patrons. Continental high culture had given Japan its sense of "classical" (*ga*), with an emphasis on the past and continuity. Late in the Heian period (794–1185), aristocrats, as a means of preserving their status and artistic authority after they had lost political power, elevated the values of elegance and refinement associated with *ga* into a nearly absolute ideal. Exclusiveness and "secret teachings" (*hiden* or *kuden*) became increasingly important in the arts from the Kamakura period (1185–1333) onward. The irony, of course, is that the best of the arts, including *waka* poetry and noh drama, usually owed their birth to energetic innovators who drew on many sources, in open competitions, and produced works that were entirely up-to-date and lively. Those who inherited the conservative legacy of high culture, however, continued to stress the primacy of *ga*—the elegant-aristocratic-traditional—over its opposite, *zoku*—art that was vulgar common contemporary. In time the *ga/zoku* dichotomy bred a canonical ideology that judged any new artistic innovation to be crude and unworthy of appreciation until it was transformed to fit within the existing tradition.

The development of *iemoto* practices was important both in high and popular culture—whether one was a Kyoto aristocrat who relied on secret teachings about the composition of *waka* poetry or an itinerant blind musician who chanted ballads—and the system contained an element of rationality in that each individual school created its own status and protected its own legitimacy. Such an orthodoxy does not, to be sure, necessarily foster continuous excellence or innovation, but it does give value to preservation, even through unstable times. On the other hand, a dogma based on restriction and exclusivity can stifle an art at the formative stages by placing too much emphasis on the past and by rejecting the energies generated by popular culture. One can understand why a school-based philosophy was attractive in Kyoto, where a long and continuous imperial history seemed to confirm the legitimacy of the courtiers' claim to act as Japan's self-appointed cultural guardians, but its core values also emerged as a model in Edo, where *iemoto* arts flourished in the late eighteenth century. Certainly in Tokugawa Japan the *ie*, or household, constituted the basic unit of business and social organization. In a society where every son expected to follow in his father's footsteps, it was not unnatural that performing traditions developed household organizations. Despite the prevalence of the *iemoto* system in the theatrical and artistic communities of Edo, however, the towering figures of the world of *jōruri* in Osaka never were especially enamored with the maintenance of a family lineage, preferring instead to mold and develop talent through uncompromising, individualistic competition.

Founding the *Jōruri* Tradition

There are no doubts as to the modest beginnings of *jōruri*; it emerged from the lowest and poorest elements of society. *Jōruri*'s origins, as noted above, can be traced back to the final years of the unstable sixteenth century when the narrative storytelling tradition was at its height and when blind minstrels were switching from the *biwa* lute to the newly imported shamisen as their accompanying instrument. About that same time, voice and accompaniment split into two, and performers began experimenting with puppets as a means of illustrating and enlivening their narratives. Early in the seventeenth century, sighted persons started to become *jōruri* chanters, although shamisen players customarily continued to be drawn from the blind community until the second half of the eighteenth century. Those sorts of changes occurred because of the development of urban, commercial theaters in the three great metropolises of Kyoto, Osaka, and Edo, and because of the art's growing popularity among aristocrats and emperors in the imperial capital. Famous chanters in particular received court titles and frequently performed in elite circles.

Although *jōruri* was evolving into a more sophisticated and complex art form, it remained essentially an extension of medieval storytelling until the last quarter of the seventeenth century, when it gradually became more theatrical in technique and contemporary in content. Crucial to the maturation of *jōruri* were a succession of famous chanters. Prominent among them were Inoue Harima no Jō, son of a Kyoto craftsman and active in Osaka during the middle decades of the seventeenth century; his disciple Kiyomizu Rihei, who later became one of Takemoto Gidayū's teachers; and Uji Kaga no Jō, an extremely influential figure who performed mostly in Kyoto and who hired both Gidayū and the playwright Chikamatsu to work under him. Kaga no Jō, as we shall see, became especially famous for enunciating artistic principles in the prefaces to collections of plays that were written under his direction.

Tokugawa Japan was clearly a hierarchical society defined by an officially decreed status system. Kyoto with its aristocracy and Edo with its samurai were both directly constructed around the precepts of those status concepts. Those two cities, of course, produced a great deal of popular art, but the commoners who worked in those cities seem as a rule always to be conscious of Japan's aristocratic-warrior heritage, either in trying to emulate that tradition or in rebelling against it, such as the case in Edo kabuki.[1] Kaga no Jō provides an example of the dilemma confronting a performer from a lowly art who tried to achieve respect for both himself and his craft in tradition-conscious Kyoto. On the one hand, Kaga no Jō was innovative; on the other, he was un-

---

1. See my "Flowers of Edo: Kabuki and its Patrons," in Gerstle, ed., *18th Century Japan: Culture and Society* (Sydney: Allen and Unwin, 1989), pp. 33–50.

Kaga no Jō. From "Seikyoku ruisan," by permission of the Tsubouchi Memorial Theatre Museum, Waseda University, Tokyo.

comfortable with any perceived deviation from classical standard or principle that popular fashion forced him to make. At mid-career, Kaga no Jō undertook a radical experiment that revealed the tension he felt about honoring the polar imperatives of being up-to-date and, at the same time, remaining true to the traditions of the past.

In the 1670s Kaga no Jō began to publish texts that contained the complete and theretofore "secret" musical notation for the voiced recitation, and he then went further to include prefaces that explicated the meanings of particular terms. Done as a response to the demands of patrons and amateur performers in the Kamigata region, which encompassed the cities of Kyoto and Osaka and their surrounding environs, Kaga no Jō's daring revelation of material that previously he had shared only with his disciples ignited a boom of interest in *jōruri*, and learning to chant *jōruri* as a hobby quickly became popular with the urban classes in Japan's major cities.

At the same time that his innovation made *jōruri* accessible to everybody, Kaga no Jō emphasized the debt that his *jōruri* texts owed to the venerated noh drama. The samurai estate long had patronized noh, and the Tokugawa shogunate had made it the warriors' exclusive preserve. Consequently, noh chanting and dance became essential elements of upper-level samurai education and training, and from the early seventeenth century publishers typically included a code of musical notation in printed texts of noh dramas.[2] Those manuscripts served as the model for Kaga no Jō's writings. In 1678, for instance, Kaga no Jō published an anthology of his most popular works under the title *Takenoko-shū* (A Collection of Bamboo Shoots), and in the preface he revealed the relationship between noh and his "secret" teachings:

> In *jōruri*, there are no teachers. However, one should understand that its parent is the noh. The reasons for this are first, at the beginning of a day's performance of *jōruri*, the puppets perform the noh dances Okina, Senzai, and Sanbasō. Then, when this ritual has ended, an opening melody from noh is played as the puppets make their entrances. Are not the robes and costumes for the important roles the same as in the noh? Therefore, the source of *jōruri* is the noh.[3]

In "A Collection of Bamboo Shoots," Kaga no Jō is both bold and cautious in his introductory "apology." His statement that there are no teachers in *jōruri* means that he claims himself as the founder, but to name the noh as parent legitimizes his infant art by placing it in a direct line of descent from Japan's most revered dramatic lineage. We know from another of his works, *Shichikushū* (A Collection of Black Bamboo), which appeared in 1697, that Kaga no Jō yearned to be a famous performer in noh. At the age of sixty-two years he reminisces:

> They say a life passes as a dream, but if I think back, my life has been one ntirely of training from the age of sixteen when I prayed to thirty shrines to achieve fame as a performer. I had a chance to enter a family of noh performers and gain training but found that even for those who work hard and have skill, unless you are a child of the family, you will not be taught the secrets of the tradition. Because I felt that I had no hope there, I turned to *jōruri*, but since there were no teachers I decided to learn from other arts and to try to improve *jōruri* by following the principles of earlier music. I studied noh, *kyōgen*, *Heike-bushi*, *kōwaka-mai* and *kouta* to create my own style.[4]

Kaga no Jō obviously had mixed feelings about the classical heritage from which he was excluded. He does, however, borrow metaphors from *Hachijō kaden sho* (The Eight-Chapter Volume of Hereditary Secrets), a popular treatise on noh published in the mid-seventeenth century, and he states clearly that the principles from this text provide a foundation for his conceptualization of

---

2. I have discussed the code for *jōruri* in my *Circles of Fantasy: Convention in the Plays of Chikamatsu* (Cambridge: Council on East Asian Studies, Harvard University, 1986), pp. 39–62, and in Gerstle, Kiyoshi Inobe, and William P. Malm, *Theater as Music: The Bunraku Play "Mt. Imo and Mt. Se: An Exemplary Tale of Womanly Virtue"* (Ann Arbor: Center for Japanese Studies, University of Michigan, 1990), pp. 39–63.

3. *Ningyō jōruri*, in Geinō-shi Kenkyūkai, ed., *Nihon shomin bunka shiryō shūsei*, vol. 7 (Tokyo: San'ichi Shobō, 1975), p. 125, and translated in my *Circles of Fantasy*, p. 183 (hereafter both works are cited by title only).

4. *Ningyō jōruri*, p. 135.

jōruri.⁵ Another quotation from "A Collection of Bamboo Shoots" shows Kaga no Jō's complex stance:

> If you take the branches of a garden tree and fashion them into various shapes, it makes them interesting, but soon they lose their charm. However, deep in the mountains near the rocks where the small pines naturally receive the blessing of rain and dew and gradually become covered with moss—such trees are so indescribably magnificent that their beauty and charm penetrate to the depths of one's soul. *Jōruri* too will retain its flavor, if the four musical styles and the enunciation of the syllabary are carefully studied, and if the text is recited to traditional melodies. However, being unable to keep to classical standard, I mix other music, such as popular songs and ballads, into *jōruri*, which makes the musical product the same as sickly bamboo or an artificially fashioned tree. Those who have discerning tastes will naturally find this music strange. Since such people are scarce, however, I must follow the whims and fashions of the times, although I myself consider them base.
>
> If one does insert other music into *jōruri*, since the transfer of other melodies to *jōruri* is like grafting bamboo onto tree branches, one must practice again and again to make it harmonize with the whole.⁶

On the one hand, Kaga no Jō wants his art (the young tree) to have the charm, elegance, and reverence of the ancient pine (noh) but, on the other, he readily innovates.

We have from his writings an image of a stern, rather severe Kaga no Jō who has a mission to raise his art in the eyes of the world, particularly those of his discerning Kyoto patrons.

> No other art is considered as base as *jōruri*, because the performance of most chanters is crude. But already a few able performers have been appreciated and have received honorary titles and offices from the court. In any type of music, is not this the case? However, those who do not understand this, or those who are not even aware of the fact that there are four basic musical styles and four essential elements, and continue to chant carelessly, are poor artists indeed, and their work is crude.⁷

Kaga no Jō completes his inaugural statement to the world with these words:

> As with all the arts, nothing is as difficult as following the dictates of one's heart: "out of the darkness, even further into the path of darkness," as the saying goes. This phrase seems most appropriate. Although I my-

---

5. *Hachijō Kaden sho*, in Hayashiya Tatsusaburō, ed., *Kodai chūsei geijutsu-ron*, Nihon Shisō Taikei 23 (Tokyo: Iwanami Shoten, 1973), pp. 511–665.
6. *Ningyō jōruri*, pp. 125–26; *Circles of Fantasy*, pp. 185–86.
7. *Ningyō jōruri*, p. 126; *Circles of Fantasy*, p. 186.

self hardly know anything about the path of art, I have relied on the writings of the sage of noh, and, while hoping that my clumsy efforts might be worthwhile, I have exhausted my mind to produce these writings and now offer them to you, my disciples. My audacity in writing this preface is truly like that of a raven who imitates the cormorant bird, tasting not the water of the sea but swallowing instead the slanders and criticisms of society. I regret divulging these secrets of the tradition.[8]

Complementing Kaga no Jō's words were the thoughts of the most famous of all Osakans, the writer Ihara Saikaku, who composed two plays for the *jōruri* chanter in 1685. That same year, Saikaku wrote in a preface to Kaga no Jō's *Kotake-shū* (The Little Bamboo Collection): "Hear ye! Hear ye! *Jōruri*, hitherto a low, vulgar thing, to be used and discarded, has been raised by Uji Kaga no Jō and his school to a level equal to noh in its depth and ability to entertain and charm its audience."[9] Saikaku then relates how everyone everywhere is singing Kaga no Jō's tunes, even the great novelist himself: "When I seek out a bit of pleasure in my old age, now too weak for football, and my eyesight too poor for archery, I look to the *Ōtake-shū* (The Great Bamboo Collection, 1681) and enjoy it from morn till night. But it is too big to carry in my pocket, so Kaga no Jō has now given us a new set of tunes and put them conveniently into this pocketbook, "The Little Bamboo Collection."[10]

Saikaku is clever here to touch just the right notes in his praise of Kaga no Jō's efforts to raise *jōruri*, but he is also half as clever again, if not whimsical, when he speaks of himself as a courtier (a football player) and as a samurai (an archer) who enjoys *jōruri* over the more lofty, traditional pastimes of his social betters. Saikaku's boldness in declaring *jōruri*'s merits as being on a par with aristocratic or samurai arts seems closer to Takemoto Gidayū's attitude than to that of Kaga no Jō. But of course Gidayū, initially an apprentice to and then a rival of Kaga no Jō, lived and worked during the Genroku cultural epoch that spanned the turn of the eighteenth century, an era when Osakans almost purposefully seem to have adopted an attitude of brash cultural self-confidence, even though the city's merchants officially were assigned to the lowest rung of the social hierarchy.

Takemoto Gidayū and Osaka Theater

Takemoto Gidayū was born in Tennōji, on the outskirts of Osaka proper. Though we have a view of Osaka as having its urban roots in the sixteenth century, the Shitennōji temple complex at Tennōji is one of Japan's oldest religious centers, dating back to the regency of Shōtoku Taishi at the end of the sixth century and beginning of the seventh. As Wakita Haruko shows, a thriving

8. *Ningyō jōruri*, pp. 126–27; *Circles of Fantasy*, p. 188.
9. *Ningyō jōruri*, p. 128.
10. Ibid.

seaside market grew up at Tennōji in the late middle ages, and the surrounding area probably was settled continuously from the early seventeenth century. Therefore, though but a farmer's son, young Gorobei—the future Gidayū— would certainly have been aware of the significance of tradition and almost certainly was possessed with a sturdy sense of local pride. He apprenticed himself to Kiyomizu Rihei, a disciple of Inoue Harima no Jō, and began performing in Osaka around 1676. The following year he is recorded to have been performing with Kaga no Jō in Kyoto under the name Kiyomizu Gorobei. At the end of 1677, when he was only twenty-six years old, Gorobei took the name Kiyomizu Ridayū and founded his own theater in Osaka. That venture failed, however, and Gorobei spent most of the next six years performing on the road. He began to call himself Takemoto Gidayū from about 1680. The name Takemoto means "the base or roots of the bamboo," so presumably the performer was following the "bamboo" metaphor for *jōruri* as expounded by Kaga no Jō. In 1684 Gidayū established the Takemoto Theater on the southern fringes of Osaka in the area commonly known as Dōtonbori. His first play at the Takemoto Theater and most thereafter were written by Chikamatsu. In 1698 he received his court title Chikugo no Jō. Gidayū's theater was continuously in debt, however, until after the reception of Chikamatsu's enormously successful *Sonezaki shinjū* (The Love Suicides at Sonezaki) in 1703, which began a new era of popularity for *jōruri*.[11]

Gidayū's rise to fame entangled him in a bitter rivalry with his onetime mentor, Kaga no Jō. The year after Gidayū established his theater at Dōtonbori in 1684, Kaga no Jō provocatively moved his troupe from aristocratic Kyoto to the burgeoning merchant city and opened a playhouse to compete side by side with Gidayū, who had been copping plays originally composed by Kaga no Jō and Chikamatsu in collaboration and performing them with great success. About this time, Gidayū launched a countergambit to woo Chikamatsu away from Kaga no Jō, a stratagem that succeeded after Gidayū took the decisive step of permitting Chikamatsu to claim credit for himself on published texts as the play's author, an acknowledgment that Kaga no Jō never had allowed. Saikaku then allied himself with Kaga no Jō and in 1685 wrote two works to be performed for the Osaka audience. The second play at least seems to have met with some success, but Kaga no Jō's theater burned to the ground and the veteran performer retreated to Kyoto, seemingly leaving Gidayū as the undisputed victor in Osaka. Gidayū's supremacy was ensured permanently when Chikamatsu eventually moved to Osaka in 1705-6 to become staff playwright at the Takemoto Theater. Not all details about the great rivalry are clear or verifiable. We do not know, for example, why Kaga no Jō took the risk of coming to Osaka to challenge Gidayū when he already was well established in Kyoto, although one can imagine the compelling attraction exerted by wealthy

---

11. Detailed accounts of Gidayū's career can be found in Mizutani Hōgin, *Jōruri kenkyū sho* (Tokyo: Dai Ichi Shobō, 1941), pp. 1-65, and Watsuji Tetsurō, *Nihon geijutsu kenkyū*, rev. ed. (Tokyo: Iwanami Shoten, 1971), pp. 486-504.

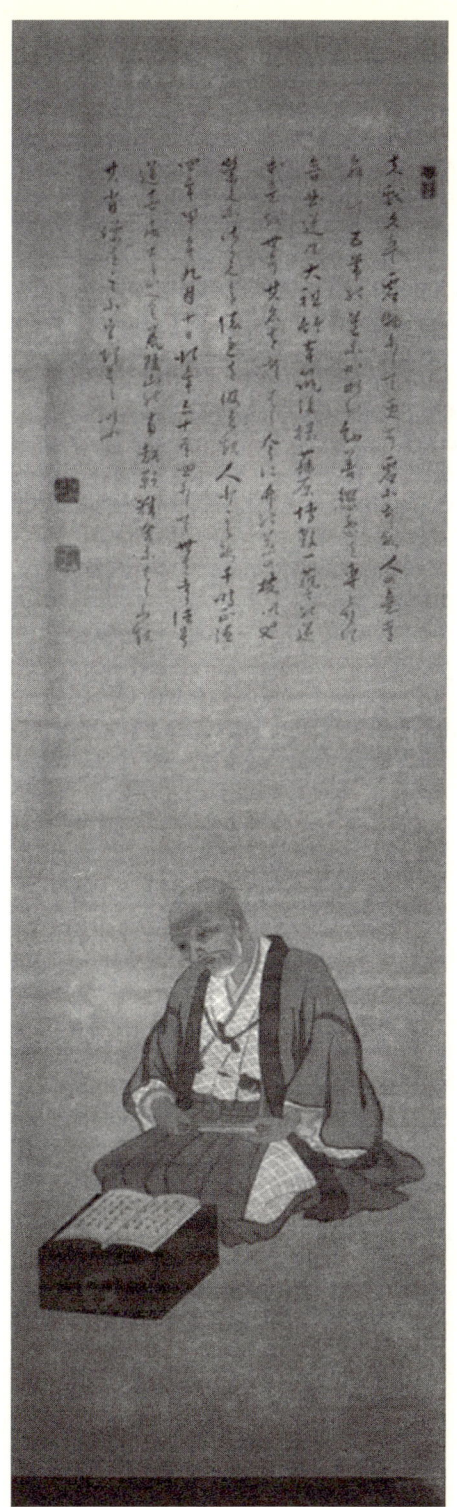

Takemoto Gidayū. Courtesy of Ōsaka Shiritsu Toshokan.

Osaka patrons at a time when the city was enjoying rapid economic growth. But the impression is of a tremendously competitive and lively atmosphere, with Osaka host to a battle between Japan's two most famous chanters, backed respectively by the most celebrated writer of the age and by an extraordinary new talent. Adding to the heady atmospherics was the irony that Osaka's Saikaku was writing for Kyotoite Kaga no Jō, while Kyoto's Chikamatsu wrote for the Osakan Gidayū.

The events of 1684–86 marked a significant moment in the career of Gidayū, and he celebrated by publishing in 1686 a collection of his pieces together with an explanatory preface—in the mode of Kaga no Jō—and titled auspiciously (and ambitiously) as *Chihiro-shū* (A Collection for a Thousand Years). This very real rivalry between the established elder generation and the young upstarts and between different styles and cities is the immediate background to Gidayū's prefaces; in fact one often feels that Gidayū is writing always with Kaga no Jō in mind. Gidayū, like Kaga no Jō, is bold in his first statement:

> These days those who chant at the crossroads are either descendants of Kanze noh or are in the *kōwaka-mai* school. . . . Here we have a new style founded by Takemoto Gidayū which is neither too strong nor too weak. . . . Above, the voices mix with the high-hatted courtiers sitting in a row chanting *waka* poetry in thirty-one syllables; below, he and his followers learn from those poor folk who sing songs as they wander about peddling their wares. There are none he does not learn from.[12]

Gidayū in subsequent prefaces is forthright and confident in his convictions. He makes fun of contemporary entertainers who claim ancient or august lineage. Tradition is useful only if it can teach you something practical. He seems, in contrast to Kaga no Jō, to have little awe for either the noh tradition or for the Kyoto aristocracy.

Gidayū's most important treatise is found in his "Collection of *Jōruri* Scenes" (*Gidayū danmono-shū*), published in 1687. It is worth quoting his words at some length to give us a feel of his personality and his conception of himself as an artist. Moreover, Gidayū's prefaces often were quoted by others, and his individualistic ideology formed the philosophical foundation for *jōruri* performers until the modern age. It begins: "The courtiers of the palace decorate their hair and hats with blossoms in their leisure as they enjoy spring's glorious beauty. Each person has his own preferred aesthetic pleasures, and *jōruri* too can be ranked alongside the flowering arts of the nobility. However, even among flowers and plants, there are old trees as well as young ones. The blos-

---

12. The preface is signed by an otherwise unknown person, Josui, but represents sentiments and attitudes echoed in later writings that can be authoritatively attributed to Gidayū; see *Ningyō jōruri*, p. 130.

soms of young cherry trees have bright colors and delightful fragrance in abundance, around which butterflies, birds, and passersby frolic in joyous play."[13] Gidayū is setting up *jōruri* as the young but mature cherry tree in full bloom, an art comparable to those of the past and of the aristocracy. He picks up on Kaga no Jō's (and others') nature metaphors for drama. His comments, however, undercut Kaga no Jō's preference for the old tree: "To be sure, the finest trees are the old ones deep in the valleys, upon which only a few scattered flowers quietly bloom, but, if one cultivates a young tree in imitation of these old ones, then its branches will not grow strong; rather, they will be stifled, and the blossoms will be feeble with little charm. The style of *jōruri* too should be lively and vigorous, like the colorful image of the dandy, the fashionable man-about-town."[14] Here Gidayū swaggers a bit with self-confidence; we have a sense of his resemblance to one of Saikaku's boastful and worldly Osakans.

Next Gidayū turns to his "secret teachings," and again directly comments on Kaga no Jō's writings.

> Recently, on a certain evening, an old and intimate friend came to visit and asked me to instruct him in the secret teachings of the art of *jōruri*. I answered in the following manner. Basically, since the art is modern, there are no traditional teachings to be learned from anyone. The music is restricted to a five-tone and twelve-note scale. The traditional songs and melodies of *kagura* sacred music, popular songs, folk songs, *kōwakamai* ballad drama, noh, and *Heike-bushi* recitation are all incorporated into *jōruri*; this is the tradition. If an artist performs well, is praised by others, and then is acknowledged by the world as a master, his words will certainly become secret teachings. However, if he slanders others while saying that only he himself is good in the hope that he will be considered a great artist, then for such a person there is the refined treatise, *Hachijō kaden sho*, by the sage of noh, which contains the secret precepts of the tradition, handed down from generation to generation. . . .
>
> It is only natural that those who teach others about the art, or are acknowledged by the world as accomplished artists, must be familiar with these matters. However, to use quotations from the *Hachijō kaden sho* in order to brandish pompously one's authority is distasteful. Those who skip their practice sessions and try to learn solely from secret teachings will never learn to perform well. Reading books on theory will neither help one's mouth to move smoothly nor one's voice to improve and become entertaining for the audience. . . . Although at the lofty Emperor's Court there are disputes about theories of art, even there the closely guarded secret teachings of poetry are of little use when com-

---

13. *Ningyō jōruri*, p. 130; *Circles of Fantasy*, p. 189.
14. *Ningyō jōruri*, p. 131; *Circles of Fantasy*, p. 190.

posing poems; they can only reassure one's heart, as Konoe Motohiro of the court has said.[15]

Gidayū is consistent: each individual can become a master, but only through constant struggle to improve.

Implicit in Gidayū's critique is that Kaga no Jō is not the grand master with the secret teachings necessary for legitimacy. He openly criticizes Kaga no Jō for claiming to be an heir of the noh lineage. Gidayū's constant references to the aristocracy are intriguing, even from a twentieth-century perspective. He matter-of-factly inserts *jōruri* into the most elevated ranks of the canon. We may be casual about such matters today, but Gidayū's boldness is remarkable here. He contests Kaga no Jō's ideas in other ways as well:

> It has been said that *jōruri* should consider the noh as its parent, and so one should learn noh chanting first, and only then begin to practice *jōruri*. My reply is that, although such an idea has its apparent merits, the artists who follow my style regard the former masters of *jōruri* as father and mother, while considering noh, *kōwaka-mai*, and other traditional music as foster parents. Children, however, do not know the hearts of their parents. Each individual has his own talent, his own sense of poetics and of the rhythm of the shamisen, and his own sensitivity to the reception by and criticism of the audience, which can never be learned from a teacher.... The ability to entertain without boring one's audience should be considered the secret tradition of the art of *jōruri*. Those who achieve this skill should be considered masters.
>
> Although *jōruri* is not as great an art as noh, what is the rhythm of the steps of the god in the noh play *Takasago* for? Is not its purpose to entertain the hearts of the audience! Our teaching is to listen to many kinds of music, drama, and storytelling, and to discard that which is not pleasing to one's heart; that which remains most likely will be effective as art. One should adhere to the golden writings of the sages, while gathering familiar childhood songs and any melodies that one finds particularly pleasing, and use them to refresh and expand one's art. One must open one's ear and mind, because no one school has the secret teachings and traditions, handed down from generation to generation. One must think that one can oneself become a master of *jōruri*. One should not, however, seek to become famous; instead, practice with full concentration to become proficient and skillful. If I consider the above to be the essentials of *jōruri*, and if I then call this my secret teachings, there will be both those who are impressed and those who will laugh.[16]

Gidayū makes a very strong stand for individual talent and hard work, although acknowledging that there is much to learn from the past. But a par-

---

15. *Ningyō jōruri*, p. 131; *Circles of Fantasy*, pp. 190–91.
16. *Ningyō jōruri*, p. 131; *Circles of Fantasy*, pp. 191–92.

ticular tenet—that a performer should learn and use any kind of music—remained a firm part of the *jōruri* tradition long after Gidayū departed the stage.

Kaga no Jō replied to Gidayū's rhetoric in his "A Collection of Black Bamboo," making a case for the importance of classical form and tradition over individual inspiration.

> Without tradition and teaching (*den*) how can *jōruri* flourish and the music be considered great? Without such discrimination, someone who lets his voice follow the rhythm or lets a bad rhythm overtake the mood and cause the chanting to fall into disarray—this is the same as someone losing his sense of self and going mad. Or, without training, when someone sets a text to music or simply copies another chanter—this is false *jōruri*, and the artist reduces himself to the level of a priest who sells dispensations. In any art, no matter how talented or original the person, without training in the tradition, how can one expect to become skillful in the Way?[17]

Both of these seminal figures view training as absolutely essential, but they fundamentally differ on their views about *jōruri* and about the individual in relation to tradition. Kaga no Jō wishes to locate *jōruri* within the tradition of the classical arts, whereas Gidayū sees *jōruri* as distinct and equal. In the *Jōruri tōryū kohyakuban* (Gidayū's Best One Hundred), published around 1702–3, Gidayū stresses that each person and each age has different tastes and preferences. Each era has its own distinctive voice (*jise no onsei*), and today it is *jōruri* that flourishes.[18]

In the last of his prefaces, published in *Ōmu ga soma* (Parrot Mountain) in 1711, just a few years before his death, Gidayū names Kaga no Jō and responds to his notion about the necessity of sticking to principles. He acknowledges criticism that a performer is the same as a madman if he lets popular tunes inserted into the performance take over from the main melody. Gidayū, however, then takes this one step further:

> If the audience happens to prefer the bits taken from outside *jōruri*, then we must look again to see why *jōruri* is considered inferior and use this as inspiration to improve.... No music can replace *jōruri*, whether from the past or present. But we must not ignore innovation, fashions, and changes in the times. Without going too far astray, we must alter our melodies and rhythms and express the depths of human emotion (*jō o fukaku kataru*). By experimenting with other styles and discovering which bits are effective and adding these to our musical brew, by taking these to spice our sauce, this increases its impact.... I have always tried to innovate through practice and training in order to go beyond the re-

---

17. *Ningyō jōruri*, p. 134.
18. *Jōruri tōryū kohyakuban*, in *Ningyō jōruri*, p. 136.

ceived teaching. Though I have tried to remember this for the more than forty years of my career, I still have not reached the furthest depths and chanted to my fullest satisfaction.[19]

Gidayū's emphasis on disciplined training is common to all the traditional arts, but his demand that each individual must follow his own artistic path is radical. Gidayū's ideas and his personal example set the bunraku theater onto its fiercely competitive and individualistic path. Gidayū's most famous student, Toyotake Wakatayū, became his most ardent rival. Wakatayū, who later was known as Echizen no Shōjō, established his Toyotake Theater in 1703 to compete with Gidayū's Takemoto Theater, located just one hundred meters away. That initial venture failed, however, and in 1705 Wakatayū is recorded as performing again at the Takemoto Theater. In 1707 he successfully reestablished his Toyotake Theater, and the two playhouses ushered in the golden age of *jōruri*, vying against each other for audiences until the 1760s. Despite the spirited competition, however, there is no record of Gidayū being antagonistic to his student-turned-rival. Toward the end of his life, Gidayū designated as his heir the young Masatayū (Harima no Shōjō), in whom he saw talent. Eventually, more than a decade later, Masatayū did come into his own as the star performer in the Takemoto Theater, but he had to earn his place; his ascent was neither automatic nor guaranteed.[20]

Bunraku did not develop family lineages, only lineages based on apprenticeship, discipline, skill, innovation, and achievement. Occasionally sons did join the troupe, but they were (and are) as likely as not to choose a different specialization from that of their fathers, opting perhaps to become a shamisen player rather than a chanter. In that regard, the practices that characterized bunraku in Osaka diverged from those associated with kabuki in Edo. Both, of course, demanded innovation from mature actors after they had mastered their roles through teaching and training, but kabuki in the eighteenth century became an exclusive world, a family lineage. As an outcast art, kabuki in general was restrictive in its practice of preferring only relatives within the troupe and in encouraging an eldest son to follow in his father's footsteps and eventually take his name, no matter what the offspring's level of skill. As a consequence of those preferences, kabuki troupes in Edo followed the strict custom of never teaching the art of acting to amateurs.

While the above observations certainly hold true for the world of Edo theater, kabuki in Osaka followed a different path. Since most of our knowledge about kabuki actors comes from the Edo tradition, a better image of Osaka's distinctiveness must await a comparative study of kabuki in those two cities over the eighteenth and nineteenth centuries. Still, it does seem clear that kabuki troupes in Osaka did not have such a strong sense of keeping alive a household tradition, as opposed to an individual style, as did their counter-

---

19. *Ōmu ga soma*, in *Ningyō jōruri*, p. 149.
20. For details, see Yūda Yoshio, *Jōruri-shi ronkō* (Tokyo: Chūō Kōronsha, 1975), pp. 384–407.

parts in Edo. In that context, the organization of Osaka kabuki may be more akin to that of bunraku than to Edo kabuki. It was of course common practice throughout Japan in the early modern period for individuals to relate to the world through the family (*ie*) business. *Jōruri* (and perhaps Osaka kabuki) seem to be exceptional in their preference for individual talent.

Another difference between the theatrical worlds of Edo and Osaka concerned the attitudes of professionals toward amateurs—Edo kabuki always jealously guarded the tools of its trade; bunraku, in contrast, was economically dependent on the teaching of amateur practitioners from its beginnings until at least recent times. During the course of the eighteenth century, nonprofessional enthusiasts began to take up chanting and shamisen playing in increasing numbers. As might be expected, those amateurs imbibed deeply from Gidayū's tradition of competitive individualism, as can be seen from publications about their performances. In 1786, "Amateur *Jōruri* Critiques" (Kishin shirōto jōruri hyōbanki) went on sale in Edo, Osaka, and Kyoto. It is a remarkable document because it reviews the public performances of amateurs at so-called benefit (*kishin*) productions, plays staged at temples or shrines with the proceeds from ticket sales going to support the religious institution. The critiques are serious and in the style of earlier books analyzing professional performances. Tribute is paid to those amateurs in the subtitle, "Mirror of Hard-Working Amateurs" (Benkyō sukanjo). The text even goes as far as to boldly criticize the general level of current professionals. The continuous publication of synopses, training guides, and fictional accounts of performers paints an interesting picture of how serious the business of amateur *jōruri* performances became.[21]

Those amateurs certainly craved the fame of being on stage and of seeing their names in print. The striving to be as good as a professional, however, was matched by the opposing ethic of the cult of the amateur, which exalted the purity expressed by performing at shrines and temples for the gods and for the benefit of others, rather than for one's own personal profit. An important word frequently employed to describe the purpose of such performances was *nagusami*. Gidayū and Chikamatsu also used to that term, often glossed as "amusement" or "entertainment," to explain the aim of *jōruri*. But *nagusami* has the additional Buddhistic meaning of calming the spirit and consoling persons as they cope with the suffering inherent in the human condition, and the "Amateur *Jōruri* Critiques" emphasizes the religious, spiritual side of that idiom to specify the purpose of amateur benefit performances.[22] Furthermore, the handbook depicts how each night all the gods in Osaka gathered to discuss the various *jōruri* performances. Amateurs perform, at least ideally, for the gods' pleasure, and the critiques come from the deities. The main text even specifically ranks the amateurs and comments candidly on their skills and

---

21. I discuss the history of nonprofessional *jōruri* in "Amateurs and the Theatre: The So-called Demented Art Gidayū," in *Senri Ethnological Studies* 40 (Spring 1995), pp. 37–57. For more on the changing nature of playwrights and performers see the chapter "Playwrights and Performers," in Gerstle, Malm, and Inobe, *Theater as Music*, pp. 103–21.

22. *Kishin shirōto jōruri hyōbanki*, in *Ningyō jōruri*, p. 493.

techniques. The focus is Osaka, but "Amateur *Jōruri* Critiques" includes lists of individuals in Kyoto, Edo, and Sakai as well. Competition both among groups or clubs and among individuals was fundamental to the organization of amateur activities. *Jōruri*, absent an *iemoto* system, always has depended on rivalry, rather than lineage, to sustain its vigor in both professional and amateur spheres.

The Legacy of Gidayū

The primacy of competition and innovation over lineage and preservation continued into the modern period when amateur *jōruri* experienced a renewed boom in popularity. *Gidayū zasshi*, which began publication in 1893 in Tokyo, was the first of a series of modern magazines devoted to *jōruri*.[23] Its opening "apology" stated the journal's mission, declaring that *jōruri* is the receptacle of Japanese popular culture; that since *jōruri* employs the only language commonly understood throughout the country, it ought to be taught as the core of the national educational curriculum and should serve as the model for a standard national language; and that Japan must keep the *jōruri* tradition alive and vigorous in order to preserve the native culture in the face of the Western challenge. The editor's push to use *jōruri* as the prototype for a national language is remarkable since this was a Tokyo-based magazine and *jōruri* is a Kansai-centered language.

The theme that *jōruri* embodies the essence of Japanese culture remained a consistent cry in similar publications until the end of World War II. The periodical *Naniwa meibutsu–Jōruri zasshi* (Osaka's Finest: The *Jōruri* Magazine) gives us a particularly detailed record of amateur competitions held throughout Japan from 1899 to 1945, complete with photographs of the winners and brief details concerning their specialty pieces. Those competitions were formal, had officials and judges, and awarded prizes. The competitive nature is fascinating, and distinctive from the *iemoto* arts which hold regular recitals for students studying under a teacher but do not arrange for competitions. Early in the century "Osaka's Finest: The *Jōruri* Magazine" occasionally featured

---

23. Issues of this magazine are not easy to locate, nor are those of similar publications such as *Jōruri zasshi* (published in Osaka, 1899–1945); *Jōruri sekai* (Kyoto, 1920–1930s?); *Gidayū kenkyū* (Tokyo, 1921–?); *Jōruri geppō* (Kurume, 1920s?–1930s?); and *Jōkyoku kenkyū* (Tokyo, 1940s). The Waseda Theatre Museum Library has all the above journals, whereas the *Jōruri zasshi* and *Jōruri sekai* can also be found at the Ōsaka Furitsu Chūō Toshokan; the Kokuritsu Bunraku Gekijō Toshokan has the latter publication as well. Other titles that I have seen, or at least seen mention of, include *Gidayūkai, Dai Nippon jōrurikai, Jōruri bunko, Seikyokukai, Kyūshū jōruri geppō, Take no Kawa, Engei,* and *Kamigata*. *Kamigata shumi* (1920s, Osaka) is a delightfully tasteful booklet (about fifty pages) with articles on various aspects of traditional Kansai culture. It is printed as if it were a woodblock from the early modern period, with folded pages and color prints on the cover and inside. Each issue includes a stamp from a temple or shrine in the area and has a seasonal aesthetic flavor. *Jōruri* naturally commands center stage in its pages honoring Osaka's contributions to the best of Japanese traditional culture. I am thankful to Yoshinaga Takao for introducing me to this publication.

stories about the scandals that arose over charging fees for amateur performances held at the Kado Theater in Dōtonbori. The journal upheld the ideal of the purity of amateur activity—that material profit is not the goal remained essential throughout this period. We know that professionals acknowledged that amateurs performed certain *jōruri* pieces in a manner that surpassed even the professionals and that professionals went to learn such pieces from them.[24] Such would be inconceivable in noh or kabuki.

Our image of bunraku from the Meiji period (1868–1912) to the end of World War II is that of a tradition which continued to pay homage to intense discipline and a competitive atmosphere. The reminiscences of performers about legendary figures give us a picture of artistic dedication taken to an extreme degree. In particular, *jōruri* training was legendary for its severity. Toyozawa Danpei, the shamisen player who trained many of the most famous chanters of the Meiji period, is representative of the Gidayū heritage. His famous phrase, *butai de shine* (die playing on stage), sums up his commitment to his art.[25] His is a tale, like Gidayū's two centuries earlier, of the personal determination to struggle, to strive constantly to improve, to perfect. Danpei was true to his purpose to the very end; his disciples relate how he did in fact pass away while performing—his notes kept getting louder and louder, until he collapsed on the stage.[26] This competitive, individualistic spirit produced some of the best performances ever in the Japanese tradition. At its peak within an atmosphere of open competition in the initial decades of the twentieth century, bunraku stood unrivaled in its dramatic intensity. That is immediately evident even today from the recordings we have of Toyotake Yamashiro no Shōjō performing in the late 1920s and 1930s.[27]

For all of its merits, *jōruri*'s individualistic spirit, as noted at the beginning of this chapter, does not necessarily see preservation of the lineage alone as a noble goal; there is no family line to keep alive, no family shrine to make offerings at or sacrifices for. As a consequence, today bunraku finds it hard to draw new performers into a profession where one has little hope of fame or financial reward until well into middle age. To survive, the art has had both to recruit outsiders and encourage its own sons to enter the profession. In recent years, the National Theater organizations in Tokyo and Osaka have come to the rescue and provided a means of keeping bunraku alive, but in saving the art form authorities have transformed bunraku into a preserved national treasure and tamed its individualistic, competitive nature. Whatever the changes

---

24. The famous Meiji-Taishō shamisen player Tsuruzawa Dōhachi said that it was not unusual for a professional to learn a particular piece from an amateur; Kōnoike Yukitake, *Dōhachi geidan* (Tokyo: privately printed, 1944), pp. 100–101. Volume 106 (1912) of *Jōruri zasshi* has an article on how amateurs were becoming as good as the professionals, and volume 109 (1912) bewails the fear that there are too few professionals. Dōhachi also said that often patrons risked bankruptcy because of the costs of hosting private performances.

25. Two works that contain details about Danpei's life and art as supplied by his disciples are Kōnoike, *Dōhachi geidan*, and Chatani Hanjirō, *Bunraku kikigaki* (Osaka: Zenkoku Shobō, 1946).

26. Kōnoike, *Dōhachi geidan*, pp. 42–47.

27. *Shigei: Toyotake Yamashiro no Shōjō*, Japan Victor, Records SJL 25016–25031.

of the postwar years, however, it is important to remember that bunraku represented an important stream of popular culture for almost four centuries, an Osaka tradition and legacy that demanded individualism and innovation through lifelong dedication.

Jōruri's origins lie in the tradition of wandering blind minstrels active long before the development of Osaka as a major urban center. Those performers were the receptacles of the popular collective heroic memory. Originality of composition was not a conscious concern for those performers; they were the voices of gods and spirits long past. *Jōruri* puppet theater, however, blossomed under Gidayū within an urban commercial context during Osaka's golden age of success and self-confidence. From Gidayū's writings and the characteristics of amateur *jōruri* chanting sprang an ideal of individuality and competitiveness that is striking not only for Japan but in world history. The ideal, at least, was not fame and fortune (though both professionals and amateurs, of course, sought public recognition); rather, dedication to training and improvement were seen as roads to artistic and, consequently, spiritual achievement. Though the context is indisputably commercial theater, *jōruri* was only rarely a financial success, even during its best years in the middle decades of the eighteenth century. The aesthetic ideal of *sui* (savoir faire, sensitivity to others), which emerged out of the harsh financial realities of the Osaka pleasure quarters, put human feelings on a pedestal and counted them as more precious and more important than monetary considerations. *Jōruri*, too, held dedication to the art to be an ideal that far surpassed financial considerations. Osaka professionals and amateurs created an anti-money ethic, which ironically, it can be argued, was a manifestation of Osaka's peculiar mercantile culture. Together with a rigorous and pragmatic rationalism that cut across convention and tradition, *jōruri* placed a subtle, shrouded emphasis on the irrational, emotional, and spiritual aspects of human existence. The plays themselves are filled with an overwhelming concern about *jō* (passion) and its often tragic consequences, while the code of performance revered a tradition of striving through training and performance to gain a spiritual, Buddhistic experience. Osaka's culture contains fascinating paradoxes whose complexity needs more study. For example, although Saikaku's metaphor for Osaka, the eternal storehouse of commercial prosperity (*eitaigura*), was certainly one ideal, the city's most representative art, *jōruri*, honored Gidayū's opposing ethic of individual achievement, a creed that denied the relevance of household or continuity of lineage and heralded an egalitarianism open to anyone who possessed talent and skill and was willing to work hard.

CHAPTER SIX

The Five Men of Naniwa: Gang Violence and Popular Culture in Genroku Osaka

— Gary P. Leupp

> The criminal produces an impression, partly moral and partly tragic, as the case may be, and in this way renders a "service" by arousing the moral and aesthetic feelings of the public. He produces not only compendia on Criminal Law, but also . . . art, belles-lettres, novels, and even tragedies. . . . The criminal breaks the monotony and everyday security of bourgeois life. In this way he keeps it from stagnation.
> —KARL MARX

Outlaws are productive people indeed. The crimes they commit keep police forces busy, justify large budgets for criminal justice bureaucracies, and nourish the academic discipline of criminology. More important, those who violate the system's rules stimulate a popular fascination with their transgressions and inspire the creation and marketing of countless novels, plays, films, and television shows. Apparently people everywhere share a fascination with crime and its perpetrators, but few have glorified outlaws as conspicuously as did urban commoners in Japan during the Tokugawa period—and residents of few cities have adulated criminals as enthusiastically as the merchants, artisans, and laborers of early modern Osaka valorized the "Five Men of Naniwa" (*Naniwa gonin otoko*).

At the end of the seventeenth century and beginning of the eighteenth, Karigane Bunshichi, Gokuin no Sen'emon, An no Heibei, Hote no Ichiemon, and Kaminari Shōkurō haunted the streets of Osaka, robbing, beating, and even killing fellow residents. In the summer of 1701 the police caught up with the violent young men, and, after an investigation, authorities publicly executed them in the Eighth Month of the following year. The brazen personalities of the ruffians and their contemptuous disregard for the law riveted the attention of Osakans, who began to create an intriguing set of myths about the motives and deeds of those ne'er-do-wells of Naniwa, a traditional name for Osaka. In time the condemned men were elevated to legendary status. Celebrated in ballads, plays, stories, and wood-block prints, the Five Men of Naniwa, thugs and murderers in real life, became transformed into protectors of ordinary people and the embodiment of the best and most noble aspirations and values espoused by the commoners of Osaka.

The incident involving the Five Men of Naniwa unfolded at the same time that the affair of the Forty-Seven Righteous Warriors of Akō was capturing the imagination of the residents of Edo. That event began in the spring of 1701 when Kira Yoshinaka, a leading shogunal official who oversaw the conduct of important rituals within Edo Castle, berated Asano Naganori, the lord of Akō domain, presumably for his uncouth behavior during a ceremonial visit from imperial envoys. Humiliated, the impetuous Asano drew his sword and wounded Kira. Before the day was done, the shogun ordered Asano to commit suicide immediately to atone for his rash actions. For a year and a half, members of Asano's former band of retainers kept their anger and intentions to themselves, and then as evening fell on the fourteenth day of the Twelfth Month of Genroku Fifteen (January 31, 1703, according to the Western calendar) they took their revenge by attacking Kira's residential compound in Edo and lopping off the head of their lord's antagonist. The warriors' bold act won them the respect and admiration of many, but participation in a secret vendetta was technically a violation of the shogun's law, and so on the afternoon of the fourth day of the Second Month, 1703, the samurai of Akō accepted the punishment decreed for them, and did still further honor to Asano's memory by taking their own lives in ritual suicide.

The people of Edo knew little about the personalities of Akō's righteous warriors or the motives that inspired them, but that hardly mattered to the city's playwrights and printmakers. As they scripted dramas for the kabuki stage and churned out wood-block prints by the score, those artists quickly mythologized the deeds of lord Asano's retainers and made them into exemplars of all that was considered good within the samurai code of ethics—courage, personal honor, absolute loyalty to one's lord, and the willingness to sacrifice one's life on his behalf. In time, the righteous warriors acquired the status of folk heroes, their legend kept alive even today in contemporary stage productions, films, and television dramas, and even enhanced by the translation of kabuki plays about the event into foreign languages.

Time has not been nearly so kind to the memory of the Five Men of Naniwa, and very few Japanese today could be expected to recall their exploits or enumerate their supposed virtues. In the eighteenth century, however, Karigane Bunshichi and his band of roughnecks—the swashbuckling offspring of economically humble merchants and artisans—were as well known as the warriors from Akō and were equally celebrated as custodians of popularly respected values. Unlike the incident in Edo, for which few reliable documentary accounts remain extant, in Osaka a police report completed in the Seventh Month of 1703 permits historians some evidentiary insights into the lives of the Five Men of Naniwa. Comparison of that record with the depiction of the Osaka outlaws in popular culture can reveal, in turn, how the creators of songs, dramas, and wood-block prints romanticized the lives of the Five Men of Naniwa and converted them from untamed troublemakers into popular heroes who represented values held dear by the merchants and artisans of Osaka and Japan's other urban centers.

Urban Gangs in Early Modern Japan

Tokugawa popular culture reserved a special place in its affections for the members of organized criminal gangs—persons referred to as *kabukimono*, *yakko*, *otokodate*, *kyōkaku* (or *kyankaku*), and *roppōsha*.[1] During the first century of the Tokugawa period such rogues were especially conspicuous in castle towns that included large samurai populations—Kanazawa, Sendai, Nagoya, and most notably the shogun's administrative headquarters, Edo. Many members of the warrior class, confined to such cities as a consequence of the imposition of the four-estate status system, became disillusioned with the social order during the early decades of the century. Often in financial difficulty, envious of the relative affluence of the despised merchant class, and disgruntled by the absence of warfare and lack of opportunities to display their martial skills, some samurai vented their frustrations by forming gangs and visiting violence upon their fellow urban dwellers.

Government ordinances provide some of the earliest information about *kabukimono*. In 1605 authorities in the castle town of Kanazawa forbade such toughs from loitering on streets or engaging in street-corner sumo. More serious offenses prompted the domain to crack down on its hoodlums in 1610, when officials rounded up sixty persons and executed them.[2] Gangsters also troubled Edo from an early date. The author of the *Daitoku Kō ki* (Record of Lord Daitoku, 1612) noted that "worthless, dissipated fellows called *kabukimono* swagger about Edo, causing trouble to its good citizens."[3] A group known as the Ōtori Gang (*Ōtorigumi*, after its leader, Ōtori Ichibei) was punished in 1612 when its members killed a ranking government official named Shibayama Masatsugu to avenge the death of a colleague at the hands of that

---

1. Some of the terms have an unclear or complicated etymology. *Kabukimono* conveys a sense of eccentricity; *yakko* connotes servility (and is felicitously rendered by Sansom as "varlet"); *otokodate* has the positive implication of "one who stands up as a man"; and *kyōkaku* suggests someone who is "brave" or "stalwart." The term *roppōsha* ("one of all six directions") apparently derives from the name of one seventeenth-century gang. For overviews of urban gang violence in this period see Kodama Kōta, *Genroku jidai* (Tokyo: Chūō Kōronsha, 1984), pp. 80–93, and George Sansom, *A History of Japan, 1615–1867* (Stanford: Stanford University Press, 1963), pp. 58–61.

2. James L. McClain, *Kanazawa: A Seventeenth-Century Japanese Castle Town* (New Haven: Yale University Press, 1982), p. 60.

3. Imagawa Tokuzō, *Edo jidai mushukunin no seikatsu* (Tokyo: Yūzankaku, 1973), p. 49.

shogunal functionary. Many died in the attack on Shibayama, and a subsequent investigation uncovered a document with the names of five hundred *kabukimono* involved in the affair, including the sons of several important daimyo. List in hand, officials apprehended a number of the thugs, who shared the same fate as the outlaws in Kanazawa.[4]

From at least the 1640s, some of the shogun's own retainers of bannerman rank (*hatamoto*) and their sons organized themselves into gangs. Dressed in outlandish clothing and swaggering about town, the *hatamoto yakko*, as the samurai hooligans were known, indulged in unlawful behavior. In 1645 one such *hatamoto yakko*, a member of the great guards (*ōban*) with an income of five hundred *koku*, was ordered to commit ritual suicide to make amends for his unruly behavior.[5] Nine years later, a lampoon circulated throughout Edo parodying two high-ranking *hatamoto* for supplementing their annual rice stipends (ten thousand and three thousand *koku* respectively) by roaming the streets at night and robbing hapless townspeople.[6]

In challenging state authority, those samurai hooligans bore some resemblance to persons Eric Hobsbawm has called "social bandits."[7] But the lawbreakers studied by Hobsbawm were either peasants or impoverished country gentlemen who, having run afoul of the law, came to be idealized as popular heroes. *Hatamoto yakko*, in contrast, were urbanized samurai who frequently targeted merchants and artisans as their victims. Even if the *hatamoto yakko* had preyed only on wealthy merchants and left the urban poor alone, the latter would not necessarily have been inclined to see the samurai rowdies as champions and avengers. Indeed, commoners came to organize bands of their own whose members, the self-styled *machi yakko*, might be regarded as genuine social bandits. Quarrels between the two *yakko* groups quickly became the stuff of legend. For example, the rivalry between the *machi yakko* Banzuiin Chōbei and the *hatamoto yakko* Mizuno Jūrōzaemon, which culminated in the Chōbei's gruesome murder in 1657, subsequently became celebrated in stories and stage retellings, and even today it inspires comic book writers and filmmakers, who usually cast Chōbei as the heroic figure and Jūrōzaemon as a treacherous villain.[8]

Such outbursts of violence prompted the shogunate to take stern measures, ordering the beheadings of several *kabukimono* in Edo in the Second Month of 1659 and expanding the system of guardhouses located in samurai neighbor-

---

4. Uno Shun'ichi et al., *Nihon zenshi (Jiapan Kuronikku)* (Tokyo: Kōdansha, 1991), p. 476; *Edogaku jiten* (Tokyo: Kōbundō, 1984), s.v. "Otokodate," by Jinbō Kazuya, p. 299; and Benito Ortolani, *The Japanese Theatre from Shamanistic Ritual to Contemporary Pluralism* (Leiden: E. J. Brill, 1990), p. 155.

5. *Kodansha Encyclopedia of Japan*, vol. 3 (Tokyo: Kodansha, 1983), s.v. "Hatamoto yakko," by George Elison [Jurgis Elisonas], p. 112.

6. Naramoto Tatsuya, ed., *Yomeru nenpyō, Edo no hen*, vol. 1 (Tokyo: Jiyūminkokusha, 1982), p. 51.

7. Eric Hobsbawm, *Bandits* (New York: Delacorte, 1969), pp. 13–15.

8. Tamura Eitarō, *Seikatsu-shi sōsho*, vol. 4, *Yakuza no seikatsu* (Tokyo: Yūzankaku, 1987), pp. 170–73. For a vivid retelling of the tale in English, see A. B. Mitford [Lord Redesdale], *Tales of Old Japan* (Rutland, Vt.: Charles E. Tuttle, 1966), pp. 90–141.

hoods of the city. Those guardhouses were staffed by two to four watchmen in the daytime, and four to six men in the evenings, who patrolled the neighborhood and took into custody anyone found acting in a suspicious manner.[9] Urban gang violence continued, however, and increasingly commoners participated in the bloodshed. There seems to have been important regional variations in the nature of such commoner gang activity. During the Genroku period (1688–1704) many *machi yakko* in Edo came from the households of rice brokers who, given their key role in marketing the tax rice of bannermen and other direct retainers of the shogun, often made fortunes that aroused the warriors' envy. In Osaka, by way of contrast, disaffected young men from the lowest stratum of society fleshed out the ranks of commoner gangs, and they directed their hostility toward wealthy merchants.[10]

During the administration of the fifth shogun, Tsunayoshi (ruled 1680–1709), Edo's streets grew more peaceful. A more intensive policing effort was partially responsible. By the end of the seventeenth century more than nine hundred guardhouses were sprinkled throughout samurai neighborhoods, and nearly a thousand similar posts, manned and supported by commoners, could be found in the residential quarters set aside for merchants and artisans. The continued meting out of severe punishments also must have helped to deter gang activity; in 1686, for instance, police arrested more than two hundred members of the Daishōjingi Gang, eleven of whom were executed.[11] Contributing to the more subdued urban climate as well, although in a manner that defies measurement, was the waning of martial culture brought about by the disappearance of warfare.

Although violent crime seems to have decreased during the final decades of the seventeenth century, such gang activities as gambling, extortion, racketeering, and protection became increasingly institutionalized, especially in Edo. Racketeers called *yashi* and rings of professional gamblers were the forbears of Japan's modern *yakuza*. Construction workers and manual laborers such as palanquin bearers also formed gangs for mutual self-protection, comparable to the *compagnonnages* of early nineteenth-century Paris. Rival squads of fire fighters brawled publicly in Edo and other cities, and, under the pretext of opening up firebreaks, even demolished the homes and shops of persons whom they disliked. Lower-ranking samurai as well as commoners continued to form all manner of illegal gangs throughout the Tokugawa period.[12]

---

9. Katō Takeshi, "Governing Edo," in James L. McClain, John M. Merriman, and Ugawa Kaoru, eds., *Edo and Paris: Urban Life and the State in the Early Modern Era* (Ithaca: Cornell University Press, 1994), pp. 50–51; Endō Motoo, comp., *Kinsei seikatsu nenpyō* (Tokyo: Yūzankaku, 1982), p. 85. By the middle of the 1650s, the Osaka castle warden also had organized an elaborate network of police officials; see Naramoto, *Yomeru nenpyō*, 1:50.

10. *Edogaku jiten*, s.v. "Otokodate," p. 299.

11. Endo, *Kinsei seikatsu nenpyō*, p. 120.

12. Tamura, *Yakuza no seikatsu*, pp. 1–168; on Japanese construction workers and French *compagnonnages*, see Yoshida Nobuyuki, "Tobi," in Takahashi Yasuo and Yoshida, eds., *Nihon toshi-shi nyūmon*, vol. 3, *Hito* (Tokyo: Tōkyō Daigaku Shuppankai, 1990), p. 220, and Louis Chevalier, *Laboring Classes and Dangerous Classes in Paris during the First Half of the Nineteenth Century*, trans. Frank Jellinek (New York: Howard Fertig, 1973), esp. pp. 420–22; and for fire-

Just as the nature of crime changed in the Genroku period, so, too, did commoners become more involved in gang activity. United in their dissatisfaction with the surrounding world, yet fiercely loyal to one another, such gang members forged a unique subculture. Some spoke in harsh nasal voices, communicating with one another (like Elizabethan rogues) in a strange argot called *roppō kotoba*.[13] Like urban gang members in contemporary American cities, some expressed their spirit of rebellion by affecting unusual appearances—they dressed exotically, defied the convention of shaving the front part of the head upon attainment of adulthood, ignored the contemporary prejudice against facial hair, and flaunted oversized, fearsome-looking weapons. The *Owari-shi* (History of Owari), for instance, describes delinquents who "wear clothing with velvet collars, have long, flowing hair, do not shave their heads, have lots of facial hair, and wander about sporting great swords and daggers at their side."[14] That sort of unruly youth surely would have been disturbing in a society where clothing and hairstyles were minutely regulated by status regulations and sumptuary legislation. Equally unsettling would have been the sobriquets which the bullies often adopted: nicknames such as Arashi no Suke (Captain Tempest), Tōken Gonbei (Chinese Dog Gonbei), Meido Kohachi (Kohachi from Hell), and Jiman no Chōbei (Chōbei the Braggart) were prevalent among gang members.

Such colorful characters could not help but fascinate bourgeois society, and the image of gang members seems to have undergone a significant transformation at the end of the seventeenth century and beginning of the eighteenth. The rogues involved in gang activity increasingly were lionized in popular culture, converted from worthless hoodlums into romantic heroes. Even the tattoo, traditionally a badge of disgrace, became a mark of rebellion and, in some quarters, distinction. Originally applied by the authorities to apprehended criminals, tattoos became an elaborate art form worked upon the bodies of paying customers by highly skilled specialists.[15] In many ways, the new images emerged from depictions of urban outlaws in key genres of urban popular culture—most notably kabuki drama, which shared its very name with the *kabukimono* and found in their unconventional behavior an endless source

---

fighting squads inclined to violence, see William W. Kelly, "Incendiary Actions: Fires and Firefighting in the Shogun's Capital and the People's City," in McClain, Merriman, and Ugawa, *Edo and Paris*, pp. 310–31.

13. Takekoshi Yosaburō, *The Economic Aspects of the History of the Civilization of Japan*, vol. 2 (London: Allen & Unwin, 1930), p. 197; for examples, see Tamura, *Yakuza no seikatsu*, pp. 154–64.

14. Cited in Ikeda Akihiko, "Edo no hikeshi seido no seiritsu to tenkai," in Nishiyama Matsunosuke, ed., *Edo chōnin no kenkyū*, vol. 5 (Tokyo: Yoshikawa Kōbunkan, 1978), p. 91; the 1832 *Owari-shi* was based in part on *Owari fudoki*, commissioned by the daimyo Tokugawa Tsunanari and completed in 1698. Similarly, an entry in the earlier *Sunpu ki* (Sunpu Chronicle, 1612), cited in *Kogo jiten* (Tokyo: Iwanami Shoten, 1974), p. 321, explains that "These people, known to the world as *kabukimono*, have long sideburns, wildly colorful crests, wear great swords with long hilts, and have an unusual appearance." For additional examples see Charles J. Dunn, *Everyday Life in Traditional Japan* (Rutland, Vt.: Charles E. Tuttle, 1969), p. 178.

15. *Jidai fūzoku kōshō jiten* (Tokyo: Kawade Shobō, 1977), p. 421f.

of material. Wood-block prints dwelled incessantly on the best-known reprobates, while ballads and a vast picaresque literary tradition recalled their deeds. Even today, memorial tablets dedicated to famous gangsters still stand on the grounds of obscure temples, testifying to the respect they once commanded among some residents of Tokugawa cities.

Osakans probably were no less fascinated by gangster tales than the residents of other cities. But Osaka during the early Tokugawa period generally was spared the worst ravages of the urban gang violence described above. An occasional incident might excite that city of merchants and artisans—rivalries over the affections of kabuki performers led to violent disagreements, and a sword fight in a theater in 1652 prompted authorities to order those establishments closed for one year.[16] On a larger scale, eleven men and women were seriously injured one evening in 1693 in a spear-throwing brawl in the residential quarter of Andōji-chō.[17] But for the most part Osaka's streets were safe under the Tokugawa shogunate—at least after the siege of the castle in 1615-16. For one thing, as Wakita Osamu points out in Chapter 11 of this book, very few samurai resided in Osaka in comparison to Edo and the nation's other castle towns, and so there were bound to be fewer confrontations between *hatamoto yakko* and *machi yakko* than in the shogun's administrative capital, where such showdowns blossomed as one of "Edo's Flowers," a symbol of the rough-and-tumble spirit of that metropolis. Moreover, as one leading scholar has suggested, Osaka's malcontents were perhaps less prone to factionalism than Edo's young and restless;[18] thus, conflagrations in Osaka never became widely anticipated popular attractions as they did in Edo, where fires were celebrated as another of that city's "flowers," *events* capable of drawing enormous crowds that turned out to thrill at the sight of rival fire-fighting squads smashing buildings and skirmishing with each other. Whatever reason one might postulate, the term Pax Tokugawa described Osaka better than many towns in Japan during the Genroku period. Despite that more peaceful facade, however, the misdeeds and subsequent execution of the Five Men of Naniwa at the beginning of the eighteenth century would galvanize the attention of all Osakans and bring the cult of the outlaw to Japan's leading commercial center.

THE FIVE MEN OF NANIWA

The Five Men of Naniwa were members of Seven's Gang (*Shichigumi*), a ragtag collection of misfits headed by Karigane Bunshichi, who used the ideograph representing the numeral seven in the compound that made up his personal name. The most reliable source about Bunshichi and his flagitious colleagues is found in what appears to be a copy of the original police report regarding

---

16. Donald Shively, "Bakufu versus Kabuki," in John W. Hall and Marius B. Jansen, eds., *Studies in the Institutional History of Early Modern Japan* (Princeton: Princeton University Press, 1968), pp. 242-43.
17. Ōsaka-shi, ed., *Ōsaka shishi*, vol. 1 (reprint; Osaka: Seibundō Shuppan, 1965), p. 510.
18. Miyamoto Mataji, *Keihan to Edo* (Tokyo: Seiabō, 1978), p. 20.

their arrest, interrogation, and punishment.[19] The title "Genroku aburemono no ki" (Record of Some Outlaws of the Genroku Era) appears on its cover, but throughout the fifty-page report, the gangsters are referred to not as *aburemono* but as *abaremono*. Although both terms can be glossed as "outlaw" or "ruffian," *aburemono* was used to refer to bandits in the classic fourteenth-century war tale *Taiheiki* and may have carried more romantic overtones than the latter appellation, which connoted a vagrant or a scoundrel.[20] Quite possibly, then, the original report bore a different title, and this one, appended decades later, indicates how the story of the Five Men of Naniwa gradually had become romanticized.

Although the manuscript was written by several hands, the first page bears the names of two police officials, Hazu Motoemon and Sugiwara Yazaemon. The next three pages describe the circumstances leading to the roundup of the men associated with Seven's Gang. Thereupon follows verbatim testimony from victims of the hoodlum's nefarious deeds, statements by eyewitnesses, explanations about the role of the various parties involved, and the confessions of the wrongdoers. A final section outlines the conclusions that the Osaka city magistrates, Nakayama Tokiharu and Matsuno Sukeyoshi, reached about the activities of Seven's Gang and details the judgments delivered upon the accused. The text sheds some light on police procedure in early modern Osaka, but even more vividly it illuminates the hardships, frustrations, and motives that led young men from the ranks of the urban poor to a life of crime.

According to the "Record of Some Outlaws of the Genroku Era," Karigane Bunshichi himself was the son of a merchant, Kariganeya Shichibei, and first earned a reputation as a troublemaker in 1696 when, at age twenty-two, he struck the night watchman at a guardhouse in the residential quarter of Naraya. Two years later, Bunshichi roughed up a certain Kiyobei in the Tateuri Horihama section of Osaka. At a loss about how to deal with their wayward son, Bunshichi's parents in the Fourth Month of 1699 asked the authorities to incarcerate him, and following an investigation, officials tossed the young man into jail. Within a month of his imprisonment, however, Bunshichi's father died of illness, and his mother, who in fact might never have favored her son's confinement, submitted an appeal for his release. Authorities pardoned Bunshichi and discharged him from jail on the twenty-seventh day of the Sixth Month, warning him that further violent acts would result in severe punishment.

Despite that admonition, however, it did not take Bunshichi long to return to his old habits, pairing up with his friend Gokuin no Sen'emon. In 1697, two years before Bunshichi was locked up temporarily, Sen'emon (then eighteen years old) provoked a series of melees in the pleasure quarter, and during the next five years, he would inflict injuries upon many persons there, as well as in the Nagahori, Obama, and Gokō-machi quarters and at the amusement

---

19. The manuscript is located at the Osaka Prefectural Central Library and is catalogued in *Ōsaka Furitsu Chūō Toshokan zōsho mokuroku, Wakan sho*, vol. 6 (Osaka: Ōsaka Furitsu Chūō Toshokan, 1971), p. 306.

20. *Daijirin* (Tokyo: Sanseidō, 1989), p. 62; *Edogo no jiten* (Tokyo: Kōdansha, 1979), p. 42.

centers that lined the approaches to the Nagahori Yotsu and Horie Sumiyoshi bridges. In the Tenth Month of 1699, just out of prison, Bunshichi teamed up with Sen'emon during an affray in the pleasure quarter, and one of them dealt a fatal blow to a Shika no Chōbei, who died after lingering in pain for several months.

Meanwhile, other young men who later joined up with Bunshichi were also beginning their criminal careers. As early as 1692, two friends and budding troublemakers—twenty-year-old An no Heibei and nineteen-year-old Hote no Ichiemon—joined a gang that included Kaitate no Kichiemon (age sixteen) and Kōshin no Kanbei (age eleven!). The names were colorful aliases: "Hermitage" Heibei, "God of Wealth" Ichiemon, "Brand-New" Kichiemon, and, loosely rendered, "Three Worms" Kanbei, the "Kōshin" in his name referring to the folk custom of staying awake throughout a particular night in the zodiacal cycle when people feared that the "three worms" said to dwell within the human body might attempt to escape and report one's transgressions to the gods.[21] Given his age, Heibei may well have been the leader of this group.

Two years after he joined that gang, Hote no Ichiemon became homeless, expelled from his father's house because of his unrepentant violent conduct. In 1697 God of Wealth landed in prison after seriously injuring a man in a brawl—having lost his sword in the scuffle, Ichiemon used a firewood log to cripple his opponent. In the First Month of the following year, Ichiemon received clemency and was released from prison, but he and his pals continued their pattern of incorrigible behavior. In the Fifth Month of 1699, Brand-New Kichiemon injured one Kasaya Gohei in the residential quarter of Gokō-machi, quickly hiding the sword he had used with Shichibei, a tobacconist-friend living in Kami Naniwa. A month later, brandishing a borrowed sword, Brand-New also cut up some people in the licensed prostitution quarter. In the Seventh Month of that same summer Hermitage Heibei, who often shared swords with Kichiemon, attacked a number of innocent people living in various neighborhoods in Osaka.

Somewhat before 1700, perhaps around the time that Bunshichi murdered the unfortunate Shika no Chōbei, Seven's Gang was born when An no Heibei, Hote no Ichiemon, Kaitate no Kichiemon, Kōshin no Kanbei, and other members of that group threw in with Bunshichi. Kaminari (Thunder) Shōkurō also began to consort with Bunshichi's gang about that time. Homeless since 1694, when he turned twenty-one years old, Thunder had injured a resident of Minami Horie in 1698 and had taken part in a chain of other violent crimes. Other enlistees in Seven's Gang as mentioned in the police report included Tonbi Kan'emon, Dōguya Yohei, Karakuri Rokubei, and Mippiki Jihei. The names of Kan'emon and Yohei apparently referred to their professions: "Construction Worker" and "Tool-Shop" respectively. Karakuri, however, was an alias meaning "Trickster." Yohei also had a nickname, Oyaji no Saburō, or "Old Man

---

21. Ichiemon's name appears in phonetic characters as "Hote," apparently a corruption of the standard "Hotei"; in later fictional treatments, he almost always is referred to as "Hotei no Ichiemon."

Saburō"; although the appellation hardly seems appropriate since he was born around 1674. The report also mentioned some past associations between members of Seven's Gang and other ruffians well known to the Osaka police—including Kenkaya Gorōemon (Goroemon the Brawler), Ueno Ibei, Mino Jinbei, Inga no Heibei (Heibei the Fated), and Jippu (True Father) no Heibei—all of whom were arrested during the investigation of Seven's Gang even though they had not actually joined Bunshichi's crew.

The following biographical information about Seven's Gang can be found in the "Record of Some Outlaws of the Genroku Era," which includes Bunshichi's confession, translated as an appendix to this chapter.

The Five Men of Naniwa

An no Heibei (ca. 1672–1702)

In a gang with Kaitate no Kichiemon, Hote no Ichiemon, Mippiki Jihei and others as of the Seventh Month of 1697. Attacked people with a sword on the sixth day, Seventh Month, 1699, which he then secreted with Kichiemon. On the evening of the sixth day, Sixth Month, 1701, stabbed Kibei, employee of Kawachiya Gohei of the residential quarter Kyūhōji, in the side with a dagger. Subsequent police investigation resulted in Heibei's arrest the following day. Beheaded at the execution grounds located at Sennichi Mae on the twenty-sixth day of the Eighth Month, 1702.

Gokuin no Sen'emon (ca. 1679–1702)

Began career of violent crime in 1697; wounded about ten people over the next five years in Gokō-machi and Obama residential quarters, inside the licensed prostitute quarter, at the approaches to Nagahori Yotsu and Horie Sumiyoshi bridges, etc. Associated with Karigane Bunshichi from at least the Tenth Month of 1699. Arrested on the twenty-second day, Sixth Month, 1701, in connection with the investigation of Seven's Gang. Beheaded on the twenty-sixth day of the Eighth Month, 1702.

Hote no Ichiemon (1673–1702)

Expelled from father's home and became homeless in 1694. Involved in violent crimes from at least 1697, when he enlisted as a member of a gang that included An no Heibei and Kaitate no Kichiemon. Imprisoned in mid-1697, he received clemency on the twenty-fourth day, First Month, 1698, but thereafter joined Seven's Gang. Imprisoned on the twenty-second day, Eleventh Month, 1701, and beheaded on the twenty-sixth day of the Eighth Month, 1702.

Kaminari Shōkurō (ca. 1671–1702)

Became homeless in 1692. Injured someone in Minami Horie in 1698; linked up with a gang led by Kenkaya Goroemon; associated with Seven's Gang from at least the Tenth Month of 1699. Formally joined the latter gang in late 1700, cutting ties with Gorōemon in the Second Month of 1701. Arrested on the tenth day, Sixth Month, 1701, in connection with the investigation of Seven's Gang. Beheaded on the twenty-sixth day of the Eighth Month, 1702.

Karigane Bunshichi (ca. 1674–1702)

Beat a night watchman in 1696, two years later injured people in the Minami Horie and Tateuri Horihama residential quarters. On the twenty-second day, Fourth Month, 1699, his own parents asked the authorities to jail him; police officials complied. Two months later, following his father's death from illness, Bunshichi was pardoned and released at the request of his mother. From the Tenth Month of 1699 he continued to commit violent crimes, in company with Gokuin no Sen'emon and Kaminari Shōkurō. In 1699 they wounded about ten people, one fatally, and started to call themselves Seven's Gang, since Bunshichi was the leader. On the nineteenth day, Sixth Month, 1701, Bunshichi was arrested in connection with the investigation of the gang. He accepted responsibility for all of the group's crimes. Beheaded on the twenty-sixth day of the Eighth Month, 1702.

Other Members of Seven's Gang

Dōguya Yohei (alias Oyaji no Saburō) (ca. 1674–?)

Adopted by one Rokubei at age five. Became involved with Seven's Gang by late 1699. Committed mayhem with Tonbi Kan'emon in the Ninth Month of 1700. Arrested on the eighteenth day, Sixth Month, 1701, in connection with the roundup of Seven's Gang. Released from prison and banished from Settsu and Kawachi Provinces on the seventh day, Eighth Month, 1703.

Kaitate no Kichiemon (ca. 1676–1701)

Began associating with An no Heibei, Hote no Ichiemon, and Kōshin no Kanbei in 1692. Injured Kasaya Gohei in Gokō-machi and committed other acts of violence in 1699. Shared swords with An no Heibei, hiding them with Tabakoya Shichibei. Arrested in the Sixth Month of 1701, in connection with the investigation of Seven's Gang. Died in prison on the twenty-second day, Eleventh Month, 1701.

Karakuri Rokubei (ca. 1671–1702)

Abandoned by his parents at age eight. Once hijacked a riverboat, together with Kenkaya Gorōemon, and stabbed someone in Gokō-machi. Arrested on the sixth day, Tenth Month, 1701, in connection with the roundup of Seven's Gang. Sentenced to a lengthy jail term, but died in prison on the twenty-ninth day, Fourth Month, 1702.

Kōshin no Kanbei (ca. 1680–?)

Began association with An no Heibei and Hote no Ichiemon at a very young age, in 1692. On the evening of the sixth day, Sixth Month, 1701, quarreled with a party of friends including Kibei, employee of Kawachiya Gohei of the residential quarter of Kyūhōji, and provoked an attack by Ichibei, servant of Itaya San'emon. Later in the evening, Kanbei encountered the party again and fought with Ichibei. At that point An no Heibei appeared and stabbed Kibei, leading to the investigation that implicated Seven's Gang. [The police report does not indicate Kanbei's fate.]

Mippiki Jihei (dates unknown)

Involved with An no Heibei and Kaitate no Kichiemon from at least 1697, and with Kaminari Shōkurō and Kenkaya Goroemon from 1700. In his confession, Bunshichi referred to Jihei as a member of his gang; he probably joined in early 1701. At the time he was homeless. [Fate unclear.]

Tonbi Kan'emon (ca. 1678–1702)

An accomplice of Dōguya Yohei from the Ninth Month of 1700. Early in 1701, following the death of his father, Tonbi joined Seven's Gang, with whom he already had links. Arrested in the Sixth Month of 1702, died in prison a month later.

The Six-Six Incident

As the "Record of Some Outlaws of the Genroku Era" indicates, the demise of Seven's Gang came when the police launched an especially efficient investigation of a relatively minor episode that erupted on the sixth day of the Sixth Month, 1701. On that evening, Three Worms (Kōshin no) Kanbei affronted several men as they strolled along Nishi Yoko Canal in the neighborhood of Hinaya-machi, enjoying the evening cool. The party included a certain Mikiya Kanbei; his servant Gorō; Kibei, the employee of a Kawachiya Gohei and friend of Gorō; and one Ichibei, the servant of another shop owner. Ichibei answered Kanbei's provocation by attacking him, and apparently got the better of the troublemaker. Later the same evening, however, Three Worms ran across the four men again, at the Hinaya Crossroads, and assaulted Ichibei. As the two tussled, and the others looked on or tried in vain to intervene, Kanbei's friend, An no Heibei, happened by and jumped into the fray. In the ensuing free-for-all, Heibei stabbed the shop hand Kibei in the stomach with a dagger, whereupon the two miscreants fled the scene. The wound, examined the next day, measured about five inches deep and two and one-half inches across, but it seems that Kibei eventually recovered from it.

Someone at the scene of the crime recognized Kōshin no Kanbei and was able to provide his address. That information was passed to the neighborhood elder (*machidoshiyori*) of the Kyūhōji quarter where the injured Kibei resided, and the following morning the elder appeared before a city magistrate to report the crime. Immediately the two police officers, Hazu Motoemon and Sugiwara Yazaemon, were dispatched to investigate. They visited Kibei, apparently at his home where he had been carried following the altercation with Kanbei and Heibei. Another official examined his injury and filed a report. Kibei had recovered enough to recount the events of the previous night to Hazu and Sugiwara, who also interviewed Mikiya Kanbei and Gorō. They completely corroborated Kibei's account.

Within two days police had tracked down, arrested, and imprisoned Kōshin no Kanbei and An no Heibei. Questioning began immediately, and no doubt the interrogators drew on their favorite tortures. With little delay the police next pulled in the ruffian Kaitate no Kichiemon. They also brought in Ichibei, questioning him closely about how the incident started, and they placed Mikiya Kanbei's servant Gorō in the custody of a trusted townsman, although he was released soon after giving his testimony. Police arrested Kaminari Shōkurō and Karakuri Rokubei, leading members of Seven's Gang, on the tenth day of the Sixth Month, and caught up with Dōguya Yohei eight days later. On the nineteenth authorities arrested Karigane Bunshichi, and Gokuin no Sen'emon joined him in prison three days after that. Hote no Ichiemon remained on the lam until the twenty-second day of the Eleventh Month, 1701, and Tonbi Kan'emon was able to avoid arrest until the Sixth Month of the following year.

After completing their investigation, city officials handed down their verdicts in the Second Month of 1702. They prescribed the death penalty for Bunshichi and four of his henchmen, and the ritual of beheading took place on the twenty-sixth day of the Eighth Month.[22] The "Record of Some Outlaws of the Genroku Era" does not describe the process, but the five condemned men probably were placed on horseback and paraded about the city.[23] Then, after crossing the Nippon Bridge over Dōton Canal, they would have been pulled down from their mounts at Sennichi Mae and led to a guardhouse. Thereupon guards would have forced the five men to cover their faces with paper, indicating the shame they were expected to feel, and then escorted the condemned men to the execution ground. There, forced to kneel before their executioner, an outcast from the nearby settlement, one by one Bunshichi, Heibei, Sen'emon, Shōkurō, and Ichiemon would have intoned the traditional request *Saa, otanomi mōshimasu*, "Well, if you please." That said, the outcast executioner would deliver a swift blow of his sword to the back of each neck. His assistants

---

22. Miyoshi Teiji, editor of *Ōsaka shiseki jiten* (Osaka: Seibundō Shuppan, 1985), indicates on p. 289 of that compilation that Gokuin no Sen'emon was executed on the seventh day of the Sixth Month, 1701, but that must be an error.

23. This reconstruction of a public execution in Osaka is based on the description in *Jidai fūzoku kōshō jiten*, pp. 569–70. Carl Streenstrup asserts, however, that in the case of murderers and robbers, "beheading took place within the prison." See his *A History of Law in Japan until 1868* (Leiden: E. J. Brill, 1991), p. 152. On the punishment of *gokumon* (decapitation followed by the public display of the head), see also Dani V. Botsman, "Punishment and Power in the Tokugawa Period," *East Asian History* 3 (June 1992), pp. 3–4.

then would line up the severed heads on a wooden platform located just outside the walls of the nearby temple Hōzenji (popularly known as Sennichi temple). A poster on an adjacent notice board explained their crimes. No doubt thousands of townspeople, out to enjoy an afternoon of theater at Dōtonbori or hoping to dally with an actor-prostitute in one of the district's teahouses, made a slight detour to pass the execution ground. They would be drawn by what Foucault called "the fascination of the abomination," and presumably they stood with gazes riveted upon the severed heads, "fearsome as tigers and wolves" in the phrasing of one commentator.[24]

Of the dozen or so gangsters apprehended in the Six-Six Incident, the authorities publicly executed only the five men put to the sword on the twenty-sixth day of the Eighth Month, 1702, and the people of Osaka very soon began to remember them as the Five Men of Naniwa. With one exception, however, all the other men rounded up in the wake of the Six-Six Incident apparently died in prison, probably as a consequence of tortures and maltreatment whose cruelty and pain surely exceeded the punishment of beheading. As far as can be determined for certain from the written record, only Oyaji no Saburō (Dōguya Yohei) escaped with his life. After indicating his earnest repentance, Old Man was exiled from Osaka and its immediate hinterland, never to be heard of again.

Seven's Gang and Lower-Class Crime in Osaka

The "Record of Some Outlaws of the Genroku Era" reveals a number of interesting details about the nature of violent crime in early modern Osaka. The typical member of Seven's Gang was young, but well past adolescence; the five men who were executed averaged twenty-eight years of age, and most had led a life of petty crime for a decade or longer. Not surprisingly, most heralded from the poorer strata of Osaka society; among Seven's Gang only Karigane Bunshichi is not identified in the police report as being a renter or homeless person. Karakuri Rokubei had been without fixed abode for fourteen years. Kaminari Shōkurō had been homeless nearly ten years at the time of his arrest; Hote no Ichiemon for eight years. Similarly, Mippiki Jihei and Kenkaya Goroemon could provide the police with no permanent address.

A number of the lawbreakers either had been abandoned by their parents or expelled from their natal homes and disinherited. The phenomenon of child abandonment indicates poverty; expulsion, more likely, reflects the fear that a son's actions might bring disaster upon the whole household, or that the son might inflict violence on his parents. Of the dozen and more members

---

24. On the reaction of French townspeople to public executions in the eighteenth century, see Michel Foucault, *Discipline and Punishment: The Birth of the Prison* (London: Peregrine Books, 1977), pp. 57–69; the tigers and wolves phrase is from Takizawa Bakin's *Chosakudō isseki-banashi* (1803), reprinted in Kishigami Shikken et al., eds., *Onchi sōsho*, vol. 9 (Tokyo: Tōkyō Hakubutsukan, 1910), p. 93.

of Seven's Gang, only Tonbi Kan'emon, who waited until his father had died before joining up with Bunshichi, seems to have been moved by the dictates of filial piety. The backgrounds of Bunshichi and Hote no Ichiemon, in contrast, suggest generational conflict, and one wonders if some of the aliases chosen by the young gangsters, such as Oyaji no Saburō (Old Man Saburō) and Jippu no Heibei (True Father Heibei), might not express mockery of the older generation.

Some members of Seven's Gang spoke bitterly about their poverty as they underwent interrogation by officials. Karakuri Rokubei, for example, began his confession, "When I was eight years old, I was abandoned by my parents, and since then I have been working on boats. I have led such a homeless, hungry life that I've never stopped behaving violently toward people all over town." As alienated young men with large chips on their shoulders, the outlaws may have taken their cue from the behavior of the samurai *yakko* whose provocative behavior has been described above. Although there were relatively few warriors in Osaka, they sometimes could claim to act with near impunity against commoners. The concept of *kirisute gomen* implied the prerogative of a samurai to cut down a commoner for a serious offense or insolence that infringed upon a samurai's honor, to then discard the body, and receive a pardon. To be certain, the authorities did not countenance many acts of *kirisute gomen*, and they frequently punished samurai who, after the fact, were judged to have drawn their swords without sufficient reason, but the mere existence of a privileged, armed estate who might abuse commoners and deal with the consequences later may well have encouraged angry young commoners to lash out at others in a similar fashion.

The "Record of Some Outlaws of the Genroku Era" also exposes some of the important divisions that existed within commoner society itself. Perhaps 15 percent of the nonsamurai population in Osaka consisted of house owners (*iemochi*) or their agents (*yamori*).[25] Those two categories of urban dwellers, and their families, constituted the true bourgeoisie, the *chōnin*. The term *chōnin* was not typically applied to the *tanagarinin*, persons who leased shops and lodgings, or to the *shakuyanin*, those who lived in rented dwellings. There was a wide status gap between the *chōnin* and the renters. The home owners paid taxes, and they (and their agents) were eligible to serve as neighborhood elders. House owners were usually well-to-do merchants and artisans, whereas tenants tended to be small-scale shopkeepers, peddlers, or wageworkers— persons who were more than likely to experience hardship and hunger, and even to suffer eviction. In this context, it is important to note that Seven's Gang often preyed upon persons specifically described as being *chōnin* or *yadomochi* ("owner of a lodging"). The confessions of Goroemon the Brawler, Thunder Shōkurō, and God of Wealth Ichiemon all indicate that they deliberately targeted such well-to-do merchants, often picking trouble with them in the prostitution quarter of Shinmachi where merchant dandies, as the novels of Ihara Saikaku attest, were particularly apt to flaunt their wealth in conspicuous fash-

25. Miyamoto Mataji, *Osaka* (Osaka: Seibundō Shuppan, 1962), p. 180.

ion. An no Heibei, Kaitate no Kichiemon, and others also frequently set upon pleasure boats in which parties of wealthy commoners were making merry with women hired for the evening. It is thus likely that the crimes of Seven's Gang reflected the antagonism that many in the urban underclass harbored for the affluent commoner elite.

One must pause and recall, however, that Karigane Bunshichi himself was a man of property. Probably the only person of such status among the gangsters under discussion, Bunshichi had inherited the shop-residence of his father, Kariganeya Shichibei, in 1699. Shichibei was doubtless a merchant, but it is not known what goods he sold in his establishment. It is possible that he dealt in a type of middle-grade green tea commonly known as *karigane*. Or he may have woven, dyed, or sold textiles, since a major textile firm in Kyoto also went by the name Kariganeya. Moreover, the ballad *Karigane Bunshichi Sennichi gonin otoko*, composed soon after Bunshichi's execution, refers to Bunshichi as "a skillful master of silk dyeing,"[26] and some later kabuki plays (e.g., *Koi goromo Bunshichi zome*, 1777) as well as comic fiction (the novel *Somenuki itsu tokoro mon*, 1790) associate him with this profession. Normally gang hierarchies reflected age differences; the boss (*oyakata* or "parent") led his followers (*kokata* or "children"). Since Bunshichi was not the eldest in his group (at least four members were older), it is possible that his standing as a property owner might have elevated him in the eyes of his collaborators—despite (or perhaps because of) his personal rejection of the social perquisites that accompanied *chōnin* status.

The members of Seven's Gang seem to have taken particular delight in provoking visitors to crowded places, such as the pleasure quarter at Shinmachi or the approaches to Horie Sumiyoshi Bridge. One imagines them loitering, mocking and ridiculing passersby, reserving the sharpest barbs for those who appeared to be wealthy but physically weak. Thus would the young delinquents express their frustration at their own social deprivation. If their rude taunts led to some pushing and shoving or even a bit of a scuffle, so much the better perhaps, for those sorts of minor incidents carried little risk of official punishment; the shogunate regarded such quarrels among commoners as private matters too tiresome to adjudicate.[27] On several occasions, however, Bunshichi and his comrades snatched coin purses, tote bags, and even items of apparel from innocent bystanders. Such pilfering constituted a more serious level of crime than did quarrels, but Osaka's police probably were not inclined to spend much time or energy on such petty thievery. Still, the gangsters stole swords and daggers, too, from at least 1699, so it is curious that they remained at large as late as 1701.

Aside from those crimes, the "Record of Some Outlaws of the Genroku Era" states that some members of Seven's Gang committed acts of piracy, hijacking

---

26. Takano Tatsuyuki, ed., *Nihon kayō shūsei*, vol. 8 (Tokyo: Shunjūsha, 1928), p. 62.

27. Takeuchi Makoto, "Festivals and Fights: The Law and the People of Edo," in McClain, Merriman, and Ugawa, *Edo and Paris*, pp. 385–86.

the riverboats which facilitated travel, commerce, and recreation within Osaka. As James L. McClain shows in Chapter 3, Osaka grew up at the juncture of the Yodo, Kizu, and several other rivers and was crisscrossed by canals, thus providing Bunshichi and his followers with ample opportunities to commandeer both cargo and pleasure craft. The issue of weapons concealment also comes up frequently in the official police report. Stolen weapons, especially those used in assaults, were handed over quickly by their users to other gang members, or to individuals not involved in the group's violence but willing to harbor the blades; Tabakoya Shichibei of the Kami Naniwa residential quarter often provided that service for Seven's Gang. This suggests a fear of police searches, but also indicates the difficulty that homeless people, or those residing in cramped lodgings, might have in concealing their weapons or stolen goods.

Folklore extends the list of crimes committed by Seven's Gang. The *Ōsaka shiseki jiten* (Dictionary of Osaka Historical Sites), for example, tells us that a certain Harimaya Genzō, the owner of a prosperous tobacco-pipe shop in the vicinity of Yotsuyabashi, had been the victim of a shakedown orchestrated by Karigane Bunshichi.[28] Such stories suggest that the importance of Seven's Gang derived as much from the popular mythologizing of the Five Men of Naniwa that took place after their executions as it did from the rather ignoble details concerning the real lives of the young thugs who perpetrated the Six-Six Incident.

The Evolution of a Myth

With the image of the five severed heads sitting next to the gate of the temple Hōzenji burned into their memories, Osaka's citizens began to forge a myth, reworking the five troublemakers into chivalrous heroes who valiantly defended the humble townsfolk against powerful and arrogant enemies. The legend of the Five Men of Naniwa, like many other storied tales, began with songs. Tokugawa cities supported countless itinerant entertainers who performed *utazaimon*, ballads that typically drew inspiration from recent tragic events and voiced the popular conception of those incidents, even while treating the actual facts in a rather free and casual manner. *Utazaimon*, for instance, constitute the oldest surviving accounts of the execution of the famous adulterers Osan and Mohei (crucified in Kyoto ca. 1683), the sad suicide of Osen the Cooper's Wife (in Osaka ca. 1685), and the death of the star-crossed shop clerk Seijūrō (decapitated in Himeji ca. 1690).[29] So it is not surprising that within a month of the beheadings of Bunshichi and his followers, the "Ballad of Kari-

---

28. *Ōsaka shiseki jiten*, p. 621.
29. Richard Lane, "Saikaku's 'Five Women'," in Ihara Saikaku, *Five Women Who Loved Love*, ed. and trans. William Theodore de Bary (Rutland, Vt.: Charles E. Tuttle, 1956), pp. 236, 245, 251.

gane Bunshichi" (*Karigane Bunshichi utazaimon*) became popular in Osaka. The song is divided into two parts. The first depicts the strenuous efforts undertaken by Bunshichi's mother to free him from prison following his first arrest, and the second deals with an issue not found in the police report: Bunshichi's relationship with a Shinmachi prostitute, Kogiku. According to the lyrics, she had struggled in vain to reform her lover and persuade him to forsake his violent ways.[30]

Soon after this, other balladeers further elaborated the heroics of the Osakan outlaws. The lyrics of *Karigane Bunshichi Sennichi gonin otoko* and its longer, revised version, *Kaeri Bunshichi utazaimon* have survived.[31] Those songs also emphasized the supposed involvement of Bunshichi with a golden-hearted courtesan, identified in the former as Kiyokawa and in the latter as Kiyotake. Bunshichi is dubbed "the root of all quarrels" and the "Commander of Quarrelers." There is mention of an uncle, whom Bunshichi treats kindly. The two ballads place special weight on Bunshichi's relationship with his mother, imagining Bunshichi as unfailingly filial and "bravely righteous." As an innocent victim of an unkind fate and bad friends, the songsters conclude, Bunshichi's was a story bathed in true pathos.

Playwrights for Osaka's puppet theaters did not tarry in adapting material about Seven's Gang for their stage productions. Just as the first kabuki treatment of the Forty-Seven Righteous Warriors of Akō apparently delighted kabuki-goers in Edo a mere ten days after the retainers committed suicide in 1703, in Osaka the curtain went up on the first puppet play depicting Bunshichi's crew of ne'er-do-wells within days of their executions. On the ninth day of the Ninth Month, 1702, the Okamoto Theater featured *Karigane Bunshichi aki no shimo* (Karigane Bunshichi: Dew of Autumn). That was, additionally, one of the first important *sewamono* (domestic plays) ever to be staged in Osaka, preceding by a year *Sonezaki shinjū* (The Love Suicides at Sonezaki), the play by Chikamatsu Monzaemon that popularized the genre. On the thirteenth day of the Ninth Month, 1702, just four days after "Dew of Autumn" debuted, *Karigane gonin otoko* appeared on the playbill at the theater founded by Uji Kaga no Jō, whose notions about what constituted good drama are detailed in C. Andrew Gerstle's chapter. At least one other such puppet play was staged before year's end, and in 1703 audiences flocked to see *Karigane Bunshichi no isshūnenki* (Commemorating the First Anniversary of Karigane Bunshichi's Death). Two years later, a similar work performed at the Masamoto Theater honored the third anniversary of the executions.[32]

The plot of the first play, "Karigane Bunshichi: Dew of Autumn," is important because it articulates several themes that would become central components in the mythologizing of the Five Men of Naniwa. "Dew of Autumn"

30. *Nihon bungaku daijiten*, vol. 2 (Tokyo: Shinchōsha, 1940), p. 81.
31. Tatsuyuki, *Nihon kayō shūsei*, 8:62–65.
32. Okamoto Ryōichi and Watanabe Takeru, *Ōsaka no sesō*, Mainichi Hōsō bunka sōsho 7 (Osaka: Mainichi Hōsō, 1973), p. 52; Iizuka Tomoichirō, *Kabuki kyōgen saiken* (Tokyo: Dai Ichi Shobō, 1932), p. 694.

opens on a hot day in the Sixth Month as Bunshichi and four of his followers, including Thunder Shōkurō, are engaged in an epic drinking bout in the home Bunshichi inherited from his father. Toward evening, the disreputable entourage, dressed informally in lightweight summer robes (*yukata*), heads off to the licensed quarter of Shinmachi. There Bunshichi harasses wealthy passersby until Kiyotaki (another variant of the prostitute's name) appears and admonishes Bunshichi, with whom she has been intimate, about his unbridled lust for fighting and his shameful lack of filial concern for his elderly mother. Bunshichi repents and agrees to mend his ways. The couple parts, promising to meet the following day.

On his way home, however, Bunshichi happens upon his comrades once more, who persuade him to join them and return to the prostitution district. Inside the gates to the quarter, they again quarrel with free-spending and arrogant "magnates" (*daijin*), killing and injuring several people in the process. Finally the police apprehend the retinue and toss the five men into prison. In the *michiyuki*, the poignant poetic-journey scene that typically draws a puppet drama toward its conclusion, Kiyotaki leaves the licensed district and makes her way to the execution grounds at Sennichi Mae. Under cover of night, she recovers Bunshichi's head from the stand near the gate to Hōzenji temple and takes it to a priest who performs a service for the soul of the deceased. The play ends with Kiyotaki becoming famous, and as a consequence, prosperous.[33]

Karigane Bunshichi aki no shimo helped to further establish the personalities of the two women who were introduced in the ballads: the pure-of-heart prostitute and the long-suffering mother (although the mother does not appear onstage in "Dew of Autumn"). The play contributes a new element to the evolving story by situating most of the action within the licensed quarter. By 1702 that had become somewhat of a convention as many puppet plays and kabuki dramas took advantage of the romanticism and eroticism of that same setting, but in this case the venue seems natural given the historical activities of Bunshichi and his fellow rogues. Perhaps even more significantly, "Dew of Autumn" suggests a motivation for Bunshichi's actions: he hates the rich, and he is loyal to his friends. In addition, Thunder Shōkurō receives a certain distinction in this account, which endows him with a reputation in his own right. Finally, although Kiyotaki's retrieval of Bunshichi's head seems implausible, it is not impossible that the climactic scene represents a real-life action undertaken by some unknown prostitute who was fond of Bunshichi. It is even less farfetched to imagine that some such woman might have arranged for the respectful disposal of Bunshichi's body, or at least hired a priest to offer a blessing upon his soul.

The plot of "Commemorating the First Anniversary of Karigane Bunshichi's Death" is similar.[34] It begins with the drinking party, whereupon the ill-

33. *Nihon bungaku daijiten*, 2:81.
34. Facsimile printing in Nakamura Yukihiko and Hino Tatsuo, eds., *Kisho fukuseikai sōsho*, vol. 16 (reprint; Tokyo: Rinsen Shoten, 1990), pp. 95–113.

fated young men set off for a night of adventure at the Shinmachi pleasure quarter. But since they "despise wealthy merchants," they provoke some of the teahouse customers visiting the district, until the sincere prostitute, identified as Kiyokawa in this play, comes out to admonish Bunshichi. She reminds him of his sad, lonely, waiting mother. Bunshichi signs a pledge to live serenely with his mother, but after leaving Kiyokawa he happens to encounter Sen'emon and the other three as they are exchanging insults and blows with a group of rich merchants. Loyalty to friends compels Bunshichi to join the melee, which results in his arrest. In this play, too, there is a concluding *michiyuki* in which Kiyokawa retrieves the head and has it blessed by a priest.

Like "Dew of Autumn," *Karigane Bunshichi no isshūnen-ki* is built around the Shinmachi connection, Bunshichi's hatred of the rich, the lonely mother, the spiritually righteous prostitute, Bunshichi's desire to reform, and the gang leader's loyalty to his friends. Sen'emon receives his moment in the spotlight in this play, largely at the expense of Kaminari Shōkurō—an appropriate plot modification, since Bunshichi had begun to associate with Gokuin no Sen'emon before Shōkurō came into his orbit. Moreover, "Commemorating the First Anniversary of Karigane Bunshichi's Death" builds on the earlier "Dew of Autumn" by further tempering and prettifying Bunshichi's character: here the hero does not go to Shinmachi with his friends and become involved in a quarrel alongside them; rather Bunshichi encounters his colleagues during a fight-in-progress and feels obligated to come to their rescue.

Plays staged in subsequent decades added new embellishments to the legend of the Five Men of Naniwa. One subset of puppet plays tended to dissolve into farce. Perhaps that strain of dramatic self-indulgence began with *Kinpira Kaminari Shōkurō* (The Swashbuckling Kaminari Shōkurō), first performed in Osaka's theaters in 1718.[35] As the title suggests, Shōkurō is highlighted in this work, which otherwise has little to do with the actual Six-Six Incident. Indeed, the action takes place in the remote past and moves from Kyoto to Kamakura and (implausibly) to the Yoshiwara prostitution district in Edo. Improbably, the plot revolves around a clash between the righteous lord Yoriyoshi and the rebellious retainer Hironaga. A member of the imperial family, a long-nosed goblin, and a ghost all make appearances. The Five Men of Naniwa enter the story when Hironaga visits Yoshiwara in an effort to wrest away from Yoriyoshi a beautiful courtesan named Takao.[36] Karigane Bunshichi and his four partners chance to be in the pleasure quarter at the same time, and Hironaga offends Bunshichi by pouring water on his hair ribbon. Enraged, the five men fall upon Hironaga and his retainers, driving them off, saving Takao, and winning praise from Yoriyoshi.[37] Similarly absurd plays, exploiting the Five Men

---

35. An alternative title is *Kinpira gonin otoko*; Wakatsuki Yasuji, ed., *Ko jōruri no kenkyū, Enpō Kyōhō hen* (Tokyo: Shingetsusha, 1939), p. 1414.

36. Takao was name taken by a long succession of Yoshiwara courtesans, of whom the second was involved with Date Tsunamune, daimyo of Sendai domain, before her death in 1659; for details on the Takao legend, see Cecilia Segawa Siegle, *Yoshiwara: The Glittering World of the Japanese Courtesan* (Honolulu: University of Hawaii Press, 1993), pp. 59–61.

37. Wakatsuki, *Ko jōruri no kenkyū*, pp. 1415–17.

of Naniwa myth but set in the Kamakura period, remained popular throughout the early modern era.

In other more serious puppet plays, written later, the Five Men of Naniwa are seen as confronting not only rich merchants but members of the samurai estate as well. In 1742, for instance, Takeda Izumo II, dramatist and manager of the Takemoto Theater located at Dōtonbori, wrote the puppet play *Otokodate itsutsu no Karigane* (Karigane's Five Gallant Stalwarts)—six years before he coauthored *Kanadehon Chūshingura* (The Treasury of Loyal Retainers), which became perhaps the most famous of all dramatic renditions of the story of the Forty-Seven Righteous Warriors of Akō after it was pirated as a kabuki play and performed in Edo.[38] *Otokodate itsutsu no Karigane* debuted at the Takemoto Theater in the Ninth Month of 1742 and delighted the audience with a scene in which Bunshichi and his followers quarrel with, and kill, a samurai named Noda Kakuzaemon.

Playwrights for the kabuki stage also contributed to the ongoing reinvention of the story of the Five Men of Naniwa. It appears that the first kabuki drama based on the Bunshichi tale was staged in the Dōtonbori theater district of Osaka in 1702. It was said to be a success, although there is disagreement about its title; some say it is unknown, others that it was called *Gonin otoko*.[39] By the 1730s kabuki versions of the Five Men of Naniwa were being performed regularly in Edo. The first such production, staged at the incomparable Nakamura Theater in 1730, was so popular it ran for more than sixty days, and it injected a note of levity into the evolving Karigane legend by including comical versions of the soliloquies performed by each of the five in earlier kabuki dramas. *Mon tsukushi gonin otoko* (1825), by the renowned Tsuruya Nanboku, and Kawatake Mokuami's *Koi goromo Karigane zome* (1852), which duplicated the title of an earlier play, added captivating new twists to the way events unfolded. Both dramas featured the warrior Noda Kakuzaemon, but audiences gasped as the Five Men of Naniwa were executed as punishment for killing the samurai. In those plays, Noda is depicted as evil and fully deserving of his fate; the punishment of the Five for his death, thus, is taken to underscore the injustice of the authorities.[40]

Perhaps the ultimate prettification of Bunshichi and his band occurred when playwrights identified them with the Soga brothers, long revered as two of Japan's most popular folk heroes, and with Sukeroku, the exemplar par excellence of a model *chōnin*. Soga no Gorō Tokimune and Soga no Jūrō Sukenari were samurai who, at the foot of Mount Fuji in 1193, heroically avenged the

---

38. Okamoto and Watanabe, *Ōsaka no sesō*, p. 52.
39. *Nihon bungaku daijiten*, 2:81.
40. Gunji Masakatsu et al., eds., *Tsuruya Nanboku zenshū* (Tokyo: San'ichi Shobō, 1973), pp. 371–442. Mokuami's play *Shiranami gonin otoko* (Five Men of the White Waves), first performed in Edo in 1862, also dips into the Five Men of Naniwa legend. The five heroes in this play are not the Osaka ruffians, but in the scene where they defiantly reveal their identities to the police they compare themselves, through clever puns, to each of the Five Men of Naniwa; see Samuel L. Leiter, *The Art of Kabuki: Famous Plays in Performance* (Berkeley: University of California Press, 1979), p. 11.

murder of their father at the cost of their own lives. Held up as paradigms of filial piety and bravery, the brothers were celebrated for centuries in noh and other dramatic presentations, and from the early Tokugawa period their story became standard stock for puppet and kabuki plays as well. During the second half of the seventeenth century, many kabuki dramas also began to glorify the feats of contemporary *otokodate*—gallant, valorous young men of commoner origin who stepped forth in times of trouble to defend fellow merchants and artisans against injustice. By the end of the seventeenth century, the fictional Sukeroku, typically identified as a rice broker, had emerged as the most illustrious *otokodate* on stages in Osaka and Kyoto.

Inevitably, perhaps, kabuki playwrights were tempted to craft works in which Soga no Gorō appeared under the guise of the *otokodate* Sukeroku, only to reveal his second identity at the climax of the play, thus bringing together in a single persona prized virtues associated with different individuals. The preeminent example of such a play was staged in Edo in 1716 under the title *Sukeroku: Edo no hana* (Sukeroku: Flower of Edo).[41] The drama (whose subtitle underscores the hero's significance as another symbol of the city's commoner class) draws its tension from a love triangle: the vile samurai Ikyū hopes to purchase the affections of Agemaki, a ranking courtesan in the Yoshiwara pleasure quarter who truly loves Sukeroku but despairs when her emotions seem not to be fully requited. After Agemaki spurns Ikyū's advances, Sukeroku realizes the depth and purity of her love for him. At that point, Sukeroku discovers that Ikyū has the sword which belonged to Soga no Gorō's slain father. In the final scene, Sukeroku/Soga no Gorō cuts down his foe and declares his love for Agemaki, thus upholding his personal honor and winning justice for the courtesan and, by implication, all townspeople.

If one could stage plays in which Sukeroku was the alter ego of Soga no Gorō, it was only a short step to mounting productions in which other *otokodate*, such as the Five Men of Naniwa, might also turn out to have double identities. Thus in the kabuki drama *Maki kaesu mikari Soga*, performed at the Morita Theater in Edo in 1776, Bunshichi and his allies take center stage, only to be revealed as mythological or historical figures in disguise. Bunshichi, predictably, turns out to be Soga no Gorō.[42] Thereafter the Bunshichi, Sukeroku, and Soga legends became deeply interwoven; paradoxically, popular myth once again had transformed the leader of the Five Men of Naniwa, converting the foe of samurai and rich merchants in Osaka into a warrior, disguised as a wealthy rice broker, who defended the honor of the townspeople of Edo!

By the late eighteenth century, writers of cheap fiction (*sharebon*) also extended the legend of the Five Men of Naniwa into new territory. *Sharebon* frequently tended to satire, and some offered wonderfully ludicrous takeoffs on

---

41. The play is analyzed in Barbara E. Thornbury, *Sukeroku's Double Identity: The Dramatic Structure of Edo Kabuki* (Ann Arbor: Center for Japanese Studies, University of Michigan, 1982).

42. Narazaki Muneshige, ed., *Pari Kokuritsu Toshokan, Hizō ukiyoe taikan* 8 (Tokyo: Kōdansha, 1989), p. 282 and plate 105.

the Five Men of Naniwa story. *Gunin otoko itsutsu Karigane* (1783), written by Hōrai Yamabito Kibashi, for instance, had nothing to do with the historical gangsters, but featured five fools (*gunin*) who were fans of sumo wrestling. There Karigane's name was written with characters that mean to "borrow money," and the title might be loosely rendered as "Five Fools Who Fell into Debt."[43]

Although some *sharebon* authors sheared Bunshichi and his friends of any threatening aspects in order to achieve humorous effects, others played with the themes set forth in the familiar theatrical renditions of the evolving myth. *Seirō itsutsu Karigane* (The Karigane Five in the Brothel Quarter, 1788) by Baigetsudō Kajihito, for example, made clever use of the Noda Kakuzaemon character.[44] Here, too, the samurai is a low-ranking member of the warrior class who lives on a samurai residential estate in Edo. But whereas Noda appeared in Takeda Izumo's puppet play as a boy-lover, a patron of actor-prostitutes who has a run-in with the Five Men of Naniwa outside an Osaka theater, in Baigetsudō's work he is recast as a suitor of Bunshichi's lover, the courtesan Kiyokawa. At the beginning of the novel, it appears that Thunder Shōkurō is in league with Noda, whom Kiyokawa's prostitute-friends regard as a *hatamoto yakko* and, by implication, an *akudama*, an "evil man." In spinning out the plot complications, "The Karigane Five in the Brothel Quarter" represents Bunshichi and his friends as heroic and as transcending traditional moral imperatives: "When people try to crush the honor of the *otokodate*, the Five Men of Naniwa, beyond right and wrong, will appear."[45] Thus Bunshichi, depicted in the earliest stage of the legend as a decent young man led astray by evil friends, continues his gradual evolution into an adversary of rich merchants, and ultimately into a foe of the sinister members of the warrior class as well.[46]

Print artists produced visual representations of the themes swirling around the Five Men of Naniwa. The first illustrations appeared in wood-block storybooks marketed soon after the executions. The pictures in *Bunshichi isshū-ki* (1703), for instance, depict the lawless behavior of Seven's Gang, the arrests of its members, and the journey of the faithful prostitute to retrieve Bunshichi's

---

43. Mizuno Minoru, ed., *Sharebon taisei*, vol. 12 (Tokyo: Chūō Kōronsha, 1981), pp. 233–46. Playwrights also engaged in parody; sometimes by substituting female for male characters. In the kabuki play *Waka Murasaki Edokko Soga* (performed in Edo in 1792), the five outlaws appear as beautiful women, and Segawa Kiku no Jō III, the famed *onnagata*, or male actor who specialized in portraying women, played the lead role of Karigane Obun; see Timothy T. Clark and Ueda Osamu, with Donald Jenkins, *The Actor's Image: Print Makers of the Katsukawa School*, ed. Naomi Noble Richard (Chicago: Chicago Art Institute in association with Princeton University Press, 1994), p. 444.

44. Mizuno, *Sharebon taisei*, vol. 14 (1981), p. 208f.

45. Ibid., p. 208.

46. Okamoto and Watanabe, *Ōsaka no sesō*, p. 53, note that all five of the men were portrayed as "the allies of the townspeople, *otokodate* who punished evil samurai." That characterization is especially applicable in the case of Bunshichi, for the plot line of betrayal as advanced in works such as *Seirō itsutsu Karigane* helps to distance him from some of the gang's most violent members, thus making Bunshichi into a more sympathetic figure.

severed head from the execution grounds.[47] As might be imagined, woodblock prints portraying leading actors became extremely popular as kabuki plays continued to broadcast the fame of the Five Men of Naniwa. Utagawa Kunimasa was especially fascinated with the Five Men of Naniwa; one of his large-size prints pictures a youthful Bunshichi, sword raised above his head, about to kill a very evil-looking Noda Kakuzaemon, and another shows a pose by the actor Ichikawa Omezō, cross-eyed and frowning, rolling up his sleeves in the role of Hote no Ichiemon.[48]

Certain conventions emerged from the visual treatments of the Five Men of Naniwa. The ruffians usually sported swords and stout *shakuhachi* flutes, which could be pressed into service as weapons if need be but which also symbolized the more genteel accomplishments of noted warrior-heroes of the past. At some point it became customary to decorate the shoulder of each man's kimono with a distinctive crest: a crane or wild goose for Bunshichi (*karigane* being the Japanese word for those birds); a drumhead over crossed sticks (emblematic of the God of Thunder) for Kaminari Shōkurō; a stylized ideograph signifying *an* (peace) for An no Heibei; a sackful of treasure (a symbol of the God of Wealth) for Hote no Ichiemon; and the ideograph for *sen* (one thousand) under crossed hammers for Gokuin no Sen'emon.[49] In 1768 Katsukawa Shunshō popularized pentaptychs that placed each of the five men on an individual single sheet against a common background. On one set, the latticed fronts of pleasure-quarter brothels provide the backdrop; on another, a river.[50]

The wood-block prints fixed new images of Bunshichi and his gang in the popular mind. Over time, the Five Men of Naniwa became younger and more slender, and Bunshichi in particular came to sport long locks.[51] Never did the Five Men of Naniwa look more handsome than in a theater poster by Juyōdō Toshikuni publicizing a kabuki performance in Kyoto in 1826, which focused tightly on the men's faces, with Bunshichi's staring out from the center of the print.[52] The new slimmer-smarter look was part of the eroticization of representations of the five men, who increasingly were associated with women. One print by Kitagawa Utamaro, for instance, portrays the courtesan-paramour Kiyokawa next to an elegant Bunshichi, while a menacing Kaminari Shōkurō looms above them, and a pentaptych by Isoda Koryūsai entitled *Karigane gonin otoko no kuruwa-nai sanpo* (The Five Men of Karigane's Gang Strolling in the Licensed Quarter) and dated 1780 features a courtesan and her attendant accompanying each of the five men, who are beardless, demure, and anything but threatening.[53]

---

47. Nakamura and Hino, *Kisho fukuseikai sōsho*, 16:100–101.
48. Kikuchi Sadao, *A Treasury of Japanese Wood Block Prints*, trans. Don Kenny (New York: Crown Publishers, 1969), plates 1099, 1100.
49. Clark and Ueda, *Actor's Image*, p. 257.
50. Ibid., p. 256.
51. See, for instance, the 1780 print by Shunshō in ibid., pp. 254–55.
52. Dean J. Schwaab, *Osaka Prints* (New York: Rizzoli, 1989), p. 117, plate 92.
53. The Utamaro print, which is not dated, appears in Sotheby & Co., *Catalogue of Highly Important Japanese Prints, Illustrated Books and Drawings, from the Henri Vever Collection: Part I*

The Five Men of Naniwa: Gang Violence and Popular Culture — 149

"Bunshichi and His Friends in Crested Outerwear," by Shunshō. Courtesy of Tokyo National Museum and the Art Institute of Chicago.

"The Five Men of Karigane's Gang Strolling in the Licensed Quarter," by Koryūsai. Courtesy of the Museum für Ostasiatische Kunst.

The Five Men of Naniwa could be found impressed upon many diverse artifacts of Japan's popular culture as well. Along with visualizations of other famous persons drawn from Japanese history, religion, literature, and folklore, for instance, their faces adorned the souvenir drawings known as "Ōtsu pictures." Ōtsu was a key post town on the Tōkaidō Highway linking the Kansai area with Edo and eastern Japan, as well as a way station for visitors to the nearby temple Miidera, and travelers and pilgrims patronized the roadside stands that sold the inexpensive Ōtsu pictures, presenting the mementos to

(Westerham: Westerham Press, 1973), p. 169, plate 198. Four sheets of the pentaptych by Koryūsai are in the possession of the Berlin Museum of Eastern Art and are reproduced in Narazaki Muneshige, comp., *Berurin Tōyō Bijutsukan*, Missho ukiyoe taikan 12 (Tokyo: Kōdansha, 1988), p. 226, plate 59. I am indebted to Takahashi Keiko of the Sackler Museum at Harvard University for this reference.

relatives and friends at home and thus helping to spread the fame of Bunshichi and his thugs-turned-folk-heroes. From the Meiwa era (1764–72), commercial print artists put the Five Men of Naniwa on calendars. One, executed in 1802 by Kubo Shunman, features an illustration of Bunshichi on the leaf for the Seventh Month (*Shichigatsu*). The month's poetic name (*Fumizuki*, or Month of Letters) figures prominently in an accompanying poem, and, to double the pun, *fumi* is written with the same ideograph as the *bun* in Bunshichi.[54] Naturally, the Bunshichi legend also had fashion implications. From the 1780s, if not earlier, a particular style of men's hair ribbon was called the "Bunshichi hair ribbon," recalling the scene from *Kinpira Kaminari Shōkurō* in which a despised samurai angers Bunshichi by pouring water on his decorative ribbon.[55] Finally, Bunshichi's severed head made its way back to the puppet stage, inspiring what became the most important male puppet head used in bunraku theater after the large-scale marionettes operated by three puppeteers became popular. That head, usually used for "good" adult males, came to be called the Bunshichi head following its appearance in the 1742 play *Otokodate itsutsu no Karigane*. Its strong lines were supposed to suggest both bravery and a secret grief.[56]

Factual Accounts of the Five Men Affair

Lore about the Five Men of Naniwa became so ubiquitous that some popular writers were motivated to look behind the popular myths and set down factual accounts about the men's careers, arrests, and executions. Perhaps the first of those was *Chosakudō isseki-banashi* (An Evening's Conversation at a Literary Salon), published in 1803 by Takizawa Bakin, one of Edo's leading authors. Bakin begins with a wry observation: "The Five Men of Naniwa were basically worthless scoundrels," and then recounts the events that happened on the evening of the sixth day of the Sixth Month, 1701, before summarizing the punishments meted out to Bunshichi's gang: "In the end, on the twenty-sixth day of the Eighth Month of the following year, the corpses of the five men, fearsome as tigers and wolves, were exposed at the temple grounds."[57]

Bakin specifies that his account is based on the "true record" which he has personally researched in Osaka, so apparently he had access to the official police report, "Record of Some Outlaws of the Genroku Era." Clearly, Bakin is attempting to debunk a major myth and to discourage the portrayal of Bunshichi and his gang as anything other than "villainous scoundrels." Ironically,

---

54. Narazaki, *Pari Kokuritsu Toshokan*, plate 105.
55. *Kogo jiten*, p. 896.
56. Saitō Seijirō, *Nihon no kashira* (Tokyo: Iwanami Bijutsusha, 1964), p. 120; Donald Keene, *Bunraku: The Art of the Japanese Puppet Theatre* (Tokyo: Kodansha, 1978), pp. 59, 210–11. Barbara C. Adachi, *Backstage at Bunraku* (Tokyo: Weatherhill, 1985), p. 179, suggests that the Bunshichi head dates from 1745.
57. Bakin, *Chosakudō isseki-banashi*, 9:93–97.

The Five Men of Naniwa: Gang Violence and Popular Culture — 151

Bakin's version of the "real" Five Men of Naniwa. Reprinted from Takizawa Bakin, Chosakudō isseki-banashi. Photograph by Gary P. Leupp.

and perhaps unwittingly, however, Bakin himself contributes to the prettification of Bunshichi when he includes an account of his search for evidence:

> Some time ago I visited Naniwa and investigated the true record. I have summed up my findings here. Beginning in Genroku 16 [1703], various works—dramas and books—were produced about the Five Men of Naniwa, and although we hear about their posthumous reputations, if we don't look below the surface, we will not uncover the truth about them. In the pagoda of the temple Shitennōji there was a votive tablet, dedicated by Karigane Bunshichi, showing the Battle of Yashima. Someone told me that it was lost at the time of the recent temple fire and no longer exists.[58]

In 1184, Minamoto no Yoshitsune led his family's armies to a major triumph at Yashima against the rival Taira clan, thus paving the way for the eventual establishment of Japan's first shogunate by his older half-brother, Yoritomo. The relationship between the two Minamoto leaders quickly deteriorated, however, and as Yoritomo grew jealous of Yoshitsune's burgeoning fame and popularity, he turned against the younger hero and forced Yoshitsune to commit

58. Ibid.

suicide in 1189. The poignant story about Yoshitsune and his sad fate quickly became a treasured staple of Japanese popular culture, and countless noh, puppet, and kabuki dramas cast Yoshitsune as the hapless victim of a ruthless, despotic, and vengeful overlord. Thus, for Bunshichi to place a votive offering portraying the Battle of Yashima at the temple Shitennōji might be construed merely as a pious gesture honoring Yoshitsune, but the episode also had the effect of identifying Bunshichi with that fallen folk hero and earned the Osakan sympathy as another figure in popular culture whose life was cut short by an oppressive regime.

After Bakin, the Osaka playwright Hamamatsu Utakuni penned his famous *Setsuyō kikan* (The Wonders of Settsu Province) as another attempt to unearth the truth about the Six-Six Incident.[59] Utakuni drew heavily from Bakin's earlier treatment, even quoting the Edoite verbatim in places, although Utakuni shunned most of Bakin's moralizing interjections. Utakuni omits, for instance, any extended discussion of the "disembodied spirits" of the Five Men of Naniwa, a subject that fascinated Bakin; nor does Utakuni preach about the need to investigate the "real historical record" so as to refute the myth. Rather, Utakuni seems more interested in satisfying his readers' curiosity for additional information about Bunshichi and his fellows-in-crime. Thus Utakuni adds details about the possible identity of Kiyokawa, explains various nuances about the mythopoeia of Bunshichi in popular culture, and explores the legends concerning Bunshichi, commenting on their plausibility. At one point, for instance, he notes that "at Sennichi Mae cemetery, among the Thunder God trees on the east side of the graveyard, there is a stone pagoda inscribed with the names of the Five Men of Naniwa."[60] Apparently several individuals erected such memorials, either out of admiration or a desire to placate the gangsters' avenging spirits. In similar fashion, according to the *Setsuyō kikan*, the manservant of a ranking samurai in Tanba left his master's service, settled down in Osaka to work as a dyer, and took the name Kariganeya Bunzaemon. His son Bunshichi, admiring his namesake, erected a stone at a temple in his home province honoring the Five Men of Naniwa.

Utakuni also attempts to affirm Bunshichi's date of execution by examining temple artifacts. He asserts that the "tombstones of Karigane Bunshichi and Gokuin no Sen'emon are located at the temple Kōzu Shōhōji," each engraved with the date of the men's death, the twenty-sixth day of the Eighth Month of 1702. Today, in fact, on the grounds of that temple, lie two pagoda-style stones which, by the late eighteenth century, had come to be identified with the two outlaws. One bears the inscription "Loving Father Hōren'in; Loving Mother Hōkūin." Etched into the base of the stone beneath those posthumous Buddhist titles is the single name Kariganeya. One can also make out the routine,

---

59. Hamamatsu's work was published in 1883 and is reprinted in Ōsaka-shi Shiryō Hensanjo, ed., *Ōsaka shishi shiryō*, vol. 3 (Osaka: Ōsaka-shi Shiryō Chōsakai, 1981), pp. 79–81. A slightly different version appears in Funakoshi Seiichirō, ed., *Naniwa sōsho*, vol. 3 (Ōsaka: Naniwa Sōsho Kankōkai, 1927), pp. 477–81.

60. Funakoshi, *Naniwa sōsho*, 3:479; *Ōsaka shishi shiryō*, 3:80.

The memorial to Bunshichi at the temple Kōzu Shōhōji. Courtesy of Gary P. Leupp.

pious statement "Through the strength of the Lotus Sutra the existing body becomes a Buddha," but no visible date appears on the monument.[61]

No simple explanation can account for the complex evolution of the tale of the Five Men of Naniwa and its extended popularity well into the nineteenth century. We can assemble the basic facts of the case from the police record. We also know the content of the earliest folk ballads about the Six-Six Incident and its aftermath, which can yield additional insights into the nature and activities of Seven's Gang since the *utazaimon* were being sung within weeks of the executions at Sennichi Mae. Finally, we are able to trace how the portrayal of the Five Men of Naniwa changed in popular literature and art over the course of the eighteenth century.

Still, there is much that we do not understand about the psychological, sociological, and cultural conditions of the time that stimulated the valorization of these outlaws from Osaka. Undoubtedly the requirements of different art forms had some impact on the curious twists and turns worked upon the story

61. The *Ōsaka shiseki jiten*, p. 289, suggests that Osaka's residents began to identify the memorial with Bunshichi late in the Tokugawa period.

of the Bunshichi and his accomplices, as did the constantly changing psychological idiosyncrasies of the authors and consumers of the myth, the evolving social and economic conditions within Osaka, political interventions such as censorship, and pan-Japanese cultural values that came to be reflected in all hero worship. Thus in studying this legend we require an interdisciplinary approach, a "historical sociology of psychology," checked by attention to the particular requirements of the genres of popular culture.[62] The progress of such interdisciplinary research ultimately may provide a full and satisfactory explanation for the mythologizing of the Five Men of Naniwa. At present we can at least offer some modest observations.

Osaka during the Genroku era was a bustling and prosperous city. But many of its residents were the impoverished victims of abandonment and homelessness. Such persons could view the affluent merchants of the city with bitter envy, and regard municipal authority with both disdain and fear. Many picked pockets, or fights; in crowded areas others filched purses, pilfered items of clothing from passersby, and swiped weapons from pedestrians. More brazenly, some shook down neighborhood merchants and pirated small riverboats. But Osaka's disaffected could also take part in crimes that seem less remunerative and more inspired by pure animosity, such as provoking wealthy passersby, stabbing them, then running off. That sort of violence suggests a very conscious, if unfocused, class hatred.

The Five Men of Naniwa seem to have despised rich persons in general, and their subsequent valorization by Osaka's commoners suggests that gradations of such feeling were widespread among the various segments of the city's population. What else can explain the transformation of Bunshichi and his followers from *abaremono*, thugs and ruffians, into *otokodate*, heroes and protectors of the common people? It is not particularly unusual that criminals such as Bunshichi might become metamorphosed into heroes. Like their near contemporaries, the English robbers Jack Sheppard and Jonathan Wild who were hanged in 1724 and 1725 respectively, the Five Men of Naniwa generated a slew of literary and artistic works, and in the manner of more recent outlaw pairs such as the James brothers and Bonnie and Clyde, Bunshichi and his partners-in-crime acted out fantasies shared by more ordinary, law-abiding men and women who also harbored indignation and bitterness toward existing economic and political authority.[63]

Thus, the murders, assaults, and piracies committed by Seven's Gang were ultimately productive. The legend of the Five Men of Naniwa rendered, as

---

62. I borrow the expression from David Halperin and his discussion of research methodology in connection with the history of sexuality; see his *One Hundred Years of Homosexuality, and Other Essays on Greek Love* (New York: Routledge, 1990), p. 40.

63. On Jack Sheppard and his impact on popular culture, see Peter Linebaugh, *The London Hanged: Crime and Civil Society in the Eighteenth Century* (Cambridge: Cambridge University Press, 1992), pp. 7–41; on Jonathan Wild, see Michael Weisser, *Crime and Punishment in Early Modern Europe* (Atlantic Highlands, N.J.: Humanities Press, 1979), pp. 123–24; and for a discussion of Frank and Jesse James, see Paul Kooistra, *Criminals as Heroes: Structure, Power, and Identity* (Bowling Green, Ohio: Bowling Green University, 1989), p. 43f.

Marx put it, the "service" of "arousing the moral and aesthetic feelings of the public" and "breaking the monotony and everyday security of bourgeois life."[64] In their celebration of the Five Men of Naniwa, the writers, actors, and print artists of Osaka and other Tokugawa cities produced countless works (many now lost) of aesthetic value, which stirred and inspired the consumers of such popular culture for generations.

64. Karl Marx, *Capital*, vol. 4, *Theories of Surplus-Value*, pt. 1 (Moscow: Progress Publishers, 1963), pp. 387–88.

APPENDIX

The Confession of Karigane Bunshichi (from "Genroku aburemono no ki")

Six years ago, in Genroku Nine [1696], I struck the night watchman of my quarter, and four years ago I injured Kiyobei in Tateuri Horihama. Since I committed other outrages throughout the city, three years ago my parents, on the twenty-second day of the Fourth Month of the Year of the Rabbit [1699], made a request to the authorities. After an investigation, I was ordered to jail. My father was seriously ill and died on the fifteenth day of the Fifth Month, however, and because I was her only child, my mother repeatedly made appeals on my behalf. So on the twenty-seventh day of the Sixth Month, I was pardoned, released from jail, and instructed not to commit any further transgressions in the city.

In the Tenth Month of the same year that I got out of prison, however, I went with Gokuin no Sen'emon to the licensed quarter and got involved in a street fight. Sen'emon and I cut up about three people, and injured another ten. Among them, Shika no Chōbei was badly hurt and died some months later. Then at Horie Sumiyoshi Bridge, aided by Kaminari Shōkurō and Dōguya Yohei, I attacked someone named Iemon of the residential quarter Tōemon. But he pushed his way through the townspeople and escaped death. I also committed many other violent acts all over the city, but I didn't kill any other people.

Since I am the leader of a gang of ruffians, I have more crimes to confess than the others. I was accompanied by Gokuin no Sen'emon, Kaminari Shōkurō, Tonbi Kan'emon, and others, but since they all played minor roles, I should naturally receive the most severe treatment. I accept responsibility for all the group's crimes. As for the five swords, the dirk, spear and dagger in my home, I took them from my victims when I committed crimes, and have not taken them from any single place.

I have just heard that Kaminari Shōkurō is to be arrested. I know he will not es-

The Confession of Karigane Bunshichi (from "Genroku aburemono no ki") — 157

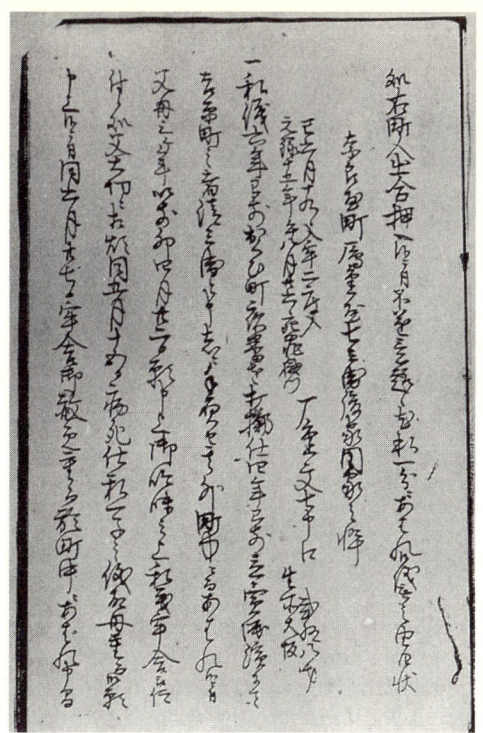

Bunshichi's confession. From "Genroku aburemono no ki," by permission of Ōsaka Furitsu Naka no Shima Toshokan.

cape. He has taken refuge at the home of his uncle Saburōbei in Akekawa village in Settsu Province. When he learned that a search for him had been ordered, he went to visit his relatives, telling them that if he returned to Osaka he would be arrested. I've heard that Mippiki Jihei, another member of our gang, went on a murderous rampage, but since he is homeless, I don't know where he is.

CHAPTER SEVEN

Osaka's Brotherhood of Mendicant Monks

— *Yoshida Nobuyuki*
TRANSLATED BY AKIO YASUHARA

Several miles north of Kyoto looms the silhouette of famous, mysterious Mount Kurama. Written today with the ideographs that mean Saddle Horse Mountain, the name Kurama derived originally from the word *kurayami*, which implies a place of darkness and secrecy, a locale where the customary norms of behavior hover in suspension. The image is fitting, for since ancient times people have venerated the slopes of Mount Kurama as the home to an amazing variety of wizards, sorcerers, and assorted mountain spirits. Few historians would forget that Kurama was where the popular hero Minamoto no Yoshitsune supposedly learned sophisticated techniques of swordplay and unarmed combat from a friendly *tengu*, one of the half-human, half-bird avatars of Japanese folklore who often protected innocents against evil. Later, when Yoshitsune descended Mount Kurama, he easily defeated the marauding warrior monk Benkei at the bridge in Kyoto where Gojō Avenue crossed the Kamo River. Overawed, Benkei vowed to become the virtuous Yoshitsune's loyal retainer, thus forming perhaps the most famous warrior duo of Japanese mythohistory.

Also dotting the slopes of Mount Kurama is an assemblage of chapels, monasteries, abbeys, and retreats known collectively as Kuramadera, the temple Kurama. Originally established in the eighth century and affiliated with several different Buddhist sects over the centuries, Kuramadera has won lasting esteem for its enshrinement of the deity Bishamon. The faithful have revered that divinity as one of four powerful gods who stand guard at the cardinal directions, protecting temples and associated lay communities from the depravities of hostile invading spirits. Since Bishamon bears responsibility for defending the northern quadrant, it is not surprising that he should be found at Mount Kurama, whose shadows overreach the passes and roadways that expose Kyoto to danger from that quarter. Even today, one of the most prized icons preserved in the treasury at Kuramadera is a carved wooden statue of Bishamon, resplendent in armor, carrying a jeweled spear, and depicted as stomping two evil demons into the ground.

Far removed from the spirit-filled, wooded slopes that shelter the temples on Mount Kurama, a group of humbly clad ecclesiastics roamed the streets of Osaka during the early modern period, pausing in front of the homes and shops of prosperous merchant families. There, the begging monks, or *gannin bōzu* as they were known, presided over the conduct of pious rituals, prayers, and supplications in hopes of receiving a small benefaction. The friars even carved out a niche for themselves in the annals of Osaka's urban popular culture, winning renown for the manner in which they shouted out witticisms, fired off parodies of well-known Buddhist scriptures, and even acted out famous scenes from kabuki and puppet plays in exchange for a few coins or a bowl of rice. Closely identified with the life of Japan's leading commercial city, Osaka's fraternity of mendicant monks nevertheless maintained close relations with the priests at Daizōin, a monastery within the complex of temples on Mount Kurama.

Osaka's streets were not the only byways frequented by ecclesiastics identified with Kurama during the early modern period. In Edo, friars affiliated with Daizōin and Enkōin, another chapel at Kuramadera, organized themselves into a brotherhood known as the *gannin bōzu nakama*, the association of mendicant monks. That order included a "vast number of friars," divided into fifty-member groups (*kumi*) and presided over by some twenty headmen (*kumigashira*) who reported to two chief headmen (*furegashira*).[1] In addition, a group of thirty bonzes under one headman entertained and begged in the castle town of Kōfu, as did twenty other monks in Sunpu, again under the oversight of a single headman. Curiously missing from the list of cities that hosted the presence of a fraternity of begging, performing clerics was Kyoto, located at the very foot of Mount Kurama.

The Tokugawa regime attempted to maintain some semblance of administrative control over the various associations of mendicant monks. The line of authority was not direct: the shogun and his commissioners of temples and shrines (*jisha bugyō*), appointed from the ranks of the allied lords (*fudai daimyō*) on a regular basis from 1635, set general religious policy. Besides sounding a major voice in the formulation of laws and codes of conduct, the commissioners supervised bureaus and departments staffed by functionaries who conveyed the regime's rules and regulations to the heads of major religious institutions across Japan, including the priestly authorities at Kuramadera. The patriarchs at Daizōin and Enkōin on Mount Kurama, in turn, maintained contact with their subordinate headmen in the various cities around Japan, thus closing the link between the highest officials of the shogunate and

---

1. For additional details, see my "Edo no gannin to toshi shakai," in Tsukada Takashi, Yoshida, and Wakita Osamu, eds., *Mibun-teki shūen* (Kyoto: Buraku Mondai Kenkyūjo Shuppanbu, 1994), pp. 83–126.

the mendicant friars. However circuitous it may have been, that administrative route provided a means for the government to monitor the behavior of the begging monks, to transmit decrees and ordinances to them, and to settle any problems that arose from their conduct.

Still today, the archives maintained at Kuramadera contain a collection of documents which can enlighten us about the activities of the brotherhood of entertainer-beggar monks in Osaka. Those materials reveal much about religious values and popular beliefs in Japan's largest commercial city and, at the same time, bring to our attention some of the differences between modes of religious behavior in that city and in the shogun's administrative headquarters in eastern Japan.

The World of the Mendicant Monks in the Late Seventeenth Century

Most of the historical records maintained in the archives at Kuramadera that concern Osaka's mendicant monks date to the years between the late Tenpō era (1830–44) and the collapse of the Tokugawa shogunate in 1868. Although we cannot know as much as we would wish about the lives of the friars during the initial half of the early modern period, a booklet bearing the title "Kuramadera shita ganningumi-chō" does illuminate something of the early history of the brotherhood. Inscribed on the cover of the manuscript is the date 1839, although in reality it is a somewhat later reproduction. Two of Osaka's mendicant monks, Umemoto Bō and Chigen, brought the original "Kuramadera shita ganningumi-chō" with them when they "climbed the mountain" to their home temple at Kurama, arriving on the twentieth day of the Second Month, 1843. At that time, the patriarchs at Daizōin made a copy of the register as "a reminder for future reference" and stored the duplicate in the chapel's "treasury."

Despite the booklet's relatively recent pedigree, it contains information about conditions as far back as the mid-seventeenth century. In particular, the manuscript provides details about a contentious incident that occurred among the monks in Osaka in 1672, and it includes a list of regulations governing their behavior that was compiled upon the settlement of that disagreement. Every time a new Osaka city magistrate took office, the headmen for the association of mendicant monks presented the register to the new official. When they did so, they updated the list of brothers present in Osaka and submitted as well an accompanying form to which all the friars set their signatures as testimony that they understood and agreed to abide by the stated regulations.

An entry dated the twenty-second day of the Twelfth Month, Kanbun 12 (1672), contains information about the dispute, although, for reasons that become clear in the document, tensions had been mounting over the days and months before that date. According to the manuscript, the number of begging monks in Osaka had increased in the years before 1672, to a total of twenty-one men. As a consequence, it was difficult for all of them to live together in a single house. "Our quarters were cramped," they complained, "and we were inconvenienced." Dissatisfied with their living arrangements, the mendicant friars at some unspecified date had submitted a request to the Osaka city magistrates seeking permission to reorganize themselves into two groups, with a certain Harunaga to serve as the headman for one and a brother named Junkai for the other. The Osaka city magistrates approved the request, and the friars divided themselves into the two bands.

Near the end of the Ninth Month, 1672, however, a bitter altercation erupted between Harunaga and Junkai. As the angers of the moment built upon themselves, pitting friar against friar, priests from Kuramadera and the Osaka city magistrates finally intervened and arranged a settlement. Enzui, the abbot at one of the leading monasteries on Mount Kurama, led the efforts to resolve the dispute, and he laid blame at the feet of Harunaga. "Nenko is a member of Harunaga's group," Enzui wrote with passion in the "Kuramadera shita ganningumi-chō." "Nenko concocted a falsehood in order to conceal his venal deeds. As the group's headman, Harunaga was supposed to prevent such misconduct. Instead, he conspired to cover up Nenko's mischief."

Another document, the "Kurama shita gannin yuishogaki," reveals the genesis of Enzui's anger.[2] "Until the middle of the Kanbun period [1661–73]," the authors of that account declared, "some mendicant monks residing in Osaka engaged in *henge kanjin*." Presumably, this meant that some friars tried to increase their income from solicitations by wandering the streets of Osaka in garb that would identify them as revered Buddhist deities, popular Shinto gods, or famous spirits and apparitions. The practice of *henge kanjin*, however, was also the preserve of *hinin* outcasts, the "nonhumans" who likewise entertained and begged for a living on the streets of Osaka. Some hereditary *hinin* were born into that status, and the government occasionally demoted to outcast status former convicts and families who had lost their shop-residences and fallen into abject poverty. In either case, the shogunate prohibited the *hinin* in Japan's major cities from engaging in commerce, artisanal enterprises, or even manual labor, and so the outcasts lived on the donations they received from engaging in *henge kanjin* and from staging street performances of *shikata nō*, abbreviated renditions of classical noh dramas, and *kado saimon*, in which the performer set up an altar in front of a person's house or on a street corner and offered prayers and songs to bring forth blessings from Buddhist and Shinto deities.

Clearly, Harunaga and his followers were the "mendicant monks residing in Osaka" who "engaged in *henge kanjin*." Their audacity in daring to conduct so brazenly solicitations usually associated with the outcasts is what provoked Enzui's wrath. "Some of Harunaga's followers were ignoramuses," another entry in the "Kurama shita gannin yuishogaki" continued. "They committed improprieties and were even mistaken as being members of the *hinin* group of so-

2. This document was compiled in 1842 (Tenpō 13) and is located in the temple archives at Kuramadera, together with the "Kuramadera shita ganningumi-chō."

cial pariahs. As a consequence, priestly authorities at the home temple issued prohibitions against such behavior." The clerics at Kurama itemized those regulations in a Notification (*oboe*), whose seventeen clauses appear in an appendix to this chapter, and in the Eleventh Month of 1672, Enzui journeyed to Osaka to present that document to the Osaka city magistrates.³

As can be seen, the Notification of 1672 did more than prohibit certain mendicancies. In sum, it represented an attempt by priestly authorities at Kuramadera to compile a code of behavior that would regulate many aspects of the lives of friars affiliated with a subsidiary temple and resident in a somewhat distant city. Moreover, Osaka's city magistrates referred to the slate of regulations as a *shioki*, or "specification of conduct." Even if one sets aside the government's predictable predilection to erect a facade of sternness and to identify itself as the arbiter of what was socially acceptable, the use of the term suggests that city officials took the Notification of 1672 as having the force of law. Put in that light, the dual nature of the seventeen clauses becomes clear: they both embodied "temple law" (*jihō*), as set forth by the prelates at Kuramadera, and became the basis for secular law when the Osaka city magistrates ratified them in the Eleventh Month of Kanbun 12.

An examination of the more important provisions within the Notification of 1672 reveals the tenor of this amalgam of religious law and government-approved code of conduct and explicates its importance for one particular religious subcommunity within the complex mosaic of Osaka society. One cluster of clauses reveals how the monks organized themselves and carried out certain pious activities in the late seventeenth century. As noted in the fourth item, the brothers in Osaka had formed their own particular communal association, which they called the *gannin nakama*. The use of the term *nakama* is suggestive. For one thing, it indicates that the two groups of monks had received formal recognition from the Osaka city officials, in the manner of the merchants' protective associations that James L. McClain describes in Chapter 3, and that the monks regulated many aspects of their own religious life, giving them the sort of communal empowerments that Wakita Haruko identifies in Chapter 2 as one legacy of medieval urbanism.

Other information from the fourth item confirms the implications advanced by the usage of the term *nakama*. The friars themselves determined who could be admitted into their brotherhood. The fourth item restricted entry into the association to "persons of this locale" and specified that prospective members had to be sponsored by one of the Osaka friars and receive the blessing of the prelates at Daizōin. That done, the officers of the association accompanied the inductee to the appropriate government office, presumably that of an Osaka

---

3. The entire edict is contained in "Kurama shita gannin yuishogaki." The Notification is dated the twenty-seventh day, Eleventh Month, Kanbun 12, or January 14, 1673, on the Gregorian calendar. Since Kanbun 12 more closely corresponds to 1672, however, the set of regulations is referred to here as the Notification of 1672. The third and eighth items of the Notification are extracted in Hashigawa Masashi, ed., *Kuramadera-shi* (Kyoto: Kuramayama Kaisen Jimukyoku, 1926), pp. 221–22.

city magistrate, who formally recorded information about the new member in an official register.

The brotherhood consisted of masters, disciples, and affiliates who lived apart from the main body of friars. The masters were the full-fledged, constituent members of the association. As suggested by the fifth and seventh items, each master was responsible for what might be termed a family group (*gannin no ie*) that included his own "natural and adopted sons" and perhaps "the single disciple who resides with him." At any given time, the total number of brothers enrolled in each of the two groups that comprised the association was not supposed to exceed a maximum of fifty persons, including all disciples. The seventeenth clause yields additional details about the supervision of the family units: the headmen and subordinate officers known as the monthly representatives, a title indicating that the various masters took turns serving in that position for a month at a time, assumed responsibility for managing budgets, overseeing the use of the alms that the friars received from begging, and disbursing daily living allowances.

Several other clauses touch on the theological concerns and religious activities of the brotherhood. According to the sixteenth item, for instance, the members of the monks' association held a grand meeting once each year as well as monthly gatherings to perform rituals of worship to Bishamon, the popular deity enshrined at Kurama. The eighth clause enumerated the "general regulations" concerning the sorts of endeavors that the friars might undertake as they roamed the streets of Osaka in quest of alms—peddling amulets, offering masses for the deceased, undertaking pilgrimages, and chanting the *nenbutsu* prayer formulas that evoked the name of the Amida Buddha in hopes of being reborn in the Western Paradise.

A document that Nishi no Bō, a headman in the association of mendicant monks, submitted to the Osaka city magistrates in the Twelfth Month of Tenpō 13 (1842) expands our understanding of the sorts of pious mendicancies that the bonzes undertook in Osaka.[4] During the middle of the nineteenth century, for instance, the friars continued to hand out good luck amulets, distributing to the faithful of Osaka talismans blessed by the priests at the chapel Bishamon Daihōzen on Mount Kurama and inscribed with propitious sayings such as Peace in the Realm (*tenka taihei*) and Prosperity of Bountiful Harvests (*gokokujōju*). Similarly, in the Seventh Month, the brothers offered masses for the dead on behalf of thankful patrons. Ringing gongs and chimes, the clerics solemnly progressed to local temples where they made offerings to the "hungry demons" who might otherwise torment the souls of the deceased. In an activity not mentioned in the Notification of 1672, the monks received alms for sitting in for believers during the Kōshin observances which, as Gary P. Leupp points out in the preceding chapter, obligated persons to stay awake throughout a particularly portentous night in the zodiacal cycle when the "three worms"

---

4. The document bears the title "Kono yaku Kurama gannin kanjin tsukamatsuri sōrō taihō" and can be found in the temple archives at Kurama.

that supposedly secret themselves within the human body might attempt to escape and report one's transgressions to the gods.

Priest Nishi also elaborates on the surrogate pilgrimages that Osaka's friars undertook to prominent Buddhist temples on behalf of true believers who were physically unable or simply too busy to complete the journeys of faith on their own. Pilgrimages that combined a fondness for sightseeing with expressions of devotion emerged as an important element in popular culture at the end of the seventeenth century and beginning of the eighteenth, and one especially rewarding destination for Osakans was Kotohira Shrine, located in Sanuki Province on the island of Shikoku and home to Konpira Daigongen. Originally a protective deity within the Buddhist pantheon of gods, Konpira came to be revered widely as an amorphous spirit with the power to do good for the human community. By the late medieval period, for instance, seafarers had come to rely on Konpira to spare them from storms and shipwrecks. Perhaps because of the association with water, townspeople during the Tokugawa era began to hang out wooden plaques engraved with his image in order to keep their homes and shops safe from fire, and they also worshipped Konpira as their protector against the diseases that often contaminated supplies of summer drinking water. Not surprisingly, at the turn of the eighteenth century many merchant and artisan families in Osaka cherished the desire to undertake a pilgrimage to visit Konpira's home shrine, and if they could not go in person, some were willing to pay a mendicant monk to complete that act of faith in their name.

Nishi no Bō's 1842 submission to Osaka's city officials pointed out that the surrogate pilgrims bound for Shikoku departed the city by the seventh day of the Third Month for the "summer trek" and that they might undertake a second "winter circuit" between the Ninth Month and the end of the calendar year. In both cases, the friars upon their return to Osaka went to the homes of their benefactors to present them with engraved plaques and other religious mementos acquired during the pilgrimage and to perform rituals of purification, the chants and dances designed to ensure their patrons a "home, safe and tranquil" (*kanai anzen*), secure against the threats of fire and disease. In exchange, the monks received a gratuity, the "first fruits of the season" in the flowery language of the document.

In similar fashion, between the Fourth and Sixth Months small groups of four or five brothers each would undertake "dancing supplications" to nearby Sumiyoshi Shrine. Upon their return, the mendicant monks appeared in front of the shops of the Osaka merchants who had commissioned their journeys to offer prayers for business success during the coming year and to receive their anticipated reward. Later, as cold weather moved into the city during the final months of the year and Osaka's residents began to light the fires that heated their shops and homes, the friars visited religious centers that hosted the presence of Akiba Daigongen, another deity believed to afford protection against calamities related to fire and whose home shrine stood on Mount Akiba in Shikoku. Back in Osaka, the friars traveled around the city, stopping in front of shops and homes to receive a gift in return for offering a "midwinter's ablution," prayers to the god of fire.

Some interesting observations arise if the information from Nishi no Bō's memorandum of the early nineteenth century is placed alongside the Notification of 1672. Rather than accept the religious supplications mentioned by Priest Nishi as examples of pious devotion, for instance, it appears evident that the secular political authorities of Osaka tended to regard them as somewhat suspect additions to Osaka's already vibrant and sometimes rowdy street culture. Consequently, the eleventh item of the Notification of 1672, which prohibited large numbers of monks from gathering to chant sutras while keeping cadence by beating together hardwood staffs, and the following twelfth item, which condemned "street preaching," invite interpretation as efforts to regulate and suppress activities that were difficult to distinguish from already flourishing street entertainments. The notion that authorities sometimes felt unsettled enough to impose regulatory decrees receives support from another item, the fourteenth, which suggests that the mendicant brothers traveled outside of Osaka frequently and expresses a kind of official nervousness about their activities while away from the city.

Another issue of note to emerge from the 1672 document concerns the relationship between the officially recognized association of mendicant monks and persons disdained in the fourth item as "outsiders." As noted above, that clause stipulated that only "persons of this locale" could become formal members of the brotherhood. But according to the thirteenth item, an annoying number of "outsiders" were coming into Osaka and engaging in the same sort of supplications as the mendicant monks. As a consequence, the association of friars inserted this clause enjoining the authorities to investigate interlopers "in accordance with official regulations." In contrast, the brotherhood showed more restraint when it came to the activities of another group of rivals identified in the ninth item. According to that article, it would "not be a matter of concern" if a full-fledged member who left the association continued to solicit alms, providing he had obtained from a temple associated with either the Tendai or Shingon sects a special shawl or shoulder surplice embroidered with Sanskrit incantations and arcane formulations designed to aid one's quest for salvation. The friars, that is, were zealous to preserve their special rights within Osaka, yet tolerant of former associates who had affiliated themselves with those influential sects that also maintained close ties to the Tokugawa regime.

The activities and lifestyles of the mendicant monks residing in Edo at the end of the seventeenth century paralleled those of their peers in Osaka, and the brothers in each city stood in approximately the same relationship to higher authority. The friars of both Osaka and Edo traced their genealogical roots back to chapels located at Kurama. Moreover, in each metropolis the monks organized themselves into associations and sought formal recognition from governmental authorities as well as the confirmation of special privileges. Finally, the regulations that governed their way of living and defined their range of permissible activities were practically indistinguishable, at least if one compares the Notification of 1672 that pertained in Osaka with extant decrees for Edo dating to the Kyōhō period (1716–36).

On the other hand, noticeable differences existed. For one thing, the administrative structure for the Edo association was more extensive and thickly layered than was the case in Osaka. Hindering comparisons is the fact that the evidentiary record is not always consistent in describing the internal configuration of the associations, thus indicating that the number of brothers and association officials varied over time. Moreover, it is difficult to find documents dating from the same era for both cities, except for the final two decades of the early modern period. Nevertheless, at that late date it seems that in Osaka there was one chief headman, who had the assistance of a single elder (*toshiyori*) in carrying out his duties. In contrast, the two chief headmen for the Edo brotherhood could call on the services of two deputies (*daiyaku*) to help them preside over approximately ten group headmen each. In addition, each group headman in Edo could expect support from a set of underlings, including assistant headmen, elders, and the heads of the five-man units that made up each of the larger groups.

The differences in how the monks organized themselves in Osaka and Edo surely had something to do with the relative numbers of friars resident in the two cities; the larger association in the nation's political capital simply required more low-level officers than did the smaller brotherhood in Japan's leading commercial city. But the attitudes of city officials in the two urban centers and their respective decisions to locate the two associations in very different administrative orbits also merit attention. In particular, the city magistrates in Edo at the end of the seventeenth century officially recognized the *gannin bōzu nakama*, the association of mendicant friars, as the approved organization for all begging monks in that city. Put differently, the phrase "association of mendicant monks" became a blanket term that covered all ecclesiastics who entertained, begged, and solicited alms, regardless of what they might name themselves. In Osaka, however, only those friars affiliated with Daizōin could claim membership in the official association of mendicant monks that bore the city magistrates' seal of approval, while certain outcasts and some bonzes, such as the "outsiders" mentioned above and other clerics described below, retained their own distinctive identities even though they carried out pious activities that resembled the supplications conducted by the brotherhood.

Religious Rivalry in the Nineteenth Century

In the Fourth Month of 1845 the Osaka city magistrates promulgated a lengthy ordinance designed to enhance their regulatory powers over certain subcommunities of Osaka's believers and proselytizers.[5] In particular, the secular authorities focused their attention on "diviners, evangelists, vergers, sisters

---

5. Ōsaka-shi, ed., *Ōsaka shishi*, vol. 5 (Osaka: Sanjikai, 1913), pp. 1767–69.

of Buddha, and begging monks claiming association with the Shingon and Tendai sects." From the perspective of the city magistrates, too many problems and complicated situations arose when such persons came into Osaka. In particular, the decree suggests that the interlopers were trespassing on the pious endeavors that secular authorities had marked off as the sole preserve of the officially recognized association of mendicant monks and a similar organization for wandering diviners. An addendum reminds persons who claimed membership in those two groups that they were required to register either with the patriarchs at Daizōin on Mount Kurama or with the Tsuchimikado family of Kyoto, which served the imperial household and was entrusted with overseeing the affairs of fellow oracles everywhere in Japan. That done, the proclamation ordained, it would be "strictly forbidden" for anyone else to conduct any supplication or act of worship that was part of the exclusive repertoires of the mendicant monks and migratory diviners.

A further indication of the regime's desire to quash the contentious disagreements generated by the doctrinal jealousies and competition over mendicancies that broke out among the religious subcommunities can be seen in another clause of the city ordinances (*machibure*), which ordered the abolition of "temple teahouses" (*jiin no chadokoro*). That euphemism applied to crude places of worship set up by those evangelists and sisters of the cloth who rented lodgings in the merchant neighborhoods of Osaka. Such enterprising ecclesiastics apparently would place a Buddhist statue or other holy icon at a conspicuous spot on the street, hang out large paper lanterns inscribed with auspicious expressions, and welcome in pilgrims and other passersby for a moment of worship and a refreshing cup of tea—together, perhaps, with a hard-to-refuse suggestion about the religious merit that could be earned by dropping a contribution into a nearby offertory box.

Nishi no Bō, the headman we encountered earlier, registered his thoughts about such matters in a letter addressed to the priests at Daizōin.[6] "The members of my original group (*hongumi*) of mendicant monks," Priest Nishi declared, "are shocked, besotted with surprise." Previously, he went on to note, the government had announced that "the seven persons of my group were entitled to practice their traditional affairs without hindrance, and prohibitions against persons carrying out supplications in front of their homes were to be strictly enforced." Despite that, the cleric moaned, priests "affiliated with such temples as Tōji in Kyoto, Ryōkōji of Awa Province, and Kohanji of Yamato Province have been coming into the city. In order to solicit alms, they call themselves *Kurama gannin*, wandering monks from Kurama, and they pretend to

---

6. The missive is contained in the second volume of the "Ōsaka haika yōki," which primarily consists of the correspondence exchanged between priests at the home temple of Daizōin and monks in the city and is located in the temple archives at Kurama. At some time, archivists separated the materials comprising the "Ōsaka haika yōki" into eight volumes, each of which bears a serial number before the title heading. The first and the fifth volume have been lost, and the extant manuscripts cover the years between Tenpō 15 and Keiō 4, that is, from 1844 until 1868, except for the period 1854–1857 (Kaei 7–Ansei 4), which appears to be the province of the missing volume five.

be members of our brotherhood. Sometimes they even have set up so-called temple teahouses at the lodgings they rent from merchants." There, the irate Nishi no Bō continued, the newcomers "display Buddhist statues and icons and pester passersby for donations." Priest Nishi dubbed the unwelcome strangers a "new group" (*shingumi*), and he concluded his letter by expressing his hope that the authorities would evict them from their rented quarters by autumn and get matters under control.

At first blush, it is tempting to read Nishi no Bō's "besotted surprise" as a mere echo of the alarm about "outsiders" that was expressed in the 1672 document discussed earlier. The coexistence of the "original group" and a larger "new group" bespoke a differently nuanced historical reality, however. As the thirteenth item in the Notification of 1672 stipulated, the association of mendicant monks sought to restrain the activities of "outsiders" who were wandering the streets of Osaka and performing the same sorts of religious rituals as the association's members. The regulations of the late seventeenth century, however, extended exemptions to former masters who had detached themselves from the brotherhood and, apparently, to "outsiders" who had a letter of introduction "from our home temple" in their possession. Monks in that latter group, the Notification of 1672 implied, would be granted provisional membership in the Osaka association and would be permitted to beg and solicit alms on a temporary basis. Priest Nishi's letter of 1845 clarifies that procedure and indicates that such ad hoc arrangements had become more common with wandering groups of monks frequently taking advantage of the opportunities available to them in Osaka. That is, in the nineteenth century, bonzes affiliated with prominent temples of the Shingon sect—Tōji, for instance, had been established by imperial decree in 796 and was the headquarters for the Kyoto-based branch of that denomination—apparently were coming into Osaka in growing numbers. More than likely, those monks were only a temporary presence at first, but by the time Nishi no Bō penned his letter, they had formed a more durable "new group" whose continued presence in the city had become a constant irritant to Nishi no Bō and his "original group."

If the two factions sought their livelihoods in differing fashion, with the friars of Nishi no Bō's "original group" engaged in the traditional supplications associated with Osaka's mendicant monks while the members of the "new group" chiefly ran "temple teahouses," residential patterns further illustrate the cleavages that separated the two camps. A register compiled in the wake of the 1845 incident indicates that the newcomers rented rooms and apartments in scattered locations within Osaka and on the fringes of the city. In contrast, the twenty-three friars mentioned in the "Kuramadera shita ganningumi-chō" as being members of the "original group" in the year 1839 lived in Nishi Kōzu Shinchi, an area that stretched along the northern bank of the Dōton Canal, straddling its intersection with the Higashi Yoko Canal. They, too, were renters, and, as was the case with Nishi no Bō, the headman of the "original group," two or more monks sometimes lived at the same address.

Interestingly enough, Nishi Kōzu was adjacent to Naga-machi, a long, narrow, and down-at-the-heels residential quarter that ran off to the south of

Dōton Canal. Naga-machi's main claim to fame was its large number of cheap boarding houses. In Edo, mendicant monks known familiarly in the argot of the day as "dormitory priests" (*ryō-bōzu*) managed such barracks-like facilities. Those, too, were very humble lodgings, often established in abandoned buildings, where each evening beggars and vagrants spread out worn, threadbare tatami-mat covers and settled down to a meal shared from a common pot. It is not unlikely that Osaka's friars ran similar boarding houses, although such cannot be confirmed from the documents.[7]

The Monks in Osaka and the Patriarchs at Daizōin

The correspondence exchanged by the priests at Daizōin and the monks in the city, as found in the "Ōsaka haika yōki," permits an examination of the relationship between the priestly authorities on Mount Kurama and the members of the brotherhood as it existed in Osaka after the events of 1845. Particularly useful is an inventory of letters and various commodities that Daizōin's patriarchs and Osaka's mendicant monks exchanged during the year 1852, as summarized in Table 7.1. In general, money and seasonal gifts of food made their way up the mountain to the temple at Kurama, and symbols flowed back down the slopes. In the intercalary Second Month of 1852, for instance, the friars submitted their traditional and expected monetary offering to the prelates. Earlier in the year the brothers had included a gift of eighty turnips with their New Year's greeting, and in the summer and winter they sent refined white sugar to the patriarchs at Daizōin. The itemized listing that accompanied the more grandiose submissions of the intercalary Second and Eighth months divided the shipments into separate portions earmarked for Daizōin itself as well as for the head priests, the lay officials who assisted with religious services, and servant personnel who helped clean the grounds and care for the ceremonial accouterments.

In addition to the seasonal foodstuffs and money, the brothers in Osaka also labored to meet an urgent demand to contribute to an "Assistance Fund" to help repair buildings at Daizōin and to replace religious paraphernalia damaged by a fire in 1842.[8] At first, the patriarchs had instructed the friars to contribute a total of fifty *ryō* of gold, to be paid in five annual installments. The association in Osaka appealed to Kurama, and the head priests acceded to their request to reduce the donation to thirty *ryō* of gold and, in 1844, further agreed to stretch the payments out over a period of seven years. Even under those

---

7. My "Edo no gannin to toshi shakai" touches on the doss houses in Edo; for a discussion of the boarding houses at Naga-machi, see Shinshū Ōsaka Shishi Hensan Iinkai, ed., *Shinshū: Ōsaka shishi*, vol. 3 (Osaka: Ōsaka-shi, 1991), pp. 847–51, and Sugimori Tetsuya, "Kinsei toshi Kyōto to 'mibun-teki shūen'," in Tsukada, Yoshida, and Wakita, *Mibun-teki shūen*, pp. 323–61.
8. Details about the fire and the fund can be found in "Tōto haika yōki." This document constitutes the basis for our understanding of Edo's mendicant brotherhood. It is similar to the contemporaneous "Ōsaka haika yōki" and is located in the temple archives at Kurama.

Table 7.1. The exchange of gifts and letters between the Osaka association of mendicant monks and Daizōin in 1852.

Date	Gifts and letters
First Month, eighth day	The association of monks in Osaka sends New Year's greetings and eighty turnips to Daizōin; letters and offering arrive on the fourteenth
First Month, twenty-eighth day	The patriarchs reply to the greetings and send the elixir *en-meigan* to the mendicant monks
Intercalary Second Month, fourth day*	Monks send gifts of money and white sugar to patriarchs, lay officials, and temple servants at Daizōin; gifts arrive on the sixth day of the intercalary Second Month
Third Month, fourteenth day	Priests at Daizōin acknowledge receipt of goods sent by the monks the previous month
Sixth Month, second day	Monks send a letter politely inquiring about the health of the patriarchs during the season of intense summer heat; one bag of white sugar accompanies the letter; letter and gift arrive on the Seventh Month, sixth day
Seventh Month, tenth day	Priests at Daizōin reply to the solicitations concerning their health and the gift of sugar
Seventh Month, eighteenth day	The monks send to Daizōin a bag of squash grown in Kawachi Province; gift arrives on the twenty-eighth day
Eighth Month, second day	Priests at Daizōin send a reply to the monks in Osaka
Eighth Month, fifteenth day*	The monks send autumn greetings and gifts of money and white sugar to patriarchs, lay officials, and temple servants at Daizōin; letter and gifts arrive on the Eighth Month, twenty-second day
Eighth Month, twenty-ninth day	The priests at Daizōin reply to the greetings and acknowledge receipt of the money and sugar
Tenth Month, fifth day	The association of monks submits a register of its membership to Daizōin
Tenth Month, tenth day	Priests at Daizōin acknowledge receipt of the membership roster
Twelfth Month, twenty-second day	The monks send year-end greetings to the patriarchs at Daizōin; a bag of white sugar and two *ryō* of gold for the Assistance Fund accompany the letter
Twelfth Month, twenty-eighth day	The priests at Daizōin reply to the greetings and acknowledge receipt of the sugar and the donation to the Assistance Fund

*Appendices to the letters of greeting dated the fourth day of the intercalary Second Month and the fifteenth day of the Eighth Month indicate that the mendicant monks wished to make the following specific gifts:

	Intercalary Second Month	Eighth Month
To Daizōin:	100 *hiki* of gold	200 *hiki* of gold
	1 bag of white sugar	1 bag of white sugar
To Daizōin (from Kishimoto Bō):	1 *ryō* of gold	1 *ryō* of silver
To high priests:	50 *hiki* of gold	50 *hiki* of gold
	1 bag of white sugar	1 bag of white sugar
To high lay officials:	1 *ryō* of silver	1 *ryō* of silver
To minor lay officials:	3 *monme* of silver	3 *monme* of silver
To servant personnel:	2 *monme* of silver	2 *monme* of silver
Offering:	80 *monme* of silver	
Other (last winter's contribution to the Assistance Fund):	1 *ryō* of gold	

relaxed conditions, however, the brothers in Osaka had difficulty raising the money and could not fulfill their obligation to the Assistance Fund until the Sixth Month of 1859, some seventeen years after the conflagration.

At the beginning of every new year, each member of the association of mendicant monks in Osaka received from the high priests at Kurama a ration of the elixir *enmeigan*, "pills to lengthen one's life." Other than that herb potion, the friars received only letters. The patriarchs at Kurama sent the expected, courteous replies to the seasonal greetings and formally acknowledged receipt of the gifts, and they bestowed patents of appointment upon each new association headman and elder. Interestingly enough, although the brotherhood sent a roster of its members to the head temple every autumn, there is no evidence that the patriarchs penned any comments about the internal structure of the association in Osaka or issued any approvals authorizing the promotion of individual friars to low-level offices within the organization, as the high priests at Daizōin did in respect to the Edo association of mendicant monks. The lack of such notices probably means that the brotherhood in Osaka was so small in scale that it had established no permanent subranks beneath the position of elder.

At first glance, the relationship between the association in Osaka and the home temple at Kurama appears very one-sided. Certainly, the financial onus was the friars' to bear. Although the association's gifts and monetary contributions to Daizōin probably did not represent a significant proportion of the total revenues received each year by the temple and priests at Kurama, it would seem likely that the offerings constituted a substantial burden for the small band of mendicant monks in Osaka who, if their lodgings are any indication, lived on the edge of impoverishment. Moreover, the wording of the documents and letters makes it clear that the priests at Daizōin assumed a position of authority and dominance, and they took the lead in articulating the expectations and obligations that would apply to the brotherhood in Osaka. "One of the duties incumbent upon our subordinates," the patriarchs averred in one missive, "is to present formal, regular offerings to the home temple."

For all of that, the relationship with the prelates at Daizōin must have held some reciprocal value for the monks in Osaka. We might well expect that the friars drew religious and psychological sustenance from the patriarchs, and it is easy to suppose that the brothers' very identity, their standing within Osaka, and their legitimacy in the eyes of Osaka's governing authorities depended heavily upon the symbolic nourishment provided by the letters and gifts from Kurama. Still, the relationship was a delicate one, subject to the kinds of tension and periodic renegotiation exhibited in a dispute about the submission of offerings that broke out in 1851.

In the Second Month of 1851 Giben and seven other friars formally wrote to "The Honorable Nishi no Bō" and "The Honorable Kishimoto Bō," respectively the headman and elder of the Osaka association of mendicant monks. It was a somewhat unusual, and certainly bold, step for the ordinary members of the organization to address a formal petition to their leaders, and Giben and his colleagues tempered their temerity by heading their missive a "Letter of

Lamentation" that they were submitting "humbly, with all due respect." The recitation of polite phrases did not prevent Giben and the others from stating their request in the very first sentence of the letter—they wanted to postpone paying that year's contribution to the Assistance Fund for Daizōin. Giben's sense of urgency arose from the fact that the previous autumn had been "a season of extremely poor harvests" and famine conditions in western Japan. Grain shortages had caused the retail price of rice "to climb precipitously," causing hardship for "people in cities and villages alike." Since the people of Osaka had little money to spare, Giben and the cosigners of the letter continued, the mendicant monks found it "virtually impossible" to raise money through their usual supplications. In fact, the petitioners added, conditions were so horrible that it would be appropriate to reschedule all the traditional offerings and gifts due that spring to the priests and other clerics at Kurama. Events of 1837, they suggested, provided a precedent: during that famine year the prelates at Daizōin graciously had agreed to defer contributions. Giben and his friends ended their letter by requesting Nishi no Bō and Kishimoto Bō to convey their appeal to the prelates at Daizōin.

The headman and elder did transmit the petition immediately to officials at Daizōin. The patriarchs, however, had little sympathy for the plight of the monks in Osaka. The mere suggestion of a deferment, the head priests of Daizōin declared, was "preposterous, totally out of the question," and they even refused to accept officially the Letter of Lamentation. Back in Osaka, the scolding from on high did not deter Giben and his seven associates from pursuing a course they felt necessary if they were to survive hard times. In the Third Month they sent a petition directly to their superiors at Daizōin. They repeated the facts—economic conditions were deteriorating because of the extended famine, rice prices had been climbing steadily since the previous summer, and not many townspeople would pay precious money to have the traditional religious rituals performed. Even begging was not easy: it was nearly impossible to get people to let go of "the smallest coin"; appeals for charity were like asking to "get one's hands squeezed between rocks."

The persistence and touch of audacity that Giben and his colleagues demonstrated in pressing their appeal are mildly surprising considering prevailing norms and the long history of honoring dictates from Daizōin. The monks' tenacity must have impressed the patriarchs, however, for in the end officials at Daizōin accepted a proposal, put forth at the conclusion of Giben's letter of the Third Month, to defer presentation of the spring offerings until the Sixth Month. Later the high priests even agreed to revise that schedule, with the consequence that the association of mendicant monks in Osaka did not forward their usual gifts and the contribution to the Assistance Fund until the very end of the year. The following spring economic conditions improved, and relations between the prelates at Daizōin and the monks in Osaka returned to normal. The incident of 1851, however, illustrates the delicate balance that existed between the "divine protection" provided to the monks by the deities and patriarchs at Daizōin and the worldly, but appreciated, gifts of money and foodstuffs that the friars presented to their home temple, just as it reveals the fundamental assumptions that defined the symmetry of the relationship and held the prelates and monks suspended together in a normally harmonious and mutually beneficial equilibrium.

More Rivals: Renegade Monks, *Yamabushi*, and the Problems of Self-Identity

The particular tensions that energized and shaped the relationship between the head temple at Kurama and the association of monks in Osaka also were evident in the process by which the friars conceptualized their self-identity. The so-called Incident of Priest Kishimoto in 1858–59 brought such matters to the foreground. Matsu no Bō and Kishimoto Bō had served as the headman and elder respectively for the Osaka association of mendicant monks from the 1840s, but the two men had never enjoyed a close relationship. The documents hint only vaguely at the antagonisms that divided the two friars, but by the late 1850s Matsu no Bō was complaining openly that his assistant was making it difficult for him "to manage the affairs of the association." Kishimoto Bō, for his part, appears to have grown weary of his nemesis and, having reached the age of sixty, was ready to consider retirement.

The friction between the two reached a flash point on the second day of the Twelfth Month, Ansei 5 (1858), when Matsu no Bō appeared at the offices of the Osaka city magistrates to lodge a complaint against Kishimoto Bō. According to the offended headman, one of Priest Kishimoto's disciples, a novice who used the religious name Bunshō, had perverted his "occupational calling." Specifically, Bunshō had begun to associate with a *yamabushi*, a mountain ascetic named Washōin whose address was given as Shin Kyōbashi-machi in Osaka. It galled Matsu no Bō that Bunshō had remained a member of the association of mendicant monks even after he had taken a second name, Daiseiin, and had begun "to practice the daily rituals of Shugendō," the Way of Mountain Asceticism. That, in the eyes of Matsu no Bō, was degenerate behavior, a corruption of religious practices, and he called on the magistrates to put a stop to it.

In some ways, it is difficult to understand Matsu no Bō's ire. After all, Shugendō had coalesced as a coherent religious tradition several centuries earlier, and its members, the *yamabushi*, usually affiliated themselves with either the Tendai or Shingon sects. Moreover, the mountain ascetics and mendicant monks engaged in similar sorts of pious activities that were intended to benefit their home communities. The friars, for instance, went on surrogate pilgrimages to certain shrines and temples, while the *yamabushi* seasonally journeyed out of Osaka to visit holy mountains. Donning distinctive costumes that included a small black cap, a tunic with baggy trousers, and a collar decorated with tufts of colored fur, and carrying Buddhist rosaries and their trademark conch-shell trumpets, the *yamabushi* trudged into the deepest recesses of sacred mountains, where they practiced austerities thought to endow them with magical or holy powers that they could use to heal the sick and exorcise the possessed among Osaka's merchant and artisan population. In the end, as we shall see, it was precisely that rivalry over the prerogative to conduct surrogate pilgrimages that aroused Matsu no Bō's consternation.

Even Matsu no Bō himself in his petition to the Osaka city magistrates admitted that the Way of Mountain Asceticism and "the business of private monks" (shisōgyō) were "parallel occupations" (niyori no shokugyō). Still, he was nettled, perhaps because of some existing rivalry with the mountain ascetics, or perhaps because the disciple's divided loyalties complicated the problem of maintaining discipline within the association. In any event, the crisis resolved itself only after Daiseiin left the association of mendicant monks and "internal negotiations" resulted in Kishimoto Bō submitting his petition to step down as elder. Matsu no Bō accepted the resignation, and in the Second Month of the subsequent year, 1859, Kishimoto Bō "parted from the brotherhood."

The events of 1858 and 1859 recall an earlier dispute between the association of mendicant monks and the mountain ascetics that also might have been preying on the mind of Matsu no Bō. That confrontation came to a head early in 1853, after the monastery Kongōin, a part of the Kotohira shrine complex, constructed a new branch chapel near the Nishi Yoko Canal in Osaka. Originally, a subgroup of *yamabushi* from Osaka had undertaken surrogate pilgrimages to Kotohira Shrine on the island of Shikoku, where they acquired amulets inscribed with "the names of the great gods" for distribution to the faithful back in Osaka. At some point in the past, however, the association of mendicant monks had started to dispatch one or two of its members to Shikoku each New Year's to acquire sacred talismans to give out to their own "true believers." The opening of the new chapel in Osaka drew attention to the question of which religious group ought to enjoy the privilege of undertaking pilgrimages, and the *yamabushi* demanded that the friars set forth a history of their expeditions to worship Konpira at Kotohira Shrine and explain why they had intruded upon what originally had been a perquisite of the mountain ascetics.

To their chagrin, the monks could discover few good reasons to justify their conduct. Consequently, on the eighth day of the Second Month, 1853, Matsu no Bō and Kishimoto Bō jointly wrote "an urgent letter" to the patriarchs at Daizōin. After recounting the background to their current predicament, the two monks asked the prelates if they could recall how the surrogate pilgrimages to Kotohira Shrine had begun and sought specific advice about how to deal with the ongoing inquisition by the *yamabushi*. Quite obviously, Matsu no Bō and Kishimoto Bō were extremely concerned about the danger of a lawsuit, as is seen in their worried observation that the whole affair "might become a source of consternation to government officials." A subsequent letter dated the twenty-first day of the Third Month expressed even greater alarm. "The mountain ascetics might continue to harass us with difficult questions," the two monks in Osaka wrote. "Since the *yamabushi* might file a complaint with the governing authorities if we ignore their inquiries," Matsu no Bō and Kishimoto Bō pleaded, "please select some clever, eloquent monks and send them to us."

Eventually, the crisis bumped along toward a negotiated settlement. At one point in the spring of 1853 everything seemed to have been "resolved peacefully," only to have tempers flare up again. For a while authorities instructed the mendicant monks to refrain from their usual "daily rituals," and, additionally burdened by the "expenses" involved in continuing the confrontation, the brothers had to appeal to Daizōin for financial help. Finally, in the Fifth Month and without further government involvement, the two sides settled their differences: the *yamabushi* agreed to tolerate the New Year's pilgrimage by the mendicant monks, and the friars met demands to eliminate the expression Elephant Head Mountain, a popular name for the location of the Kotohira religious center, from the amulets they brought back to confer upon Osaka's merchant and artisan families.

The two moments of contention at the beginning and at the end of the decade of the 1850s illustrate the difficulties that the mendicant monks faced in projecting a distinctive religious personality. The brotherhood of friars in Osaka certainly was a discrete group that attempted to preserve its own self-identity in many ways: by living in near proximity to one another, by cooperatively deciding who could and could not enter the brotherhood, by maintaining a collective allegiance to the home temple at Kurama, by venturing out together onto the streets of Osaka to seek alms, and by obeying the rules of behavior as formulated by the patriarchs at Daizōin and confirmed by the Osaka city magistrates. But the dispute between the monks and the mountain ascetics over the issue of surrogate pilgrimages to Kotohira Shrine demonstrates that both engaged in religious practices that were nearly indistinguishable. The headman Matsu no Bō again admitted to that conclusion during his dispute with Kishimoto Bō when he confessed to the city magistrates that the Way of Mountain Asceticism and "the business of private monks" were "parallel occupations." Unable to sufficiently differentiate themselves from other similar groups whose pious activities also took them onto Osaka's streets, the association of mendicant monks found it difficult to claim an enduring monopoly over any particular set of special religious privileges.

In the Eleventh Month of 1798 the Osaka city magistrates issued an announcement declaring that they would not tolerate "corrupt clerics" in the city.[9] In recent years, the magistrates complained, bonzes "who consumed meat and cohabited with women" had been posing as "ecclesiastics of virtue" who practiced religious mendicancy. "From times past," the magistrates intoned, ordinances clearly had specified that only the brotherhood of friars associated with Daizōin at Kurama as well as "monks affiliated with the temples Gyōzanji and Rokusaiji" could carry out pious supplications in Osaka; for others to do so was "contrary to the law." Consequently, the magistrates instructed, the "corrupt clerics" either had to return to "an ordinary, secular existence" or else had to join the officially recognized association of mendicant monks or certify their affiliation with "the ecclesiastical brotherhoods at Gyōzanji or Rokusaiji."

9. *Ōsaka shishi*, vol. 4 (1912), p. 325.

The exact identity of "the ecclesiastical brotherhoods at Gyōzanji and Rokusaiji" is not clear, although it seems likely that the former were members of the monastery Saihōji at Nishigamo in Kyoto and the latter associated themselves with the temple Senbaji (Kōfukuji), located at Kami Yanagi-machi in the imperial capital. Despite that ambiguity, however, the document does confirm that those two groups had solicited from political authorities the privilege to conduct certain mendicancies in Osaka, just as the association of monks from Kurama and the *yamabushi* had done for their activities. The only other source of information about the friars from Gyōzanji and Rokusaiji comes from research on Edo, where they roamed the streets soliciting alms in exchange for their ritualized chanting of *nenbutsu*, the prayer verses offered to the Amida Buddha in hopes of obtaining salvation.

The problem of "corrupt clerics" also appeared in Edo. There, in the shogun's administrative capital, governing officials by the end of the seventeenth century had incorporated nearly all mendicant ecclesiastics, whether "corrupt clerics" or "virtuous priests," into that city's Kurama-linked brotherhood of monks. In Osaka, matters developed differently. Administrative integration did not take place in Japan's largest commercial city, where diverse groups continued to entertain, beg, and cater to the religious needs of the people of the city. In one part, Osaka developed its own religious personality because the *yamabushi*, diviners, sisters of Buddha, and myriad other clerics in the city cultivated particular specialties that they insisted were theirs to practice. In another part, street religion in Osaka retained its own distinctive flavor because the association of mendicant monks stressed the friars' uniqueness by living together in specific residential neighborhoods, by claiming an exclusive right to engage in certain pious endeavors such as leading memorial masses and participating in Kōshin observances, and by attempting to marshal the support of civil officials and the patriarchs at Daizōin behind their claims.

Despite the friars' best efforts to establish a particular identity for themselves, however, confusion about their persona remained commonplace. Sometimes, that was the fault of the brothers themselves, such as in the 1670s when some of them went around town garbed as deities, spirits, and apparitions, an appropriation of *henge kanjin* that associated the monks with the *hinin* outcasts in many people's minds. In similar fashion, the friars' insistence that they be permitted to conduct surrogate pilgrimages to worship Konpira at New Year's blurred distinctions between themselves and the *yamabushi*. At other times, visiting diviners, the dreaded "outsiders" mentioned in the Notification of 1672, and the despised "corrupt clerics" condemned in complaints during the early nineteenth century all poached on the brotherhood's religious preserve. As a consequence, the monks became difficult to distinguish from other groups whose religious mendicancies and street entertainments did so much to enrich the lives of Osakans, and the friars have passed into historical memory as just one among several groups that helped to create popular religion and fuse it with commoner culture during the early modern era.

APPENDIX

The Notification of 1672 (from "Kurama shita gannin yuishogaki")

NOTIFICATION

Item [1]: None shall transgress the rules as set forth by the shogun's officials. Any violation shall be reported to the political authorities immediately. Matters that are left to the discretion of the association shall be settled at a meeting of the headmen. If they are unable to reach a resolution, the matter shall be referred to the governing officials.

Item [2]: Gambling and games of chance are strictly forbidden.

Item [3]: The small Five-Striped shawl shall not exceed eight *sun* [approximately twenty-four centimeters] in width. Monks shall be permitted to wear shawls made of ordinary cloth and shoulder surplices inscribed with Sanskrit phrases; both may be decorated with gold threads. Monks are not permitted to wear shawls done in a knotted design or Five-Striped shawls interwoven with gold threads.

Item [4]: Outsiders (*tasho no mono*) shall not be allowed to join the association of mendicant monks (*gannin nakama*), even if they apply to do so. Persons of this locale (*tōchi no mono*) may be admitted to the brotherhood, but they need to be sponsored by a member and must receive the endorsement of the prelates at Daizōin. Prospective members shall be introduced to both groups that comprise the association and shall visit the home temple at Kurama. Afterward, in the company of the headmen, the monthly representative (*gatsu gyōji*), and the head of his five-man unit (*goningumi*), the inductee shall visit the appropriate government office and have his name entered into the official register.

Item [5]: Each master shall have no more than the single disciple who resides with him. After securing a sponsor and the approval of the priests at Daizōin, . . . [illegible]. One may begin to engage in mendicancies after his name is entered into the official government register; before that occasion one may not engage in any mendicant activity.

Item [6]: An inductee who does not reside with a master, but, rather, lives apart shall not, even upon admission into the brotherhood, take a vow to become the disciple of a master.

Item [7]: As for the number of mendicant monks, there may be no more than fifty persons in each group, including natural and adopted sons as well as disciples.

Item [8]: The general regulations allow the following mendicancies: to distribute at New Year's amulets obtained at Kurama; to make surrogate processions on behalf of patrons to shrines and temples while ringing gongs and chimes and there to offer masses for the dead; to undertake surrogate pilgrimages to Sumiyoshi Shrine between the Fourth and Sixth months; to undertake "dancing supplications" (*odori kanjin*) to the same shrine; to conduct masses for the repose of the dead during the Seventh Month; to recite *nenbutsu* prayer formulas to the accompaniment of chimes and gongs; and to chant sutras, write out sutras, and beg with rice bowl in hand. Groups engaged in such mendicancies shall not include more than four or five monks.

Addendum: If someone who is not a member of the association of mendicant monks undertakes any of the above activities, except for the distribution of talismans acquired at Kurama, prelates from the home temple will insist that he cease such practices.

Item [9]: It will not be a matter of concern if a person who has been a full-fledged member of the association leaves the brotherhood and continues to engage in the above mendicant activities, providing that person has received a special shawl embossed with Sanskrit prayer formulas from a temple affiliated with the Tendai or Shingon sects. If a person who is only a disciple in the association leaves the brotherhood, he may not receive a special shawl embossed with Sanskrit prayer formulas from a temple affiliated with the Tendai or Shingon sects and then engage in the above mendicant activities. Former disciples may engage in other kinds of similar supplications.

Item [10]: When a temple or shrine asks a member or members of the association to perform rituals, the brother(s) should request permission from both groups within the association. The rituals may be performed after the two groups give their approval. The falsification of requests is prohibited.

Item [11]: It is forbidden for several monks to gather and chant sutras to the rhythmic beat of hardwood staffs.

Item [12]: An ordinance against street preaching was issued in Edo in the remote past. Eight years ago, the commissioners of temples and shrines again instructed the association of mendicant monks in Edo about that prohibition. Likewise, street preaching is forbidden here.

Item [13]: If outsiders come into Osaka and engage in mendicant activities, ... [illegible] ... from the shogunal authorities ... [illegible] ... they

The Notification of 1672 (from "Kurama shita gannin yuishogaki") — 179

shall be investigated in accordance with official regulations. Outsiders who claim to have a letter of introduction from our home temple but who are unable to produce such a letter . . . [illegible] . . . investigated and shall be reported to the governing authorities.

Item [14]: If a member of the association goes to another region to carry out mendicant activities and does not return to Osaka by the scheduled date, the reasons must be examined carefully. [Illegible] . . . the association will make a report to the governing authorities and that report will be entered into the official register.

Item [15]: Members of the association may not rent lodgings, stand as guarantors, or provide introductions for anyone.

Addendum: Even if a begging cleric from another region makes contract with one of the brothers in Osaka, the brother will not provide the outsider with lodgings, even for a single evening.

Item [16]: At the grand meeting held once each year, the celebratory communal meal shall consist of a bowl of miso soup with vegetables, a dish of tofu, and a toast of saké for each brother. Other than that, not even side dishes of pickles may be served. No saké or sweets will be served when the brothers gather monthly to conduct the rituals of worship to Bishamon.

Item [17]: Each month the heads of the two groups and the monthly representatives are to meet and record in detail that month's expenditures and daily outlays in an account book.

The above regulations are to be observed absolutely.

[From:] Enzui, abbot of Jūfukuin Retreat
Representative of Kuramadera, head temple for the association of mendicant monks in Osaka

[Date:] Kanbun 12, Eleventh Month, twenty-seventh day

[To:] Headmen of the two groups comprising the Kurama association of mendicant monks resident in Osaka
The entire membership of both groups

CHAPTER EIGHT

Inari Worship in Early Modern Osaka

— *Nakagawa Sugane*
TRANSLATED BY ANDREA C. DAMON

During the early modern period, Inari Daimyōjin was one of the most widely worshipped deities in Japan. Certainly, his pedigree glowed with distinction. The earliest Japanese written works, the *Kojiki* and *Nihon shoki*, identify Inari as a manifestation of Uka no Mitama no Kami, Toyouke Ōkami, Ukemochi no Kami, and several other exalted Shinto gods whose names contain the ideographs *uka*, *uke*, *ke*, and *ge*, all of which refer in some fashion to the production of grains. The exact etymology of Inari's own name is not certain, but one theory holds that it derives from the phrase *ine nari*, the ripening of rice. In the popular mind, Inari's name and his close association with a particular group of agricultural gods singled him out as the primary deity of rice and cereals, the protector of the nation's harvests.

Inari's importance to the rhythm of the seasons and the cycle of life earned him enshrinement at Fushimi Inari Taisha from an early date. The Hata family, migrants from the continent who achieved considerable political and economic prominence after settling in the Kyoto region, established a place to worship its tutelary deity on Mount Inari, southeast of Kyoto, and shrine records maintain that Inari Daimyōjin, in the guise of Uka no Mitama no Kami, was installed there as the central deity on the First Day of the Horse (*Hatsuuma*) in the Second Month of 711. The Fushimi Inari Taisha, or Grand Shrine, as it became known, moved to the foot of the mountain in 816 and subsequently emerged as one of the most significant centers of worship in the Kyoto area, particularly for farmers of the area.

Inari's popularity continued to spread throughout the medieval period, as people came to revere him not only as the guardian deity of agriculture but also as the protector of commerce and the defender of certain artisanal groups, such as smiths. By the end of the middle ages believers could worship Inari in his various manifestations and guises at thousands of village shrines and at several major religious institutions, including Takekoma Inari Shrine in northern Japan, Kasama Inari Shrine in the Kantō region, Tokokawa Inari Shrine in central Japan, and Yūtoku Inari Shrine on the island of Kyūshū. At the same time, people began to associate Inari with the figure of the fox. One reason for that, perhaps, was that foxes possess an uncanny ability to sense danger and escape enemies, and such slyness and adroitness afoot made it easy for ordinary people to conceive of them as Inari's messengers.

Inari became an urban god in the early modern period when samurai and commoner alike moved into the castle towns and trading centers that sprang up across the country. Inari's conversion during the seventeenth and eighteenth centuries into a "popular deity" (*hayarigami*) venerated by members of all social classes heralded yet another redefinition of the god. Increasingly, Japan's urban residents understood Inari to be *the* Fox Deity, and they attributed to him the supernatural, occult powers that ancient folk beliefs bestowed upon that animal. Convinced that Inari could influence the course of events in this world, the ordinary people of Japan's cities built innumerable neighborhood shrines, often adorned with a stone statue of a fox, where they could beseech the deity to vanquish their cares and worries, set right their problems, and confer upon them blessings that would open up the prospect of a more hopeful future.

Most of our knowledge about the transformation of Inari worship during the early modern period has come from scholars working within the disciplines of religious and folk studies. Only recently have historians tried to sketch out the evolution of Inari worship over a broad temporal span so that we might better understand the dissemination of Inari worship, comprehend Inari's metamorphosis into a popular urban deity, and appreciate the relationship between Inari's burgeoning popularity and the social and economic dislocations that became increasingly evident during the course of the eighteenth century.[1] Most of the new historiography, however, has focused on the shogun's capital, Edo. But Edo, as several contributors to this volume note, was not Japan, and developments in the shogun's town did not always parallel events in the country's other major cities. Consequently, this chapter will extend the discussion of Inari worship to Osaka, Japan's merchant and commercial capital, in order to better understand the explosion of interest in that deity, the nature of this new veneration, and the reaction it provoked among orthodox religious institutions and government authorities.

THE DECLINE OF COMMUNITY SHRINES

The rise of Inari worship came at a particular moment in the latter half of the eighteenth century when local shrines, the traditional centers of religious ac-

---

1. Of particular importance are the studies by Miyata Noboru, "Edo no chōnin shinkō," in Nishiyama Matsunosuke, ed., *Edo chōnin no kenkyū*, vol. 2 (Tokyo: Yoshikawa Kōbunkan, 1973), pp. 227–71, and Ōmori Keiko, *Inari shinkō to shūkyō minzoku* (Tokyo: Iwata Shoten, 1994).

The Fox Deity at Fushimi Inari Grand Shrine. Photograph by Nakagawa Sugane.

tivity for most people, were on the decline. In the Osaka region, *ujigamisha*, or village and neighborhood shrines dedicated to the local deity who protected the inhabitants of a specific geographic encompassment, had occupied a central role in popular Shinto worship from the beginning of the early modern era.[2] In contradistinction to the geographically complicated relationships that often existed between Buddhist temples and their congregations, which sometimes came from a wide and spatially discontiguous area, worship at community shrines usually developed in tandem with a particular village's or neighborhood's emerging sense of itself as a distinct and coherent communal group (*kyōdōtai*). In general, most such local shrines did not own any sustenance lands or other property, and so the parishioners collectively shouldered the financial responsibility for their management and upkeep, using the income from designated village lands and from donations or solicitations.

A variegated priesthood ministered to the village and neighborhood congregations, at least according to such contemporary sources as census registers

---

2. The terms *ujigamisha* and *ubusunasha* are easily confused because they were used in different ways in the Kansai and Kantō regions. In the Osaka area, an *ujigamisha* was dedicated to the local god who protected all the residents of a particular village or urban neighborhood, and it served as the focus of worship for those persons; it is translated here as a community, neighborhood, or village shrine, depending on context. In contrast, such local shrines in the Kantō region were known as *ubusunasha*, and there *ujigamisha* referred to tutelary shrines dedicated to the founding deity of a consanguineous family group.

and the reports that local clerics submitted to shogunal authorities. Rarely did professional clergy live on the grounds of a shrine and conduct services on a regular basis, except for the few very large institutions whose worshippers came from a multitude of villages. Perhaps the chief reason that most communities went without a resident pastor was because they could not, or did not wish to, bear the expense of his household bills and the costs associated with his formal initiation into the Yoshida or Shirakawa houses, the Kyoto families who controlled access to respected sacerdotal titles. In the absence of a professional priesthood, most neighborhood and village shrines relied on prominent members of local shrine guilds, traveling clerics who went from town to town performing religious ceremonies, and priests who held appointments at more than one locale. Indeed, some communities did not consider it necessary even to have a priest preside over traditional religious services, and it was common for the lay primates identified with splinter groups of the Pure Land sect, Shugendō (the Way of the Mountain Asceticism), and other popular folk religions to supervise some community shrines.

In similar fashion, most neighborhood and village shrines could not support the regular complement of subordinate ecclesiastics who were necessary to the successful conduct of religious ceremonies and thus had to depend on the supplemental services of itinerant folk religionists. Even those community shrines prosperous enough to have a full-time priest, for instance, seldom could afford to employ on a permanent basis a so-called shrine maiden (*miko*) who performed the sacred *kagura* dances that constituted such an essential and popularly anticipated part of annual festivals at local shrines. Consequently, most village and neighborhood shrines simply hired a *miko* only at festival time, taking on either a young woman who danced at nearby large shrines or one of the more renowned "Ōhara maidens" who hailed from that mountainous district north of Kyoto and traveled from village to village, town to town.

However much community shrines contributed to the religious life of the neighborhoods of Osaka and the villages surrounding the city at the beginning of the early modern period, they began to lose their vitality during the eighteenth century, declining in importance as centers of communal worship. That trend was particularly noticeable in communities with highly mobile populations, where neighborhood ties were correspondingly weak. By the Kansei period (1789–1801), for instance, only a few neighborhood shrines in Osaka could count on enthusiastic backing from their parishioners. In reaction, many community shrines sought to redefine the divine roots of the local deities by attempting to link them with gods worshipped as imperial ancestors.[3] The same tendency could be observed in the farming settlements around Osaka, especially those that were becoming more urbanized as commercialized agriculture spread across the region.

The Ikota and Kureha shrines in the town of Ikeda provide a clear example of such a decline in religious vitality. Located in the Teshima District of Settsu

3. Inoue Tomokatsu, "Kansei-ki ni okeru ujigami, hayarigami to chōtei ken'i," *Nihon-shi kenkyū* 365 (January 1993), pp. 1–26.

Province, the settlement of Ikeda nestled along the banks of the Ina River and overlooked fertile rice fields spread out beneath mountains lying to the north. Blessed with pure water and easy access to well-traveled transportation routes, the community evolved during the early modern period into a prosperous local town where saké brewers thrived and a flourishing commodity market drew customers from the surrounding villages. The townsfolk referred to Ikota and Kureha respectively as the upper and lower shrines (*kami no miya, shimo no miya*), and roughly half of Ikeda's residential quarters worshipped at each. Both shrines could boast of a lustrous past and had earned mention in the *Engi shiki* (The Procedures of the Engi Period), the tenth-century compilation that provides such a wealth of valuable detail concerning festivals and rituals conducted under the auspices of the Office of Shinto Worship (jingikan). In addition, both Ikota and Kureha enshrined the spirit of Achi no Omi, a manifestation of the famous envoy Inatsu Hiko, who, according to legend, escorted two female weavers from China to Japan in the fifth century during the reign of Emperor Yūryaku, and who by the early modern period had become a principal figure in the Tanabata Festival.

Ikota and Kureha shrines were important centers of community worship at the beginning of the early modern era. The journal of the Kawamura family of hereditary priests at Ikota informs us, however, that worshippers started to shun the shrines' festivals in the early nineteenth century, as indicated by a steep decline in the number of vendors setting up booths and stalls on the feast days dedicated to the enshrined deities.[4] Furthermore, donations of money and crops from parishioners, traditionally a main source of support, began to shrink as well. That tightfisted attitude surely resulted from the economic troubles that plagued Ikeda at the time, as a depression in the brewing business and a general rise in commodity prices prompted townspeople to draw in their purse strings. Moreover, it seems likely that the economic gap between the town's wealthy merchants and its more humble residents was widening, thus eroding the communal spirit that previously had bound parishioners together and motivated them to lend financial support to the two shrines.

Kureha Shrine, in particular, fell on exceptionally hard times and could not afford to continue supporting its family of hereditary head priests. According to the journal of the Kawamura family, the presiding cleric at Kureha during the Bunka era (1804–18) was Baba Buzen. Originally, Baba made his living as a merchant and later moved to Kyoto to pursue a career as an artist. On a return visit to Ikeda one day, the desire to become a priest suddenly seized him, and Baba became affiliated with Kureha Shrine. At one point, he took as his adopted son Yoshida Hyūga, who had earned a bit of a reputation as the kind of entrepreneurial, roguish street preacher described by Yoshida Nobuyuki in the previous chapter. Yoshida no Hyūga had set himself up near the Kan-

---

4. The discussion of Ikota and Kureha shrines is informed by documents contained in Ikeda Shishi Hensan Iinkai, ed., *Ikeda shishi, shiryō-hen*, vols. 2 and 3, *Ikota Jinja nikki* (Ikeda: Ikeda Shiyakusho, 1968).

nondō temple, located at Shiraga-machi in the south of Osaka and home to both Buddhist deities and Shinto spirits. There Yoshida put out a statue of Saruta Hiko and his consort, Ame no Uzume. Saruta is a Shinto god who plays a key role in the Kōshin rituals conducted on that ominous night when, as Gary P. Leupp explains in Chapter 6, the "three worms" attempt to escape the human body and report one's misbehavior to the gods. The custom of staying awake during a Kōshin night was extremely popular among merchant and artisan families in Osaka during the early modern period. Moreover, Saruta and his wife were worshipped as symbols of a robust, satisfying sexual life, and many people came to pray in front of Yoshida's statue and to drop a hopeful coin in his collection box.

Enthralled, perhaps, by the fine reputation of Kureha Shrine, Yoshida agreed to become Baba's adopted son and promised to care for his new mother upon Baba's death. But Yoshida quickly became disillusioned with his future prospects. In Yoshida's estimation "Ikeda is a rough, uncultured town, very different from Osaka.... Kureha Shrine has a sterling reputation, but it receives very little popular support or respect." Yoshida, that is to say, felt disappointed in the townspeople's lack of religious faith and was frustrated by the economic hardship that religious disinterest imposed upon the shrine and its clerics. Discouraged, Yoshida looked into the possibility of being adopted into the family of a policeman or constable; unsuccessful, he moved to Kyoto, intending to perform *kyōgen* as a way to supplement the shrine's income. In the end, Yoshida Hyūga resigned his post at Kureha and drifted away to some unknown place. Despite the deflating conclusion to Yoshida's story, it is remarkable how both father and adopted son worked so hard to raise funds for their shrine. Not only did they take other jobs, but they also put Kureha's holy relics on display at leading temples and shrines in Osaka and hawked amulets inscribed with propitious sayings on that city's streets. Their ultimate goal was to ensure Kureha's future by creating an image that transcended its status as a relatively minor community shrine; that is, they sought to establish a reputation among the merchants and artisans of Osaka and to convert Kureha's deities into popular gods worshipped by great numbers of people, who then would financially support the shrine in Ikeda. Despite their best efforts, however, the two priests never were able to overcome the economic challenges that confronted them.

The prelates at Ikota Shrine, in contrast, scouted out a different path in their quest for financial stability. The Kawamura family had served as the hereditary head priests at Ikota for generations beyond memory, and they enjoyed a more intimate and firmly grounded relationship with their parishioners than did the clerics at Kureha. Capitalizing on those bonds of trust, members of the Kawamura family began to supplement their income during the Bunka-Bunsei periods (1804–30) by teaching calligraphy, managing rental houses, providing miscellaneous services to the town office, and pursuing other activities outside their traditional liturgical role. The priests of Ikota Shrine also ingratiated themselves with the Arisugawa no Miya family of Kyoto, an aristocratic lineage with influence at the Office of Shinto Worship, and they reframed and embellished upon the shrine's official history.[5]

In a complementary effort to enhance the shrine's prestige, the Kawamura family moved nimbly in 1815 when workers unearthed some ancient bones in a stone vault during renovations undertaken at Uho Inari Shrine, located to the south of Ikeda. Since local legend had long held that Uho Inari Shrine stood atop the tumulus of Inatsu Hiko, the Kawamura family acquired the remains and moved them to Ikota Shrine, dedicated to the spirit of that well-known figure. Disappointingly, however, few parishioners turned out to view the relics and make a grateful offering. Before long, the Kawamura head priest came to regard the bones as polluted, and he threw them into the woods. Meanwhile, the priests of Uho Inari Shrine garnered enough money by selling the stones from the tumulus to undertake extensive repairs of their halls of worship, which suggests that the people of Ikeda placed more value on maintaining that Inari shrine on the outskirts of their town than on demonstrating respect for the spirit of Inatsu Hiko at their own community shrine.[6]

The large-scale Ise pilgrimage (*okage mairi*) of 1830, which included persons from all over western Japan, and the wildly popular dances of thanksgiving (*okage odori*) that erupted in the Ikeda region that same autumn drove a further wedge between the priestly family at Ikota, bent as it was on making the shrine once again the religious focal point of the community, and the people of the parish, who remained disinterested in the Kawamura's efforts. The massive pilgrimage of 1830 to the abode of Amaterasu Ōmikami, progenitor of the imperial line itself, began in the intercalary Third Month when peasants in Shikoku reported that talismans from the Grand Shrines of Ise had descended upon them from the sky. That divine omen ignited the imagination of villagers and townspeople across western Japan, who abandoned homes and businesses to make the journey to Ise, alone and in groups, often with only a few coins in their pocket, so that they could give thanks to the gods for their august blessings. The enthusiasm of that year was nearly unimaginable, and by the time the maples had turned crimson perhaps as many as five million pilgrims had passed through the shrine gates at Ise. Just as the "Ise fever" seemed to be dying down that fall and farmers began to return to their fields and merchants to their shops, a new round of celebrations erupted in Settsu, Kawachi, and Yamato Provinces, as men and women poured onto the streets of their home communities to strut their stuff in ecstatic dances, the *okage odori*, which expressed both thanks to the gods for the events of that year and appreciation to neighbors whose largesse had comforted indigent pilgrims. That second round of celebrations peaked toward the end of 1830 but continued intermittently through the following spring, disrupting normal patterns of life and work for days and sometimes weeks on end.

5. Funagasaki Masataka, "Ayaha, Kureha densetsu o meguru shomondai," in Ikeda Shishi Hensan Iinkai, ed., *Ikeda shishi, kakusetsu-hen* (Ikeda: Ikeda Shiyakusho, 1959), pp. 345–404.
6. Inoue Masao, ed. and pub., *Ōsaka-fu zenshi*, vol. 3 (Osaka, 1921), pp. 1097–98.

The kagura *stage at Ikota Shrine. Photograph by Nakagawa Sugane.*

The carnivalesque festivity of 1830–31 deeply offended the priest at Ikota. According to the household diary, the head of the Kawamura family damned the Ise pilgrims for mixing immaculate religious motives with sometimes bizarre and frequently ribald behavior in a way that simply was beyond his ken. He looked with scarcely less askance upon members of his parish who thronged to join the local dances of thanksgiving, condemning them for wasting time and money and causing unnecessary trouble for the residential quarters that gave them gifts of food and drink. Even so, Kawamura more than once acceded to requests from the people of Ikeda to use his shrine's rather expansive grounds as a place to hold dances of thanksgiving, only to become cross when the revelers did not reciprocate his generosity with bountiful offerings to the shrine's coffers. Adding to the priest's ire was the fact that the annual presentation of sacred *kagura* dances attracted few worshippers.

Understandably, Kawamura experienced disappointment when his parishioners showed little interested in worshipping the local deity. More than that, however, the cleric felt alarmed about the bleak economic prospects that seemed to await his family and the shrine that it was supposed to preserve. If few people were visiting the shrine, even fewer were making offerings. The depth of Kawamura's concern about diminishing income was so great that he recorded the contributions to Ikota Shrine in minute detail in his diary, weighing the four *kanmon* of earnings that the grand shrine of Tenma Tenjin in Osaka received each day during its annual Sunamochi Festival against the scant two or three coins that he scraped daily from his shrine's collection boxes. The two shrines held the same official rank, Kawamura lamented, but they were as different as heaven and earth.

The Flowering of Inari Worship

As unpredictable and meager as those casual daily offerings at Ikota had become, the evidence suggests that they represented a much more important portion of the shrine's total annual income than ever had been the case. It was a disquieting moment, and the priestly family at Ikota Shrine realized that it was necessary to try somehow to bridge the gap that had opened up between the shrine and its parishioners. To that end, the Kawamura family decided to broaden the shrine's basis of support by enshrining on its precincts popular deities such as Benzaiten, one of the Seven Gods of Good Fortune and often represented as the muse of music and a defender against calamity, and Inari, whose popularity at the nearby shrine of Uho was so apparent. Most neighborhood and village shrines in the Osaka region faced a similar challenge at the beginning of the nineteenth century as their parishioners turned to popular gods and goddesses for the religious succor that the community's traditional Shinto deities no longer seemed to provide. Although the shifting tides of religious sentiment flowed across the entire Osaka region, the documentation allows us to follow the enshrinement of Inari at Ikota Shrine in some detail and thus to appreciate the subtle relationships that linked the rise of popular deities with other historical changes washing across Japan.

By the beginning of the nineteenth century people could worship at any number of Inari shrines located in Yamanokuchi, Kita Shinmachi, and numerous other towns and villages close to Ikeda. For example, entries in the household diary of the Inatsuka family, prosperous saké brewers in Ikeda, indicate that an Inari devotional confraternity (*Inari kō*) had become active in the town by 1791 at the latest.[7] In the Kyōwa period (1801–4), the members of that organization sponsored both the Hatsuuma Festival, held on the first Day of the Horse in the Second Month as determined by zodiacal calculation, and the Fire Festival of the Eleventh Month. Both of those celebrations honored Inari and were observed at a chapel established in his honor on the grounds of the Inatsuka's country estate, located at Yokooka on the slopes of Mount Satsuki. Furthermore, by the beginning of Tenpō period (1830–44), ordinary members of the surrounding rural community at Yokooka participated jointly with the devotional confraternity in the Hatsuuma Festival, and the Inatsuka family appointed a clerk to collect offerings, an unambiguous sign that Inari worship had attained substantial popularity in the Ikeda region by the beginning of the nineteenth century.

---

7. The documents can be found in *Ikeda shishi, shiryō-hen*, vols. 4 and 5, *Inatsuka-ke nikki* (1970, 1971).

Considering such circumstances, authorities at Ikota Shrine in Ikeda undertook to build a subsidiary chapel dedicated to Inari as part of a larger maintenance and reconstruction program that began in 1809 and concluded in 1811. Shrine officials held each neighborhood in the parish responsible for funding a specified portion of the project. A disruptive incident arose, however, when Hoshikaya Rokubei, an important saké brewer in the residential quarter Yanagiya-chō, refused to contribute to the building fund; as a committed Buddhist and longtime member of the Ikkō sect, he considered the worship of popular folk deities to be an abomination. Despite the saké brewer's standing in the community, one child from the quarter claimed to be possessed by the spirit of a fox and, in no uncertain terms, called Hoshikaya to account for his unwillingness to support the local shrine. As might be expected, some of the residents of Ikeda approved enshrining the Inari deity at Ikota and others did not, although this episode suggests that Ikkō adherents generally were on the side of the opposition. In the end, however, resistance to the new Inari chapel subsided after the possessed child castigated several other persons for dragging their feet. It seems clear, then, that many inhabitants of Ikeda had become enthusiastic about Inari's enshrinement, and latent dissatisfaction against anyone opposed to that move produced the local phenomena of fox possession.

Once the funding was in place, the merchant Aburaya Mohei, who was in charge of the construction project, journeyed to Fushimi Inari Taisha as a representative of Ikota Shrine. In a special ceremony, Aburaya received from the prelates of the Fushimi Inari Grand Shrine a paulownia box containing a sacred amulet signifying the presence of Inari and an accompanying Certificate of Authenticity, which constituted authority to consecrate the Inari chapel at Ikota Shrine. Those facts suggest that a lay parishioner conducted the enshrinement ceremonies and that the parishioners of Ikota Shrine constituted the main driving force behind the effort to have Inari enshrined at their local place of worship. Moreover, since the Inari chapel was situated a considerable distance from the main hall of worship at Ikota, we can imagine that while the priests at Ikota accepted the presence of the popular deity on their precincts, they intended to keep Inari worship segregated from the religious activities of the main shrine itself.

The consecration of the Inari chapel injected fresh enthusiasm into the religious routine at Ikota as neighbors in the nearby residential quarters came together to sponsor festivities at the new worship hall. For the Hatsuuma Festival of the Second Month, for instance, the residential quarters donated banners and lanterns to decorate the chapel, and home owners donated *mochi* and *manjū*, the pounded rice cakes and steamed bean-jam buns that are a staple of cold-weather celebrations, for distribution to festival-goers and to the ordinary residents of the town. In sharp contrast to the ill-attended celebrations of recent years that had featured *kagura* dances at the main shrine, home owners and renters alike thronged to the Hatsuuma Festival, and the coins tossed into the offertory boxes at the Inari chapel piled higher and higher, growing into a small mountain in the eyes of the shrine's clerics.

Torii marking the entry to the Inari chapel at Ikota Shrine. Photograph by Nakagawa Sugane.

INARI DIVINERS AND *MIKO* SHAMANS

The popularity of Inari worship among Ikeda's residents raised hopes among the chief priests at Ikota Shrine that they might successfully revive the traditional sense of communal spirit, which had fallen into such disrepair at the end of the eighteenth century, and reinvigorate the communal festivals that by custom and nature were supposed to take place at a local neighborhood shrine. However, the priests always kept themselves a step removed from the Inari devotions supported by the parishioners; persistently they preferred to see Inari worship merely as a pragmatic means to achieve prosperity for their shrine rather than as a legitimate form of religious supplication. The clerics' reasoning sprang chiefly from an unwavering conviction that the best way to reestablish Ikota's traditional prestige and authority was to advance the shrine's ranking in the officially decreed hierarchy of Shinto institutions.

Another reason, however, was also at work—Ikota's priests distrusted the supernatural aspects of Inari worship that, although not part of public festivals, played an extremely important role in private devotions. In particular, the Shinto clerics scorned the phenomenon, widely popular among the people of Ikeda, known as "the descent of Inari" (*Inari oroshi, Inari sage*) in which a person would consult an oracle, either a male diviner or a female *miko* possessed by the deity's spirit. The priests at Ikota endeavored to have as little contact as possible with that mystical side of Inari worship, but they were unable to avoid being touched by it after the consecration of the subsidiary Inari chapel on the grounds of their shrine.

Late on the evening the eighth day of the Seventh Month, 1817, the head priest of Ikota Shrine went to check on some worshippers who were lingering on the shrine grounds. The glow of oil lamps drew him to the nave of the Inari chapel, where he discovered "the carpenter Mohei, possessed by the spirit of Inari. A man identified as Abura Mo——— was also there, listening to the prophesies and posing questions to the deity through Mohei." "Abura Mo———" obviously refers to Aburaya Mohei, a leading sponsor of the construction program of 1809–11 and the person who presided over the consecration of the Inari chapel. The questions he had for Inari on the night on the eighth concerned the severity of an illness that had befallen his pregnant wife and the matter of selecting the best doctor for her. Historically, it was said, carpenters had a special affinity with deities, perhaps because they shaped special woods from the forest into sacred shrine buildings and constructed ordinary residences in accordance with Shinto building traditions, and the carpenter Mohei probably could be called a semiprofessional Inari diviner.

Besides the carpenter Mohei, other persons from Ikeda also possessed a special talent for communicating with Inari. Prominent among them was Araki Sakura, who was the daughter of Kōdaya Kōhei, a man of peasant status who lived in Ikeda's Tsukinoki-chō and also went by the name Inari Kōhei. Later Sakura began to call herself Tonoe, and together with her daughter Naka, who also used the name Sagami when appearing as a shaman, conducted seances and led prayer sessions to Inari. A famous local saké brewing family also claimed the surname Araki, and for a while that household caused a fuss, charging that the two *miko* oracles wrongfully were usurping its distinguished name, a controversy which shows that the two women never belonged to the upper strata of Ikeda's merchant society.

Other examples also testify to how widespread Inari worship had become in the town of Ikeda. In the Twelfth Month of Tenpō 4 (1833), for instance, an old woman visited Ikota Shrine and conducted an ablution and purification ceremony known as Nakatomi no Harae. According to the head priest at Ikota, that woman made her living performing Inari divination and prayers while serving concurrently as the shrine guardian at Tenjingū, situated in Tanaka-chō in Ikeda and dedicated to the spirit of Sugawara no Michizane, patron saint of learning and scholarship. The old woman once had lived near the Hirota Shrine in Nishinomiya but moved to Ikeda after losing her son, who had been an oracle for the Tsuchimikado family of Kyoto, diviners for the imperial household. In similar fashion Yasa, married to a farmer from Ozone village in the Teshima District of Settsu Province, took the name Miyamoto Orie and performed as a *miko* shaman at local Inari shrines. These types of Inari oracles and shamans carried out exorcisms and rituals of purification, presided over seances where they became possessed, and led prayer sessions at altars and miniature Inari shrines set up within their own homes, at chapels located on the precincts of Shinto shrines, and at the homes of their patrons. We also know from recent fieldwork by ethnologists that many folk religionists built small Inari shrines over the top of fox dens in the Osaka region and that countless other mystics divined people's fortunes while being possessed by the spirit of a fox.

Mountain ascetics, sorcerers, seers, clairvoyants, and all manner of other folk religionists also were busy communicating with Inari on behalf of grateful clients. According to the records of Nakamura Tokubei, a saké brewer living in Tondabayashi in Kawachi Province, the Nakamura family frequently got together with a certain Saichi, another man named Yamaguchi Kosaburō, and others from the nearby village of Shindō to worship the Inari deity enshrined in their various homes. Both at Nakamura's large town residence and at the more humble village homesteads, the faithful gathered to conduct divination and prayer sessions to Inari, to perform exorcisms and other rituals of ablution and purification, and to invoke Inari's spirit in order to fend off malevolent gods infamous for visiting illness and disease on the unsuspecting.[8] Saichi and Kosaburō had local reputations as holy men who maintained ties respectively with Hongan Aisenji chapel at Fushimi Inari Taisha and with the chapel Sanchikurin'in, located in the Yoshino mountain range of Yamato and Kii Provinces, whose slopes sheltered a multitude of temples associated with Shugendō.

Toyoda Mitsugi, whom the government condemned to death in 1829 for being a Christian, was another famous *miko* who presided over "descents of Inari." According to some accounts, Mitsugi was born in a village in rural Etchū Province and came from a long line of impoverished local Shinto ritualists. Driven by poverty, Mitsugi's family later moved to the capital, where her older brother became a self-ordained priest who, according to one contemporary observer, "passed through this sad world" by wandering around the city telling fortunes, performing ritual ablutions, and conducting other religious rites.[9] Mitsugi followed a troubled path to a similar calling: her family apprenticed her as a maid at age twelve; her first husband sold her to a house of prostitution; and her second divorced her. Despite all that, Mitsugi set up house with yet a third husband, but left him after she tired of his extramarital affairs. After all those years of grief, Mitsugi found herself alone and adrift in the Yasaka section of Kyoto, where the popular Gionsha (Yasaka Shrine) sat in the middle of a neighborhood of taverns and inns of less than shining repute. The principal deity enshrined at Gionsha represented a syncretistic manifestation of Susanoo no Mikoto, the native Shinto god, and Gozu Tennō, a Buddhist figure who had arrived in Japan from South Asia. Thus doubly empowered, the deity was said to be capable of pacifying vengeful spirits and sparing the people of Kyoto from illness, and Gionsha became one of the most popular shrines in the city. Impressed, perhaps, by the swirl of religious activity around her, Mitsugi decided to try her hand at fortune-telling and Inari div-

---

8. See the relevant documents in Ōtani Joshi Daigaku Shiryōkan, ed. and pub., *Nakamura-ke nenjūroku*, vols. 1–4 (Tondabayashi, 1986–89).

9. "Ukiyo no arisama," in Asakura Haruhiko, comp., *Nihon shomin seikatsu shiryō shūsei* 11 (Tokyo: San'ichi Shobō, 1970), pp. 58–69.

ination, practices she learned from Saitō Iori, a son of her third husband and priest at a Hachiman shrine in Ōmi Province.

Mitsugi and her disciples, women with names like Kinu and Sano, practiced their mysticism in the hills around the Fushimi Inari Grand Shrine. Their custom was "to bathe in the water of a well or a waterfall, climb a lonesome mountain in the dark of the night, concentrate one's mind, and finally become absolutely still in spirit."[10] After mastering such rites of asceticism, Mitsugi learned at least the superficial aspects of what she called "the Christian tradition" from Mizuno Gunki, a masterless samurai and devotee of Christ who lived in Kyoto. Morally rearmed, Mitsugi prospered, becoming rather well known for advocating that people use the power of prayer to improve their lot in "this sad world." Eventually, government authorities arrested Mitsugi and her followers and convicted them of using Inari divination as a front for propagating the prohibited Christian religion. Clearly, however, Mitsugi and her followers chiefly spread the mystical practices usually associated with Inari worship, as leavened by the few scraps of Christian beliefs and rituals that they had picked up from Mizuno.[11] In that regard, their faith might be understood as the beginnings of the formulation of a syncretistic new religion, not unlike Tenrikyō and Kurozumikyō, popular faiths that emerged in the late Tokugawa period and won great followings among the common people of central Japan.[12]

The number of Inari spiritualists proliferated during the latter half of the early modern era as *miko* became a common sight in the local towns and rural villages around Osaka. Several reasons account for their increased popularity. Surely many people found value in the oracles they dispensed. Moreover, spiritualists-to-be could learn shamanistic prayers and theurgical rituals easily, merely by observing other mystics, and it was not difficult for them to claim a special province over Inari divination since custom decreed that orthodox, properly ordained Shinto priests and Buddhist monks should not practice necromancy. Finally, most *miko* came from the lower rungs of society; indeed, divination and theurgy were among the very few occupations open to lower-class women in general and to the wives and daughters of poor folk religionists in particular. This meant that the *miko* were intimately familiar with the anguish and misfortunes that burdened their clients, especially those who lived at the economic margins, and could draw on their personal knowledge when speaking in the name of Inari.

Such shared experiences enabled the shamans to communicate easily with the common people, who relied on the folk religionists to perform Inari divinations when they were ill, overwhelmed by natural disasters, or beaten down by financial difficulties. Such persons were little concerned with the fate of their immortal souls but, rather, wished to receive instructions and help from

10. Ishii Ryōsuke, ed., *Oshioki-rei ruishū*, vol. 12 (Tokyo: Meicho Shuppan, 1973), pp. 161–63.
11. Anna Marie Bouchy, "Inari shinkō to fugeki," in Gorai Shigeaki, ed., *Inari shinkō no kenkyū* (Okayama: San'yō Shinbunsha, 1985), pp. 171–305.
12. Yamane Chiyomi, "Kirishitan kinsei-shi ni okeru Keihan kirishitan ikken no igi," *Ōshio kenkyū* 19 (1985), pp. 20–43.

the gods so that they could overcome the problems they were experiencing "in this sad world of troubles." Some practitioners, such as Toyoda Mitsugi, won fame for wielding supernatural powers and magically curing illness through their prayers. In most cases, however, as the examples concerning the merchants of Ikeda and the Nakamura family of Tondabayashi suggest, most diviners simply provided a medium for communicating with the Inari deity so that their clients could receive needed practical and worldly advice, such as which doctor to choose or where to locate a well in order to find good drinking water.

Inari Spiritualists and the Institutions of Orthodox Religion

It is not unusual for scholars to lump together the many different popular spiritualists of the early modern period who communicated with the dead, conjured up spirits, divined oracles, told fortunes, exorcised demons, exercised powers of sorcery, and worked their other acts of magic. Ultimately, of course, most such mystics did share common ground; the great majority placed Inari worship at the center of their religious universe and spent their time ministering to the needs of society's underprivileged. Although one might expect that those Inari folk religionists who emphasized the supernatural and catered to the needs of people far removed from centers of power and wealth would live in relative autonomy, in fact a variety of orthodox religious institutions and powerful families at the apex of Japan's religious establishment sought to exert control over subsets of popular spiritualists. The Yoshida and Shirakawa families of Kyoto, for instance, claimed jurisdiction over the folk religionists who identified themselves as practitioners of Shinto-based rituals; the Tsuchimikado house regulated the activities of oracles; and the *yamabushi* ascetics of Shugendō had to belong either to the Honzan faction, headquartered at the Tendai sect's Shōgoin chapel in Kyoto, or to the Tōzan faction, affiliated with the Sanbō chapel of the Shingon sect's great Daigoji temple located in the foothills around Fushimi Inari Taisha.

Such associations provided the folk religionists with access to the highest echelons of Japanese society. For example, Araki Sakura and Miyamoto Orie were listed as disciples in the ledger maintained by Shirakawa house, which instructed the two women in the proper worship of Shinto deities and authorized them to wear white ceremonial robes decorated with special cotton sleeve-cords.[13] The Tsuchimikado house oversaw the activities of Toyoda Mitsugi, considering her to be the successor to the well-known oracle Toyoda Tango. Interestingly enough, the names of other persons closely associated with the Tsuchimikado family also appear in the register of the Shirakawa house, suggesting that jurisdictional divisions were not always exclusive. Fur-

---

13. Kondō Yoshihiro, ed., *Shirakawa-ke monjin-chō* (Osaka: Seibundō Shuppan, 1973), pp. 311–17.

thermore, just as the priests at Ikota Shrine took advantage of their relationship with the Arisugawa no Miya family, Mitsugi exploited her connections with the Tsuchimikado and Yoshida families to gain entrée to other aristocratic households, seeking prestige and material benefit for herself.

Mitsugi, for instance, was a regular visitor to the house of the noble Yamanoi family, although she once became involved in an embarrassing incident while making a surrogate pilgrimage on their behalf to Kotohiragū, the official name for the home shrine of Konpira Daigongen and the pilgrimage destination for the mendicant monks discussed in the previous chapter. On that occasion Mitsugi clobbered a village official with a fan over a dispute involving a palanquin carrier, and she had to spend several days in jail.[14] The Yamanoi house certainly cannot be considered high nobility, since it held only the Senior Third Rank and received a meager stipend of approximately thirty *koku* of rice, but over the generations the Yamanoi built extensive ties with the lower classes to whom it dispensed licenses to make and sell certain patent medicines. Since Mitsugi garnered considerable income from her religious activities, it was perhaps the hope of tapping into her wealth that inspired the Yamanoi to overlook Mitsugi's sometimes outrageous behavior and to invite the shaman to its home on a regular basis. Indeed, social intercourse between affluent necromancers and struggling aristocratic households was not uncommon in the closing decades of the early modern period, and Mitsugi created an aura of prestige for herself by riding in a palanquin and surrounding herself with a retinue of sycophants when she visited the Tsuchimikado, Yoshida, and Yamanoi residential compounds in Kyoto.

As relations between folk religionists and aristocratic families became more intimate, the great Kyoto families struck up associations with the powerful religious institutions that sought to control Inari worship: Fushimi Inari Taisha on the outskirts of Kyoto, Kashima Inari Shrine (also known as Kagahashi Shrine) located just outside Osaka, and Tsumagoi Inari Shrine in Kōzuke Province in the northern Kantō region. For some time cordiality reigned. When the Shirakawa family decided to establish an Inari shrine at its household in 1785, for instance, it called on representatives from the Fushimi Inari Grand Shrine to preside over the consecration ceremonies.[15]

In the Bunsei era (1818–30), however, the prelates at Fushimi Inari Taisha become embroiled with the Yoshida and Shirakawa houses when each side asserted the exclusive right to conduct Inari enshrinements.[16] The head priests at Fushimi had acted first, staking out their claim at the end of the eighteenth century when folk religionists began to conduct unofficial Inari enshrinements on a rather extensive scale. In 1792, the theurgist Imamura Tanomo enshrined

14. *Oshioki-rei ruishū*, vol. 10 (1973), pp. 55–56.
15. Fushimi Inari Taisha Gochinza 1250-nen Taisai Hōshuku Kinen Hōsankai, ed. and pub., *Fushimi Inari Taisha nenpyō* (Kyoto, 1962), p. 247.
16. By this time the Yoshida and Shirakawa houses also were competing for the right to license unranked priests and to control the teaching of Shinto rituals; see Mase Kumiko, "Bakuhansei kokka ni okeru jinja sōron to chō–baku kankei," *Nihon-shi kenkyū* 277 (September 1985), pp. 63–93.

"Senior First Rank Toyokatsu Inari Daimyōjin," a manifestation of Inari, near a fox's den in a wooded thicket belonging to a farmer in the Kitayama section of Kyoto. When one of the Kyoto city magistrates inquired about the propriety of such an act, officials at the Fushimi Inari Grand Shrine replied that they alone possessed knowledge of the proper rituals, averred that tradition endowed them with the sole right to conduct all enshrinement ceremonies concerning Senior First Rank Inari Daimyōjin, and declared that consecrations by unauthorized folk religionists infringed upon the Grand Shrine's ability to control the transmission of its esoteric teachings.[17]

By the closing years of the Bunsei period, the prelates at Fushimi had to contend with more serious rivals as the Shirakawa family, whose head served as the chief official in the Office of Shinto Worship, set about fervently authorizing Senior First Rank Inari enshrinements. According to its household records, the number of consecration ceremonies performed by the Shirakawa house jumped suddenly in 1827, from the usual twenty or thirty a year to more than 230, and most of those involved the dedication of new Inari shrines and chapels.[18] At about the same time, the Yoshida house also began to sponsor Inari enshrinements in earnest, and the two aristocratic houses proclaimed that only they could authorize new places of worship for certain deities, including Inari, and concurrently took action to restrict activities by the clerics at Fushimi Inari Taisha. In reaction, the Fushimi Inari Grand Shrine lowered its profile in places like Ikeda, where historically it had been very influential in helping to spread Inari worship through devotional confraternities and had exercised a near monopoly over enshrinement ceremonies. Humbled, Fushimi's priests maneuvered to avoid a confrontation with the Shirakawa house, their intermediary to the Imperial court, by claiming that they were engaged merely in distributing protective charms to people.

At first the Shirakawa house focused its attention on supervising Inari enshrinements in the distant provinces of the Tōhoku, Kantō, and Hokuriku regions, and it oversaw surprisingly few consecrations of Inari in the area surrounding Osaka.[19] For instance, of the some 230 enshrinements carried out in 1827, just five took place in the towns and villages that lie between Osaka and Kyoto. That phenomenon perhaps may be attributed to the manner in which the Shirakawa house recruited the owners of certain inns to act as its agents in spreading the worship of Inari and prominent Shinto deities. In particular, the Shirakawa house attempted to enlist the goodwill of innkeepers who put up pilgrims journeying to the Grand Shrines at Ise and to the thirty-three temples and shrines that made up the Great Western Circuit (*Saigoku junrei*). Many of the travelers who visited those popular centers of worship came from the far-

---

17. "Inarisha jijitsu kōshō-ki," in Shintō Taikei Hensankai, ed. and pub., *Shintō taikei, jinja-hen: Inari* (Tokyo, 1991), pp. 364–67.
18. Konkō Shinsei, "Shirakawa-ke shokoku kansen todome," *Shintō shūkyō* 89 (1977), pp. 15–36.
19. "Shokoku kansen tome," manuscript collection, Konkō Toshokan (Konkōkyō Sect Library, Okayama).

off Tōhoku, Kantō, and Hokuriku regions and carried home with them a belief in the efficacy of Inari worship.

During the Tenpō period, however, the number of new enshrinements in the Osaka region increased steadily after the Shirakawa house began to offer incentives to its shrines and adherents to found new chapels dedicated to Inari. A large proportion of those consecration ceremonies took place within the city of Osaka, although several new shrines sprang up in the Teshima District of Settsu Province as well. The *miko* Miyamoto Orie of Ozone village in Teshima, for instance, served as an agent for the Shirakawa family, visiting farm families all across the Teshima District to dedicate household altars for the worship of Inari. Along with presiding over enshrinement ceremonies in farmers' homes, Miyamoto probably also acted as an oracle on their behalf, thus further widening her remarkably large circle of patrons.

The common people of early modern Japan generally welcomed the presence of Inari necromancers and *miko* like Miyamoto Orie, but it is also evident that such folk religionists experienced social discrimination. Thus, while the Shirakawa house accepted Inari devotees as disciples, it also forbade them to establish orthodox Shinto shrines, just as it instructed its pupils of mainstream Shinto not to become involved in divination or other mystical practices associated with Inari worship.[20] As the example of Kureha Shrine reveals, however, not much in the real world actually separated the priests of local community shrines from the oracles who communicated with Inari. Furthermore, we have discovered examples where *miko* who served as Inari theurgists simultaneously worked as guardians in low-ranking shrines. As we shall see below, however, the humble origins of Inari devotees and *miko*, and their apparent lack of formal knowledge about official Shinto doctrine, were not the only reasons that the Shirakawa house tried both to maintain a formal detachment from the practice of Inari worship and to make a sharp distinction between shrine priests, on the one hand, and Inari devotees and shamans, on the other.

Osaka as a Center of Popular Religion

The explosive increase in Inari worship evident during the late nineteenth century did not self-germinate in the rural towns and villages of the Osaka region. Rather, veneration of the popular deity flourished first in the city of Osaka and then spread into the hinterland, pollinating the stigmata that blossomed with such profusion into Inari chapels, festivals and midnight seances, and the processions of *miko* and diviners seen hurrying here and there in such remote locales as Ikeda, Tondabayashi, Shindō, and Ozone. The *Settsu meisho zue*, the comprehensive gazetteer-guidebook to the Osaka region compiled between 1796 and 1798, provides ample evidence about the growing popularity of Inari worship in Japan's leading commercial city. Nearly every single shrine and

20. *Ikeda shishi, shiryō-hen*, 3:1395–96.

temple included in that encyclopedic listing of places to see and visit in Osaka contained an Inari chapel within its precincts. Furthermore, believers could pay their respects to the deity at altars commonly found in the homes of merchant families and at chapels located on the warehousing estates maintained by daimyo in the city.

Significantly, large segments of Osaka's merchant and artisan populations came to believe that most manifestations of Inari worshipped at those private shrines possessed a special ability to cure particular afflictions or to offer certain kinds of divine assistance. Religious guidebooks such as the *Shinbutsu reigenki zue*, completed in 1824, introduced those deities to the people of the Osaka region and listed the miraculous interventions that were their specialties. Townspeople from the residential quarters that lined the banks of the Tosabori River, for instance, believed that prayers to the deity inhabiting Kasa Inari Shrine, situated within the warehousing estate belonging to the daimyo of Matsue domain, could help their children overcome bouts of smallpox.[21] Similarly, the deity who dwelled at a shrine located inside the residence of the influential Yasui merchant family, who lived on the northern bank of Dōton Canal, supposedly granted easy childbirth.[22]

A long history of Inari worship in Osaka's immediate hinterland had produced an environment congenial to the new religious sproutings evident at the middle of the eighteenth century. Some rural Inari shrines, for instance, first had come into existence as community shrines centuries earlier, during the late middle ages, when they served as the venues for autumn harvest festivals and other celebrations of the agricultural calendar. Examples include the Kashima Inari Shrine, mentioned earlier, and Tamatsukuri (Toyotsu) Inari Shrine, located on the banks of the Kanzaki River in an area that would become attached to Osaka's urban fringe by the middle of the eighteenth century. In addition, scholars long have been aware that Inari chapels found hospitable shelter within the precincts of temples associated with such mainstream Buddhist denominations as the Tendai, Shingon, and Jōdo sects. Moreover, the decades that bracketed the end of the seventeenth century and the beginning of the eighteenth witnessed the completion of several large-scale land development projects that opened up new fields on reclaimed river deltas in the Osaka region and along the valleys and highlands made arable by reengineering the course of the Yamato River. People considered some newly cleared spots to be hallowed ground, especially the wooded lots where foxes roamed and the hills that unexpectedly turned out to be ancient aristocratic burial tombs. Predictably perhaps, the faithful established new centers of worship at

21. Funakoshi Seiichirō, ed., *Naniwa sōsho*, vol. entitled *Keiroku* (Osaka: Naniwa Sōsho Kankōkai, 1930).

22. *Naniwa hyakuji-dan* in Kokusho Kankōkai, ed. and pub., *Shin'enseki jusshū*, vol. 1 (Tokyo, 1912), pp. 455–56. For examples of the sorts of powers attributed to manifestations of Inari enshrined in Edo, see Miyata Noboru, "Edo chōnin no shinkō," and James L. McClain, "Edobashi: Power, Space, and Popular Culture in Edo," in McClain, John M. Merriman, and Ugawa Kaoru, eds., *Edo and Paris: Urban Life and the State in the Early Modern Era* (Ithaca: Cornell University Press, 1994), p. 121.

such locations—villagers constructed Asakayama Shrine in 1704 on land made available by the diversion of the Yamato River, for instance, and others, according to an entry in the *Setsuyō kikan* (The Wonders of Settsu Province) dated 1706, built Mitsuana ("Three Hole") Inari Shrine near the abundant fox dens that once pockmarked the slopes of Sanadayama, a high knoll straddling the boundary between Obase village and Osaka city proper.[23]

As Inari worship became popular in Osaka in the middle decades of the eighteenth century, new religious tenets began to emerge. The proposition that different manifestations of Inari possessed certain specialized powers that could help ordinary people overcome the ordeals and hardships of "this sad world" was one of those. Moreover, the relationship between the Inari deity and foxes, an aspect of folk religion from at least the medieval period, became more fixed in the popular mind, as demonstrated in examples where people in the eighteenth century actually began to worship the foxes themselves. The ancient notion that foxes possessed a puissant spirit and supernatural powers stemmed from a belief that they have an intellect (*chi*) which approximates human wisdom and from folk convictions that sometimes credited the beasts with miraculous undertakings. However, people both scorned and feared the fox for lacking moral virtue (*toku*), a shortcoming which predisposed the animal to surrender itself to its selfish impulses and crude, base desires and to lash out maliciously at times against its human neighbors. Those common conceptualizations about the fox first appeared in ancient Chinese legends, but they also owed something to native folk beliefs, such as the idea that one could foretell an impending bad harvest by listening to the cry of a fox or by observing its manner of eating special offerings of food, as well as to the ghost stories and urban legends that spread across Japan at the beginning of the early modern period.

Religious tracts also promoted the cross-identification of Inari with foxes. One exposition published in 1700, for instance, raised the animals to the status of "empowered fox deities" (*kitsune myōjin*), even though it still referred to them as "wicked spirits" (*yokoshima naru kami*).[24] Moreover, that sort of flawed fox spirit, according to the text, still ranked so low in the order of things that it required instruction from humans. In contrast, a history of Inari worship in Yamashiro Province, written in 1761 by a holy man with ties to Fushimi Inari Grand Shrine, held foxes in higher esteem.[25] That cleric praised them as beasts of "holy virtue," recounted stories of foxes divining the future and faithfully honoring debts of gratitude, and concluded that it was proper to place one's belief in the moral rectitude that foxes represented. In this manner foxes became revered in Osaka, just as they did throughout all of Japan, as animals

---

23. Mitsuana Inari Shrine became very popular with pilgrims for the divine favors they received from the priests; see the *Setsuyō kikan* as reprinted in *Naniwa sōsho*, vol. 3 (1927), p. 17.

24. Fushimi Inari Taisha, ed. and pub., *Inari Taisha yuisho ki shūsei, kyōka chosaku-hen* (Kyoto, 1976), p. 15.

25. *Inari Taisha yuisho ki shūsei, hoi-hen* (1983), pp. 100–101.

who possessed "virtue," and people came to regard aged, white foxes in particular as deified spirits who inhabited a sphere somewhere between regular animals of the field and the god worshipped at Inari shrines.[26]

Popular culture also contributed to the growing fascination with foxes and the popularization of Inari worship. Wood-block prints, for instance, made urban dwellers familiar with stories about foxes. Likewise, during the Hōreki and Meiwa periods (1751–72) tales concerning the strange and supernatural powers of foxes became extremely popular additions to the standard repertoire of kabuki and puppet troupes. The drama *Shinoda-zuma*, for instance, made famous a white fox whom a certain Abe no Yasuna rescued one day from a stream where he was fishing. Grateful, the fox swore to repay the kindness and then vanished. Days later a young woman appeared at Abe's door and begged to work for him as a maid. Abe let the woman stay at his house, and eventually she bore him a child. One day the child saw his mother sweeping the yard with her tail and told his father. When Abe returned to the house, he discovered a note instructing him to visit the springs in Shinoda forest if he ever wanted to see her again. In all those various ways, then, the fox, first blessed with special unearthly powers in the legends of rural folklore, gained a greater following as its feats were retold and embellished in urban popular culture. By the middle of the early modern period, the fox finally had become sanctified as a holy creature, and the animals had come to occupy a central place in popular religion, so much so that most ordinary people commonly spoke of Inari as the Fox Deity.

Although the evidentiary record certainly testifies to the growing enthusiasm for Inari worship during the latter half of the eighteenth century, the exact reasons behind the deity's increasing popularity in Osaka at precisely that moment are less easy to fathom. It deserves note, however, that the spread of Inari worship and the fox's acquisition of new religious attributes came at a time when the people of Osaka felt increasingly divorced from the world of nature that previously had seemed always to surround and comfort them. Migrants from the rural countryside crowded into the city's residential quarters during the Hōreki and Meiwa eras, contributing to a growing urban population that reached its premodern peak in the 1760s. Moreover, some of those newly arriving families took up jobs as artisans or clerks in merchant shops but set up their households on the rural fringes of Osaka, thus pushing the physical boundaries of the city outward. At the same time, the Tokugawa government adopted a policy of encouraging schemes to increase the amount of cultivated farmland on territories it directly administered as a way of increasing the regime's tax base, and Osakans responded by sponsoring efforts to convert previously uncultivated areas on the edge of the city, as well as swampy areas around the mouths of the Kizu and Aji Rivers, into productive

---

26. In Mutsu Province in northern Japan as well, Inari worship came to be based on the veneration of foxes; see Miyata Noboru, "Inari shinkō no shintō," in Shimode Sekiyo, ed., *Nihon-shi ni okeru minshū to shūkyō* (Tokyo: Yamakawa Shuppansha, 1976), pp. 237–56.

"The Fox Woman Leaving Her Child," by Yoshitoshi. Courtesy of the Collection of John Stevenson.

rice paddies. Those projects, needless to say, drew still more newcomers from Osaka's more distant hinterland who populated the agricultural settlements that sprang up on the recently tamed land.

Those farming families, as well as the migrants who settled within Osaka proper and spilled over into the increasingly urbanized villages that ringed it, brought with them a wealth of folklore concerning foxes. However, urban growth and the creation of new farmland meant that Osaka and the half-rural, half-urban communities that surrounded it grew ever more separated from the world of nature, both physically and psychologically. As a consequence, the sight of a fox, which previously had been common even in the neighborhoods that bordered the Uemachi Plateau in central Osaka, became rare during the latter half of the eighteenth century. When the inhabitants of a residential quarter located on the banks of the Itachi Canal spied a fox in broad daylight in 1759, for instance, that event became the talk of the town. The people of that neighborhood captured the fox and tended to its needs for some time before releasing the unfortunate creature into the wild near Jūsō village, to the north of the city.[27] For the residents of Osaka, the fox was a symbol of nature, and the spurt of urbanization in the middle of the eighteenth century contributed to an impulse to deify an animal that seemed to be disappearing before one's very eyes.

Additionally, it is useful to recall the relationship between growing social unrest in Edo and the spread of popular interest in the Fox Deity in eastern Japan. In Osaka as well, the latter half of the eighteenth century was an unhappy period, as the people of the city and its environs lived through a trying sequence of unsettled weather, serious famines, riots protesting high food prices, devastating fires, and the human suffering and spiritual trepidation that followed in the wake of such disasters. As those events piled one upon the other, the influx of migrants mentioned above drove the population of Osaka to levels that the city's commercial production and infrastructure could not sustain and exacerbated inflationary pressures that impinged on everyone. The propensity of the government periodically to impose unscheduled, extraordinary tax levies on Osaka merchants and the difficulties experienced by wealthier peasants, who had provided a degree of stability in rural areas by carrying their tenants through hard times in previous generations, complicated matters and further eroded economic conditions in and around the city.

In the midst of such economic instability, few individuals or their families could count on a certain future, and many turned to Inari for help. Even the Osaka merchant families who previously had considered themselves as well-to-do lined up to have prayers read at Kashima Inari Shrine during the Hōreki years (1751–64), when the economic downturn drove them to the brink of insolvency.[28] The consequences of a deteriorating urban economy vividly comes to life as well in the *Shinpen: Hōreki zatsuroku*, which contains an account of a sickly, middle-aged clerk who seeks assistance from the Fox Deity after he falls out of favor with his employer, the owner of a shop purveying candles and other lighting supplies.

In the midst of such social distress and economic dislocations, the world of Inari worship could offer hope of an additional kind by bringing people together for festivals and other public religious ceremonies where they might make supplications to the deity and celebrate his blessings and advice. Thus, for example, the Sunamochi Festival held at Tamatsukuri Inari Shrine in the Sixth Month of 1789 enjoyed unprecedented popularity and marked the evolution of that celebration into a true communal ritual in which all the people of Osaka could participate. A spirit of play and an unforgettable lightness of being permeated the festival, and the participants spoke of it as an auspicious event, portending a fruitful year.

---

27. *Shinpen: Hōreki zatsuroku*, in Iguchi Hiroshi et al., eds., *Kamigata kōdan-shū* (Osaka: Kamigata Geibun Sōkan Kankōkai, 1983), pp. 98–99.

28. Ninomiya Masahiko and Sonoda Kōyū, eds., *Kaguhashi Jinja sennen-shi* (Osaka: Kaguhashi Jinja, 1959), pp. 112–18.

Inari Worship in Early Modern Osaka — 203

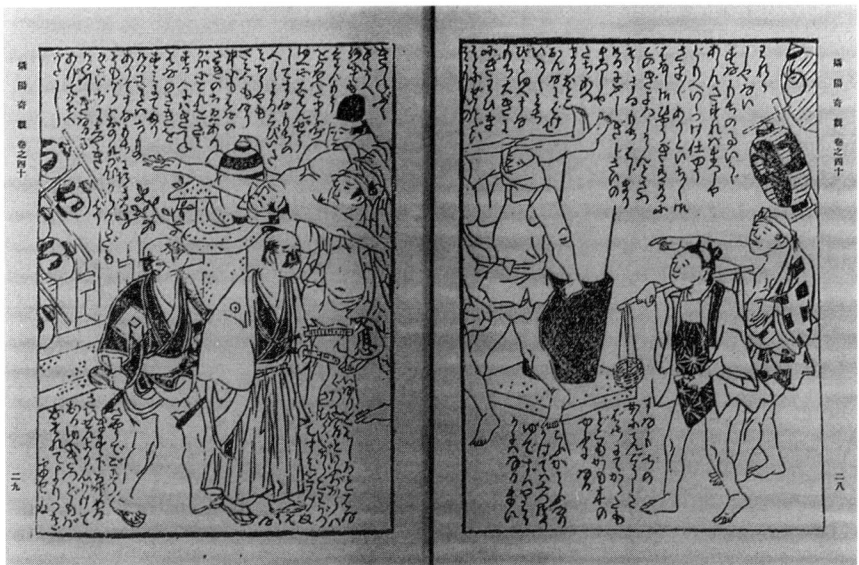

Mischief-makers at the Sunamochi Festival. From Setsuyō kikan. *Courtesy of Nakagawa Sugane.*

Picture books (*ezōshi*) and other publications of the time suggest the religious zeal that Osaka's merchants and artisans brought to such pious activities. During the Sunamochi Festival, for instance, various rumors made their way through the city, such as "those who shun the festivities at Sunamochi have black noses," and the festival-goers themselves drew up a set of rules warranting that anyone who made mischief with women or partook in other such illicit activities would be subject to divine retribution. Picture books that depicted "The Tale of the Sunamochi Black Nose" and "Tamatsukuri Inari Sunamochi Produces Great Luck and Prosperity in This World" enjoyed great circulation, and, according to one document, "from this time" members of the Osaka association of booksellers and independent dealers "sold picture books and broadsheets that went for a single *mon*."[29] Similarly, as that Inari fad mushroomed during the 1760s, popular opinion held that good would come to those who visited fifteen designated Inari shrines in the city of Osaka. That journey of worship became so popular that it was featured in broadsides publicizing pilgrimage circuits, and the number of member shrines grew to twenty-eight by the late 1770s.[30]

29. "Sashisadame-chō," part 2, in Ōsaka Furitsu Naka no Shima Toshokan, ed. and pub., *Osaka hon'ya nakama kiroku*, vol. 8 (Osaka, 1981), pp. 105–6.
30. Tanaka Tomohiko, "Kinsei Ōsaka ni okeru junrei," *Ōsaka Shōgyō Daigaku: Shōgyō-shi Kenkyūsho kiyō* 3 (1994), pp. 97–121.

Inari Travels from Osaka to the Hinterland

Given the combination of a favorable historical predisposition toward Inari worship and the new religious impulses reverberating in the city of Osaka, it is not surprising that as the eighteenth century approached its end people across the entire Osaka region became fascinated with the supernatural powers of foxes and increasingly turned to venerating Inari. The events at Ikota, the community shrine where Inari worship came to overshadow devotion to the traditional deities, and the appearance of *miko* and diviners such as Mitsugi and the carpenter Mohei amply illustrate that trend. So, too, does anecdotal evidence, such as reports that the number of persons worshipping at Kashima Inari Shrine increased dramatically after parishioners spread the word that the assistant head priest could evoke the spirit of a wild fox to exorcise evil demons. Written records contain similar accounts: according to an entry dated 1771 in the *Setsuyō kikan*, for instance, a manifestation of the deity known locally as Kojorō Inari lived on the pine-shrouded banks of the Yamato River near Nanba village and tended to the prayers of the villagers without fail.[31]

It is tempting to think that the activities of the oracles and *miko* who presided over "descents of Inari" may have been a critical precursor to the sanctification of the Fox Deity, although that remains a topic for future research. However, we do know that beginning in the Hōreki and Meiwa eras, the entries for Settsu Province in the *Shirakawa-ke monjin-chō*, a compendium of Shinto officialdom, began to include initiates and postulants as well as ordained priests, and from the 1790s through the 1810s the names of persons receiving "certificates of practice" appeared in ever increasing numbers. From that evidence, we can infer that a considerable population of Inari spiritualists and *miko* had begun to perform their mystical craft in Osaka and the surrounding countryside during the final decades of the eighteenth century.

A numerical count of shrines and chapels could provide a more concrete index with which to measure the diffusion of Inari beliefs. Unfortunately, no reliable listing of such religious centers exists for the latter half of the early modern era. It is possible, however, to use data included in the *Ōsaka-fu jinja-shi shiryō*, a compendium assembled in the 1930s, to document the history of shrines in Osaka Metropolitan Prefecture.[32] Incorporated in that collection of materials is an earlier account of the modern prefecture, the *Ōsaka-fu zenshi*, which draws upon such sources as Tokugawa period gazetteers and detailed reports about shrines and temples written soon after the Restoration of 1868. Table 8.1 employs the information contained in the *Ōsaka-fu jinja-shi shiryō* to show the most commonly worshipped popular deities in the Osaka area at the close of the early modern period and to provide an estimate of the relative number of Inari shrines. To suit the purposes of this inquiry, the data is rearranged to provide counts for the traditional, premodern provinces, with a

---

31. *Naniwa sōsho*, vol. 1 (1926), p. 425.
32. Tsujio Norihiko, ed. and pub., *Ōsaka-fu jinja-shi shiryō* (Osaka, 1933).

Table 8.1. Veneration of Inari and other popular deities in the Osaka region

	Village and other higher shrines		Unranked shrines and subsidiary chapels	
	Deity	Percentage of shrines	Deity	Percentage of shrines
City of Osaka and Settsu Province, excluding Teshima District (7 Districts, 542 villages)	Gozu Tennō	19	Inari	17
	Hachiman	11	Hachiman	7
	Tenma	9	Tenma	6
	Inari	8[a]	Ise	6
	Kasuga	7	Sai	5
			Kasuga	4
			Kotohira (Konpira)	4
			Ebisu	4
	Total number of shrines = 367		Total number of shrines = 898	
Settsu Province, Teshima District	Gozu Tennō	22	Inari	14
	Hachiman	16	Ise	14
	Inari	13[b]	Tenma	11
	Sumiyoshi	13	Hachiman	9
			Atago	8
	Total number of shrines = 45		Total number of shrines = 111	
Kawachi Province (16 Districts, 561 villages)	Hachiman	15	Inari	15
	Tenma	13	Ise	7
	Gozu Tennō	12	Mizu	7
	Sumiyoshi	6	Hachiman	7
	Kasuga	5	Kotohira (Konpira)	6
	Inari	1[c]	Tenma	5
			Kasuga	4
	Total number of shrines = 428		Total number of shrines = 510	
Izumi Province (4 Districts, 337 villages)	Tenma	17	Itsukushima	9
	Gozu Tennō	10	Ise	7
	Hachiman	10	Inari	5
	Itsukushima	7	Ebisu	5
	Kasuga	4	Kasuga	5
	Inari	4[d]	Konpira	4
			Tenma	4
			Gozu Tennō	4
	Total number of shrines = 587		Total number of shrines = 391	

Source: Based on Tsujio Norihiko, ed. and pub., Ōsaka-fu jinja-shi shiryō (Osaka, 1933).

[a] Uka no Mitama no Mikoto was the manifestation of the deity worshipped at 18 Inari shrines, Ukemochi no Kami at 5, Toyouke Ōkami at 3, and other manifestations at 2.

[b] Uka no Mitama no Mikoto was the manifestation worshipped at 3 Inari shrines, Ukemochi no Kami at 3.

[c] Uka no Mitama no Mikoto was the manifestation worshipped at 4 Inari shrines, Ukemochi no Kami at 2.

[d] Uka no Mitama no Mikoto was the manifestation worshipped at 4 Inari shrines, Ukemochi no Kami at 12, Toyouke Ōkami at 5, and another manifestation at 1 shrine.

separate entry for Teshima District of Settsu Province, which includes the town of Ikeda.

The tabulation is not without its weaknesses, even besides the obvious possibility that recording errors mar the data. In some locales, for instance, people venerated numerous deities at a single shrine, in which case the shrine has been assigned to the principal deity, if identifiable. Where that information is not known, the shrine has been included in the total calculation for the province but is not credited to any particular deity, a means of accounting that may underrepresent the proportion of shrines designated for the worship of Gozu Tennō, Hachiman, Tenma, Kasuga, and Sumiyoshi. Moreover, the calculations do not include Inari household altars, Inari chapels located within temple precincts, and shrines that escaped mention in official gazetteers, all of which are impossible to estimate even roughly. Finally, there is no reliable way to adjust the figures to take into account changes in the identity of enshrined deities and the status of individual shrines that occurred when the government officially separated Shinto and Buddhism at the beginning of the Meiji period.

Despite those limitations, the data do provide several clues that permit a greater understanding of the approximate number and type of shrines dedicated to Inari and other popular deities at the conclusion of the early modern era. First, we learn that there were at least 3,300 shrines in the Osaka region, an average of somewhat more than two for each town and village. Densely populated Settsu Province, which included the city of Osaka, had a disproportionately large number of shrines, most designated as unranked or as subsidiary chapels. In Izumi and Kawachi Provinces, however, Meiji officials categorized a comparatively large percentage of shrines as "village and other higher shrines," suggesting that they were rather large, independent establishments.

Shrines dedicated to Tenma, Gozu Tennō, and Hachiman predominated within the category of shrines ranked as village shrines and higher, accounting for nearly 40 percent of the total in each of the three provinces of Settsu, Kawachi, and Izumi. Looking closer, we find that particular deities won popular favor in different regions: Gozu Tennō in northern Settsu; Kasuga in northern Kawachi and eastern Settsu, which adjoined Yamashiro Province; Hachiman in the mountainous regions of southern Kawachi and southern Izumi; Sumiyoshi in the vicinity of Osaka Bay; and Tenma from central Kawachi into northern Izumi. In the aggregate, those leading gods from among the heavenly deities prevailed in the Osaka region.

Even though the percentage of Inari shrines trailed behind those dedicated to certain other popular deities, a relatively large number of Inari shrines provided a sanctuary for worship in Settsu Province, especially in Teshima District where Ikeda is located. The particular spirits worshipped at the various Inari shrines also form an interesting pattern. In general, parishioners venerated major figures in the Shinto hierarchy at Inari shrines ranked in the higher category. In particular, Uka no Mitama no Mikoto, identified as Kurainetama no Mikoto in the *Nihon shoki*, Japan's oldest official history, was the chief deity venerated at Inari chapels in Settsu Province; Ukemochi no Kami (Ōgetsu Hime no Mikoto) predominated in Izumi; and manifestations of Toyouke Ōkami, whose spirit resided at the Outer Shrine at Ise, appeared at many places of worship. The cross-identification of Inari with that particular set of deities, all of whom wielded influence over weather and the crops, for better or for worse, confirms that the people of the Osaka region originally conceived of Inari as a god of agriculture.

In contrast, popular deities such as Benzaiten, Konpira (also known familiarly as Kotohira), and Ebisu (god of commerce and guardian of fishermen and farmers) were present in conspicuous numbers at unranked shrines and subsidiary chapels. In almost all cases, those popular gods were latecomers, gaining enshrinement long after the original dedication of the shrine or chapel, in the same manner that parishioners introduced a popular deity to Ikota Shrine through the establishment of an Inari chapel. In that sense, the spirits worshipped at the small-scale unranked shrines and subsidiary chapels constituted the true deities of the early modern age. Moreover, Inari prevailed in the unranked and subsidiary shrines in Settsu and Kawachi Provinces, a sure indication of the widespread popularity of the Fox Deity.

Reining in Inari Worship

For a century and more after its founding, the shogunate attempted to wrap itself in Shinto doctrines in order to help legitimate its claims to political authority, but it did not advance any policy of strict control over popular religious sentiment. The state sometimes did act against Buddhist movements that it regarded with suspicion, such as when it proscribed the Fuju Fuse sect in 1655 and put many of its members to death. A decade later, in 1665, the shogunate issued the *Shoshū jiin hatto* (Ordinances Regarding the Temples of the Various Sects), which prohibited "new interpretations" and "strange doctrines" that broke with orthodox beliefs. That same year, authorities banned from Edo and other bustling urban centers wandering monks who chanted the unusual *nenbutsu* or other prayer formulas on street corners and in front of merchant shops, and the previous chapter discussed the regulations that Osaka's officials imposed on that city's association of mendicant monks in 1672. Somewhat later, in 1742, the shogunate went so far as to specify punishments for clerics who "gathered crowds" and advocated "peculiar heterodoxies," although sanctions tended to be mild, such as banishment from the immediate area. In contrast to its actions against iconoclastic Buddhist faiths, the shogunate seldom imposed any restrictions or punishments upon Shinto sects before the nineteenth century.

Beginning in the Bunka and Bunsei periods, however, the shogunate set about asserting more comprehensive controls over folk religionists such as the Inari adherents associated with Shinto sects. In 1810, for instance, officials at Nishinomiya, a village turned fledgling commercial town located on territory directly administered by the shogunate, rounded up the physician Shibukawa Shūsai and his followers and exiled them to lonely offshore islands after they were deemed guilty of conjuring wild foxes, indulging in matters of the occult, and coveting wealth.[33] In the Fourth Month of that same year, the city magistrates in Osaka announced prohibitions against the same activities that had earned the wrath of officials in Nishinomiya and included especially harsh sanctions against mediums who presided over "descents of Inari." In Edo, the authorities ordered the destruction of Sadakichi Inari Shrine in 1825, and two years later they forbade pilgrims from visiting Morikawa Inari Shrine after a "miraculous happening" began to attract large crowds that were difficult to police.

The Christian Incident of 1829, which ended with the conviction and punishment of Toyoda Mitsugi and her followers, represented an epochal event in the history of Inari worship. As described above, Mitsugi broke onto the folk religion scene as an Inari *miko*, a calling pursued by her pupils Sano and Kinu as well as several other women from Kawasaki, a settlement on the banks of the Yodo River that earlier had gravitated into Osaka's urban orbit. Ironically, the official who pressed the case against Mitsugi and her followers was Ōshio Heihachirō, then a police investigator working under the supervision of the Osaka city magistrates. As an uncompromising advocate of political and economic justice for the common person, Ōshio dedicated his police career to fighting corruption wherever he found it, and he gained considerable fame by breaking up prostitution rings in Osaka and rooting out Buddhist clerics deemed guilty of subverting Neo-Confucian orthodoxy. Later, that same sense of moral righteousness would turn Ōshio against the Tokugawa regime, which he came to condemn as the ultimate source of all political oppression and economic hardship, and in 1837 Ōshio became a people's hero when he rallied peasants around Osaka and attacked shogunal officials. In the late 1820s, however, Ōshio still proclaimed firm allegiance to the shogunate, and his peers initially hailed his determination to persecute Mitsugi and other Christians allegedly disguised as adherents of the Fox Deity.

The Christian Incident originated when Ōshio lodged charges of fraud against Sano. The policeman began to investigate the case intensively in the Fourth Month of 1827, and the trial of the women ended in the Eighth Month. At that point the shogunate's Supreme Court of Justice (hyōjōsho) entered the proceedings, and its officials passed sentence during the Twelfth Month of Bunsei 12 (1829). However, as can be perceived from the way that the case dragged on, it was not clear that Mitsugi and her disciples truly were Christians. Gradually, praise for Ōshio faded away, and his supervisor, the Osaka city magistrate Takai Yamashiro no Kami, even felt compelled to "rebuke the investigation." According to Takai, "in this case, it cannot be determined easily whether the accused are practitioners of Christianity," and the city magistrate asked the Supreme Court of Justice to reopen the proceedings.[34]

---

33. Mutō Makoto and Arisaka Takamichi, eds., *Nishinomiya shishi*, vol. 5 (Nishinomiya: Nishinomiya Shiyakusho, 1963), p. 746; Ōsaka Shiritsu Chūō Toshokan, ed. and pub., *Ōsaka hennen-shi*, vol. 15 (Osaka, 1973), pp. 321–22.

34. *Oshioki-rei ruishū*, vol. 11 (1973), pp. 492–94.

Although members of the court shared Takai's misgivings, they were reluctant to review the case. To overturn earlier decisions and suggest publicly that Mitsugi and her followers were not Christians, the court said, would raise "popular suspicions not easily dispelled" and potentially might lead to "a relaxed attitude toward official regulations that would be difficult to correct." Consequently, the court excluded from the official record certain awkward testimony, such as evidence that Sano had demonstrated her innocence by trampling on crucifixion tablets at Nagasaki, and concluded that the women were Christians, "just as they give the outward appearance of being." In the end, Mitsugi and the others received death sentences, although the women died in prison before the executions could take place. The shogunate then punished more than one hundred other persons connected to Mitsugi, considering them to be guilty by association.

It is unclear what prompted Ōshio to conclude that Mitsugi and her followers were Christians. There was no physical evidence, such as the possession of religious icons, that could tie the women to the proscribed foreign sect. In fact, the only material evidence unearthed during the investigation were the so-called Jesus Papers, which belonged to Fujita Kenzō, an Osaka physician. Those documents consisted chiefly of translations from Western medical texts, but fears about Christianity, that subversive foreign creed, ran so high in the late 1820s that the mere existence of such materials prompted some to label Fujita as Mitsugi's coconspirator. Nor was there convincing evidence that the women acted as disciples of Mizuno Gunki, Kyoto's famous calligrapher and self-identified Christian. To be certain, some years earlier Mizuno had instructed Mitsugi and her followers about certain Christian rituals and doctrines. Those teachings, however, were not related to Christian beliefs or practices in any meaningful way, and, in any event, Mizuno died in 1825, four years before Ōshio brought charges against Mitsugi.[35]

It may well be that even before launching his investigation Ōshio had made up his mind that Mitsugi and her colleagues represented a danger to social stability and to a political structure that he was sworn to uphold. Indeed, it is possible to see Mitsugi's group as a forerunner to the various "new religions" such as Tenrikyō and Kurozumikyō that proliferated in the final decades of the early modern era. Each of those new formulations venerated a transcendent, monotheistic god, maintained that supplications for worldly benefits constituted a legitimate expression of religious beliefs, and promised the construction of a new moral order that would free ordinary people from the temporal miseries fostered by incompetent officials, an unfair polity, and an unjust political economy. In that gloss, Ōshio's trepidation concerning the new religions may have prompted his unrelenting attack against Mitsugi and her fellow *miko*.

Mitsugi and the women may have had a very practical reason for studying the fundamentals of Christianity with Mizuno. Not all of Mitsugi's prayers cured illnesses and not all of her prophesies were accurate—as the oracle her-

---

35. Yamane, "Kirishitan kinsei-shi."

self admitted, she sometimes felt that she was "playing tricks on people, deceiving old men and women" when she "asked foxes to deliver blessings upon the common people and made Shinto offerings to calm those who were shaking with despair." In that context, Mitsugi's flirtation with Christianity can be seen as a simple attempt to acquire additional spiritual powers so as to improve upon the skills that were crucial to her livelihood and religious mission. Kinu, Mitsugi's pupil, also pursued Christian learning because she wanted, in her own words, "to help those suffering from illness and to bring prosperity to others, and of course to myself as well."[36] Consequently, Mitsugi and her followers felt constrained by the limits of Inari divination and desired to emancipate people from their suffering by acquiring higher spiritual powers. Furthermore, Mitsugi perceived that "descents of Inari," which she had performed for many years, were not entirely effective. That is to say, Mitsugi was beginning to reject the divinity of the fox, the core concept of the reformulated Inari worship that had begun in Osaka and swept across the region.

In combination, the above developments doomed any possibility of converting Inari into a transcendent, monotheistic deity. Mitsugi had performed her religious rituals and ceremonies in order to help ordinary people and to bring them some succor in this world of troubles, and in doing so she tried to conjure up a kind of Absolute Being whose nature surpassed by far the human attributes of "wisdom" and "virtue" previously assigned to the fox. However, Mitsugi's actual religious activities, such as prayer sessions, divinations, and rites of purification and exorcism, were no different from the supplications and acts of devotion undertaken by Inari *miko*. That fact suggests the possibility that a new populist religion could have evolved out of Inari worship, just as happened with the syncretic faiths of Tenrikyō and Kurozumikyō. In reality, however, Inari existed on a different plane than other popular deities such as Konpira Daigongen, the Buddhist-Shinto syncretic deity enshrined at Kotohira Shrine in Sanuki Province and widely venerated in the Tokugawa period as a protector deity, and Konjin (Konkō Daijin), the central deity of Konkōkyō, yet another syncretistic Shinto-based sect founded in 1859 in Bitchū Province by Kawate Bunjirō, who taught that all beings are equal and that diligence and selflessness will earn one countless blessings from on high. That is, Inari might serve as the nucleus around which fox worship could coalesce, but Inari was not capable of transmutation into an absolute supreme being.

The Christian Incident made all forms of Inari worship subject to government surveillance and imparted a serious blow to folk religionists everywhere. During 1829, the so-called three magistrates—the commissioners of temples and shrines, the Edo city magistrates, and the commissioners of finance—ordered investigations into the existence and activities of Christian cults throughout Japan, although in reality their main target was Inari worship. In the Third Month of the following year, officials in Takatsuki investigated the enshrinement of Inari in the homes of umbrella makers, and the artisans pre-

---

36. See the manuscript "Ōsaka kirishitan ikken" in the archives at Seishin Women's University (Seishin Joshi Daigaku).

sented an explanatory note stating that they were not Christians and that they did not perform delusive prayers or divinations.[37] Furthermore, in 1835 authorities demolished the household shrine of the peasant Chūzaemon, who lived in Miyake village of Tanhoku District, Kawachi Province.[38] In Uhara District in Settsu Province, the religious authorities of the great Honganji temple ordered the destruction of Inari altars in the homes of its adherents, on the pretext that they were acting in accordance with government directives to suppress heretical religions, an action that caused no little discord between the clerics and the village faithful.[39]

In similar fashion, leading authorities within the Shinto establishment began to issue exhortations against Inari possession and fox worship, and attempted to surgically remove those practices from Shinto doctrine and ritual. Perhaps in response to the shogunate's concentrated efforts to exercise closer regulation over Inari worship, the separation of fox worship from the veneration of Inari became the goal of many Shinto officials. Thus, in 1835 Ban Nobutomo, the renowned scholar-philologist and pupil of Motoori Norinaga, argued against honoring the fox as a beast that possessed people, averring instead that humans ought to respect the animal only in its capacity as Inari's messenger. At the same time, Ban warned against shamans and others who might manipulate those beliefs "to deceive and lead astray the ignorant people."[40] Moreover, Watanabe Masaka, a noted scholar associated with the Shirakawa house, declared that it was demented for humans, who stand at the forefront of all creation, to worship a four-legged creature. Rejecting the traditional tenet that equated foxes with virtue, Watanabe branded fox worship as an unforgivable heresy and labeled rural chapels as nothing more than "wicked little shrines stuck away deep in mountain valleys."[41] In response to such arguments and changes in attitude, people turned away from venerating Inari as a popular god who answered pleas from the common people for worldly benefits in the here and now, and, instead, began once again to emphasize Inari's attributes as a national, agricultural deity and to conceive of him as an amorphous, generalized spirit who stood guard over the harvest. The changing perception of Inari, advanced by such important arbitrators of religious fashion as the Fushimi Inari Grand Shrine and the Shirakawa house, found expression in the preaching of lower clerics and the activities of folk religionists, so that ultimately the revised ideas and conceptions from on high had a decisive impact on Inari worship at the popular level. Despite the enormous conceptual changes that took place, however, its critics never completely transformed the fundamental nature of popular Inari worship or drained it

---

37. Takatsuki Shishi Hensan Iinkai, ed. and pub., *Takatsuki shishi*, vol. 4, pt. 2 (Takatsuki: Takatsuki Shiyakusho, 1974), pp. 650–51.

38. Fujimoto Yukio, "Kinsei no Inari shinkō ni tsuite," *Hisutoria* 76 (September 1977), pp. 41–53.

39. Ashiya Shishi Hensan Iinkai, ed., *Shinshū: Ashiya shishi, shiryō-hen*, vol. 2 (Ashiya: Ashiya Shiyakusho, 1986), pp. 297–99.

40. *Shintō taikei, jinja-hen: Inari*, pp. 427–29.

41. *Inari Taisha yuisho ki shūsei, kyōka chosaku-hen*, p. 203.

of its worldly folk content, and today the veneration of Inari still occupies an important niche in popular religion.

From his ancient origins as an agricultural deity, Inari gained a new following in Japan's urban centers during the early modern period. In the middle decades of the eighteenth century, the merchants and artisans who lived in Osaka reinvented Inari, imbuing the old protector of the harvest with mystical powers, infusing him with recondite abilities associated with supernatural foxes, and transforming him into a god deemed capable of assisting people who were struggling through an era of social and economic distress. From Osaka, enthusiasm for the refashioned Inari spread outward in concentric circles, its transmission aided by diviners and *miko*—folk religionists who performed oracles, presided over "descents of Inari," and conducted other spiritual acts of necromancy that offered people the hope of obtaining worldly benefits. That sort of Inari cum fox worship replaced the traditional community celebrations held at local village and neighborhood shrines, which were losing their relevancy for ordinary people, or perhaps it is more appropriate to say that, in some cases, the emerging brand of Inari worship manifested itself as new communal festivals and rituals that parishioners welcomed with open arms and that supplemented and coexisted with the older, customary celebrations.

By the 1820s, the growing popularity of Inari raised for government officials and the leaders of orthodox sects the specter that Inari worship might evolve into a mass religious movement that would represent the antithesis of the moral principles underpinning the social and political order. Challenged, the governing regime and organized religion moved swiftly to regulate folk religions and suppress their leading spokespersons, such as Mitsugi. As a consequence, common people moved away from venerating foxes, the chief constituent element in the reformulation of Inari belief, and Inari worship lost its opportunity to develop into a monotheistic, salvational religion that offered the promise of a better life in this world. Nevertheless, that Inari worship has endured until this day provides, perhaps, a degree of evidence that the ubiquitous vermilion torii we still see around us are not mere stage props but, rather, constitute a means, however modest, for ordinary people to defy modern rationalism as it tries to crush underfoot the feelings of reverence toward nature, and to resist an omnipotent state that so often seems bent on denying happiness in this life.

CHAPTER NINE

Ambiguous Encounters: Ogata Kōan and International Studies in Late Tokugawa Osaka

— Tetsuo Najita

Widely acclaimed for its brilliant accomplishments in the literary and theatrical arts, Osaka deserves to be remembered equally for its bold assertion that international trade and the accompanying search for new ideas must be unburdened of prejudice and fear. This city of commerce—this "merchants' capital" in Wakita Osamu's phrasing in his concluding chapter to this volume—was a pivotal conduit, purveying to the rest of the nation ideas and objects from other parts of Asia and the Western world, brought by the Dutch to Nagasaki. The life of Ogata Kōan reveals a rarely told story about the international character of his adopted home city of Osaka. A leading proponent of Dutch Studies—Rangaku—Kōan studied European science and medicine in Edo during the early 1830s before establishing his own private academy in Osaka in 1838. Slightly more than two decades later, with Kōan's reputation as one of Japan's leading experts on Rangaku secure beyond dispute, the Tokugawa regime commanded him to go to Edo and assume the headship of a newly founded school of Western medicine. Having moved to Edo much against his will and desire, Kōan would die there suddenly the following year, in 1863, from hemoptysis.

Kōan lived through the turbulent decades that led toward the downfall of the Tokugawa shogunate. The momentous events of those years, when combined with the equally dramatic transformations that accompanied the rise of the new Meiji state, rendered Osaka (as well as dozens of castle towns across

Ogata Kōan. Osaka University Archives.

the Japanese countryside) "regional" and "provincial" in relation to an Edo that was being turned into the cosmopolitan capital city of Tokyo. But Kōan was a man of western as well as eastern Japan, and his career cautions us against being too quick to dismiss Osaka's profoundly important contributions to the vitality of late Tokugawa intellectual discourse, just as it flags the dangers of marking Japan's history at that critical junction exclusively in terms of the unproblematic separation of the globe into West and East, a division upon which much subsequent modern Japanese history and historiography have come to rely.

Ogata Kōan named his school of medicine and Dutch Studies in Osaka the Tekitekisaijuku, or the Tekijuku, as it is more commonly known. Kōan felt at home in Osaka partly because he frequented the city as a youth with his father, who managed the granary for the domain of Ashimori, located in Bitchū Province. But he also chose Osaka because it was a city of merchant commoners who were relatively open to independent study and teaching. And, as is clearly evident from the site of his academy, just a few streets from the shipping docks

The Tekijuku. Osaka University Archives.

where goods from western Japan arrived, Osaka was at that time the entrepôt for the most recent knowledge in Dutch medicine and science. Dutch envoys from Nagasaki en route to and from Edo to pay their formal respects to the shogun invariably spent their nights in Osaka at inns for the "red beards" which were close to the Tekijuku.

Large numbers of students from all parts of the country came to Osaka to study the Dutch language with Kōan. While some six hundred students formally registered at the Tekijuku over the years, most historians concur that several times that number actually studied with Kōan. Their primary interest, as was true of Kōan and his school, was to acquire the knowledge and skills of Western medicine. Mastering the Dutch language was considered the crucial first step in that process, but it also opened up the entire corpus of Western learning, and Kōan exposed his students to texts besides those directly related to medicine. Consequently, the students who studied at the Tekijuku went on to diverse careers. Ōmura Masujirō, for instance, used his knowledge of Western military science to organize the rebel army of Chōshū domain that finally overthrew the shogunate in 1868. When felled prematurely in 1869 by assassins loyal to the old domainal order, Ōmura held a status as military commander comparable only to the great Saigō Takamori himself.

Besides Ōmura some fifty other students from Chōshū studied at the Tekijuku, among them Kusaka Genki (brother of the famous activist Genzui), who prepared a lengthy report on coastal defenses for Chōshū and also stood at the forefront of the movement to establish smallpox inoculation stations in Japan.

Hashimoto Sanae served as an advisor to the lord of Echizen and advocated political reforms and the opening of the country, for which the shogunate executed him during the infamous Ansei Purge of 1858–60. Kōan's ties with Echizen were complex, and several of his students, Itō Shinzō most notably, taught Dutch at its domainal school, the Meidōkan. Others among Kōan's students became intellectual leaders of the Civilization and Enlightenment movement in the Meiji era, among them Mitsukuri Shūhei, who joined the Meiji Six Society (Meirokusha) and advocated Western learning and the reform of the Japanese educational system. Nagayo Sensai became instrumental in the promotion of hygienic studies, even coining the modern term for it (*eisei*) and serving as the first chief of public health in the new Meiji government. Sugi Kōji, to cite a final example, taught mathematics and introduced statistical methodology to the compilation of census data.[1]

Besides teaching Dutch and training future physicians and leaders, Kōan took a prominent role in the fight against smallpox and cholera. In that effort, he drew ideas from Western medical ethics that were harmonious with the ideals within his intellectual universe, and, as we shall see, he left a profound legacy in the shaping of medical ethics in Japan.

Forsaking Dualities: Ogata and Fukuzawa, Osaka and Edo, Past and Future

To a large measure, the reminiscences of Fukuzawa Yukichi, the great intellectual leader of the early Meiji period, have shaped our image of Kōan's Tekijuku. Born in Osaka, Fukuzawa shared with Kōan a similar social background —he, too, grew up as the son of a manager of a granary, that of Nakatsu domain. For a time in the 1850s, Fukuzawa studied Dutch and Western sciences at Kōan's Tekijuku before moving to Edo, where in 1858 he founded an academy of Western studies that he named Keiō Gijuku a decade later. Some fourteen years after that, in 1882, Fukuzawa started the *Jiji shinpō* newspaper, the capstone to a career of teaching and writing that earned him a reputation as Japan's most widely read social pundit and most staunch advocate of Western learning.

Fukuzawa's intellectual upbringing was syncretic, with influences drawn from such texts as the *Tso chuan*, an early compilation on Confucian times, as well as from the ideas of men like Itō Jinsai, often cited as the founder of the scholarly tradition known as Kogigaku (Study of Ancient Meaning), and Hoashi Banri, a follower of the naturalist philosopher Miura Baien. Banri's works commingled Western learning with tenets of Confucian and Buddhist

---

1. Details about Kōan's students can be found in Ogata Tomio, *Ogata Kōan den* (Tokyo: Iwanami Shoten, 1963); Momose Meiji, *Tekijuku no kenkyū* (Tokyo: PHP Bunko, 1989); Ban Tadayasu, *Tekijuku o meguru hitobito* (Tokyo: Sōgensha, 1978); Wakita Osamu, *Kinsei Ōsaka no machi to hito* (Kyoto: Jinbun Shoin, 1986), pp. 255–63; and Akagi Akio, *Rangaku no jidai* (Tokyo: Chūō Kōronsha, 1980). Also very informative is Umetani Noboru, Wakita Osamu, et al., *Ōsaka no gakumon* (Osaka: Isshinsha, 1980).

philosophies, and he fostered close intellectual ties with the Kaitokudō, the school for merchant youth founded in Osaka in 1724 whose curriculum centered on the study of Neo-Confucian texts. More specifically, Banri stressed the importance of mathematics, urged the translation of Western works on science, and prescribed education for all commoners, ideas that struck a special resonance with Fukuzawa and figured prominently in his later writings.

Fukuzawa's advocacy of Western-style Enlightenment thought included a broadside attack on religions and superstitions of all kinds, but his claim that this view was distinctive to him is exaggerated: the idea permeated the intellectual environment where he grew up. The attack on "spirits" was a consistent position taught by Goi Ranju at the Kaitokudō from the 1730s, and Yamagata Bantō condemned fallacious concepts in his great work *Yume no shiro* (In Place of Dreams), which he wrote over a ten-year period in the early 1800s. As late as 1848, just a few years before Fukuzawa studied at the Tekijuku, the last head teacher at the Kaitokudō, Namikawa Kansen, drew on that tradition to compile an instructional handbook whose title, *Benkai*, means to maintain reason against magic and superstition.[2] The common pedagogical ground shared by those scholars was an uncompromising insistence that the mind should question all ideas and books, religious and otherwise. Hence, it was better to have no books at all than to believe everything one read. That theme of provisional doubt, which is clearly present in Fukuzawa's writings on developing one's critical faculties through education, was part of the immediate intellectual milieu where he studied—the Kaitokudō being a few minutes' walk from the Tekijuku.

The historiography on Japan's modernization tends to situate Fukuzawa in relation to an Edo-based political theory whose origins usually are traced to the seminal Confucian thinker Ogyū Sorai. There is some justification for that, since Fukuzawa sometimes used language that appears to have been lifted almost directly from Sorai's writings. For example, this excerpt from a speech was obviously inspired by Sorai's treatise *Benmei* (Distinguishing Names), conventionally dated to 1717: "Education cannot alter what a man has been endowed with by nature. No matter how hard one tries, he will not be able to force a cucumber to bear an eggplant. The tiny wrestler in the lower ranks cannot ever become the champion no matter how hard he tries. Educators are not being honest when they claim that an education is all that is needed to turn a man into a great scholar or a great hero."[3]

For all of that, however, Fukuzawa readily admitted his identity with Osaka—a city where merchant scholars at the Kaitokudō often criticized Sorai sharply for lavishing excessive adulation on the ancients and for privileging elitist political values. As Fukuzawa wrote in his memoirs, he grew up speaking with an "Osaka dialect" and, more significantly, participating in Osaka's

---

2. A modern edition of *Benkai* has not yet been published. For views against superstition taught at the Kaitokudō, see my *Visions of Virtue in Tokugawa Japan: The Kaitokudō Merchant Academy of Osaka* (Chicago: University of Chicago Press, 1987), pp. 121–48, 248–84.

3. *The Speeches of Fukuzawa*, trans. Wayne H. Oxford (Tokyo: Hokuseidō Press, 1973), p. 174.

unashamed celebration of commerce and economic well-being. Above all, he did not have the slightest doubt as to the intellectual superiority of Osaka over Edo, as suggested in this passage from his autobiography: "Every now and then a student came from Yedo to Ogata's school to study, but never did anyone leave it for that purpose. If any went to Yedo, it was for teaching and not for more study. We often talked about this fact among ourselves, and said proudly that we, the Osaka students, were above any in the country. But it could not have been that all the good students gathered in Osaka and no able ones lived in Yedo. It seems to me that the situation of the country then created this contrasting standard of scholarship in the two cities."[4] Fukuzawa explained that variance between Osaka and Edo as being fundamentally political in nature. Students studying in Edo always were conscious of the political utility of their knowledge, so that "anyone able to read foreign books, or make any translation, secured the reward of ... patronage. There was even the possibility of a poor language student being made a high salaried samurai of several hundred *koku* overnight."[5]

Osaka, however, was different. Knowledge there was not pegged to immediate political patronage and utility. Learning Dutch had nothing to do with "gaining a livelihood or making a name for ourselves." Why then, Fukuzawa asked, "did we work so hard to learn Dutch? It would seem that we were simply laboring at difficult foreign texts for no clear purpose."[6] Unlike Edo, where the acquisition of knowledge invariably was tied to political advantage, in Osaka the students sought knowledge without such an explicit goal, which made their quest that much more intense and committed. In short, the very idea that the pursuit of knowledge should be divorced from political calculations was an ethic derived from Osaka, the "merchants' capital." This was a view of knowledge that Fukuzawa would adapt to a point of proximity with Western liberal thought and incorporate fully into his influential essays encouraging the individual pursuit of knowledge.

Here again, Fukuzawa's views resonated with other intellectuals in Osaka, such as the eccentric scholar Nakai Riken, son of a founder of the Kaitokudō, who interacted with the physicians and astronomers in Dutch Studies and engaged deeply in classical textual studies. To Riken, scholars with high reputations in Edo had compromised their integrity by accepting patronage from shogunal officials who showed themselves insensitive to the sufferings of the people. Riken's contemptuous attitude and high principles sparked an incident that became famous throughout Osaka—when Matsudaira Sadanobu, senior councilor in the shogunate, called on Nakai and his brother Chikuzan to hear their views about the state of the political economy, Riken refused to attend the meeting, condemning it as a shameless denigration of ethical integrity.[7]

---

4. *The Autobiography of Yukichi Fukuzawa*, trans. Eiichi Kiyooka (reprint; New York: Columbia University Press, 1980), p. 90.
5. Ibid.
6. Ibid.
7. Najita, *Visions of Virtue in Tokugawa Japan*, pp. 186–221.

Fukuzawa's attempt to distance himself from politics drew attention to the contrasts between his Osaka and contemporary Edo, dissimilarities that Riken and Kōan also appreciated. But Fukuzawa was being a bit disingenuous; his proposition that the pursuit of knowledge as undertaken at the Tekijuku was done solely for its own sake, with "no clear purpose" in mind, is not precisely an accurate representation of Kōan's teaching. Indeed, at the heart of Kōan's philosophy was the directive that knowledge, including the study of the Dutch language, had a utilitarian nature in that it was oriented toward the ethical and social purpose of saving others. In particular, Kōan argued that knowledge should be deployed to aid the poor, the indigent, and those who suffered from the depredations of this world—all the unfortunates who were embraced by the terms *saimin* and *kyūmin*. In his effort to orient his upbringing toward the Western Enlightenment, Fukuzawa tended to overstate the "anti-Chinese" dimension of Kōan's school, and for that reason he did not reflect sufficiently on the Asian epistemology and ethical philosophy underlying the quest for Dutch learning.

Indeed, the official name of Kōan's school, Tekitekisaijuku, was drawn from a Confucian tenet which may be transliterated here as the prescription of addressing the needs of the body and the spirit in ways that are most appropriate to their well-being. Kōan believed in the basic action ethic related to this idea, that to save others was a human imperative. It was a concept taught in all Confucian academies in the country and widely accepted throughout the intellectual strata of Kōan's society—it was also the essential intellectual drive underlying Dutch Studies. What energized Japan's scholars of Rangaku was not a simplistic wish to become more Western; rather, their hope was to uncover better ways to satisfy the ethical obligation to act on behalf of others. Thus, to somehow become "Western," as compared with other groups of thinkers who supposedly remained "traditional," did not call for a disengagement from the Tokugawa action ethic. Unfortunately, the intellectual debates of the post-Restoration era intensified the contrastive image between the two positions, as can be detected in this quote from Fukuzawa: "The only subject that bore our constant attack was Chinese medicine. And by hating Chinese medicine so thoroughly, we came to dislike everything that had any connection with Chinese culture. Our general opinion was that we should rid our country of the influences of the Chinese altogether."[8]

This memory of Fukuzawa's is misleading, however, since it presents Dutch Studies at Kōan's Tekijuku as being anti-Asian when such was not the case. Before they could enroll at the Tekijuku, Kōan's students were expected to master the principles of Tokugawa Confucian thought, undertaken at such well-known academies as Hirose Tansō's Enshirō in Ōita. Kōan believed that every student should study ethics based on the Chinese classics until the age of twenty-one. Only in that way, Kōan averred, could one construct a basis for seeking technical knowledge—a view somewhat akin to the nineteenth-

---

8. *Autobiography of Yukichi Fukuzawa*, p. 91; see also Wakita, *Kinsei Ōsaka no machi to hito*, p. 259.

century Western ideal of the liberal arts as being grounded in ancient Greek and Latin studies. When his own two sons circumvented that schedule and prematurely discontinued their study of the classics to turn their attention fully to Dutch, Kōan disowned them, an extremely harsh measure to take in Tokugawa times. Kōan's fury was clearly evident in letters referring to his sons' actions as reckless and disobedient (*fukutsu shigoku; daitan futeki no itari*), and it took much skillful negotiating by his wife Yae before Kōan's anger finally subsided.[9]

It is thus not surprising to find that Kōan's injunctions to his students conveyed a much different tone from the one remembered by Fukuzawa. Although Kōan taught that one need not accept the views and methods of traditional physicians, criticisms had to be delivered in good faith (*zen'i*) and with measured, sure evaluations that permitted no room for emotional outpourings. One of Kōan's credos as a teacher reads as follows:

> Toward fellow physicians be respectful and affectionate. Even if such might not seem possible, be restrained. Do not question another physician. To point out the weakness of another person is contrary to sagely wisdom. To speak with exaggeration about others is the limiting virtue of a small person. A person may simply criticize the excesses done in a day while we may lose the virtue of human life. What are the issues here? Each physician possesses the teachings handed down by his house and a methodology that is his own. These should not be recklessly criticized. Elderly physicians should be extended respect. Younger colleagues should be treated with affection. Those who wish to query the advantages and disadvantages of physicians from the past should base their decisions on actual effectiveness, and their healing methods should also be gauged with reference to observable illness.[10]

At another point, Kōan addressed the need to be decisive in making diagnostic decisions, but he also clearly underscored the importance of fully comprehending any treatment in process before deciding to intervene. For Kōan, the crucial issue never was to find fault with another physician, but always was to save the life of the human being for which the earlier physician had assumed ultimate responsibility: "When a patient discards a physician to whom trust had been placed and secretly seeks the counsel of another physician, do not carelessly take part in such a tactic. Unless the view of the previous physician is heard, do not go along. However, should a physician know there has in fact been an erroneous diagnosis and he still disregards it, this too is contrary to the responsibility of a physician. Indeed, when a dangerous illness is involved, do not be indecisive."[11]

---

9. Ogata Tomio, comp., *Ogata Kōan no tegami* (Osaka: Isshinsha, 1980), p. 13.

10. From "Fushi ikai no ryaku," in *Ogata Kōan den*, pp. 146–49; also quoted in Momose, *Tekijuku no kenkyū*, pp. 33–34.

11. "Fushi ikai no ryaku," in *Ogata Kōan den*, pp. 146–49; Momose, *Tekijuku no kenkyū*, pp. 33–34.

Kōan's compassion for another's life was quite sympathetic with the ethical teachings of the philosopher Itō Jinsai, who wrote that compassion (*jin*) must always be actualized outside the self as action or practice. Compassion, that is, was never a stable reference within the self but, rather, manifested itself as an activity, an extension of the process of endless life (*seisei shite yamazu*). Thus, for Jinsai, pure compassion for the other preceded authentication of the ethical self. One did not possess an innate ideal of compassion first and then practice it. Compassion was in the very exercise of doing good for the other in suffering. It followed that in acting to alleviate the pain and suffering of the other, compassion was carrying out love for the other (*jin sunawachi tasha ai*). Put differently, the value was in the act for the other, not the status or wealth of that other. Ogata Kōan phrased it thus:

> The work of the physician is only to help other human beings and not to promote the self. This is the basic tenet of the profession. Not seeking idleness or thinking about fame, one must simply abandon the self and pledge to save others. No other work is involved than protecting lives, restoring people from illness, and relieving their pain.
>
> When encountering a patient, see only the patient. See not high or low, poor or wealthy. Consider the gain within yourself in comparing the tears of gratitude in the eyes of the poor with the handful of gold given by the wealthy.[12]

In another statement, Kōan speaks specifically to the basic value of compassionate healing in the context of commerce: "Reflect on the lack of wealth of the patient. In seeking to extend life, should the capital that ties that life together be taken away, what sort of profit is there? Weigh this thoughtfully in treating the poor."[13]

As the previous quotations indicate, Kōan combined the ethic of compassion with a commitment to objective attitude and method, expressed in the ideographic compound *jinjutsu*. The expression usually is traced to Mencius, and it referred to the special skill that a benevolent prince possessed in governing so as to not cause harm to the populace. It meant ruling with the feelings of the people in mind.

Of special importance is the second ideograph in the compound, *jutsu*, which in Tokugawa times, as it does today, meant "method" or "technique," which in its more adaptive and expansive capacity functioned as a rhetoric equivalent for *gei*, a "skill" or an "art." For example, Ogyū Sorai and many other Tokugawa period intellectuals employed the phrase *gei ni asobu*, "immersion in the arts," to designate a range of methodological possibilities. Thus *jutsu* could apply to governance, ancient philology, market transactions, the

---

12. "Fushi ikai no ryaku," in *Ogata Kōan den*, pp. 146–49; Momose, *Tekijuku no kenkyū*, pp. 33–34.
13. "Fushi ikai no ryaku," in *Ogata Kōan den*, pp. 146–49; Momose, *Tekijuku no kenkyū*, pp. 33–34.

martial arts, music, board games, mathematics, painting, even printmaking. And it certainly included the disciplined work of physicians. In Tokugawa times, therefore, the compound of compassion and method, *jin* and *jutsu*, was synonymous with the art of compassionate healing and referred specifically to the work of physicians who, regardless of their social status—and many came from commoner backgrounds—dedicated themselves to caring for others.

The importance of being systematic in one's practice, of being sure of one's method, grew out of another epistemological postulate regarding the natural order. According to that premise, widely propounded in Tokugawa times, the entire natural order sprang from a single and infinite material energy, a ceaseless process of motion with neither a beginning nor an end. The vast universe was not to be cognized on the basis of a dualism of spirit and matter, physics and metaphysics, heaven and earth, or, in the most radical articulation of the theory, on the constant duality of male and female—rather, this gloss allowed only the single category of human life as natural energy meshed with other infinite life processes.

By reducing all conceptualizations to this single-energy theory of the universe, scholars deprived dualisms such as good/evil or life/death of their philosophical and theological significance as stable categories. That is, the theory compressed good and evil into goodness only, or into the relative propensity in humans to practice it, a prescription for action advanced earlier by such notable scholars as Itō Jinsai in Kyoto and Kaibara Ekken in the countryside near today's Fukuoka in Kyūshū. Similarly, the single-energy premise denied the dialectic of life and death and instead reduced the distinction between life and death—or, for example, the Buddhist view that life is impermanent while death is transcendent and eternal—to the notion of "life only" or "life-life only" (*seisei nomi*). Death, in this naturalist philosophy, could be comprehended only within the infinite process of life and renewal.

The life-only theory took on an ethical significance of its own when life was confirmed as a fundamental "gift" (*on*) of the natural order, a term obviously drawn from the tradition of popular Buddhism. One was born with that "gift," and the practice of compassion, the relative propensity in humans to feel empathy and hence to do things for others, was anchored to nourishing and saving that "gift" of natural life. The theory of life-only, in other words, necessitated ethical action in the world of everyday life. It sustained agronomy, or scientific farming, and it supported the call to revitalize the village community, a movement of considerable importance derived from this theory and identified with such diverse figures as Kaibara Ekken and the philosopher and agricultural technologist Ninomiya Sontoku. Most of all, the life-only abstraction lent powerful reinforcement to the ethical commitment to engage in the art of healing and saving human lives, to nourish the gift of life which was the blessing of every human being.

For those engaged in Dutch Studies, the life-only concept dismissed the ethical "why" question and addressed the methodological one of "how" to save lives. Whether one practiced Asian or Dutch medicine made little difference in this regard. Since the natural order was conceptualized as being infinite, with neither beginning nor end, human knowledge of that order always would be incomplete, limited, and relative in time and place. By that logic, human minds in the Tokugawa present knew more about natural phenomena than the ancients did; what intellectuals in the present did not understand, others would know eventually. Only knowledge of the infinite would remain forever incomplete. That is not to be confused with the Western idea of the progressive betterment of the material conditions of human existence. It was rather a theory of knowledge that recognized the limits of human understanding but challenged those boundaries in an effort to better nourish life. What the theory allowed was the recognition that the Dutch knew more about certain things. And while that knowledge was worth mastering, it, too, was relative, an epistemological presupposition that would persist into the early industrial era.

The question might then be asked, Why did their ethics and theory of the natural order lead Tokugawa scholars to the conclusion that it was the Dutch language they needed to master as a "method"? It may seem obvious that to acquire the knowledge of another society, one must first strive to become fluent in its language. Yet, it is not entirely self-evident that to learn and control a scientific method one must also master another language. Thus, the turn from the ethic of compassion to the study of the Dutch language as "method" deserves discussion.

The Beginnings of Dutch Studies

It may be well worth recalling that Dutch Studies grew out of an "historicist" movement begun by Itō Jinsai and Ogyū Sorai to search for and identify original or genetic propositions that might be embedded in ancient texts.[14] Where, such men asked, might one turn for answers if meditation and intuitive philosophical speculation about cosmology and metaphysical absolutes could not explain the origins of goodness or resolve the question as to why humans, alone among the species in the natural order, possessed history, rules, social hierarchy, and ethics? Practitioners of the "art of compassionate healing" followed the philological route to ancient texts to clarify those large epistemological issues. That meant shifting their focus from "modern" readings (that is, those that prevailed in China during the Song period, 960–1279) to more ancient practices of diagnosis and healing, especially in the prescription of herbal medication. But while to eighteenth-century scholars "contemporary" texts might have been overly metaphysical and misleading, unrelated to "physical" reality, ancient texts also proved to be less than satisfactory, or perhaps more to the point, were always excruciatingly difficult to decipher, frequently incomprehensible, and sometimes beyond empirical sense. To their

---

14. Fujiwara Noboru, *Nihon kinsei no kenkyū* (Tokyo: Hōritsu Bunkasha, 1971), pp. 69–75; Akagi, *Rangaku no jidai*; Haga Tōru ed., *Sugita Genpaku, Hiraga Gennai, Shiba Kōkan*, Nihon no meicho 22 (Tokyo: Chūō Kōronsha, 1971); and Grant Goodman, *The Dutch Impact on Japan, 1640–1853* (Leiden: E. J. Brill, 1967).

chagrin, the Japanese scholars discovered that the ancient prescriptions usually did not specify what illness was being treated and left vague which particular internal organ might be the source of trouble.

The shift away from the uncertainties of the ancient texts toward a concern with the concrete, physical human "body" as it presented itself to the physician is the point that marked the beginning of the complex history of Dutch Studies in Japan. How, the inquiry began, might one know with truthfulness the interiority of the human body as a physical "text," as a "grammar" of interrelated organs, that, in illness, careened into suffering and death? The conclusion that ancient language would not help was confirmed by pictorial evidence found in Dutch medical handbooks on human anatomy. The importance of "language" as a "method" or *jutsu*, however, remained intact in the epistemological shift that took place from ancient to Dutch texts.

The history briefly outlined above clearly indicates that Dutch Studies was deeply entwined with the Tokugawa Confucian discourse on history, language, and knowledge. It further suggests that physicians engaging in that discourse honored the secular ethic to "save others" out of compassion and did not harbor simple aspirations to become Westernized, as a great deal of historiography on the subject makes their motive out to be. Thus, "language" might continue to serve as the basis of national identity for certain scholars, such as those in the movement known as National Studies (Kokugaku) where a foreign language, whether Chinese or Dutch, constituted a source of contamination to the human interiority. Rangaku, in contrast, advanced the important concept of "language" as an indispensable "method" with which to accurately unscramble the grammar of the human body and thereby establish better ways to practice the art of healing.

The retreat from ancient texts to the view that the concrete human body contained the infinite life spirit coincided with the appearance of illustrated handbooks on human anatomy following the shogunate's decision in 1720 to lift its ban on Western books, Christian texts excepted. The newly imported volumes on medicine contained detailed drawings of internal organs and their relationships with one another. In a parallel development, Japanese physicians began to witness and take part in surgery and vivisection. A pivotal point in the evolution of interest in the new international learning came in 1771, when Sugita Genpaku, Maeno Ryōtaku, and a coterie of inquisitive scholars observed the dissection of the body of a female criminal executed in Edo and compared what they saw with information contained in a Dutch translation of *Anatomische Tabellen*, written by Johann Adam Kulmus in 1722. Impressed by the accuracy of its information, Sugita's group immediately began to translate the foreign medical text into Japanese.

Sugita and his circle, which came to include Nakagawa Jun'an, Ōtsuki Gentaku, and Katsuragawa Hoshū, had set a difficult task for themselves, for while many of their number would become luminaries in the Rangaku movement, in the 1770s they had only an awkward, beginner's knowledge of Dutch. As a first step, then, the translators set out to decode the Dutch language. Happily, they were able to identify certain basic linguistic features that aided them in their work. Dutch, for instance, was syllabic and hence analogous to the Japanese *iroha* phonetic system; sentences unfolded in a direct sequence of subject, verb, object, in a manner similar to Chinese; and the technical vocabulary was not itself Dutch but Latin, a mixing of languages comparable to the Japanese practice of placing Chinese ideographic compounds within Japanese grammatical constructions—a mode of deciphering sinographic sentences known as *kanbun* that proved especially pertinent. Sugita and his colleagues therefore turned to a widely used manual that offered guidance about rendering Chinese into Japanese. The primer was authored by Dazai Shundai, one of Ogyū Sorai's leading students in matters of political economy and, as one had to be in Sorai's school, a dedicated student of language. Entitled *Wabun yōryō* (1729), Shundai's guide stressed the importance of discovering the "principle" in a language as the basic first step in the decoding process. Thus, while Shundai referred to "Chinese prose" or *kanbun*, Sugita's seminar cited "Western prose," *seibun*.

Despite constant fear of surveillance and arrest by shogunal authorities for having taken part in an illegal autopsy, Sugita and his fellow scholars in 1774 produced the *Kaitai shinsho* (A New Text on Human Anatomy). Some forty years later, in 1815, Sugita detailed the arduous struggle to complete the first Japanese rendering of a European medical work in his *Rangaku kotohajime* (The Beginnings of Rangaku),[15] and he noted with satisfaction that *Kaitai shinsho* had become a standard reference in every domainal school in the country. How a group of inquisitive and dedicated physicians, on their own and armed only with a rudimentary guide to comprehending a foreign language, managed to translate a complicated and detailed text on Western medicine into Japanese is, of course, one of the great triumphs within Tokugawa intellectual history, and it would be erroneous to disengage that accomplishment from the broader discourse on knowledge. Moreover, Sugita and his companions did not see the study of the Dutch language as a departure from Asia or from national history. They stayed fundamentally anchored to the ethical purpose of compassionate healing, and the commitment to language study remained as the basic, crucial method, the *jutsu*, for achieving that end.

In that context, it is also important to remember that the appearance of *Kaitai shinsho* stimulated the preparation of additional reference aids for translating Dutch, such as Ōtsuki Gentaku's *Rangaku kaitei* (1788) and *Ranshaku teikō* (1817), works that circulated in manuscript well before publication. One especially significant undertaking, directed by Ōtsuki's student Inamura Sanpaku, was the completion in 1796 of a twenty-seven-volume Dutch-Japanese dictionary containing eighty thousand entries and entitled *Haruma wage* (Halma Translated), a rendering into Dutch-Japanese of the Dutch-French dictionary

---

15. Sugita's work has been translated into English as *Dawn of Western Science in Japan, or Rangaku Kotohajime*, trans. Ryozo Matsumoto, supervised by Tomio Ogata (Tokyo: Hokuseidō, 1969).

Woordenboek der Nederduitsche en Fransche Taalen (1708) edited by François Halma. Variations of Inamura's work appeared as *Edo Haruma* and *Nagasaki Haruma*, the latter also known as *Zūfu Haruma*, after its editor, Henkrik Doeff (Zūfu), who served as the director of the Dutch trading outpost at Nagasaki from 1803 to 1817. Those dictionaries, like Sugita's textbook on anatomy, became basic manuals in domainal schools and private academies in the late Tokugawa period. It is worth noting in passing that students called one of the "dreaded" study rooms at Kōan's Tekijuku the "Zūfu room."

The new Rangaku was not without its critics. The main charge levied against Dutch medicine concerned its limitations; it excelled in anatomy and invasive surgery, its opponents argued, but did not demonstrate dramatic superiority in therapeutic and internal medicine. As the controversy escalated, the distinction between surgery and internal medicine—between *geka* and *naika*—became part of Japan's scientific vocabulary. There was some validity to that reproach. The physicians in the employ of the Royal Dutch Navy stationed at Nagasaki were mainly military physicians and specialists in anatomy and surgery, and their appeal to Japanese physicians may have been in this shared history of military strife. But in truth, the basis seems to have been broader, as the physicians in Nagasaki were scientists and inquisitive culturalists who were not in Japan to proselytize Christianity, as some earlier Western "scientists" had been, and they were remarkably unprejudiced in teaching aspiring Japanese physicians.

Kōan's Early Career

Only the bare outlines are known of Ogata Kōan's life. He was born to the samurai Saeki (Saheki) Sezaemon in 1810 and received the given name Sanpei. As Sezaemon's third son, Sanpei could not hope to be designated as heir to the Saeki house, and he assumed instead the ancestral name of Ogata. During his youth, Ogata apparently suffered from frail health, the presumed motive behind his commitment to a life as a private physician. Subsequently, in 1825, when he turned fifteen, Ogata moved from his native Bitchū to Osaka and began to study Dutch under the tutelage of the well-known teacher Naka Ten'yū at his academy, the Shishisaijuku, a decision that meant formally severing relations with the domain of Ashimori that his father served.

As Ten'yū's student, Ogata was a recipient of a Rangaku legacy which, by the 1820s, had decreed the study of the Dutch language and, more precisely, the translation of it, as indispensable to gaining objective medical knowledge. By the time Ogata began his effort to master Dutch in order to teach and practice medicine, the basic ethic and pattern of training were well established. Although a certification was not given, one could assume a special scholarly name after roughly a twelve-year cycle of study. Such was the name Kōan, which, like the appellations Ten'yū, (Sugita) Genpaku, and (Ōtsuki) Gentaku, proclaimed Ogata's identity as an independent scholar and teacher.

Kōan did not leave for historians any record revealing why he chose Dutch over Asian medicine, but a scholarly tradition in Dutch Studies already had been firmly planted in Osaka by the time Kōan arrived in that city. In addition to his own teacher, such figures as Asada Gōryū, Hashimoto Sōkichi, and Hazama Shigetomi were acclaimed throughout the city. Asada, a colleague of Miura Baien, had settled in Osaka to teach Western science, astronomy in particular, and he became a close friend of scholars at the Kaitokudō such as Nakai Riken and Yamagata Bantō. Hashimoto and Hazama, both offspring of merchant families, taught Dutch medicine and astronomy, experimented with generating electricity, and helped to persuade the shogunate to revise Japan's calendar along Western lines. Thus, within the vibrant intellectual milieu of early nineteenth-century Osaka, Kōan's decision to study Dutch medicine with Ten'yū would not appear to have been worthy of special note, and neither his contemporaries then nor historians later have queried his decision as being somehow out of the ordinary.

After five years of study, Ten'yū sent Kōan to Edo in 1830, and the next year the young scholar began to study with Tsuboi Shindō, a leading disciple of Ōtsuki Gentaku, and also with Udagawa Shinsai, a noted physician and translator of Dutch medical manuals. In 1836, after establishing a firm reputation for mastery of the Dutch language, as evidenced by his being elevated to the level of Shindō's instructional assistant, Kōan made the obligatory pilgrimage to Nagasaki, where he studied language with the chief of the Dutch trading commission. That same year, he adopted the formal given name of Kōan, and in 1838, some thirteen years after he had first committed himself to Dutch Studies, Ogata returned to Osaka to found his Tekijuku.[16]

Contributing to the Scholarship on International Studies

Kōan began teaching during the troubled Tenpō era (1830–44) when a confluence of tumultuous events suggested that the Tokugawa state was approaching a decisive moment in its history. Devastating famines spawned riots in Osaka in 1834 and 1836, and in the Second Month of 1837 fires set by Ōshio Heihachirō in his rebellion against the shogunate consumed a good quarter of the city, leaving in ashes the commercial area where Kōan would establish his academy a year later. In the summer of 1837 Japanese shore batteries fired upon an American merchant vessel, the *Morrison*, as it approached the Japanese coast near Edo for the ostensible purpose of repatriating seven shipwrecked Japanese sailors. When an informal group of scholars calling themselves the Bangaku Shachū, or "Companions of Barbarian Studies," wrote a series of tracts criticizing the shogunate for its actions and advocating a more

---

16. Details about Ogata's career are contained in *Ogata Kōan den*, and Ogata Kōan Kinenkai, ed. and pub., *Ogata Kōan to Tekijuku* (Osaka, 1977).

hospitable policy toward Western learning, the shogunate arrested twenty-six of their number, two of whom, Watanabe Kazan and Takano Chōei, eventually committed suicide while in confinement. In the wake of that incident, the shogunate revealed its growing rigidity and defensiveness by imposing tighter scrutiny over the publication of books related to Dutch Studies and by severely limiting the number of volumes that it would officially approve. Concurrently, officials in Edo called for sweeping reforms to strengthen the regime's authority, even proposing that certain allied lords (*fudai daimyō*) exchange their holdings near Edo for lands elsewhere. The daimyo adamantly opposed that initiative, and some even dared to call for closer consultation in the formulation of national policies and to hint at the need for far-reaching structural reforms. During those same years, the Opium War between Great Britain and the Qing Court broke open along the China coast, ushering in the era of gunboat diplomacy in East Asia.

Against that backdrop of portentous events, Kōan proceeded with quiet optimism to fulfill his vision of teaching the art of healing. His Tekijuku became known as a school for commoners where warrior or aristocratic status was not a privilege. The level of competition was extraordinary and the debates loud. In the words of one of the students, no one looked about from their study with casually "folded arms" (*komanuki*)—a reference to samurai who tended to do so as a way of conveying a sense of indifference. Frustration levels also ran high. Many students were known to counter the pressures from their intensive study with youthful and boisterous play in the nearby Osaka streets, glimpses of which are provided by Fukuzawa in his autobiography, while others released their tensions by slashing their swords against the central pillar of the main boarding hall, leaving gashes and nicks still visible today.

Kōan apparently viewed such extracurricular diversions with benign tolerance and did not impose disciplinary measures, preferring instead to emphasize the competitive study of the Dutch language within the academy. Nagayo Sensai, who enrolled at the Tekijuku in 1854, shortly after Fukuzawa, gives a sense of Kōan's pedagogical approach in the following recollection:

> The academy was called the Tekijuku. Over a hundred students had come there from all four directions to study. Readings and discussions went on without interruption. It was the very best academy of Dutch Studies in the entire country. The students were divided into eight reading and discussion ranks. On six specified days in every month, students in each rank drew straws to shift their sitting place. The students at the head of each rank would hold forth on several lines or so of a basic text and then pass on a question to the next person, and so on down the line to the last person. After each query, the chief assistant would determine the pluses and minuses and assign white and black marks accordingly. After the chief assistant had given the summary lecture, the session was ended for the day. Upon compiling the white and black marks for a month, those with the greatest number of whites advanced to a

Ambiguous Encounters: Ogata Kōan and International Studies — 229

The sword-slashed pillar at the Tekijuku. Photograph by Tetsuo Najita.

higher position within their rank, and, after three successive months of improvement proceeded to a more advanced rank.[17]

Ogata Kōan's importance in the history of Dutch Studies derived from the special emphasis he gave to diseases and internal therapeutics. He thus addressed the criticism levied against physicians in this lineage as being more knowledgeable in anatomy and surgery than in internal medicine. Rather than anatomy, Kōan's major works focused on the taxonomy and therapeutics of diseases broadly conceived. He developed that particular interest while in Edo, especially after he assisted Udagawa in translating technical medicinal

17. Ban Tadayasu, *Tekijuku to Nagayo Sensai* (Osaka: Sōgensha, 1987), pp. 100–101; Soda Hajime, *Nihon iryō bunka-shi* (Tokyo: Shibunkaku, 1970), pp. 299–300; and Akagi, *Rangaku no jidai*, pp. 23–38.

terms from Dutch and Latin and compiling tables of weights and measurements. Based on that early experience with practical medicine, Kōan wrote a general summary of diseases and therapeutics, *Byōgaku tsūron*, which he eventually published in three volumes in 1849. Although Kōan originally had thought that his work would run to thirteen volumes, he set the project aside early in order to begin a translation (done with the assistance of his adopted stepbrother Ogata Ikuzō) of a work by Christoph W. Hufeland entitled *Enchiridion Medicum*, a treatise on "the practical art of healing."[18]

A well-known physician and professor of medicine in Berlin, Hufeland published that opus—an exhaustive taxonomy of human illnesses and their treatment that established his reputation as a leading scholar of diseases and internal medicine—upon his retirement in 1836, after fifty years of medical practice. Hufeland saw the work both as his legacy and as an "act of charity," for, as noted in the introduction to *Enchiridion Medicum*, "the proceeds went to a fund for the support of indigent physicians." The tome quickly was translated into Dutch in 1838 and English in 1842. Kōan completed portions of his draft from the Dutch version in 1842 under the title "Practical Instructions of Mr. Fu" (*Fushi keiken ikun*). The *Fu* in the title is an abbreviated reference for Hufeland, *hu* and *fu* being virtually indistinguishable sounds in Japanese phonetics. Circulated among physicians in handwritten form, Kōan's translation from *Enchiridion Medicum* solidified his reputation as a scholar par excellence, especially for his mastery of the Dutch scientific language, and it contributed as well to the growing popularity of his academy. After a long delay by shogunal officials to formally approve publication, Kōan's full translation finally appeared in thirty volumes between 1857 and 1860.

In his instructions on practical medicine, Hufeland had included a lengthy essay containing special admonitions and personal advice. Kōan transliterated those into an abridged twelve-point summary that he entitled "Fushi ikai no ryaku" (Mr. Fu's Advice to Physicians). Circulated in hand-copied form, "Fushi ikai no ryaku" served as instructional guidelines for students enrolled at the Tekijuku and is translated as an appendix to this chapter. Although the summary is drawn from Hufeland, the ethical language Kōan used in translation definitely places this work in a close mutual relationship with the Tokugawa ethical philosophy of "saving others."

Honoring the Action Ethic

Kōan's commitment to a medical action ethic is clearly evident in his early and dedicated effort to combat epidemics, first smallpox and then, more desper-

18. The edition I have reviewed is referenced as *Enchiridion Medicum, Manual of the Practice of Medicine—The Result of Fifty Years' Experience*, by C. W. Hufeland, Counsellor of State, Physician in Ordinary to the Late King of Prussia, Professor in the University of Berlin. From the Sixth German Edition. Translated by Caspar Bruchausen. M.S. Revised for the Proprietor by Robert Nelson, M.D. (New York: William Radde, 1842). The introduction contains a brief biography of Hufeland.

ately, cholera. Kōan championed the cause of utilizing vaccinations against smallpox, as proposed by the English physician Edward Jenner, who at the turn of the century had begun the practice of inoculating children with lymph contained in cowpox vesicles. During the 1840s Japanese physicians advocated that a live culture be brought into Japan so that they might begin to establish vaccination stations. That task was not easily accomplished, however, since the fragile lymph was carried over long distances most effectively in the bodies of human patients, typically young men who were injected with the virus for the purpose of getting the antibody from one location to the next. Finally, in the Seventh Month of 1849, a Dutch ship arrived in Nagasaki with an active culture, in the form of scabs, and the Hino brothers, Teisai and Katsutami (the latter was Kōan's student), arranged to have a portion of the antibody transferred to Kyoto. Kōan quickly made his way to Kyoto, received a sample of the virus, and returned to Osaka where he opened an inoculation station at Furute-machi in the Eleventh Month. Adhering to Hufeland's advice that inoculations were the best defense against outbreaks of smallpox, a hard-earned reward for that doctor's personal experiences in Weimar, Kōan subsequently led a campaign over a eleven-year period that in 1860 finally won official support for vaccination stations in Japan.[19]

During the long struggle against smallpox, many of Kōan's colleagues would fall victim to the disease that they were trying to tame. Two who were especially close to him, his student Hino Katsutami and the Osaka merchant Yamatoya Zenbei, died in 1857 and 1860 respectively. Throughout the lengthy ordeal, Kōan vowed "never to surrender our basic ethical commitment" (*jinjutsu no hon'i o ushinawazu*). Emphasizing the value of saving human lives as his sole objective, Kōan explicitly disavowed seeking profit or fame. He recorded his views and those of his companions Hino and Yamatoya in the following language, which resonates both with his summary of Hufeland's advice as well as the Tokugawa ethic of compassionate healing: "From the beginning, the three of us . . . agreed to a pledge. This project would have compassionate healing [*jinjutsu*] as its sole purpose. The plan was to spread the new method of vaccination throughout society. Thus, no matter how much money we received in gratitude, we would not take any of it for personal profit, nor would we accept it as payment for compassionate treatment. That was the first principle we agreed on."[20] Ultimately, the heroic efforts and self-sacrifice of Kōan and his colleagues brought about the desired end. Remarkably, the widespread establishment of inoculation stations in Osaka and western Japan brought smallpox under control in the late Tokugawa period.

Cholera presented a more complex challenge as there was no cure comparable to that for smallpox. Nor did Hufeland's manual of practical medicine turn out to be of much assistance in the case of cholera, which, in turn, cast

---

19. Akagi, *Rangaku no jidai*, pp. 161–81; *Ogata Kōan den*, pp. 51–70; and Ann Bowman Jannetta, "The Introduction of Jennerian Vaccination in Nineteenth-Century Japan," *Japan Foundation Newsletter* 23:2 (September 1995), pp. 6–9.

20. *Ogata Kōan den*, pp. 62, 67–71; *Kōan to Tekijuku*, p. 39.

doubts on his therapeutics more generally. Cholera thus offers a perspective into the interfacing of Dutch and Tokugawa medical science that deserves special comment. The disease first struck Japan in 1825 at the tail end of a worldwide pandemic. It entered through Shimonoseki, spread to Osaka and Kyoto, and then subsided just before reaching Edo. A report out of Osaka in 1825 described the basic symptoms of cholera and the dread it provoked:

> In Osaka today enormous numbers of people are dying from a severe epidemic. There are funeral rites for two and three hundred persons every day. The disease begins with diarrhea, and the stomach is severely distorted and twisted out of shape. Abdominal pains, vomiting, and cramps in the arms and legs soon follow. In this disease, after one or two diarrhetic movements, the arms and legs turn cold, and the vital pulse disappears. The eyes recede upward, and the person dies within half-a-day....
>
> Although I have no idea at all regarding the basic nature of this disease, how such a violent poison enters the body, and what sorts of damage it causes, it seems to attack directly the nervous system, much like the poison of a globefish or a viper. It appears that the virus penetrates even the skin, though most often it enters through the mouth and then turns the stomach gangrene. Just now a neighbor has requested a diagnosis, and I shall hold off on further detailing my observations....
>
> I have heard that about forty thousand people have died in Korea as well. In the town of Hagi in Chōshū domain, 583 deaths were recorded between the fourteenth and twenty-fifth days of the Eighth Month. I hear that some 234 people died in the castle town of Kashiwada, near Osaka, on the thirteenth and fourteenth days of the Ninth Month. How can one expect to live for another day under these circumstances? It seems like we have been made to stand before flintlocks and arrows of fire. Please understand our situation.[21]

From the time of this first epidemic, cholera came to be known as an especially frightening disease where people would "fall dead in three days" or sometimes "within the moment"—*mikka korori* and *nanji korori*, with *korori* or "collapsing suddenly" being a homophone sometimes used to pronounce "cholera." Everywhere, people assumed it to be just a matter of time before another epidemic reached Japan, and apprehensions rose when news of a second pandemic began to filter into the country in the 1830s. Such alarm was justified, for cholera did strike again, with enormous virulence, killing over 250,000 people during the Ansei Epidemic of 1858 when it spread as far as Edo, where perhaps as many as 100,000 persons died. Over the next fifty years, the dreaded disease returned periodically and claimed another 375,000 lives.

21. Yamamoto Shun'ichi, *Nihon korera-shi* (Tokyo: Tōkyō Daigaku Shuppankai, 1982), pp. 10–11.

The Ansei Epidemic erupted in the midst of tremendous domestic turmoil that many Japanese interpreted as portending the demise of the Tokugawa regime. The devastation wrought by the great Ansei earthquake of 1855, when perhaps another hundred thousand persons died in Edo, led people to believe that they were living through the anarchic chaos that preceded, inevitably, the turn to a better future, one in which the moral order would be restored. The coming of Perry's "black ships" in the early 1850s ultimately compelled the shogunate to sign the unequal treaties, first with the United States in 1858 and then with the other powers, that compromised Japan's national sovereignty and threatened its independence. A second British victory over China in the "*Arrow* War" of 1856–57 (the so-called Second Opium War) carried ominous tidings about the loss of historical certitudes. Within Japan, the Ansei Purge of 1858–60 saw the shogunate defend its hegemony by summarily executing young samurai activists seeking political change. When their sympathizers retaliated in 1860 by assassinating the shogun's chief senior counselor, Ii Naosuke, violent internecine strife spread to Kyoto and other parts of the country. The cholera epidemic that began in the spring of 1858 added enormously to the feelings of disorientation and uncertainty that pervaded the social landscape.

The source of the epidemic was traced to American sailors at Nagasaki, thus leading to rumors that the disease was a foreign poison, like opium along the China coast, and prompting people to refer to it, in somewhat understandable confusion, as *Eijin no doku*, the "Englishman's poison." Johannes Lydius Catherinus Pompe Van Meerdevoort, the chief Dutch physician in Nagasaki at that time, went so far as to note that it was not at all desirable to be a foreigner in Japan, and he even asserted that his life would have been in danger when he joined a funeral procession, had not a Japanese acquaintance vouched for him. "The sense of uncertainty encountered among the populace simply grew in bounds," one account put it, "and there is a feeling of being in a state of war." Fearful, some Japanese filled straw boats with effigies of Westerners and floated them downriver to the sea, symbolically banishing the foreigner from Japan's shores.[22]

In Osaka and Kyoto, commoners rushed into the streets to join what were called "cholera dances" and "cholera festivals" (*korori odori, korori matsuri*), adding to the frenzied, hysterical revelry that was sweeping up Japan's urban population during the 1860s. In contrast to participants in the "dances of thanksgiving" and "world renewal" (*okage mairi, yonaoshi odori*), who were reacting to a general sense of malaise and impending doom, the cholera dancers hoped to ward off the specific and devastating crisis of an uncontrollable epidemic. As part of the new rituals, shrines distributed papier-mâché tigers to children as good-luck charms to fight off the "tiger-wolf-badger disease," pairing the ideograph for "tiger" (*ko*) with the characters for wolf (*rō*) and the

---

22. Tatsukawa Shōji, *Byōki no shakai-shi* (Tokyo: NHK Bukkusu, 1971); idem, *Kinsei byōsō-shi* (Tokyo: Heibonsha, 1979), pp. 177–204; Yamamoto, *Nihon korera-shi*, pp. 745–99; Yokohama-shi Eisei Kyoku, ed. and pub., *Yokohama shippei-shi* (Yokohama, 1980), pp. 60–72.

contriving *tanuki*, or badger (*ri*), to sound out a rendering of the word cholera into Japanese and to signify the tricky, unpredictable, and fierce nature of the disease.[23]

Hufeland's description of cholera in his taxonomy or "classification" of human diseases was compellingly accurate. Rapid dehydration, due to the loss of liquid and food through diarrhetic attacks, led in quick order to high fever, internal gangrene, convulsion, and death within the space of just two or three days. Hufeland spelled out that deadly sequence in concise language in just a page or so. For therapeutics, however, the German physician could only prescribe techniques that he relied on as constants in his treatment of illnesses in general. At the end of his treatise on diseases, Hufeland appended an essay declaring vomiting, venesection (phlebotomy, or bleeding), and the administering of opium to be the "three cardinal means of the art of healing," what was known among scholars of Dutch Studies as *saisei sanpō*, the "three treasures of saving lives."[24]

Crude in comparison to later treatments, the inducing of vomiting may be appreciated as being essential in an era prior to refrigeration. Opium, it should be remembered, was a miraculous drug in Hufeland's world, valued as a sedative for patients in great pain or facing certain death. Above all, however, Hufeland celebrated venesection as ranking without question "first among all remedies," an endorsement that was in keeping with the mainstream of medical practices in Europe at that time. Practiced primarily among "barbers" in the medieval era, the method was continued among reputable physicians. As one account put it, "Doctors had bled their patients for hundreds of years in season and out of season, and they continued to do so well into the nineteenth century."[25] As late as 1850 when Sir Robert Peel was thrown from his horse and suffered multiple internal injuries, the leading doctors in London prescribed the application of twenty leeches on his body. It should come as no surprise, then, that in the portion of the appendix to his *Enchiridion Medicum* that dealt with specific therapeutics for cholera, Hufeland simply wrote: "As soon as the pains become violent and burning . . . a venesection is immediately to be made." If the attacks did not abate and "the pulse becomes small, the extremities cold, and fits of fainting set in, then there remains no other salvative for life but opium. . . . In extreme prostration, besides opium a strong warming wine might be administered, best old malaga [a sweet Spanish wine]."[26]

Kōan soon realized the limited efficacy of malaga as well as the so-called "Osaka remedy" of *shōchū*, the grain-distilled liquor which some physicians prescribed for internal consumption and as a rubbing compound. At a loss, Kōan sent an appeal to Pompe Van Meerdevoort in Nagasaki asking for more

---

23. Ban, *Tekijuku to Nagayo Sensai*, p. 16; Soda, *Nihon iryō bunka-shi*, pp. 299–301.
24. Hufeland, *Enchiridion Medicum*, appendix on "The Three Cardinal Means."
25. A. J. Youngson, *The Scientific Revolution in Victorian Medicine* (New York: Holmes and Meier Publishers, 1979), pp. 18–19; Audrey Davis and Toby Appel, *Bloodletting Instruments*, Smithsonian Studies in History and Technology 41 (Washington: Smithsonian Institution Press, 1979).
26. Hufeland, *Enchiridion Medicum*, appendix on "The Three Cardinal Means."

precise and effective guidance on therapeutics. A physician of considerable ability and decency whose Socratic style of teaching Kōan came to admire, Pompe Van Meerdevoort sent his response in the form of a lecture that he had prepared on the subject and had it delivered through Matsumoto Ryōjun, Kōan's colleague who served as the Dutch doctor's chief interpreter and assistant. Pompe Van Meerdervoort focused his attention almost entirely on preventive measures rather than on therapeutics per se. In particular, he argued that more good would come from improving sanitary conditions and controlling the environment than from distributing medication to patients who were already dying. Political agencies, Pompe Van Meerdervoort told shogunal officials stationed in Nagasaki, had the obligation to provide directives instructing the public to boil water, shun fresh vegetables and seafood, stay out of evening breezes, keep covered when sleeping, avoid stress and excessive drinking, and seek the attention of a physician at the first outbreak of diarrhea.

The Dutch medical officer was correct of course. There was no known cure for cholera, and sanitation was the most effective long-term remedy. Students and colleagues of Kōan studying in Nagasaki, men such as Matsumoto and Nagayo Sensai, would learn this lesson from Pompe Van Meerdervoort and introduce the idea of "public hygiene," or *eisei*, as an instrument of public policy and a method for saving lives during epidemics. It was a concept that went beyond the Tokugawa practices designed to preserve the nation's health, and in the early 1870s Kōan's students lobbied to incorporate hygienic studies into the curricula of medical schools throughout the country. Not surprisingly, the Meiji government appointed Nagayo its first chief of public health.

In 1858, however, forging a long-term legacy for public health was not an uppermost concern for Kōan, who was losing his battle against the Ansei Epidemic. Faced with the desperate situation of thousands dying around him, Kōan found the response from Pompe Van Meerdervoort to be, in his own wording, *fukanzen*, a term usually used to mean "incomplete" but here carrying the connotation of "inadequate." The problem, to Kōan's way of thinking, was that the Dutch doctor outlined a single remedy, whereas the disease itself progressed in stages, each of which seemed to demand a separate kind of treatment. Kōan set out his thoughts in a letter he sent late in the summer of 1858 to his student Mitsukuri Shūhei, then working in Edo:

> Here too, from the middle of the Eighth Month, the epidemic has spread enormously. The number of dead since then is about ten thousand. Okuno Yatarō and Shinozaki Chōtei have both died of cholera. Luckily, Gotō recovered from it. Many other acquaintances and friends have also died. . . . No area has been spared from this disease. Thanks very much for sending the lecture of Pompe Van Meerdervoort. I had received earlier a copy of it from Matsumoto Ryōjun. As you note, it is quite incomplete (*fukanzen*). But it has been widely circulated, and physicians and non-physicians have come to rely on it far too much. Without distinguishing different phases in the illness, people are being greatly misled to make continuous use of the prescription. Finding this too painful, I

hurriedly edited a volume [*Korera chijun*] and circulated it as widely as possible.... As it is a work done in a great hurry, even the pages may not be in order. I did it only with the deepest aim of helping people.... To complete the volume, I worked through night and day between seventeenth and twenty-third days of the Eighth Month, while also attending to the needs of patients without pause.[27]

Thus, Kōan worked feverishly, hoping to defy "the punishment of heaven" (*ten no bassuru tokoro ka*) by putting together a working handbook of his own addressed specifically to the treatment of cholera. Kōan's decision to circulate the manuscript among his colleagues in 1858 came just a year after his translation of Hufeland's *Enchiridion Medicum* had begun to be published formally, and the brief, handwritten treatise constituted an admission that Hufeland's therapeutics on this illness were not reliable. Perhaps even Hufeland had become frustrated with his own methods, for in the 1830s he experimented with the belladonna plant as an antispasmodic. Kōan does not seem to have been aware of that fact, however, probably because the results had not been translated into Dutch. Consequently, the Osaka physician's hurried compilation of his experiences during the epidemic in that city called into question Hufeland's treatment of cholera through bleeding, and Kōan's objections prefigured a more thorough questioning of the therapeutics of the "three treasures" as a remedy for all diseases.

Kōan's booklet on cholera refers to physicians such as G. F. Most, G. Ganstatt, and J. W. H. Canradi, whose names, unlike Hufeland's, are no longer remembered; but, more important, Kōan made no mention of the German doctor's prescriptions for cholera as set forth in the *Enchiridion Medicum*. Instead, Kōan described his own experimentation in 1858 with certain opiates and especially quinine, used mainly for malaria but presumably effective in reducing fever and thus capable of giving patients at least a fighting chance to survive. After describing the symptoms of cholera, Kōan suggested the following prescription to a colleague.

At the onset of diarrhea, the application of emetine or opiate substances will save eight or nine patients out of ten. When the diarrhea is severe, quinine salts must be used as a preventive. I have experimented with quinine a great deal this year. The efficacy is quite noticeable. I have added a few items here and there in my book on the treatment of cholera, which I forward to you. I have tried varying amounts of quinine, and there is a point where a reaction to the medication sets in. Thus I use about one-half or one-third of the usual amount once every two hours or so. Should the epidemic reach your area, try these measures.[28]

27. *Ogata Kōan no tegami*, pp. 250–51.
28. The letter is dated the first day of the Eighth Month, 1859, and is included in *Ogata Kōan no tegami*, pp. 424–25.

Ambiguous Encounters: Ogata Kōan and International Studies — 237

After the epidemic subsided, Kōan eventually softened his position toward Pompe Van Meerdervoort, in part due to Matsumoto Ryōjun's stern reply to the Osaka doctor explaining the significance of the Dutch physician's recommendations regarding sanitation and public health. From Kōan, however, Hufeland's predilection for bleeding cholera victims received no further comment.[29] Significantly, Kōan's dismissive attitude toward venesection was in keeping with a broader reassessment of medical therapeutics that took place after Hufeland's time and that swept aside the "three treasures in the art of healing," techniques so confidently endorsed by Hufeland.

Kōan and Hufeland

As things turned out, history has remembered Hufeland not for the therapeutics he promoted in his massive *Enchiridion Medicum*, upon which Kōan staked his own scholarly reputation, but for his advocacy of preventive care as set forth in a much briefer treatise entitled *Makrobiotik*, published in 1796 and translated into English, French, Italian, and Dutch within two years.[30] Hufeland wrote that work to advise individuals not to succumb to the "present melancholy age, so destructive to mankind," referring to the Napoleonic Wars, and to encourage people to take personal responsibility for prolonging their own lives. Preventive care for the body, Hufeland argued in his widely read and highly influential essay, paid better dividends than did reliance on physicians to repair the damages of an illness after its onset. Diseases, the enemy of life, attacked humans, Hufeland claimed, because persons persisted in disregarding commonsense health habits, ingested excessive amounts of food and drink, and disdained proper exercise, especially long hikes in mountains blessed with fresh, bracing air. Expressing a philosophy that, unknown to him, was also central to Tokugawa thought, Hufeland emphasized the importance of nourishing the vital energy or power within the human body: "The vital power is, without dispute, one of the most general, the most incomprehensible, and the most powerful of all the powers of nature. It fills and gives motion to everything, and, in all probability, is the grand source from which all the power of the physical or at least the organized world proceeds. It is that which produces, supports, and renews everything."[31]

Kōan never did select Hufeland's *Makrobiotik* as a text to be rendered into Japanese, despite the fact that it was translated into all the major European lan-

---

29. Soda, *Nihon iryō bunka-shi*, pp. 299–300; Tatsukawa, *Byōki no shakai-shi*, p. 670.

30. The work was also known as *Macrobioticon* and was published in English as *The Art of Prolonging Life* (London: J. Bell, 1797).

31. Hufeland, *Art of Prolonging Life*, pp. 40–41, 167. Hufeland's essay prompted Immanuel Kant to write a letter to "Privy Councillor and Professor Hufeland" headed "On the Power of the Mind to Master its Morbid Feelings by Sheer Resolution." The title reflects Kant's somewhat ponderous (if in retrospect humorous) way of valorizing his own "sheer" mental, that is to say "philosophical," resolution to live to his ripe old age; Immanuel Kant, *The Conflict of the Faculties*, trans. Mary J. Gregor (New York: Janus Library, 1978), pp. 175–211.

guages. In all likelihood, his reasoning on this matter will never be known, but it may well be that the *Makrobiotik* contained little that was new to Kōan and his colleagues. Indeed, most of Hufeland's perceptions and practices merely echoed ideas that Japanese scholars already had articulated for themselves in such well-known and best-selling works as Kaibara Ekken's *Yōjōkun* (Instructions on Nourishing Life). Published in 1713, that work explicated Ekken's fundamental premise that a single infinite energy, the grace of life—the "vital power" in Hufeland's later conceptualization—permeated the universe and was the essence of life in each human being. Ekken spoke in everyday language about the responsibility of each person to sustain this gift of life through exercising properly, practicing moderation in food and drink, and avoiding extremes in all matters concerning the maintenance of health. In short, he spoke of the nourishment of "life" as being, in the first and crucial instance, the obligation of each individual.[32]

Hufeland and Kōan shared a common belief that a vital energy sustained life in each individual and that each person and each physician alike was accountable for nourishing that gift. Both men taught "the doctrine of the mean," the necessity, in Hufeland's phrasing, of remaining vigilant against "all extremes, either too much or too little, too high or too low," that might impede the prolongation of life. That language coincided with the universally acknowledged ethic of reason and accuracy in Tokugawa times that taught the avoidance of excesses as the way to approximate the mean, often stated as "exceeding [the mean] is the same thing as falling short of it" (*sugitaru wa oyobazaru ga gotoshi*). With the hindsight of history, we can see how closely Kōan and Hufeland actually stood to each other as the two men, each in his own way, shaped a similar philosophy of life and elaborated the common view that the art of healing consisted of acts of compassion and moral commitment. A physician without moral values, as Hufeland put it, was a "monster."[33]

The great divide between East and West that we are accustomed to rely upon in viewing late Tokugawa history obscures this important relationship. Indeed, the gulf that separates Hufeland and Western medical science as practiced today probably is much greater than the intellectual distance between Hufeland and Kōan's generation of Tokugawa physicians. In the decades after the two men struggled to save their patients from cholera, revolutionary advances in medical knowledge and technology would discredit Hufeland's therapeutics, something Kōan already had begun to sense. Soon enough, that same explosion of scientific information, combined with a broadening flow of epistemological transactions, would render obsolete Kōan's dedication to the Dutch language as the entry point into the study of medicine. Kōan did not fully appreciate the fact that much of the scientific scholarship he taught to his students consisted of "translations" from German into Dutch; Berlin and

---

32. Matsuda Michio, *Kaibara Ekken*, Nihon no meicho 14 (Tokyo: Chūō Kōronsha, 1969), pp. 7–54, 319–456.
33. Hufeland, *Art of Prolonging Life*, pp. 167, 301.

Amsterdam remained largely undifferentiated in his view of the world. In the early Meiji era, however, scholars would use translations from German, French, and English sources to create a new vocabulary for the natural as well as the social and human sciences, and such learning would become the intellectual property of all East Asia.

Still, the mastery of foreign and especially Western languages as a methodology to seek new information and ideas remained a key legacy of Dutch Studies. Because Kōan and his colleagues believed in the study of the Dutch language as the basic method, the *jutsu*, by which to acquire new knowledge, the practice of teaching language for the purpose of translation would have far-reaching consequences. The use of dictionaries by scholars and students at the Tekijuku to decode and translate Dutch, and in turn other Western languages, would be of fundamental importance in Japan's modern transformation. It is an intellectual history that from the late Tokugawa into the modern eras remained in continuous opposition to the view that language ought to be the source of uncontaminated identity, as theorized in National Studies.

International studies as Kōan taught them at the Tekijuku would be overwhelmed by the rapid turn of events within the country and along the Asian coasts on the eve of the Meiji Restoration. Comments scattered in his letters indicate that Kōan was aware of contemporary affairs and that he accepted the inevitability of change that the swirling clouds signaled. The flow of news from the China coast led Kōan to lament the outbreak of the "*Arrow* War" between the Qing Court and the British in 1856, and he realized that such gunboat diplomacy left Ii Naosuke, the shogunate's chief policymaker, with little choice but to accede to the commercial treaty that Townsend Harris, America's consular representative, was pressing for so hard. When the shogunate signed trade agreements with the United States and several other Western powers in 1858, Kōan described the action as *atarimae*, a "reasonable" course that would permit international trade. Nevertheless, he knew that radical activists saw the so-called Ansei commercial treaties as a humiliating assault upon Japan's sovereignty and national honor, and he expected that domestic disturbances would follow. So, too, did Ii, who moved harshly to suppress the shogunate's critics—placing opposition daimyo under house arrest, dismissing antiforeign court nobles from office, and executing such proimperial activists as the Chōshū radical Yoshida Shōin and Kōan's own student, Hashimoto Sanae, who was in the service of the reformist daimyo of Echizen.

The turmoil of the late 1850s led Kōan to believe that further change was on its way, and he began to foresee, however dimly, a future that was vastly different from his own present. In the wake of Britain's second military victory over China and America's diplomatic successes against Japan, Kōan recognized that English would become the key international language to master, and he began teaching it at the Tekijuku in 1860. Still, the past would not be easy to abandon; Kōan complained bitterly about the exorbitant price he had to pay for a Dutch-English dictionary, and he continued to use Dutch terms in his letters as code words, as though communicating within a clandestine society. Ii's purge, he wrote, was *sondaaru*, or "cruel," *sondalle* in Dutch. For transformation or revolution, Kōan used *omuenteringu* (*omwenteling*), and to describe the changing political system, he turned to the word *staat*. But if the language of the intellectual past could not protect against continuing political change, Kōan at least hoped that the process of revolution would be as brief and painless as possible. Without much commentary, he noted that he had witnessed the working of an electrical device and had purchased a rifle and a pistol—but Kōan's hopes for a peaceful political experiment would not transpire.[34]

In a time made precarious by epidemics, political purges, the threat of civil war, and the danger of foreign siege, the declining Tokugawa regime in 1862 summoned Kōan to Edo to become the headmaster at a new school of Western medicine founded just four years earlier. Having declined the position three times previously, another refusal would have been tantamount to treason, and Kōan had no choice but to make the journey east. He would not return again to Osaka; nor would Kōan live to see the West that he translated. Frail in health throughout his life, Kōan succumbed to the enormous stress imposed on him by his official tasks in Edo, and he died there in 1863 of a massive internal hemorrhage. The project that he undertook would serve as the cornerstone for the new school of medicine at Tokyo University, and Ikeda Kensai, Kōan's student at the Tekijuku, would become its first dean. In Osaka, the smallpox inoculation station near the Tekijuku would become a hospital named after Ogata Kōan.

The appointment in Edo was for Kōan a "thankless burden," and he set out on this journey as though facing "certain death." A participant in poetry writing groups in the classical Japanese style from an early age and through all those years when he taught Dutch, Kōan revealed his deep feelings of regret in having to leave his Osaka in the following lines:[35]

yorube zo to	This Osaka by the bay,
omohishi mono o	This dear locale
naniwagata	Of which I am so very fond—
ashinokarine to	Were you for me
narinikeru ka na	But a temporary place to rest?

Kōan's school in Osaka closed its doors to Dutch and international studies in 1864. The Tekijuku thus came to an end, like its neighbor the Kaitokudō and all the other diverse domainal and private academies that had flourished in cities and castle towns throughout the country within the once seemingly indestructible confines of the Tokugawa regime. Today Kōan's Tekijuku is a well-preserved museum under the care of Osaka University.

---

34. *Ogata Kōan no tegami*, pp. 29–30, 80–81, 258–336.
35. Wakita, *Kinsei Ōsaka no machi to hito*, p. 263.

APPENDIX

Mr. Fu's Advice to Physicians (Fushi ikai no ryaku)

The work of the physician is only to help other human beings and not to promote the self. This is the basic tenet of the profession. Not seeking idleness or thinking about fame, one must simply abandon the self and pledge to save others. No other work is involved than protecting lives, restoring people from illness, and relieving their pain.

When encountering a patient, see only the patient. See not high or low, poor or wealthy. Consider the gain within yourself in comparing the tears of gratitude in the eyes of the poor with the handful of gold given by the wealthy. Think deeply about this.

When applying your method address the afflicted person as the exclusive subject. Never rely on the hit-or-miss method. Do not cling to biases or rely on careless testing. Always be disciplined and detailed.

Besides perfecting medical skills, one also must strive to speak and act in ways that will encourage trust in the patient. However, simply to rely on the latest trends and present deceptive theories to become persuasive is truly shameful.

Every evening review once again the cases treated during the day, and document these in detail. As they accumulate toward a book, these may be of use to yourself and to the patients as well as to others more broadly.

In calling on a patient, it is best to concentrate on making a detailed diagnosis in a single visit rather than on making several visits. However, to be so overly self-confident as to deny the need for repeated examinations is detestable.

It is the calling of the physician to provide relief to the suffering of even the incurably ill. To turn away from this without reflection is contrary to the human way. Even though there is no hope of saving the patient, to provide relief is to practice the method of compassion [*jinjutsu*]. Try to prolong that life even for a minute. Do not say that recovery is impossible and convey this in your language and manner.

Reflect on the lack of wealth of the patient. In seeking to extend life, should the capital that ties that life together be taken away, what sort of profit is there? Weigh this thoughtfully in treating the poor.

Based on the text contained in Ogata Tomio, *Ogata Kōan den* (Tokyo: Iwanami Shoten, 1963), pp. 146–48, and Momose Meiji, *Tekijuku no kenkyū* (Tokyo: PHP Bunko, 1989), pp. 34–36. A translation also appears in *Readings in Tokugawa Thought*, 2d ed., Select Papers, vol. 9 (Center for East Asian Studies, University of Chicago, 1994), pp. 253–55.

In dealing with the community, gaining the good wishes of the people is desired. Though excellent in medical skill and strict in language and manner, one's virtue cannot be put to use without having gained the trust of the people who are to be saved. There must be sensitivity with the world of everyday affairs. In particular physicians are entrusted with human lives, view the naked body, speak about deeply held secrets, and listen to humiliating confessions. Hold always a feeling of warmth and generosity within, and speak sparingly. Strive to be silent. It goes without much saying that gambling, wining, playing in the gay quarters, and gaining a name in the world of luxury should all be avoided.

Toward fellow physicians be respectful and affectionate. Even if such might not seem possible, be restrained. Do not question another physician. To point out the weakness of another person is contrary to sagely wisdom. To speak with exaggeration about others is the limiting virtue of a small person. A person may simply criticize the excesses done in a day while we may lose the virtue of a human life. What are the issues here? Each physician possesses the teachings handed down by his house and a methodology that is his own. These should not be recklessly criticized. Elderly physicians should be extended respect. Younger colleagues should be treated with affection. Those who wish to query the advantages and disadvantages of physicians from the past should base their decisions on actual effectiveness, and their healing methods should also be gauged with reference to observable illness.

In holding a conference to discuss medical treatment, the group should be as small as possible. At the most there should be no more than three persons. Special care should be given to selecting the right people. The sole purpose should be the health of the patient, no other matter should be under consideration, and disputes should be avoided absolutely.

When a patient discards a physician to whom trust had been placed and secretly seeks the counsel of another physician, do not carelessly take part in such a tactic. Unless the view of the previous physician is heard, do not go along. However, should a physician know there has in fact been an erroneous diagnosis and he still disregards it, this too is contrary to the responsibility of a physician. Indeed, when a dangerous illness is involved, do not be indecisive.

CHAPTER TEN

Osaka as a Center of Regional Governance

— *Murata Michihito*

TRANSLATED BY KIKUKO YAMASHITA

As James L. McClain suggests in Chapter 3, early modern Osaka was a multifaceted city, a focal point of power and samurai governance as well as a repository of wealth and merchant culture. Subsequent chapters have elaborated upon the significance of the city's commoner population, detailing the manner in which artistic innovations, popular beliefs, religious values, and intellectual breakthroughs emanated outward from Osaka, washing over people in the nearby provinces and all of Japan. As we approach the conclusion to this volume, it is appropriate to return to Osaka's centrality to the exercise of political power and to investigate in more detail the city's importance as a center of regional governance.

Scholars have long conceived of an "Osaka region" that consisted of the villages and hamlets adjacent to the city as well as the surrounding provinces of Settsu, Kawachi, and Izumi. To a very large extent, most of those same scholars have been intent on describing the functioning of the marketing structures that linked Osaka commercially with its extended hinterland.[1] In addition to economic leadership, however, Osaka exerted a kind of political dominance over the surrounding region. To restate a point made in earlier chapters, Osaka was a shogunal city, a bastion of Tokugawa authority in western Japan. With an eye toward ensuring stability throughout central Japan, the shogunate built a major castle at Osaka, and it stationed in the community around the fortress many of its officials, such as the rural intendants (*daikan*) who conveyed the regime's laws, decrees, and tax bills to villagers residing on the shogun's holdings scattered across the region.

---

1. See, for instance, the extensive bibliographic listings found in the reference sections of Shinshū Ōsaka Shishi Hensan Iinkai, ed., *Shinshū: Ōsaka shishi*, vols. 3 and 4 (Osaka: Ōsaka-shi, 1991, 1990).

Despite the city's prominence as a center of shogunal administration, only a handful of scholarly studies have probed deeply into the political aspects of Osaka's urbanism. The compilers of a multivolume prewar history of Osaka and, more recently, Yasuoka Shigeaki and Yabuta Yutaka have investigated the prerogatives exercised by the Osaka city magistrates (*Ōsaka machi bugyō*), explicating their role in handling juridical matters both in the city and the surrounding provinces.[2] My own research into the scope and effectiveness of the Tokugawa shogunate's authority in central Japan, meanwhile, has focused on the duties assigned to the so-called *tsutsumi bugyō*, or supervisors for riparian matters, and the *kawa bugyō*, the river wardens who adjudicated rights concerning the use of rivers and their waters in the provinces of Settsu and Kawachi.[3]

Needless to say, members of the samurai estate filled all of the administrative posts mentioned above. Relatively high-ranking bannermen (*hatamoto*) served as city magistrates and rural intendants; somewhat lesser members of the shogun's retainer corps received appointments as supervisors for riparian matters; and constables (*yoriki*) assigned to the city magistrates did double duty as river wardens. What has been left unexplored in the existing scholarship is a related issue of considerable historiographic consequence—the possible contributions that commoners, urban or rural, might have made to the conduct of government throughout the Osaka region. That commoners have not received more attention is somewhat curious, for as McClain points out in his chapter, merchants played a key role in the political life of Osaka during the early modern period by serving as city and neighborhood elders. Moreover, studies about how authority was translated from edicts on paper to concrete actions in Edo and elsewhere have revealed the importance of merchant functionaries to the governing process.[4]

Perhaps the nature of scholarly discourse concerning the Osaka region is the primary reason that we do not see more traces of commoners in that city's hinterland. Most researchers have been interested chiefly in specifying the exact content of the government directives authored by the samurai rulers in their Osaka offices and with assessing the impact that the regime's policies had upon the ruled, that is, the villagers of the Osaka region. Very little effort, in

---

2. Ōsaka-shi, ed., *Ōsaka shishi*, vol. 1 (reprint; Osaka: Seibundō Shuppan, 1965), pp. 486–93; Yasuoka Shigeaki, *Nihon hōken keizai seisaku shiron: Keizai tōsei to bakuhan taisei* (Osaka: Ōsaka Daigaku Keizaigakubu, Shakai Keizai Kenkyū Shitsu, 1959; reprinted by Kōyō Shobō, 1985); and Yabuta Yutaka, " 'Sekka shihai-koku'-ron—Nihon kinsei ni okeru chiiki to kōsei," in Wakita Osamu, ed., *Kinsei Ōsaka chiiki no shiteki bunseki* (Tokyo: Ochanomizu Shobō, 1980), pp. 13–59.

3. Murata Michihito, "Kinsei Sekka ni okeru kasen shihai no jittai to seikaku—Tsutsumi bugyō to kawa bugyō o tōshite," *Hisutoria* 85 (December 1979), pp. 56–76; idem, *Kinsei kōiki shihai no kenkyū* (Osaka: Ōsaka Daigaku Shuppankai, 1995), pp. 171–209.

4. In English, for instance, see Katō Takashi, "Governing Edo," in James L. McClain, John M. Merriman, and Ugawa Kaoru, eds., *Edo and Paris: Urban Life and the State in the Early Modern Era* (Ithaca: Cornell University Press, 1994), pp. 41–67, and James L. McClain, *Kanazawa: A Seventeenth-Century Japanese Castle Town* (New Haven: Yale University Press, 1982), pp. 85–101.

contrast, has gone into learning how policies actually were formulated and then implemented. Consequently, this chapter will examine the conception and execution of government policy in the Osaka region from the middle of the seventeenth century through the early eighteenth. In particular, it asks how the city magistrates and rural intendants, officials who were stationed in Osaka but whose responsibilities stretched into the surrounding region, carried out their administrative duties. That inquiry, in turn, will draw our attention to a group of assistants who emerged from Osaka's burgeoning merchant community to assume significant administrative and governing duties. The activities of those functionaries should suggest new perspectives for understanding the nature of governance and yield a greater appreciation of Osaka's role as a center of political authority during the early modern era.

THE GEOGRAPHY OF GOVERNANCE IN CENTRAL JAPAN

The region surrounding the city of Osaka was split into a complicated mosaic of fragmented territorial jurisdictions, many claimed by military lords and religious institutions headquartered in other parts of Japan. The construction of castles at Osaka and Kyoto signaled the shogun's awareness of the strategic and economic importance of Osaka and its hinterland. The shogunate augmented its influence in central Japan by assigning fiefs to many of its bannermen and by reserving for itself a set of holdings, looked after by rural intendants who reported to the commissioners of finance (*kanjō bugyō*) in Edo. In addition, a number of outside lords (*tozama daimyō*), many of whom had been rivals to the House of Tokugawa at one time or another, asserted claim to a welter of relatively small territories, their avenue for tapping into the economic and cultural wealth of the Osaka region. To counterbalance their presence, the shogunate granted domains in the Kinai provinces to several of its more trusted allied lords (*fudai daimyō*). In addition, many Shinto and Buddhist sects had their head shrines and temples in central Japan and possessed extensive territorial holdings there, as did some of Kyoto's aristocratic families, whose more modest landed prerogatives often stretched far back into the medieval period.

The complex geography of central Japan gave birth to an equally complicated, and richly layered, approach to political administration. Proprietary rights implied administrative responsibilities, and each person or institution with holdings in the Osaka region had to devise some means to oversee local affairs, collect rents, and maintain law and order within his own particular bailiwick. Thus, those allied lords whose lands were situated entirely within the Kinai region typically governed from offices located inside the domain. In other cases, authority over a given holding might be exercised in a more indirect manner. The bannermen, for instance, resided permanently in Edo, and so they usually opened facilities on their fiefs in central Japan and relied on influential local peasants to carry out routine aspects of taxation and administration.

In several instances, administrative affairs and matters of governance cut across the quilt work of territorial jurisdictions, requiring the Tokugawa shogunate to craft a variety of offices that could address those problems that called for a more coordinated, regional approach. Broadly conceived, therefore, administrative authority in the Kinai region was divided into two parts: those prerogatives that individual lords and proprietors exercised within their own domains and the pan-regional responsibilities that the shogun assigned to its magistrates and other functionaries. As one example of the latter, the Tokugawa government entrusted to its supervisors for riparian matters the task of keeping riverbanks, dikes, and levees in good repair along all major waterways throughout the entirety of Settsu and Kawachi Provinces. Similarly, as occasion demanded, the Tokugawa government assigned to particular daimyo the task of making certain that landslides from nearby mountains and other acts of nature did not silt up the riverbeds that traversed several territorial holdings.[5]

The administration of justice illustrates how extensive and penetrating was the authority that the shogunate delegated to its subordinate officials. In the first half of the century, for instance, the Kyoto city magistrates handled all juridical matters concerning land disputes among villagers in Tanba, Ōmi, Harima, and the five Kinai provinces. Subsequently, in 1722, the Osaka city magistrates assumed responsibility for adjudicating such matters in Settsu, Kawachi, Izumi, and Harima, while the Kyoto city magistrates retained jurisdiction in the remaining four provinces.[6] Concurrently, in those provinces under their sway, the Osaka city magistrates carried out policing duties and enforced justice in all cases of violent crime and in civil disputes that involved persons residing in different jurisdictions. Furthermore, the Osaka city magistrates took charge of proclaiming and distributing official notices and decrees in all towns and villages in Settsu and Kawachi Provinces. For example, a ledger maintained by the elders of Komagatani village shows that all seven government edicts concerning that village which were promulgated in 1708 originated with the Osaka city magistrates—despite the fact that the village physically was located in Furuichi District of Kawachi Province and officially was part of a geographically dispersed domain belonging to the Watanabe daimyo family, whose core holdings lay in Izumi Province.[7]

The location of most of the administrative offices described above demonstrates Osaka's pivotal role in the process of governing central Japan. Among those daimyo whose castles and principal domains were far removed from

---

5. Lords tapped for this duty were known as *doshadome tantō daimyō* and are the subject of the following studies by Mizumoto Kunihiko: "Doshadome yakunin to nōmin—Yodogawa • Yamatogawa ryūiki ni okeru," *Shirin* 64:5 (September 1981), pp. 1–49; *Kinsei no mura shakai to kokka* (Tokyo: Tōkyō Daigaku Shuppankai, 1987), pp. 221–73; and *Kinsei no gōson jichi to gyōsei* (Tokyo: Tōkyō Daigaku Shuppankai, 1993), pp. 225–66.

6. For additional details see Ōsaka Shishi Hensanjo, ed. and pub., *Ōsaka shishi shiryō*, vol. 41, *Ōsaka machi bugyōsho kyūki* 1 (Osaka, 1994), pp. 21–25.

7. The ledger records all edicts transmitted to Komagatani village between 1707 and 1730; it bears the title "Ōsaka gobansho yori ofurejōdome-chō" and is located in archives of the Habikino City Office (Habikino shiyakusho).

their subordinate holdings in the Osaka region, some established branch offices on the Kinai fief itself, but many others decided to use Osaka as a base for their local administration. Moreover, the shogunate stationed its powerful rural intendants in Osaka, just as it posted others in Kyoto, Ōtsu, and Uji. In addition, the Osaka city magistrates, who constituted the chief agency for the administration of justice throughout the Kinai region, and the supervisors for riparian matters, who could be found under the rural intendants on the shogunate's table of organization, had their offices in Osaka as well. It is fair to say, therefore, that most of the people residing in the rural towns and villages surrounding Osaka felt the touch, in one way or another, of the governing powers exercised by officials who lived in, and worked out of, Osaka.

Merchant Delegates as Agents of Political Authority

All the daimyo lords, city magistrates, and rural intendants who exercised the governing prerogatives outlined above were, as noted, members of the samurai estate, the status group that laid preponderant claim to political authority during the Tokugawa period. Nevertheless, many of Osaka's merchant families also became intimately involved in the administration of rural areas around the city and helped to facilitate the implementation of government policies during the early modern era. Such functionaries were known interchangeably as *yōkiki* and *yōtashi*—the former appellation was used from the late seventeenth century until the end of the Tokugawa era, whereas the latter became increasingly commonplace from the middle of the eighteenth century—and both terms might be rendered as "merchant delegate." Some of the *yōkiki* worked for the shogunate's rural intendants, others assisted the city magistrates, and still others served the daimyo lords and aristocratic families with proprietary claims in the Kinai region.[8]

The Osaka merchant delegates performed a variety of significant governing functions. One of their primary responsibilities was to guarantee the payment of what can be termed regional levies (*kōiki yaku*) of corvée for riparian projects and for the construction and maintenance of shogunal facilities.[9] The shogunate made such imposts on all villagers in the Kinai region, even those that belonged to individual daimyo or other independent proprietors. Shogunal officials calculated the total amount of the levy, which was then apportioned among the subject villages in accordance with each settlement's officially reg-

---

8. Iwaki Takuji, "Kamigata hachikakoku bakuryō shihai ni tsuite," in Arisaka Takamichi-sensei Koki Kinenkai, ed., *Nihon bunka-shi ronshū* (Osaka: Dōhōsha Shuppan, 1991), pp. 481–93; idem, "Ōsaka machi bugyōsho to yōtashi," *Nihon-shi kenkyū* 349 (September 1991), pp. 31–50.

9. For addition details and examples of such levies, see my "Yōkiki no shokinō to kinsei-teki shihai no tokushitsu," *Kyōto Tachibana Joshi Daigaku kenkyū kiyō* 17 (December 1990), pp. 45–74, and "Kinsei Kinai no bakufu kōiki yaku—Ōsaka-jō • kura shūfuku yaku o chūshin ni," *Kyōto Tachibana Joshi Daigaku kenkyū kiyō* 20 (December 1993), pp. 87–129.

istered productive capacity, as expressed in units of *koku* of rice. In principle, each village then produced the requisite number of men for the specified number of days, and it was the responsibility of the merchant delegates who were associated with the daimyo whose villagers were being taxed to make certain that the peasant laborers turned out as required or, as became somewhat standard practice later, to collect a cash sum from the villagers with which to hire laborers.

Specific examples can help to clarify the merchants' role when they assumed responsibility for the regional levies. To repair and maintain dikes and riverbanks in Settsu and Kawachi, for instance, the Tokugawa government frequently compelled farmers living on both shogunal and daimyo lands in those provinces to provide labor service, typically five to eight man-days of work for each one hundred *koku* of a village's total assessed productivity. In addition, the regime periodically required peasants living on shogunal lands in the four provinces of Settsu, Kawachi, Izumi, and Harima to provide labor and specified quantities of bamboo, rope, and other building materials in order to help keep Osaka Castle and the shogun's warehouses in the city in good repair. The merchant functionaries from Osaka were held fully liable for ascertaining that the villagers supplied the required requisitions in a timely fashion, receiving in turn a commission for their services. In some cases, the merchant officials used their own funds to hire laborers and purchase materials on behalf of the villagers, and then collected a sum from the villages that covered their costs and commissions.[10]

A second task assigned to the Osaka merchant delegates was to communicate government edicts and other expressions of official will to villagers living in the provinces around Osaka. On the sixteenth day of the Tenth Month, 1721, for instance, the merchant functionary Atarashiya Yahei, who worked under the Osaka-based rural intendant Kuge Tōjūrō, transmitted instructions concerning the payment of the annual land taxes to ten villages in Ōtori District, Izumi Province, that fell under Kuge's jurisdiction:

> In response to requests from several villages expressing a desire to pay this year's land tax both with older silver coins known as Yotsu Hōgin and with "new silver," I have been instructed to inform the villagers about the following procedure. For payments due in the Eleventh Month, villagers may pay with a mix of the two currencies, but they must use only the new silver for payments due from the Twelfth Month. When I asked the rural intendant whether this procedure should be announced only to the villages that initiated the original petitions, Rural Intendant

---

10. It should be noted that those procedures concerning riparian projects were revised in 1722, when the shogunate began to impose a cash levy on each village, and later in the century the government also began to require cash payments from villages that it then used to acquire building materials and hire laborers for the repair and maintenance of the castle and warehousing facilities in Osaka; further details can be found in my "Kinsei Kinai no bakufu kōiki yaku," pp. 62–105.

Kuge explained confidentially that any village can make this same request. Therefore, I am informing everyone simultaneously.
• Addendum •
Because this office will be overburdened if all villages make the same request individually, they should submit a single group petition.[11]

It is evident that Atarashiya very effectively conveyed the intentions of the rural intendant to the villagers of Ōtori District, but the events of 1721 reveal an additional significant aspect of Atarashiya's performance: the merchant delegate did not act merely as a passive conduit for decisions made by officialdom to rural areas. Rather, Atarashiya subtly put into motion some independent actions that helped to shape policy. For example, taking the initiative, he asked his superior, Kuge, which villages ought be informed of the decision to have taxes paid in a mix of currencies in the Eleventh Month and in new silver beginning from the Twelfth. The result was that all villages, even those that had not been party to the original petitions, received the opportunity to use the older coinage through the Eleventh Month. Accompanying documents indicate that Kuge initially wanted each village to make all payments in the new currency, but he changed his mind after private conversations with Atarashiya and agreed to the procedures announced on the sixteenth day of the Tenth Month, an arrangement that was to the villagers' advantage. Moreover, through his addendum, Atarashiya provided a convenient means for all villages to be treated in a uniform manner, thus heading off potential discord. Thus, in addition to making important suggestions and inputs during the decision making, Atarashiya consistently kept officials and peasants informed about each other's desires and intentions, thus promoting efficient government and encouraging harmonious relations between higher political authorities and the villagers of the Osaka region.

The merchant delegates who worked under the Osaka city magistrates carried out duties analogous to Atarashiya's services to the rural intendant. In 1762, for example, three farmers from Settsu Province together with an Osaka merchant jointly directed a request to the Osaka city magistrates.[12] In their submission, the four men pointed out that the bed of the Yodo River had silted up in recent years, making dangerous flooding likely, and they asked the magistrates to arrange to have the river dredged. In order to solve the silting problems on the Yodo River, however, it was necessary to clean up as well the riverbeds of the Katsura, Uji, Kizu, and Ō Rivers. Since a project that extensive would entail great expense, the men suggested that some three hundred villages adjacent to the rivers in Yamashiro, Kawachi, and Settsu Provinces

---

11. The document is included in the assemblage of materials entitled "Kōgi goyōfuredome-chō," dated Shōtoku 5 (1715) to Kyōhō 7 (1722), and can be found in Mori Sugio, "Sakai-mawari nōson no goyōdome-chō," *Sakai kenkyū* 20 (March 1989), p. 130.

12. Details are taken from the document "Sesshū • Kawashū goryō • shiryō yōkiki," the records of the Nishihara family of Takahama village, Shima Kami District, Settsu Province, and located in the manuscript collection at the Kansai University Central Library (Kansai Daigaku Sōgō Toshokan).

annually pay one *monme* of silver per each *koku* of assessed productivity for the next ten years and that other villages benefiting from the project contribute half of that amount each year. After receiving the petition, the Osaka city magistrates in the Fifth Month of 1762 instructed the merchant functionaries who customarily liaised with the affected villages to conduct inquiries and sound out reactions to the scheme.

The manner in which one merchant delegate, Hiya Ichirōbei, fulfilled his assignment yields some important insights into the nature of governance in the Osaka area. Hiya's sphere of responsibility included a mix of villages, some on lands belonging to the Karasuma aristocratic family of Kyoto and some on fiefs assigned to the Edo bannermen Suzuki Seizaemon and Suzuki Gonnosuke. When Hiya explained the proposed plan to the villagers, he asked them to signal their agreement or opposition. That is, at the same time that the merchant functionary served as a conduit for communicating the Osaka city magistrates' thoughts about river dredging to the rural population, he also had the task of summarizing the opinions of the villagers and explaining their response to the project. In that way, the Osaka city magistrates were able to weigh the views of the rural residents before formulating a final plan of action, and this style of governance by mutual negotiation was made possible by the dedicated efforts of merchant delegates such as Atarashiya Yahei and Hiya Ichirōbei.

A third duty assigned to the merchant functionaries was to house and feed village representatives who journeyed to Osaka on official business. On the first day of the Ninth Month, 1722, for instance, Honda Chūemon, the chief manager at Kuge Tōjūrō's office, issued the following announcement to the villages within the rural magistrate's jurisdiction. "From times past, the rural intendant's merchant delegate, Atarashiya Yahei, has been assigned to provide lodging and board in Osaka for village officials who come to the city on government business. In the future, those village officials should continue to stay with the same person. They are not to lodge at any other place. This announcement is being issued since additional villages have been placed under Kuge's jurisdiction this year."[13] The purpose of requiring village officials to stay at the residences of merchant functionaries such as Atarashiya, even though Honda's announcement suggests that alternative arrangements were possible, was to facilitate communication between the village representatives and the merchant delegates. That is, meetings and discussion sessions between the two sides could be easily arranged, and from the perspective of the merchant functionaries, the intimate housing arrangements virtually insured that their opinions would find expression in any petitions or statements about policy decisions that the village leaders might prepare for submission to higher officials.

Finally, the merchant delegates frequently helped to mediate civil disputes in the rural areas around Osaka. Whenever a disagreement involved persons living on holdings that belonged to a single proprietor, daimyo, or bannerman,

---

13. "Kōgi goyōfuredome-chō," as found in Mori, "Sakai-mawari nōson no goyōdome-chō," p. 152.

village officials would attempt to negotiate a settlement. When they failed to do so, the merchant delegate then might enter the arbitration process. Moreover, if an altercation broke out between people from different jurisdictions, then the merchant assistants for all of the area jointly undertook to reach a satisfactory resolution. In 1739, for example, a dispute erupted concerning tax imposts due on some paddy located in Shinke village of Nishikibe District, Kawachi Province.[14] Shinke was part of the proprietary holdings of the daimyo Honda Tadamune, but the peasant who claimed cultivation rights to the fields, a certain Sugiyama Gizaemon, actually resided in Tondabayashi village in neighboring Ishikawa District, which was part of the domain belonging to Matsudaira Norimura, one of the shogunate's senior councilors (*rōjū*). Consequently, Yorozuya Ihei and Hinoya Shōsuke, the merchant delegates in the service of Honda and Matsudaira respectively, huddled with the village elders from Tondabayashi and the village headmen of two other nearby communities. Collectively, those men worked out a settlement that clarified Sugiyama's rights to the land and specified the taxes owed.

Besides the major responsibilities outlined above, the merchant delegates performed several additional functions. Among other things, they oversaw the erection and maintenance of the official signboards where the shogunate posted its decrees and proclamations, arranged messenger services for higher officials, and provided palanquins and porters for rural intendants and their chief lieutenants when those samurai officials traveled out to the countryside. In addition, the merchant functionaries had to verify the facts and cosign the rather complicated recommendations that villages were required to submit to higher officialdom concerning the disposition of fields and the other real property of persons who for one reason or another, ranging from romantic entanglements to financial difficulties, decided to steal away and lose themselves in some far-off province or a crowded neighborhood in one of Japan's major cities.

THE EVOLVING ROLE OF MERCHANT ASSISTANTS

The materials that provide us with the most comprehensive information about the *yōkiki* merchant delegates and the responsibilities they discharged date to the early and middle decades of the eighteenth century. The content and phrasing of those documents make it clear that merchant functionaries already had been active in the Osaka region for several decades. Equally evident is that an evolutionary process was at work; the first merchant assistants were mere tax commissioners, entrusted with helping to collect levies of corvée and matériel that the government imposed on rural villagers, whereas the later *yōkiki* delegates exercised considerably more extensive prerogatives as gov-

---

14. The documents concerning the case can be found in Tondabayashi Shishi Shiryō Hensan Iinkai, ed., *Tondabayashi shishi*, vol. 5 (Tondabayashi: Tondabayashi Shiyakusho, 1973), pp. 25–26.

erning agents within the Tokugawa system of samurai-centric rule. Although the seventeenth-century record concerning the origins of the merchant functionaries is not always as rich one might wish, the documents and circumstantial evidence are sufficient for us to understand how this system, in which samurai officials depended on merchant delegates to administer the peasant population, came into being during the seventeenth century.

The peasants of Japan quickly learned that the Tokugawa shoguns had a voracious appetite for corvée. We know, for instance, that from the very first years of its existence the shogunate was imposing levies on villages in Settsu, Kawachi, and Izumi Provinces for the repair and maintenance of local rivers. Moreover, from the Shōhō period (1644–48) on, the Tokugawa government regularly required villagers to help repair and maintain its castle and warehouses in Osaka, and starting in 1653 officials imposed annual corvée levies on village residents in Settsu and Kawachi to keep rivers and dikes in good condition. Peasants had to contend with a plethora of other exactions: at various times they might be required to supply rice for payment to those who performed miscellaneous labor and carrier duties at Edo Castle, contribute to restoration projects at the imperial palace and the shogunate's Nijō Castle in Kyoto, submit harvests of Chinese matrimony vine, gather and transport raw materials used to produce gunpowder for the musket bearers stationed at Osaka Castle, and perform miscellaneous duties at the imperial palace when the emperor had audiences with the retired emperor or crown prince. In addition they often were called to provide porter services—for shogunal envoys processing to Kyoto, for the ceremonial retinue that accompanied Iemitsu's daughter from Edo when she married into an aristocratic family in 1649, for distinguished visitors from Korea and the Ryūkyū Islands as they journeyed up the Tōkaidō Highway, and for aristocrats and priests on their pilgrimages to Ieyasu's mausoleum at Mount Nikkō.

Peasants from villages in different locales had to bear the levies, depending upon the kind of supplies or type of labor service that the political elites required. For example, the impositions for riparian projects fell chiefly on the villagers residing on the shogun's holdings and daimyo domains in Settsu and Kawachi Provinces, whereas peasants from the shogun's direct holdings in Settsu, Kawachi, Izumi, and Harima became more familiar than perhaps they wished concerning the need to keep Osaka Castle and the hegemon's warehouses in that city in good repair. Meanwhile, farmers from the shogun's lands in Harima, joined by fellow cultivators from shogunal and daimyo lands in Ōmi, Tanba, and the five Kinai provinces, had to turn out to cart the bags of the envoys from Korea and the Ryūkyū Islands. As can be seen in Table 10.1, the government imposed on a regular, permanent basis levies to carry out riparian projects, maintain Osaka Castle and the shogun's warehouses, and support labor and carrier services at Edo Castle, whereas the authorities decreed the others as circumstances demanded.

During the seventeenth century, highly placed shogunal officials—the regional supervisor of rural intendants (*Kamigata gundai*), the Kyoto city magistrates, the Osaka city magistrates, or some combination thereof, depending

Table 10.1. Regional levies imposed in Settsu, Kawachi, and Izumi Provinces during the seventeenth century

A. Levies of corvée and matériel made on a permanent, regular basis
  1. Imposts made on territories administered by the shogunate
     • For payments to those who performed miscellaneous labor and carrier duties at Edo Castle
     • For the repair and maintenance of Osaka Castle
     • For the construction and upkeep of the shogunate's warehouses in Osaka
  2. Imposts made both on territories administered by the shogunate and on holdings belonging to other proprietors
     • For riparian projects (from 1653, and only in Settsu and Kawachi Provinces)
B. Levies of corvée and matériel made on an extraordinary, ad hoc basis
  1. Imposts made on territories administered by the shogunate
     • For porters to accompany aristocrats and priests journeying to Mount Nikkō
     • For the upkeep of the imperial palace and residence
     • For the harvesting of Chinese matrimony vine
     • For the collection and transportation of materials used to manufacture ammunition for musket bearers at Osaka Castle
  2. Imposts made both on territories administered by the shogunate and on holdings belonging to other proprietors
     • For porters to accompany envoys from the Ryūkyū Islands
     • For porters to accompany the bridal procession of Iemitsu's daughter from Edo in 1649 when she married into an aristocratic household
     • For miscellaneous duties at the imperial palace when the emperor had audiences with the retired emperor or crown prince
     • For porters to accompany envoys from Korea
     • Corvée for riparian projects (before 1653, and only in Settsu and Kawachi Provinces)
     • For porters to accompany shogunal envoys making courtesy visits to the emperor

Note: Levies of corvée and matériel to repair and maintain Nijō Castle in Kyoto were made on an ad hoc basis on unspecified lands.

upon the circumstances and particular time period—informed each individual proprietor (or rural magistrate, in the case of the shogun's direct holdings) about the amount of corvée and matériel that would be required from him (or from the villages within his particular jurisdiction). The proprietor and rural magistrates in turn relied upon the services of certain merchants from Osaka who served in essence as tax commissioners, taking responsibility for guaranteeing that the government received its levies in a timely fashion. A petition dated to the Fourth Month of 1648 provides some informative insights into how that was accomplished. In that document Naraya Chōzaemon, a merchant residing in Osaka, addressed a request to Kogō Kichiemon, who was an assistant to Ishiko Katsumasa, the locally prominent shogunal official who served jointly as a city magistrate of Sakai and as a rural intendant.[15] Naraya was concerned about some twenty-two villages under Ishiko's supervision, all

15. A document containing the proclamations issued by the Sakai city magistrates between the Fourth Month of 1648 (Keian 1) and the spring of the following year can be found in Sakai-shi, ed., *Sakai shishi, zoku-hen*, vol. 5 (Sakai: Sakai Shiyakusho, 1973), pp. 989–1012; see pp. 990–91 for the petition cited here. For additional details about the merchant delegates, see my "Yaku no jitsugen kikō to bugashira • yōkiki no yakuwari," *Nihon-shi kenkyū* 349 (September 1991), pp. 1–30.

located in Ōtori District of Izumi Province. According to Naraya, the residents of those communities were seriously in arrears in their taxes; they had failed, he charged, to submit assessments of matériel and labor for the repair of the government's grain warehouse at Takatsuki in 1646, and the following year the villagers had ignored a levy of medicinal herbs, had neglected to supply porters and horses for a pilgrimage of Kyoto notables to Mount Nikkō, and had not responded to calls for matériel and labor to repair official warehouses in Osaka. Therefore, Naraya concluded, he hoped that Kogō, in his capacity as the magistrate's assistant, would intercede and compel the village headmen to make certain that the residents of their settlements complied with the assessments made upon them.

This example reveals that the villages subject to the government's regional corvée levies did not submit the requisitions directly to tax authorities. Rather, intermediaries such as Naraya, who was so designated by the rural intendant, either made alternative arrangements to have the services performed or tendered a single cash payment to the government equivalent to the corvée levy, with the villagers then reimbursing him the amount of the impost. The documents refer to intermediaries such as Naraya as *bugashira*, a term that might be rendered as tax commissioner or tax contractor. The *bugashira*, that is, were in charge of submitting taxes as representatives of governing authorities, and evidence confirming their responsibilities and functions can be found in a wide variety of mid-seventeenth-century documents concerning the shogunate's direct holdings in Settsu and Kawachi.

Tax contractors such as Naraya were fundamental to the smooth functioning of the multitiered taxation system. Specifically, the officials at the apex, such as the Kyoto and Osaka city magistrates, issued decrees that announced and specified the total amount of taxes to be collected. It was then up to the domain lords, proprietors, and rural magistrates to insure that the villages within their specific jurisdictions submitted the shogunate's regional tax assessments expeditiously and efficiently. Consequently, the rural magistrates and domain lords found the use of tax contractors to be a very convenient way to discharge that responsibility. The magistrates and lords selected trusted and dependable members of Osaka's merchant community to serve as their assistants, and the merchant tax commissioners, when necessary, would even pay the assessment out of their own pockets and then be recompensed by the villagers at a later date.

Although the tax contractor system worked fairly smoothly for some time, important transformations took place during the final years of the seventeenth century and the beginning decades of the eighteenth. By the early eighteenth century, for example, the Tokugawa regime had relaxed the number and variety of regional levies. Table 10.2 summarizes the principal modifications. The shogun's government regularly continued to levy imposts for riparian works on peasant families residing both on its own lands and on territories belonging to other proprietors, and it still demanded from villages on the shogun's direct holdings contributions to help repair and maintain Osaka Castle and the hegemon's warehouses, produce gunpowder, and cover the costs of those

Table 10.2. Regional levies imposed in Settsu, Kawachi, and Izumi Provinces after 1722

A. Levies of corvée and matériel made on a permanent, regular basis
  1. Imposts made on territories administered by the shogunate
     - The so-called *takagakari san'yaku*, which included payments to those who performed miscellaneous labor and carrier duties at Edo Castle (see Table 10.1); payments to keep in good repair the shogunal rice warehouse at Asakusa in Edo; and payments to help maintain inns and compensate merchant associations patronized by the shogunate and public officials at post towns located along major highways
     - For the repair and maintenance of Osaka Castle
     - For the construction and upkeep of the shogunate's warehouses in Osaka
     - For the collection and transportation of materials used to manufacture ammunition for musket bearers at Osaka Castle
  2. Imposts made both on territories administered by the shogunate and on holdings belonging to other proprietors
     - For riparian projects
B. Levies of corvée and matériel made on an extraordinary, ad hoc basis
  1. Imposts made on territories administered by the shogunate
     - For the upkeep of the imperial palace and residence
  2. Imposts made both on territories administered by the shogunate and on holdings belonging to other proprietors
     - For porters to accompany envoys from Korea

who performed miscellaneous labor and porter duties at Edo Castle. The number of extraordinary, ad hoc requisitions made on the shogun's own direct holdings, however, was reduced to corvée levies for the upkeep of the emperor's residence and imperial palace buildings and, on the shogun's lands and private holdings, to demands for porters to accompany delegations of Korean envoys.

Simultaneously, the evidentiary record also indicates that authorities began to calculate the corvée assessments in new ways and in some cases routinely demanded monetary payments in place of labor contributions. That was the case concerning the regional levies used for riparian projects, for instance. Beginning in 1722, the Tokugawa government annually contributed from its coffers one-tenth of the funds needed for the upkeep of banks, levees, and dikes in the five Kinai provinces. The village residents of Yamato, Yamashiro, Kawachi, Settsu, and Izumi Provinces then had to submit a cash tax to cover the remaining 90 percent of the cost of maintaining the region's waterways. A corresponding change took place in the assessment of levies to repair Osaka Castle and warehouses in the city. Until the late seventeenth century, the *bugashira* tax commissioners contracted to deliver laborers and materials such as bamboo and rope, with specific levies apportioned among the liable villages located on territories administered by the rural intendants according to the officially determined rice production of each community. After that date, however, it became standard for the government to require each village to make a specific cash payment, based as before on the community's assessed productivity, to cover the costs of materials and workmen.

As the above changes took hold during the final years of the seventeenth century and opening decades of the eighteenth, the documentation refers less often to the *bugashira* tax commissioners and mentions more frequently merchant delegates known as *yōkiki*. Initially, the profile of the new merchant delegates corresponded closely to the contours of the outgoing tax contractors since the delegates' chief responsibility was to guarantee delivery of the regional corvée assessments imposed on villages under the jurisdiction of the rural magistrates and the lords of private domains. Consequently, one can hypothesize that the roles of the *yōkiki* merchant delegates evolved out of the duties originally performed by the *bugashira* tax commissioners. A look at some specific documents lends credence to that suggestion. In official records dated 1647 and 1648 the Osaka merchant Edoya Gen'emon appears as a tax commissioner in the service of Toshima Jūzaemon, the Osaka-based rural magistrate who administered affairs in Jūhachijō village, located in Nishi Nari District, Settsu Province. The name Edoya Gen'emon also can be found in the "Kokon ashiwakezuru taizen," a comprehensive directory to Osaka administration compiled in 1681.[16] In that guide to officialdom, Edoya is listed as a *yōkiki*, a merchant functionary, in the service of Toshima Gonnojō, who had succeeded his father Jūzaemon as a rural magistrate. It is not clear whether the Edoya in the 1681 document was the same person as in the preceding records or whether he was the earlier Gen'emon's son, but, in either event, the case demonstrates the close relationship that existed between samurai officials and merchant assistants, and it also provides some clues about how the position of tax commissioner grew into that of the merchant delegate, who eventually carried out a broader range of duties as specified above.

The collection of the Tokugawa regime's regional corvée imposts was one agency that helped to cement and strengthen the relationship between rural magistrates and domain officials, on the one hand, and the merchant assistants who were responsible for actually delivering the taxes, on the other. In essence, the tax contractors and merchant delegates who succeeded them were taking responsibility for implementing the authority of higher officials. In that context, it is important to note that by the early eighteenth century, at the latest, the Osaka city magistrates utilized the merchant delegates to circulate decrees and pronouncements to various districts under their supervision. As discussed earlier, the village of Komagatani in Furuichi District of Kawachi Province received seven decrees that originated with the Osaka city magistrates. Of those seven, the merchant functionaries themselves authored and put their seals to two announcements, after having received guiding instructions from the city magistrates. In those two instances, the merchant delegates who propagated the edicts were not acting on behalf of the Watanabe daimyo family, which claimed the village as part of its domain, but rather were in the employ of a different daimyo who had territorial holdings in Furuichi District. This is convincing evidence that by the early years of the Kyōhō period (1716–36), it had become standard procedure for merchant delegates to receive in-

16. Located in the archives of the Osaka City History Research Institute (Ōsaka Shishi Hensanjo).

structions and hear the intentions of the Osaka city magistrates and then to circulate decrees throughout the provinces surrounding the city of Osaka.[17] Thus, beginning with the collection of the government's regional corvée levies in the seventeenth century, the merchant functionaries broadened their activities so that by the middle of the eighteenth century they carried out many governing functions noted earlier on behalf of daimyo proprietors, the Osaka city magistrates, and rural intendants.

Osaka as a Center of Governance

It may be useful, by way of leading toward a conclusion, to elaborate on the activities of the merchant delegates by discussing the evolution of that office within the broader context of Osaka's early modern urbanism. First of all, while the *yōkiki* delegates were all members of the Osaka merchant community, their combined office-residences were clustered within a fairly compact part of the city. The map "Office-residences of Osaka's merchant delegates in 1728" shows the distribution of the known residences of some sixty-eight merchant delegates, as derived from information about eighty-two such functionaries mentioned in the "Naniwa sode kagami zen," a document compiled in 1728.[18] As can be seen, a great many of the merchant functionaries conducted their affairs from properties located in the neighborhoods that lay between Osaka Castle and Higashi Yoko Canal. Not unexpectedly, that was a matter of convenience. The office compounds of such authorities as the Osaka city magistrates and the Osaka rural intendants also could be found in the same section of the city, thus facilitating communication between those higher-level samurai officials and the commoner delegates who assisted them and helped to govern in their names.

As the position of *yōkiki* became a permanent part of the administrative system during the late seventeenth century, certain Osaka families came to serve as delegates on a permanent basis. Evidence from the "Settsu Naniwa maru," thought to have been completed in 1696, shows how deeply imbedded the merchant deputies had become in the administrative system.[19] According to that document, for instance, Kohashiya Chōbei served as a merchant delegate on behalf of the magistrate of armaments (*teppō bugyō*) and a total of seventeen daimyo and bannermen, and Iwataya Rizaemon performed the same taxing and administrative duties for eight daimyo and bannermen. In addition, later eighteenth-century guides to Osaka administration similar to the "Kokon ashiwakezuru taizen" and the "Settsu Naniwa maru" consistently listed the head of the Iwataya family as a *yōkiki* for generation after generation, an indication of how the position of merchant delegate had become hereditary.

17. Iwaki Takuji, "Kinsei sonraku no tenkai to shihai kōzō—'Shihai-koku' ni okeru yōtashi o chūshin ni," *Nihon-shi kenkyū* 355 (March 1992), pp. 55–76.
18. Archives, Osaka City History Research Institute.
19. Ibid.

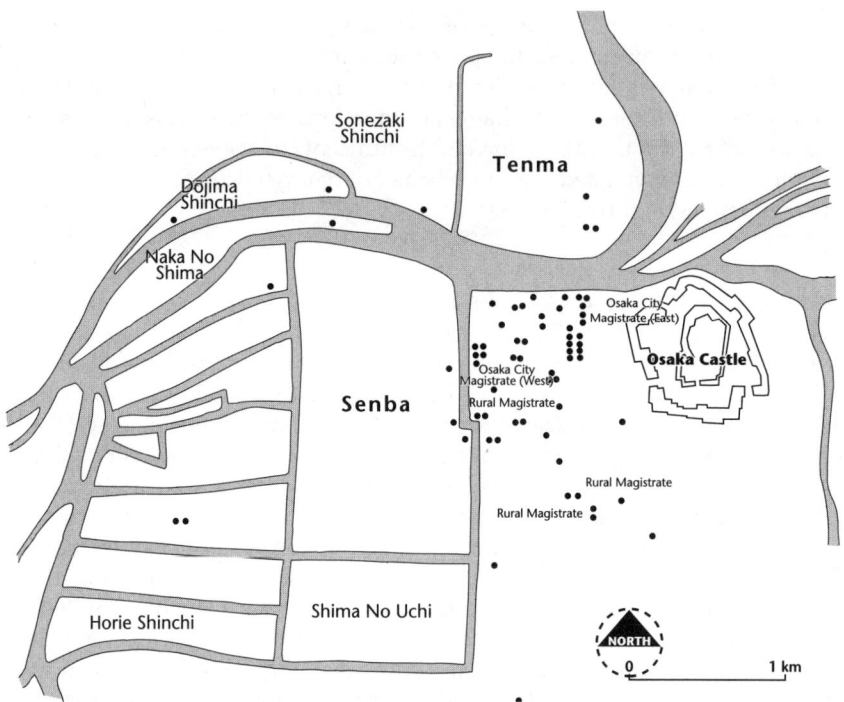

Map 10. Office-residences of Osaka's merchant delegates in 1728

Concurrently, Osaka's merchant delegates were forming associations among themselves. One example of that comes from a letter dated the Eleventh Month of 1727. The document bears the seal of Iwataya Rizaemon, who was acting in his capacity as the merchant delegate for the bannerman Nagai Naotsune, and it is addressed to fourteen villages on that samurai's scattered holdings in the Mamuta, Katano, and Wakae Districts of Kawachi Province.[20] "In previous years," Iwataya's missive began, "our association of merchant delegates collectively handled the details concerning assessments of corvée for riparian projects in Settsu and Kawachi Provinces." The expression "previous years" refers to the period before 1722, when the system of making assessments was changed from actual levies of manpower and materials to an equivalent monetary contribution, and the document indicates that an association of merchant delegates bore responsibility for overseeing the imposition of the taxes for riparian projects until that date. Although the documents do not reveal very much about the circumstances or activities of the associations of merchant delegates, it probably would not be too remiss to suppose that the associations originally came into being when merchant delegates had to me-

---

20. The specific document bears the title "Go-kōgi furejō no tome" and is part of the records of the Ohara family of Katano District, Kawachi Province, preserved at the Hirakata City Office (Hirakata shiyakusho).

diate taxation or other civil disputes among villages under the jurisdiction of different proprietors and rural intendants. Of course the supervisors for riparian matters were the principal officials entrusted with determining the levies of corvée and matériel used to keep riverbanks, dikes, and levees in good repair, but, judging from the contents of the 1727 document, it appears likely that associations of merchant delegates in Osaka, functioning under the authority of samurai supervisors, collectively decided most details concerning the actual assessment and collection of the levies.

As the above examples indicate, by the end of the seventeenth century the merchant delegates occupied a key niche in the structure of governance for the region surrounding Osaka, shouldering an important part of the actual administration of the region. In understanding how this came about, we need to bear in mind that the existence of so many fragmented territorial holdings and political jurisdictions created certain particular problems concerning governance in the Osaka region. From the very first years of its existence, the shogunate imposed regional levies of corvée and matériel on all villagers in Osaka's hinterland, and the officials who bore the highest degree of administrative responsibility for collecting those taxes, the Osaka city magistrates and the rural intendants, were headquartered in the city. The fact that individual proprietors and the rural intendants were responsible for actually delivering those imposts (for their own holdings or for the shogun's lands) necessitated the existence of lower-level functionaries who, as tax commissioners, could handle the details of the process. In time, the prerogatives exercised by the merchant assistants broadened, going beyond matters related to the collection of the shogunate's regional levies to embrace a range of governing responsibilities that their successors, the merchant delegates, performed on behalf of the Osaka city magistrates, the rural intendants, and individual proprietors. The transition from acting essentially as tax collectors to being more significant agents of governance took place during the late seventeenth century.

As the offices of regional and shogunal government matured during the course of the seventeenth and early eighteenth centuries, Osaka became something more than a mere assemblage of bureaucratic offices. Rather, Osaka emerged as a true headquarters of governance. The elites at the apex of the political hierarchy, of course, were the rulers, the magistrates and intendants of samurai pedigree who enjoyed the prerogative of formulating the policies that did so much to shape the conditions under which the urban and rural commoners of the Osaka region lived out their lives. The ruling officials were few in number, however, and the area of their jurisdiction was broad, both in geographical extent and in terms of the range of responsibilities they had to assume. Consequently, the rulers reached into the ranks of the ruled commoners and tapped some to act as their agents. The research presented in this chapter illustrates how one group of merchant assistants, the *bugashira* tax collectors, first came into existence and then evolved into more influential *yōkiki* delegates whose activities and negotiations with superiors helped to mold and modulate policies. In that sense, the merchant delegates entered the realm of the rulers, and their inclusion within the pyramid of political leadership added to Osaka's importance as a nodal point for both the formulation and execution of governmental authority. No historian would dispute Osaka's importance as a center of commerce and production, and other chapters in this volume have expounded its contributions to the cultural, religious, intellectual vitality of the early modern era. In addition to those guises, Osaka appears on Japan's urban landscape as a nucleus of political power.

CHAPTER ELEVEN

The Distinguishing Characteristics of Osaka's Early Modern Urbanism

— *Wakita Osamu*

TRANSLATED BY JAMES L. MCCLAIN

Osaka was born in an age of ferment and strife, the tumultuous Sengoku era when Japan was a Country at War with itself. Centuries before that, at the dawn of Japan's recorded history, people settled the Uemachi Plateau, and in the seventh century contenders for national hegemony had established there a center of imperial authority, short lived though it was. In subsequent centuries, the Watanabe clan put down roots on the estuary of the Yodo and Yamato Rivers, and thriving trading communities eventually grew up nearby at Tennōji, Sumiyoshi, and Sakai. Osaka's conception as an urban center of lasting and permanent significance, however, came only when the prelates of the Honganji branch of the True Pure Land sect (Jōdo Shinshū) founded a temple-fortress on the Uemachi Plateau in 1496. Quickly, a prospering town grew up around the religious redoubt, and the Ishiyama Honganji became a center of commerce and culture, as well as the political nerve center for the denomination's far-flung religious monarchy, which at its height embraced tens of thousands of adherents in several provinces.

During the 1570s, Oda Nobunaga saw the sect as standing in the way of his drive to extend hegemony over central Japan, and the warlord threw his legions against the religious armies mobilized by Kennyo Kōsa, the eleventh abbot of the Honganji. Many considered the temple-fortress at Osaka to be impregnable, and the citadel's adherents defended themselves with great resolve during the first half of the decade. In 1577, however, Nobunaga shifted tactics and launched a determined campaign against the Honganji's outer defenses, successfully cutting off the religious stronghold from its affiliated congregations in other parts of Japan. In the Third Month of 1580, the ambitious warlord persuaded Emperor Ōgimachi to send Abbot Kennyo a Letter of Advice, counseling him to negotiate a peaceful settlement. Isolated and running short of supplies, Kennyo agreed to lay down his arms and to surrender the Ishiyama Honganji. On the second day of the Eighth Month, the abbot's son, Kyōnyo Kōju, threw open the gates to the fortress; that very day the Ishiyama Honganji burned to the ground, apparently on the prelate's orders.

As Toyotomi Hideyoshi fought to secure his control over central Japan in the months and years following Nobunaga's death in 1582, he decided to build a new castle on the site of the former Ishiyama Honganji. Hideyoshi's thinking, presumably, followed from strategic concerns: to grasp Japan's economic heartland for himself and to protect the southern approaches to Kyoto. Hideyoshi's ambitions also demanded monuments to his newfound power and glory, and he set about erecting a citadel that would rival Nobunaga's magnificent Azuchi Castle, completed at the end of the 1570s. Hideyoshi's engineers began construction in the Eighth Month of 1583, and with as many as a hundred thousand workers laboring on the project, the warlord was able to move into Osaka Castle on the eighth day of the Eighth Month, 1584. When finally finished, the castle grounds measured more than seven miles in circumference and contained, as described in the first chapter of this volume, several spacious enceintes, a multistoried donjon, and splendid residential mansions gilded with gold leaf.

Even in an era marked by extraordinary architectural flamboyance, Osaka Castle stood as Japan's most celebrated and majestic fortress complex. Quickly, daimyo who wished to be counted as Hideyoshi's loyal allies built elaborate mansions nearby, and merchant and artisan families thronged to the Uemachi Plateau, where they settled down and began to supply the needs of the thriving assemblage of warriors and their families. As the adjoining merchant town began to grow anew, Hideyoshi invited important religious institutions to construct shrines and temples in Osaka, and he included the Honganji in his largesse, although in this instance one suspects that the opportunity to keep a close eye on a potential enemy counted more with Hideyoshi than did pious thoughts. As a consequence of such policies, Osaka expanded rapidly during the Toyotomi years and eventually enveloped such satellite additions as Tennōji, Sumiyoshi, and Sakai, which previously had existed as separate communities.

The Winter and Summer Campaigns of 1614–15 laid waste to the Toyotomi fortress and did great destruction to the surrounding merchant neighborhoods. Nevertheless, by the beginning of the seventeenth century the strategic and economic importance of the Osaka region was undeniable to all, and so it was only natural that the Tokugawa shogunate would rebuild Osaka Castle to serve as its defense anchor in western Japan. Quite naturally, too, it sought to promote the development of a flourishing city of production and trade, as symbolized by Iemitsu's dramatic unfurling of the great golden banner in 1634 announcing an exemption to property taxes. Over the next century, Osaka would grow to enormous proportions and, as the chapters in this volume bear witness, assume its place as one of the Three Metropoles atop Japan's urban hierarchy.

Hideyoshi's Osaka

In a variety of ways, the Osaka that emerged at the end of the sixteenth century and beginning of the seventeenth simultaneously recapitulated the past and announced the future. As different persons staked their claim to the Uemachi Plateau over the course of nearly a thousand years, they had made it in turn a home to government, commerce, religion, and culture. Hideyoshi's Osaka was all of that—and considerably more as well. That is, the warlord's efforts to create an urban environment that reflected his accomplishments and aspirations as Japan's unifier and military master, along with his attempts to nurture commercial and religious life within the city, made Osaka a prototype for other castle towns and defined a number of the enduring characteristics that came to distinguish Osaka's future urbanism.

One of Hideyoshi's most consequential initiatives was to decree that Osaka's geography articulate a correspondence between space, function, and status. He intended his castle to be at the heart of the new community, and he located his direct vassals in close proximity to his imposing citadel. Somewhat further away, but still in positions of convenience and comfort, were the estates of leading daimyo who came to Osaka to pay obeisance to their lord. Geographically distinct from those warrior residences were the neighborhoods, mostly to the south and west of the castle, inhabited by Osaka's growing merchant and artisan population. Further distant, as seen in the map "Osaka under Toyotomi Hideyoshi" in Chapter 1, districts set aside for temples and shrines ringed the outskirts of the community, and outcast families lived on the far northern fringes of Osaka, in villages strung out along the marshy banks of the Yodo River.

Hideyoshi also strove to induce the commercial development of Osaka, an initiative that other daimyo would repeat when they established their castle towns. Certainly, the names of individual neighborhoods and residential quarters within Osaka indicate that considerable numbers of aspiring merchants and artisans migrated to Osaka from towns and villages in the surrounding hinterland during the Toyotomi years. Thus, the names of provinces within the Kinai region such as Ise, Ōmi, Kii, and Awaji reappear as appellations for specific Osaka neighborhoods that presumably were home to persons from those locales. Similarly, the existence of Azuchi-machi suggests a mass migration to Osaka after Azuchi Castle was demolished, while yet other place names in the city derived from individual families (the Yasui of Kyūhōji village and the Nariyasu and Sukeyoshi from the town of Hirano) who played important roles in developing Osaka's economic potential after moving to the city from surrounding communities.

In part, the movement of individuals and families into Osaka was spontaneous; knowledge about the area's past economic significance imparted a clear message to contemporaries about the commercial gains they might hope to reap by taking up residence around Hideyoshi's grand edifice. But while many families found their way to Osaka on their own, others were responding more directly to specific policies authored by the powerful warlord. Toward the end of his life, for instance, Hideyoshi sponsored the development of wharves and anchorages along the Yodo River to facilitate the shipment of goods into Osaka, and he formulated plans to plat new residential quarters for merchants and artisans in the Senba area. Moreover, according to the diaries of several of the so-called five commissioners (*go bugyō*) who handled routine administrative affairs on behalf of Hideyoshi, the exchange market for gold and silver coinage rotated monthly between Fushimi, Sakai, and Osaka, a policy that signified Osaka's emerging economic importance and drew traders to the city.[1]

As part of the campaign to make Osaka an important node of exchange and production, Hideyoshi threw his weight behind an ongoing effort to create "free markets and open guilds" (*rakuichi to rakuza*). Earlier, daimyo such as the Rokkaku family of Ōmi Province and Shibata Katsuie on his own holdings had pursued that goal by abolishing local marketing taxes that religious institutions and aristocratic houses previously had imposed and by eliminating the monopolistic privileges that medieval guilds had enjoyed under the patronage of those powerful Kyoto-based religious and social elites. Hideyoshi extended that initiative across all of central Japan, with the consequence that the market economy and networks of commercial exchange came to center on the emerging castle towns. In the case of Osaka, to cite one example, many merchant and artisan families who had specialized in the production of oil in the late medieval period abandoned their homes in Ōyamazaki, Settsu, and Yamashiro and moved into Osaka.

Hideyoshi also manipulated tax policies as a means of compelling people to pull up stakes and migrate to Osaka. In 1591, Hideyoshi declared that merchant and artisan families in Osaka would be exempt from property taxes (*jishigin*). In contrast, villagers had to pay high taxes, the burdensome *nengu* that was calculated as a proportion of the yield of their paddy, as did the residents of former temple towns, such as Tondabayashi, that were legally redefined as villages after falling to the military hegemons. The merchant and artisan families that lived in other cities also faced higher levies than did their counterparts in Osaka. Commoners in nearby Sakai, for instance, had to pay a stiff property tax, and artisanal guilds bore the responsibility for submitting business taxes. Moreover, all merchants and artisans in Sakai occasionally had to dig into their purses to meet extraordinary demands, such as in the Third Month of 1586 when Hideyoshi required them to cover the cost of supplying 250 boats to convey materials for the construction of Osaka Castle. Needless to

---

1. For additional details, see my *Kinsei hōken shakai no keizai kōzō* (Tokyo: Ochanomizu Shobō, 1963), pp. 15–41.

say, such differentials, deliberately created by Hideyoshi, encouraged migration to Osaka from surrounding towns and villages.

As noted in the introductory chapter, it is impossible to know the exact population of Osaka during the Toyotomi years. The physical size of the community, however, as well as claims that authorities relocated as many as seventeen thousand merchant households in order to make room for castle expansion in 1598, would suggest that Osaka's population at the end of the sixteenth century numbered in the several tens of thousands of persons. Whatever the size that the city obtained, however, the dynamics of growth clearly relied on both the spontaneous desires of ordinary men and women to come live in the city and the calculated efforts of the military overlords to promote urban growth, a dualism that would continue to define Osaka's urban experience throughout the early modern era.

From Castle Town to "Merchants' Capital"

After the armies of Tokugawa Ieyasu and Hidetada obliterated the Toyotomi pedigree in the ferocious campaigns of 1614–15, the Tokugawa overlords duplicated many of Hideyoshi's policies in order to promote Osaka's renascence as a bastion of military and economic prowess. As James L. McClain describes in Chapter 3, Matsudaira Tadaakira encouraged important markets to reopen and cooperated with leading merchants to expand the city's infrastructure of waterways and shipping facilities. By the end of 1620, Osaka's entrepreneurs could move their goods along the completed Nishi Yoko, Dōton, Edo, and Kyōmachi waterways, and engineering corps were at work digging channels for the Naga and Itachi Canals. Early that same decade, government survey teams had finished platting Senba, which soon fulfilled its potential by becoming the heart of merchant Osaka.

In the 1620s, Hidetada defined a geographical linchpin for the shogunate's Osaka when he required daimyo from western Japan to expend vast sums to reconstruct Osaka Castle and then reserved space near the castle for the regime's vassals. In the next decade, Iemitsu more vigorously encouraged merchants and artisans to migrate to the city by reinstituting the exemption from urban land taxes that Hideyoshi originally had established in 1591. Later tax exemptions took more imaginative forms. When authorities platted Dōjima Shinchi for merchant use in 1688, for example, they held new residents liable for paying a property tax but exempted them from the standard house tax.[2] A decade after that, merchant and artisan families moving into newly developed North and South Horie successfully petitioned for a ten-year exemption from property taxes; in 1708 taxes were remitted for fifteen years for persons settling at Sonezaki Shinchi; and a ten-year reprieve on taxes was granted to families taking up residence at Nishi Kōzu in 1745.

2. See "Fujii Zenpachi oboegaki," in Ōsaka-shi, ed., *Ōsaka shishi*, vol. 5 (Osaka: Sanjikai, 1913), pp. 29–30.

At times, the shogunate even went so far as to confiscate land for merchant and artisan use. Hideyoshi occasionally had done likewise, such as when he compelled Ikutama and Zama shrines to relocate to make room for arriving merchant and artisan families, but the Tokugawa shogunate more frequently asserted its rights of eminent domain. In 1620, for instance, the families of Mitsudera village "offered up all their farmland to the lord, and it was converted to use for merchant and artisan housing."[3] The verb "offered up" is a euphemism, of course, masking the reality that the farmers were being compelled to move to undeveloped lands so that the government could divide their old paddy into eleven urban neighborhoods.

For a while in the 1620s and 1630s, the reborn Osaka appeared destined to relive its former incarnation as a castle town. That was particularly evident in the physical layout of the city. The new Tokugawa battlements loomed over the surrounding community; the lord's vassals lived adjacent to the castle; daimyo began to move into elaborate estates along the banks of the Yodo River; merchants and artisans settled into residential quarters geographically discrete from their warrior neighbors; and temples remained clustered together. Indeed, for many persons the predominant image of Osaka was its castle and the adjacent military community. That certainly seems to have been so in the case of the cartographers who in 1657 drew the oldest extant map of the city, reproduced in Chapter 3, which lavishes more attention on the details of the castle complex than it does on the merchant neighborhoods of Osaka.

Osaka's persona changed during the course of the seventeenth century, however, as the emerging city gradually shed its identity as the shogunate's headquarters in western Japan and, instead, became what legitimately can be called Japan's *chōnin no miyako*, the merchants' capital. By the midpoint of the early modern epoch, Osaka was acknowledged as the economic hub of Japan, the "country's kitchen" in the later words of the respected city magistrate Kusumi Sukeyoshi. That phrase encapsulated Osaka's emergence as the country's leading center for the production and processing of a vast array of goods, from rapeseed oil to cotton cloth and leather wear, as well as the country's most significant transshipment axis, where such commodities as rice, tea, saké, vinegar, soy sauce, medicines, and household furnishings were brought together and then dispatched to customers throughout the Osaka region and as far away as Edo and other population centers in eastern Japan.

Many reasons account for Osaka's transformation from the shogun's castle town into the merchants' capital. Prominent among those was the overall rise of the Kinai region, beginning in the late medieval period, as Japan's leading center of craft production and agricultural output. That phenomenon gave life to Osaka's role as the pivotal commercial node in the complicated supply network that collected basic necessities and moved them into Edo and the emerging Kantō region, and perhaps more than anything else, it also ensured the success of the policies undertaken by the overlords in the 1610s and 1620s to revitalize Osaka, as well as later government initiatives such as the completion

---

3. *Mitsudera monjo*, located in the manuscript collection at the shrine Mitsu Hachimangū.

of the eastern and western shipping circuits under the direction of Kawamura Zuiken. Yet, as many authors in this volume emphasize, merchant initiative—the efforts of individuals and their families to secure their own livelihoods—must be taken into account, for without their enterprise and labors all government policies would have ended in naught. It is that sort of merchant enterprise that came to characterize Osaka's urbanism.

Other noneconomic factors also came into play as the merchant and artisan families of Osaka reinvented the city during the seventeenth century. The decision of the shogun not to station a major garrison at Osaka meant that demographically Osaka would be a commoners' city with the samurai constituting only a very small fraction of the population. The warrior residents of Osaka included merely the castle warden and the bannermen who captained the guard units under his supervision, the constables and patrolmen assigned to those regiments, shogunal civil officials such as the city magistrates and their subordinate staffs, and the samurai dispatched from individual domains to work on their master's warehousing estates. In all, it is unlikely that the total number of samurai residents, even including all the warriors from daimyo domains who were in the city temporarily, living on their lord's warehousing estates, amounted to more than a couple of thousand persons. That was a minuscule number compared to the more than three hundred thousand commoners who were resident in the city at any time during the eighteenth and early nineteenth centuries.

The population imbalance carried with it political implications. Merchant self-management of their own political affairs, a hallmark of medieval urbanism as discussed by Wakita Haruko in her contribution to this volume, became the norm in Osaka during the early modern epoch. Self-management is not to be confused, of course, with complete autonomy from outside authority. In the early modern era, cities were the cornerstone upon which the shogun and individual daimyo erected their structures of power, and the overlords went to great lengths to secure their control over Japan's urban centers and to make certain that their prerogatives as rulers would be respected. Within that context, however, the shogun and daimyo entrusted many aspects of urban administration to the merchant and artisan population, especially as conditions of peace, the great Pax Tokugawa, extended over the country from the middle decades of the seventeenth century.

The registration of property provides one barometer of that transition toward merchant self-management. Since the possession of land endowed one with the status of *chōnin*, together with all of its attendant privileges and obligations, deciding which individuals were entitled to possess, rent out, sell, and bequeath specified parcels of land was of particular importance. In the early years of Tokugawa rule, it appears that samurai officials had the responsibility to approve and keep track of most property transactions, thus in practice determining who would have *chōnin* status. When Iemitsu visited Osaka in 1634 and declared a general exemption from property taxes, however, he also shifted responsibility for verifying the transfer and possession of property to the neighborhood elders (*machidoshiyori*), the leaders of the merchant and artisan residential quarters who reported to the city elders and city magistrates, with the consequence that merchant representatives came to wield a veto power over who might reside in their jurisdiction and enjoy the status of being a property owner.

A review of how the ordinary merchant and artisan residents of Osaka shouldered a variety of burdens and duties associated with urban administration provides another perspective about self-management. Various clerks and other low-level functionaries were stationed at the city offices (*machi kaisho*) to carry out administrative functions, and the inhabitants of individual neighborhoods bore the collective responsibility for compiling and preserving census records, dredging the city's canals and waterways, fighting fires, managing and keeping in good repair water and sewage systems, roads, and bridges, and generally looking out for each other's welfare. Moreover, while the city magistrates retained ultimate jurisdiction over criminal matters and acted as judges in civil and criminal cases, the residents of each residential quarter shared in policing duties by maintaining night guards (*yaban, jishiban*) and apprehending troublemakers. Indeed, by the turn of the seventeenth century, commoner self-management of the city had become so marked that the haiku poet Konishi Raizan would write in his diary that "another year has passed without my even learning the names of the Osaka city magistrates."

Exploring the Merchants' Capital

The growing economic prowess of Osaka's merchant and artisan estates, together with their expanding role in the administration of their own neighborhoods and their assumption of control over many governing duties that impinged directly on their lives, constituted two characteristics that defined Osaka's early modern urbanism. In turn, growing economic and political self-confidence spawned what might be called second generation examples of increasing merchant and artisan influence. Indeed, so adept at political administration did some leading Osakans become that they assisted samurai officials in conducting government business in towns and villages around Osaka, as Murata Michihito explains in his chapter. But Uchida Kusuo also cautions us that harmony did not always prevail and that sometimes official policy did not accord with merchant thoughts about the proper course of governmental action. In such cases, as Uchida makes clear, Osaka's commoners did not permit themselves to be trampled upon by the samurai overlords, and they remonstrated against unpopular policies, finding ways to make their voices heard about matters most dear to them.

The conversion of Osaka into the merchants' capital was multidimensional, moving well beyond political and economic spheres of conduct. As McClain shows in his chapter, the merchants and artisans of Osaka came to possess the city physically, shifting the geographical center of gravity away from the castle and pushing it toward the neighborhoods of the Senba area and the network of canals and waterways used to transport the economic lifeblood of the city.

By the Genroku era, merchant Osaka also became a setting for experimenting with new proclivities in arts and for creating fresh cultural motifs. In Chapter 5, C. Andrew Gerstle argues that the famous chanter Takemoto Gidayū achieved success in the world of puppetry because he was innovative, fiercely competitive, and willing to set off in new directions—characteristics widely evident throughout Osaka's merchant and artisan population. Moreover, *jōruri*, which Gerstle characterizes as "indisputably commercial theater," reaffirmed other ideals that many Osakans wished to believe about themselves as they moved about their city: that hard work, dedication, and self-sacrifice formed the basis for action; that rewards came to persons who worked for them rather than inherited them; and that egalitarianism made a place for anyone who possessed talent and was willing to labor to develop his or her talents.

Osaka's playwrights and print artists, according to Gary P. Leupp's carefully detailed reconstruction of the memory of the Five Men of Naniwa, contributed to another self-image—that ordinary merchants and artisans were virtuous commoners vulnerable to the predatory behavior of wealthy magnates, unscrupulous landlords, and arrogant and bullying samurai neighbors. In actuality, according to Leupp, Bunshichi and his band of roughnecks were common criminals who committed outrages against fellow commoners, but they reemerged in artistic mythohistory as victim-heroes who could right society's wrongs by protecting ordinary men and women from the injustices perpetuated by haughty samurai and unscrupulous businessmen. It is worth noting that the romantic aura that grew up around Bunshichi, what Leupp calls the prettification of the outlaw, took on its glow at roughly the same time that theater-goers thrilled to accounts of the Forty-Seven Righteous Warriors of Akō as acted out on the kabuki stages of Edo. But whereas the outlaws of Osaka became the custodians of commoner values in Osaka, in Edo the mythologized deeds of the forty-seven warriors converted them into folk heroes who represented all that was good within the samurai code of ethics.

Leupp's chapter draws our attention to another notable consideration. The story of Bunshichi featured conflict between commoners and warriors, but Leupp also is careful to note how extant police records suggest that gang members came from the lower economic rungs of Osaka's merchant and artisan estates and that their actual crimes reflected an acute alienation from their more well-to-do neighbors. The significance of economic distinctions among merchants and artisans as another distinguishing feature of Osaka's early modern urbanism also is revealed in a delineation of living patterns, with the economically and socially marginalized segments of the population being relegated to the fringes of the city. Yet, it is also important to remember that Osaka's commoner population could act in unison. The petition drive, as Uchida so clearly demonstrates, brought together otherwise disparate elements of the commoner population in common cause to remonstrate against particular government policies.

Economically humble Osakans also helped to create and disseminate new religious beliefs and practices. The chapters by Yoshida Nobuyuki and Nakagawa Sugane reveal the myriad activities of mendicant monks and popular shamans. The monks were extraordinarily poor and existed outside the official four-status system, yet their mendicancies contributed to a lively street culture cum popular religion that entertained even as it helped impart spiritual meaning to people's lives. The shamans, who as often as not had experienced poverty as children and difficult marriages as young women, ministered to those who sought their assistance to probe the mysteries of existence and to plot strategies that would enable them to cope with the sorrows of "this sad world."

Interestingly, both Yoshida and Nakagawa also touch upon another aspect of urban life that is imbedded in other chapters, the ambiguity of popular attitudes toward government. For merchants and for protesters, government might be an ally who could build an infrastructure and implement programs that brought well-being to the city, or it might be a foe whose policies crippled economic development and threatened to make people pay unreasonable, even immoral, prices for the necessities of life. In the case of popular religion, Osaka's mendicant monks sought out government intervention to protect their prerogatives concerning certain pious activities, whereas the devotees of Inari fell victim to a government campaign to suppress what it saw as a dangerous, unorthodox cult, led, ironically, by an official who later would organize a popular rebellion against the shogunate. For officials and the governed alike, then, stable relations could never be taken as a given, but were characterized by constant renegotiation as each side sought to advance its interests.

Osaka also emerges from these pages as a city of intellectual vitality and philosophical contestation. Early in the Tokugawa period, the poet-scholar Shimokōbe Nagaru (Chōryū) and the priest-scholar Keichū contributed to the nascent field of ancient studies, which placed a particular emphasis on the traditions of Japanese culture, and an ethnocentric consciousness flowered more fully in the writings of Motoori Norinaga. Not all Osakans, however, wished to travel down that road of philosophical inquiry: Ueda Akinari, born to a woman in Osaka's prostitution quarters and later adopted by a masterless samurai who had become a paper merchant, vigorously attacked Motoori's contentions in philology and classical studies. Similarly, Miyake Sekian, Tominaga Nakamoto, and other scholars associated with the Kaitokudō, the merchant academy where Ueda studied for a time, advanced the notion that empirical rationalism (*keiken-teki gōrishugi*) could provide the basis for knowledge and conduct. In this volume, Tetsuo Najita's chapter about Ogata Kōan and his Tekijuku reveals another aspect of that humanistic and rational quest for knowledge and, at the same time, suggests that to some degree Osaka was an international city, even in a country known for restricting its contacts with the outside world, where ideas as well as physical commodities would be welcomed and then disseminated to other people in Japan.

It might be argued, by way of a final comment, that the rise of Osaka as Japan's economic hub, together with the merchants' ever increasing demographic, political, cultural, religious, and philosophical importance, created an "Osaka personality," whose elements included a boastful self-confidence, a determined self-reliance, and pride in family, shop, and neighborhood, as well as what I have characterized elsewhere as a cold, empirically rational approach to the management of money, a tightfisted closeness with a penny, and a devilish persistence to see things through to an end.[4] Perhaps the scholar Hirose Kyokusō, however, was the first to attempt to articulate the essentials of the Osaka temperament in the early nineteenth century when he wrote that the people of Kyoto were extremely "haughty" and "consider Edo and Osaka to be rustic and backward." Edoites, Hirose groused, "are filled with mere bravado" and "value office and bureaucratic rank above all else." The men and women of Osaka, in admirable contrast, "put their hand to merchant activity, and there is no one else in the world who prizes wealth more than do the people of Osaka."[5]

In the estimation of some, Hirose's musings might seem to lean toward caricature—for as the chapters in this volume show, Osakans concerned themselves with far more than economic calculations. Still, his thoughts draw our attention to one of the underlying touchstones of this volume: Osaka's transformation—from an ordinary castle town, the shogun's military outpost in western Japan, to the country's leading center of trade and production—defined a community that was different from Japan's two other great conurbations. For many of today's historians as well as contemporaries such as Hirose, Edo stands as Japan's political headquarters, where samurai administrators composed about half of the population; and Kyoto is seen as a monument to Japan's high culture, an imperial city where patrician courtiers carefully preserved the arts of the past.

The notion of Osaka's distinctiveness returns us to the other two central themes of this volume: that the enormous changes which coursed through all of Japan during the early modern period, leading to a stronger, more cohesively organized polity, a more commercialized economy, and a more variegated social and cultural milieu than at any prior time in Japanese history, defined in a broad sense the dynamics that shaped the city's development; and as Osakans coped with those swirling changes, they created new commercial products, networks of economic exchange, administrative practices, cultural motifs, religious beliefs, and modes of thought that in turn changed the lives of people in the surrounding hinterland and across all of Japan. In common with other great world cities, Osaka encapsulated the highly distilled characteristics of the civilization that produced it while simultaneously bringing together the concentrations of wealth, power, and ideas that remade society.

4. Wakita Osamu, "Ōsaka chōnin no seikatsu to bunka," in Toyoda Takeshi, Harada Tomohiko, and Yamori Kazuhiko, eds., *Kōza Nihon no hōken toshi*, vol. 2, *Kinō to kōzō* (Tokyo: Bun'ichi Sōgō Shuppan, 1983), pp. 475–95.

5. This and other reflections about life in Osaka can be found in Hirose Kyokusō Zenshū Henshū Iinkai, ed., *Hirose Kyokusō zenshū: Zuihitsu-hen* (Kyoto: Shibunkaku Shuppan, 1987).

Glossary

allied lord	*See* fudai daimyō
alternate attendance and residence system	*See* sankin kōtai
bakufu 幕府	The shogunate; the house government of the Tokugawa shogun; presided over the affairs of the nation
bannerman	*See* hatamoto
bu 分	As a unit of value for gold and silver coins, one *bu* was the equivalent of one-quarter *ryō*; *see also fun*
bunraku 文楽	Commonly used to refer to professional puppet theater, the term derives from the name of a puppet theater established by Uemura Bunrakuken in Osaka at the beginning of the nineteenth century
chō 町	A residential quarter for merchants and artisans (also read as *machi*); an officially defined administrative subdivision within a city; each *chō* was jointly responsible for certain self-administering functions, and each was represented by a neighborhood elder (*machidoshiyori*); a unit of land measurement, roughly 2.94 acres until Hideyoshi redefined it in 1594, making it equivalent to approximately 2.45 acres
chōnin 町人	Used in various contexts to mean (1) merchant and artisan landholders; that is, persons who were entitled to possess, rent out, sell, and bequeath specified parcels of land, who paid taxes and levies on those plots, and who were eligible to serve as neighborhood elders; (2) merchants and artisans in general; and (3) all nonsamurai who lived in cities
city elder	*See* sōdoshiyori
city magistrate	*See* machi bugyō
daikan 代官	Rural intendant; responsible for administering the villages on the shogun's direct holdings

daimyo 大名	Territorial lords who ruled over holdings with an assessed productive capacity of ten thousand or more *koku* of rice
District	*See* gun
fudai daimyō 譜代大名	Allied lord; a daimyo who was elevated to that status by the Tokugawa family or who, as an independent lord, allied himself with Ieyasu before the Battle of Sekigahara in 1600
fun 分	A unit of value for silver coins, with ten *fun* equal to one *monme*; see also *bu*
fusuma 襖	Sliding screens used to partition rooms; often decorated with paintings
gatsu gyōji 月行司	Monthly delegate; assisted the neighborhood elder and served as his representative when the elder was away from the city; also glossed as *tsuki gyōji*
Genroku 元禄	The era name for the years 1688–1704; refers more generally to the decades at the end of the seventeenth century and beginning of the eighteenth that witnessed the flowering of urban culture
gun 郡	District; an administrative division of a province; the administrative functions tended to disappear during the medieval period but the districts retained an organizational and geographical identity in the early modern period
hatamoto 旗元	Bannerman; a direct retainer of the shogun who received an annual rice stipend of less than ten thousand *koku*
Heike-bushi 平家節	Chanted ballads about the Taira family and its defeat in the hands of the Minamoto family in the twelfth century
hiki 疋	A unit of value for gold coins, with one thousand *hiki* equal to 2.5 *ryō*
hinin 非人	"Nonhumans"; outcasts who entertained and begged for a living; the shogunate enlisted some to carry out such tasks as assisting at executions and caring for victims of contagious diseases
Hokuriku 北陸	A common designation for the provinces of Wakasa, Echizen, Kaga, Noto, Etchū, Echigo, and Sado
ie 家	The household, as it exists through generations and includes current living members, their deceased predecessors, and future successors; the primary unit of social organization in traditional Japan

iemoto 家元	The founder or current head of a school of artistic production
jinaichō 寺内町	Literally, a town within the precincts of a temple; a phenomenon of the Muromachi period (1333–1568) when many temple towns associated with the True Pure Land sect acquired extensive self-governing powers and became important centers of commerce and trade; also glossed as *jinaimachi*
jinaimachi	*See* jinaichō
jishigin 地子銀	A property tax levied on land belonging to merchants and artisans
jōruri 浄瑠璃	A generic term for any performance that featured the narrative chanting of stories accompanied by the shamisen
kagura 神楽	A diverse genre of performances featuring songs and masked dancing performed at Shinto festivals and ceremonies
Kamigata 上方	Osaka, Kyoto, and the region surrounding those cities
kan 貫	A unit of weight measurement (3.75 kilograms or 8.72 pounds); as a unit of value for copper coins, one *kan* (or *kanmon*) consisted of one thousand *mon*; as a unit of value for silver coins, one *kan* (or *kanme*) consisted of one thousand *monme*
kanme 貫目	One thousand *monme* of silver coins
kanmon 貫文	One thousand *mon* of copper coins; four *kanmon* were equivalent to one *ryō* of gold
Kansai 関西	(1) All of Japan west of the Hakone barrier in Sagami; (2) the region around Kyoto and Osaka, including the provinces of Ōmi, Yamashiro, Tanba, Tango, Izumi, Kawachi, Yamato, Kii, Ise, Iga, Tajima, Settsu, Harima, and Awaji
Kantō 関東	(1) Eastern Japan from Shinano and Tōtōmi to Shimotsuke and Hitachi; (2) the seven provinces of Hitachi, Shimotsuke, Kōzuke, Musashi, Shimōsa, Kazusa, and Awa, to which Sagami is sometimes added to make the *Kantō hasshū*, the Eight Kantō Provinces
Kinai 畿内	The five so-called Capital Provinces of Yamato, Yamashiro, Kawachi, Settsu, and Izumi
koku 石	A measure of volume equal to approximately five bushels; theoretically enough rice to feed one person for one year; used to calculate samurai stipends as well as the productive capacity of villages and daimyo domains

Konkōkyō 金光教	A syncretic, Shinto-based religious sect founded in the middle of the nineteenth century by Kawate Bunjirō
kouta 小唄	"Short songs"; ballads with shamisen accompaniment; highly popular in the Edo period
kōwaka-mai 幸若舞	A genre of musical narratives dealing chiefly with episodes from warrior tales
kuni 国	A province; in the Tokugawa period, Japan was divided into sixty-six regular and two island provinces
kura yashiki 蔵屋敷	Warehousing facilities and estates maintained by daimyo in Osaka
Kurozumikyō 黒住教	A syncretic, Shinto-based religious sect founded in the early nineteenth century by Kurozumi Munetada
kyōdōtai 共同体	A communally based social or economic group that functioned as a collective and quasi legal entity
kyōgen 狂言	A form of comic drama that flourished from the middle of the fourteenth century; comic roles within a noh play; comic interludes performed between plays on a slate of noh dramas
machi	See chō
machi bugyō 町奉行	City magistrates; samurai officials who exercised general responsibility for administrating the merchant and artisan residential quarters
machidoshiyori 町年寄	A neighborhood elder in Osaka; a functionary representing one or more residential quarters where merchants and artisans lived; reported to the city elders (*sōdoshiyori*) and was responsible for maintaining census registers, mediating neighborhood disputes, insuring that the residents of his quarter knew and obeyed all laws, etc.; in Edo, equivalent officials were known as *nanushi* and the term *machidoshiyori* referred to city elders
merchant delegate	See yōkiki
miko 巫女	A female attendant who presided over Shinto rituals; a female shaman who acted as a medium for supernatural beings
mon 文	A unit of value for copper coinage; one thousand *mon* equaled one *kanmon*
monme 匁	A measurement of weight (3.75 grams or 0.1325 ounces) and a unit of value for silver coins; one thousand *monme* equaled one *kanme*; the shogunate fixed an exchange rate of fifty (later sixty) *monme* of silver at one *ryō* of gold

mountain ascetic	*See* yamabushi
nakama 仲間	An officially authorized association whose members determined qualifications for membership and set regulations concerning many aspects of their own activities
nanushi 名主	The term for neighborhood elders in Edo; in Osaka the equivalent officials were known as *machidoshiyori*
national seclusion policy	*See* sakoku
neighborhood elder	*See* machidoshiyori
nenbutsu 念仏	Prayer formula; an invocation of the name of the Amida Buddha uttered in hopes of receiving divine grace and being reborn in the Western Paradise
nengu 年貢	The land tax or dues that estate proprietors collected from the peasantry during the Heian period and that warrior governments levied on villages in the late medieval and early modern periods
outside lord	*See* tozama daimyō
protective association	*See* nakama
province	*See* kuni
residential quarter	*See* chō
rōnin 浪人	A masterless samurai
rural intendant	*See* daikan
ryō 両	A unit of value for gold and silver coins; the standard gold coin issued by the shogunate, the *koban*, was equivalent to one *ryō* in the early seventeenth century and contained almost exactly fifteen grams of gold, although it was periodically devalued thereafter; the shogunate fixed the exchange rate of one *ryō* of gold at fifty (later sixty) *monme* of silver or four *kan* (*kanmon*) of copper coins; one silver *ryō* generally was equivalent to four or five *monme* of that metal
sakoku 鎖国	National seclusion; the policy, implemented by the Tokugawa shogunate, to permit only diplomatic representatives from Korea and the Ryūkyū Islands to visit Japan and to restrict official trade to Dutch and Chinese agents who could import goods only through Nagasaki
samurai 侍	(1) A warrior with the rank of bannerman or higher; (2) a warrior with the privilege of personal attendance upon his lord; (3) any warrior

sankin kōtai 参勤交代	Alternate attendance and residence system; the requirement that daimyo reside periodically in Edo (generally every other year) and that their legal wives, immediate heirs, and appropriate retinues of service personnel remain in the city at all times
shakuyanin 借家人	Persons who rented lodgings; were not considered as *chōnin*
shōen 荘園	Private landed estate characterized by multiple levels of proprietary rights
shogunate	*See* bakufu
Shugendō 修験道	The Way of Mountain Asceticism; a religious order, popular in the Tokugawa period, that prescribes ascetic practices in mountains as a way to acquire magical powers that might be used to the benefit of the home community
sōdoshiyori 惣年寄	City elders; merchant officials appointed to assist the city magistrates; in Edo such officials were known as *machidoshiyori*
tanagarinin 店借人	Persons who rented shops and lodgings; were not considered as *chōnin*
temple town	*See* jinaichō
Tenrikyō 天理教	A syncretic, Shinto-based religious sect founded in the early nineteenth century by Nakayama Miki
Tōhoku 東北	A common designation for the northern portion of Japan corresponding to the ancient provinces of Dewa and Mutsu
tozama daimyō 外様大名	Outside lord; a daimyo who achieved that status independently or by alliance with Oda Nobunaga or Toyotomi Hideyoshi
tsuki gyōji	*See* gatsu gyōji
waka 和歌	"Japanese poetry"; a synonym for *tanka*, a form of courtly poetry consisting of thirty-one syllables arranged in five lines of 5-7-5-7-7 syllables each; used to signify courtly as opposed to popular poems, and to refer to poetry written in Japanese rather than in Chinese
the Way of Mountain Asceticism	*See* Shugendo
yamabushi 山伏	Mountain ascetic; a practicing member of Shugendō
yamori 家守	An agent of a merchant or artisan landholder; had the status of *chōnin*

yōkiki 用聞		Merchant delegate; helped to collect taxes, disseminate laws, mediate disputes, and conduct other government business on behalf of the Osaka city magistrates, rural intendants, and other proprietors in the Osaka region; also known as *yōtashi*
yōtashi 用達		*See* yōkiki

Contributors

C. ANDREW GERSTLE received his doctorate from Harvard University and is a member of the faculty of the School of Oriental and African Studies, University of London. Professor Gerstle is best known for his work on the puppet theater, and his *Circles of Fantasy: Convention in the Plays of Chikamatsu* was published by the Council on East Asian Studies, Harvard University. He edited the anthology *18th Century Japan: Culture and Society* (Allen and Unwin), and, together with Kiyoshi Inobe and William P. Malm, produced *Theater as Music: The Bunraku Play "Mt. Imo and Mt. Se: An Exemplary Tale of Womanly Virtue"* (Center for Japanese Studies, University of Michigan). He currently is organizing a series of symposiums on the history of modern Osaka.

GARY P. LEUPP has written extensively on questions of ethnic consciousness, sexuality, and labor in early modern Japan. His most recent book is *Male Colors: The Construction of Homosexuality in Tokugawa Japan* (University of California Press), and he is the author of *Servants, Shophands, and Laborers in the Cities of Tokugawa Japan* (Princeton University Press). Professor Leupp is a member of the History Department at Tufts University and heads the Asian Studies Program there. Currently he is completing a volume concerning relationships between Japanese women and Western men from 1524 to 1869, and he has begun a study of the lives of silk weavers in the Nishijin district of Kyoto during the early modern period.

JAMES L. MCCLAIN is the Chair of the Department of History and a professor of East Asian Studies at Brown University. He is the author of *Kanazawa: A Seventeenth-Century Japanese Castle Town* (Yale University Press), and his *Edo and Paris: Urban Life and the State in the Early Modern Era* (coedited with John M. Merriman and Ugawa Kaoru and published by Cornell University Press) received a Hiromi Arisawa Memorial Award from the American Association of University Presses. Professor McClain has been an Invited Research Scholar at the Research Institute for Japanese Culture, Tōhoku University, and a Visiting Sangyung Scholar at Yonsei University. He is completing *Japan's Quest for Modernity*, an interpretive history of Japan from 1600 to the present to be published by W. W. Norton.

MURATA MICHIHITO teaches Japanese history at the University of Osaka. Professor Murata has done extensive research on the evolution of the Tokugawa shogunate and the extension of its authority into the Kansai region. He has published numerous articles in such leading journals as *Nihon-shi kenkyū* and *Hisutoria*. His *Kinsei kōiki shihai no kenkyū* appeared recently from Ōsaka Daigaku Shuppankai.

TETSUO NAJITA is an expert on the intellectual history of the early modern period. His *Visions of Virtue in Tokugawa Japan: The Kaitokudō Merchant Academy of Osaka* (University of Chicago Press) received the Yamagata Bantō Prize from Osaka Municipal Prefecture, and the American Historical Association awarded his *Hara Kei and the Politics of Compromise* (Harvard University Press) the John King Fairbank Prize. Professor Najita has authored numerous articles for leading journals, published four books in Japanese, and coedited, with Irwin Scheiner, *Japanese Thought in the Tokugawa Period, 1600–1868* (University of Chicago Press) and, with J. Victor Koschmann, *Conflict in Modern Japanese History: The Neglected Tradition* (Princeton University Press). He has served as vice-president and president of the Association of Asian Studies and is a fellow of the American Academy of Arts and Sciences. Professor Najita teaches at the University of Chicago, where he is the Robert S. Ingersoll Distinguished Service Professor in History and East Asian Languages and Civilizations.

NAKAGAWA SUGANE received her graduate education at the University of Osaka and is a member of the Department of Cross Cultural Studies at Koshien University. Together with Wakita Osamu, she compiled and edited the documentary collection *Bakumatsu ishin Ōsaka chōnin kiroku* (Seibundō), and her "Ōsaka hon ryōgai nakama no soshiki to kinō" appeared in *Kinsei no shakai-teki kenryoku*, edited by Yoshida Nobuyuki and Kurushima Hiroshi and published by Yamakawa Shuppansha. Professor Nakagawa is an expert on the social and economic history of the early modern era, and currently she is engaged in research on currency markets and money changers in Osaka.

UCHIDA KUSUO has made his scholarly reputation through his work on the history of Osaka in the early modern era. For many years, he served as a curator at the Osaka Castle Museum and helped to prepare for publication many volumes that describe and analyze the documents and other materials held in that collection. Professor Kusuo also has written several chapters for the recent five-volume *Shinshū: Ōsaka shishi* (published by the Osaka City Government), and he frequently contributes articles to scholarly anthologies. His influential "Ōsaka sangō no seiritsu: Shigaichi no keisei o chūshin to shite" appeared in *Ōsaka no rekishi* (Ōsaka Shishi Hensanjo, ed. and pub.). Professor Uchida is on the faculty at Ehime University.

WAKITA HARUKO teaches Japanese history at Shiga Prefectural University. Professor Wakita is a specialist on medieval economic and urban history, and her widely acclaimed *Nihon chūsei shōgyō hattatsu-shi no kenkyū* and *Nihon chūsei toshi-ron* appeared from Ochanomizu Shobō and Tōkyō Daigaku Shuppankai respectively. More recently, Professor Wakita has directed her research toward gender studies and has published *Nihon chūsei joshi-shi no kenkyū* (Tōkyō Daigaku Shuppankai) and *Chūsei ni ikiru onnatachi* (Iwanami Shoten). She is the author of many other books, including *Muromachi jidai* (Chūō Kōronsha) and *Sengoku daimyō* (Shōgakukan). Professor Wakita frequently participates in international symposiums on Japanese history, and her "Dimensions of Development: Cities in Fifteenth- and Sixteenth-Century Japan" appeared in *Japan before Tokugawa: Political Consolidation and Economic Growth, 1500–1650*, edited by John W. Hall, Nagahara Keiji, and Kozo Yamamura and published by Princeton University Press.

WAKITA OSAMU is a foremost expert on the history of early modern Japan. His pathbreaking *Kinsei shakai no keizai kōzō* was published by Ochanomizu Shobō. Professor Wakita is also the author of the influential *Genroku no shakai* (Hanawa Shobō) and a two-volume study of Oda Nobunaga and Toyotomi Hideyoshi that appeared from Tōkyō Daigaku Shuppankai. He has authored several volumes concerning the history of Osaka, including *Kinsei Ōsaka no machi to hito* and *Kinsei Ōsaka no keizai to bunka*, both published by Jinbun Shoin. Professor Wakita writes often for Western-language journals, and his "The Emergence of the State in Sixteenth-Century Japan: From Oda to Tokugawa" and "The Kokudaka System: A Device for Unification" appeared in the *Journal of Japanese Studies*. He contributed "The Social and Economic Consequences of Unification" to volume 4 of the *Cambridge History of Japan*. Professor Wakita taught for many years at the University of Osaka, served as the first director of Osaka University Press (Ōsaka Daigaku Shuppankai), and currently is the Chancellor of the Tezukayama College system.

YOSHIDA NOBUYUKI is a specialist on the social and urban history of early modern Japan. Professor Yoshida is a frequent contributor to leading journals, and his *Kinsei kyodai toshi no shakai kōzō* appeared from Tōkyō Daigaku Shuppankai, as did the three-volume *Nihon toshi-shi nyūmon*, which he coedited with Takahashi Yasuo. More recently, Professor Yoshida's *Toshi no jidai* was published by Chūō Kōron as volume 9 in its important series *Nihon no kinsei*. Professor Yoshida is a member of the faculty of the Department of Letters at the University of Tokyo.

Index

Aburaya Mohei, 189, 191
actors, 138, 147. *See also* kabuki, prostitutes and prostitution, theater
Akō domain, 58, 61, 126
allied lords (*fudai daimyō*), 50, 159, 228, 245
alternate attendance and residence system (*sankin kōtai*), 45, 82
Amagasaki, 30, 40. *See also* Kawajiri
Amaterasu Ōmikami (Sun Goddess), 1, 6, 186
"Amateur *Jōruri* Critiques." See *Kishin shirōto jōruri hyōbanki*
Amida Buddha, 8, 163, 176
An no Heibei ("Hermitage" Heibei, 1672?–1702), 125, 133–37, 140, 148
Anatomische Tabellen, 224. See also *Kaitai shinsho*
Ansei earthquake (1855), 233
Ansei Epidemic (1858), 232–37
Ansei Purge (1858–60), 216, 233
aristocrats and aristocracy, 7–9, 23, 25–30, 34, 38, 45–46, 68, 108, 109, 113, 116, 195–96, 198, 228, 245, 247, 252, 254, 264, 271, *table*, 253
Arisugawa no Miya family, 185–86, 195
the "*Arrow* War." *See under* Opium War
artisans and artisanal families, 8, 10, 14, 17–19, 22, 30–31, 39, 41–43, 51–54, 67–75, 80–84, 92–103, 127–29, 139, 146, 164, 174–75, 180, 185, 198, 200, 203, 210–11, 262–69
"As I Crossed a Bridge of Dreams." See *Sarashina nikki*
Asada Gōryū (1734–99), 227
Asano daimyo, 58; Asano Naganori (1665–1701), 126
Ashikaga family and shogunate, 40–42
Ashikari (The Reed Cutter), 33–34
Ashimori domain, 214, 226
association of mendicant monks: Edo (*gannin bōzu nakama*), 159, 166, 171, 207; Osaka (*gannin nakama*), 160, 162–63, 165, 167–68, 169–71, 173–74, 176, 179, 270, *table*, 170

Awa (Awaza) Canal, 68; *map*, 51; *table*, 52
Awaji, domain and province, 57, 64, 263
Azuchi and Azuchi Castle, 12–13, 262–63

bakufu. See shoguns and shogunate
"Ballad of Karigane Bunshichi." See *Karigane Bunshichi utazaimon*
ballads (*utazaimon*), 108, 112, 126, 131, 141–42, 153
bamboo, 8, 36, 248, 255, *table*, 62–63
Ban Nobutomo (1773–1846), 211
bannermen (*hatamoto*), 128, 244–45, 250–51, 257, 267; Nagai Naotsune, 258; Suzuki Gonnosuke, 250; Suzuki Seizaemon, 250
Battle of Yashima, 26, 151–52
"Beginnings of Rangaku, The." See *Rangaku kotohajime*
Benzaiten, 188, 207
Bishamon, 158–59; Bishamon Daihōzen chapel, 163
Bitchū Province, 57, 210, 214, 226
Buddhism and Buddhists, 7–8, 15, 23–24, 105, 121, 124, 158–60, 166–67, 198, 206, 207–8, 216–17, 222, 245
bugashira. See tax commissioners
Buke shohatto, 45
bunraku, 104–7, 120–21, 123–24, 150. See also *jōruri*; theater, puppet
bushi. See samurai
Byōgaku tsūron, 230

canals, 50–53, 65, 268; *map*, 51; *table*, 52. *See also* waterways and water transportation
carpenters, 8, 10, 17, 23, 52, 71, 191, 204
castles and castle towns, 12–15, 22, 48, 82, 107, 127, 131, 181, 213–14, 232, 240, 246, 263–64, 266, 271
chabune. See tea boats
Chihiro-shū (A Collection for a Thousand Years), 116
Chikamatsu Monzaemon (1653–1724), 106, 109, 114, 116, 121, 142
China and Chinese, 5, 17, 28, 39, 65, 184, 199, 219, 223–25, 228, 239

chō. See residential quarters
cholera, 231–37, 238
chōnin, 139–40, 189, 267
Chosakudō isseki-banashi (An Evening's Conversation at a Literary Salon), 150–52
Chōshū domain, 61, 215, 232, 239
Christians and Christianity, 91, 192–93, 208–211, 224, 226; the Christian Incident, 208–210
city elders (*sōdoshiyori*), 53, 87, 90–95, 98–103, 244, 268; Sumiyoshi Sōzaemon, 94; in Edo (*machidoshiyori*), 82
city magistrates (*machi bugyō*)
    Edo, 83, 85, 87, 95–96, 210
    Kyoto, 196, 246, 252, 254
    Osaka, 53, 56, 71, 84–86, 90, 92–103, 137, 160–63, 166–67, 173–75, 208, 244–47, 249–50, 252, 254, 256–57, 259, 267–68, *map*, 258; Kusumi Sukeyoshi (1796–1864), 54–55, 266; Matsuno Sukeyoshi, 132; Nakayama Tokiharu, 132; Takai Yamashiro no Kami, 208–209
    Sakai, 253
clerics 8, 14, 17, 19, 166–67, 176, 183–88, 190, 196, 199, 208. *See also* priests, spiritualists
"A Collection of Bamboo Shoots." See *Takenoko-shū*
"A Collection of Black Bamboo." See *Shichiku-shū*
"Collection of Jōruri Scenes." See *Gidayū danmono-shū*
"A Collection for a Thousand Years." See *Chihiro-shū*
collective violence, 80–81, 202
"Commemorating the First Anniversary of Karigane Bunshichi's Death." See *Karigane Bunshichi no isshūnen-ki*
commissioners, of finance (*kanjō bugyō*), 210, 245; of temples and shrines (*jisha bugyō*), 159–60, 178, 210
constables (*yoriki*), 50, 53, 244, 267
construction trades and workers, 52–53, 129, 129n. 12
copper and refining, 67, 68–71, *table*, 62–63. *See also* Izumiya (Sumitomo) family
cotton and cotton cloth, 39, 59–61, 64, 67–68, 72–73, 266, *table*, 62–63. *See also* textiles
crime and criminals, 125–31, 141, 154–55, 160–61, 224, 246, 268–69; *yakuza*, 129

daikan. See rural intendants
daimyo and daimyo domains (*han*), 12, 14–18, 45, 48–50, 61, 64–67, 80–86, 128, 245–48, 250–52, 254, 256–57, 262, 264–65, 267; Asano, 58; Date, 15, 64; Inari, 180–212; Maeda, 15, 58, 61; warehouses (*kura yashiki*), 61, 64–67, 84–85, 87, 93, 95–96, 198, 267, *map*, 66

Daizōin monastery, 159, 160, 162, 166–67, 169–76, 177, *table*, 170
"dancing supplications" (*odori kanjin*), 164–65, 178
Date daimyo, 15, 64; Date Tsunamune (1640–1711), 144n. 36
Dazai Shundai (1680–1747), 225
debt moratoriums, 11, 41
direct remonstration (*jikiso*), 93, 98–99, 103
diviners, 21, 166–67, 190–94, 197, 204, 210, 212. *See also* spiritualists
Doeff, Henkrik, 226. See also *Haruma wage*
Dōguya Yohei ("Tool-Shop" Yohei, also known as Oyaji no Saburō, or "Old Man Saburō," 1674?–?), 133–38, 139, 156
Dōjima and Dōjima Shinchi, 58, 61, 64, 84, 265, *maps*, 66, 258. *See also* markets
Dōjima River, 53, 58, *maps*, 51, 66
domains (*han*). *See* daimyo and daimyo domains
dōshin. See patrolmen
Dōton Canal and Dōtonbori, 51, 53, 67–69, 72, 77, 114, 123, 137–38, 145, 168–69, 198, 265; *maps*, 47, 51, 66; *table*, 52
Dutch and Dutch language, 213, 215–16, 218, 220, 223, 225, 226–28, 230–31, 233, 235–40; Dutch Studies (Rangaku), 213–16, 218–19, 222, 223–29, 234, 239
dyers, 10, 72, 152

Echigoya (Mitsui) dry goods store, 73
Echizen domain and province, 37, 216, 239
Edo, 19–20, 48, 59–61, 64–65, 68, 72, 80–81, 83, 92, 102, 108, 109, 120–22, 126–31, 142, 145–47, 149, 159, 165–66, 176, 178, 181, 202, 207–8, 214–15, 216, 219, 227–29, 232–33, 235, 240, 244–45, 252, 266, 269, 271, *tables*, 253, 255; Tokyo, 122–23, 214, 218, 224
Edo Canal, 51, 57, 67, 265; *map*, 51; *table*, 52
Edo Castle, 126, 252, 255, *tables*, 253, 255
Edo Haruma. See Haruma wage
egōshū. See self-governance
"The Eight Chapter Volume of Hereditary Secrets." See *Hachijō kadensho*
Eizon (Eison, 1201–90), 8
emperors and empresses, 1–7, 12, 17, 25, 40–41, 44–46, 109, 144, 252, 255, *table*, 253; Genmei (r. 707–15), 6; Fushimi (r. 1287–98), 30; Go-Mizunoo (r. 1611–29), 44–45; Go-Nara (r. 1526–57), 41; Go-Shirakawa (r. 1155–58), 26; Jimmu (legendary), 1; Jitō (r. 686–97), 6; Kōtoku (r. 645–54), 5; Meishō (r. 1629–43), 45; Nintoku (early fifth century), 2, 6; Ōgimachi, (r. 1557–86), 262; Ōjin (late fourth to early fifth century), 6; Shōmu (r. 724–49), 23; Tenmu (r. 672–86), 5; Yūryaku (late fifth century), 184. *See also* Yamato lineage and court

Enchiridion Medicum, 230, 234, 236, 237
Engi shiki (The Procedures of the Engi Period), 184
Enzui, 161–62, 179
eta. *See* outcasts
"Evening's Conversation at a Literary Salon, An." *See Chosakudō isseki-banashi*

farmers and farm families. *See* villages and villagers
fertilizers, 65, 67–68, *table*, 62–63
festivals, 36, 38–39, 87, 183–84, 189, 190–91, 197–98, 202–3; "cholera festivals," 233–34; Fire Festival, 188; Hatsuuma Festival, 188–89; Hollyhock Festival, 37; Sunamochi Festival, 188, 202–203; Tanabata Festival, 184. *See also* urban popular culture and entertainments
fires and firefighting services, 90, 99–102, 129, 129n. 12, 131, 169, 202, 268
fish and fish dealers, 8, 17, 25, 56–57, 65, *table*, 62–63. *See also* markets
"Five Fools Who Fell into Debt." *See Gunin otoko itsutsu Karigane*
"Five Men of Karigane's Gang Strolling in the Licensed Quarter, The." *See Karigane gonin otoko no kuruwa-nai sanpo*
foreign relations and trade, 36, 56, 65–67, 69, 71, 213–16, 233, 239
Forty-Seven Righteous Warriors of Akō, 126, 142, 145, 269
Fox Deity. *See* Inari (Daimyōjin)
Frois, Luis (1532–97), 12–13, 15
fudai daimyō. *See* allied lords
Fujita Kenzō (1781–1829), 209
Fujiwara no Michinaga (966-1028), 26
Fujiwarakyō, 6
Fuku, 31–32, 39
Fukuzawa Yukichi (1834–1901), 216–20, 228
Furuichi District (Kawachi Province), 246, 256
"Fushi ikai no ryaku" (Mr. Fu's Advice to Physicians), 230, 241–42
Fushi keiken ikun (Practical Instructions of Mr. Fu), 230
Fushimi and Fushimi Castle, 17–18, 48, 51–52, 264
Fushimi Inari Grand Shrine (Fushimi Inari Taisha), 180, 189, 192–96, 199

ga (elegant, aristocratic, traditional), 108
gagaku, 107
gatsu gyōji (*tsuki gyōji*). *See* monthly delegates
"Genroku aburemono no ki" (Record of Some Outlaws of the Genroku Era), 132, 134, 136–41, 150, 156–57
Gidayū danmono-shū (Collection of *Jōruri* Scenes), 116

gidayū and *gidayū-bushi*, 106. *See also jōruri*, Takemoto Gidayū
"Gidayū's Best One Hundred." *See Jōruri tōryū kohyakuban*
Goi Ranju (Ranshū, 1697–1762), 217
Gokuin no Sen'emon (1679?–1702), 125, 132, 134–35, 137, 148, 152, 156
Gonin otoko (kabuki play), 145
Gozū Tennō, 192, 206, *table*, 205
"The Great Bamboo Collection." *See Ōtake-shū*
guards, great (*ōban*), 50, 128, 267; regular (*jōban*), 50, 267
Gunin otoko itsutsu Karigane (Five Fools Who Fell into Debt, *sharebon*), 147
guilds (*za*), 34–38, 264. *See also* protective associations

Hachijō kadensho (The Eight-Chapter Volume of Hereditary Secrets), 111–12, 117
Hachiman (the deity), 206, *table*, 205
Halma, François (1653–1722), 225–26. *See also Woordenboek de Nederduitsche en Fransche Taalen*
"Halma Translated." *See Haruma wage*
Hamamatsu Utakuni (1776–1827), 152
han. *See* daimyo and daimyo domains
Harima no Jō. *See* Inoue Harima no Jō
Harima Province, 29, 31, 49, 57, 61, 246, 248, 252
Haruma wage (Halma Translated; editions include *Edo Haruma, Nagasaki Haruma,* and *Zūfu Haruma*), 225–26
Hashimoto Sanae (1834–59), 216, 239
Hashimoto Sōkichi (1763–1836), 227
hatamoto. *See* bannermen
hatamoto yakko, 128, 131, 139, 147
Hazama Shigetomi (1756–1816), 227
Heian and Heiankyō. *See* Kyoto
Heijōkyō. *See* Nara
Heike-bushi, 111, 117
Heike monogatari (The Tale of Heike), 26
henge kanjin, 161, 176
Higashi Nari District (Settsu Province), 56
Higashi Yoko Canal, 17, 53, 57, 67, 68, 92, 257; *maps*, 16, 47, 51; *table*, 52
hinin. *See* outcasts
Hino Katsutami (?–1857), 231
Hino Teisai (1797–1850), 231
Hiranogō, 34, 263
Hirose Kyokusō (1807–63), 271
Hirose Tansō (1782–1856), 219
Hoashi Banri (1778–1852), 216
Hokuriku region, 9, 11, 12, 196–97
Honganji sect and temple, 9–11, 15, 40, 41–42, 211, 261, *map*, 16. *See also* Ishiyama Honganji
Honnōji Incident and the temple Honnōji, 12
Horie Canal, *map*, 51, *table*, 52

Horie Shinchi, 265, *maps*, 66, 258
Horie Sumiyoshi Bridge, 133–34, 140, 156
Hosoda Tanba no Kami, 85–86, 87–88, 92, 95–97
Hosokawa warrior family, 40–42; Harumoto (1514–63), 40–41; Katsumoto (1430–73), 40; Mochihisa, 40; Takakuni (1484–1531), 40
Hote (Hotei) no Ichiemon ("God of Wealth" Ichiemon, 1673–1702), 125, 133–37, 133n. 21, 138–39, 148
Hōzenji temple, 138, 141, 143
Hufeland, Christoph Wilhelm (1762–1836), 230, 234, 236, 237–39
Hyōgo, 29, 31
hyōjōsho. See Supreme Court of Justice

ie, 108–9, 121
iemoto (headmaster) system, 107–9, 120, 122
Ihara Saikaku (1642–93), 113, 114, 117, 124, 139
Ii Naosuke (1815–1860), 233, 239–40
Ikasuri Shrine, 26, *map*, 26
Ikeda (town), 183–85, 188–94, 196, 197
Ikeda Kensai (1841–1918), 240
Ikkō sect. *See* True Pure Land sect
Ikota Shrine, 183–91, 195, 204, 207
Ikutama and Ikutama Shrine, 9, 266
Ima Bridge, 67, *map*, 66
"In Place of Dreams." *See Yume no shiro*
Inamura Senpaku (1757–1827), 225–26
Inari (Daimyōjin), 180–212
Inari Kōhei. *See under* spiritualists
Inland Sea. *See* Seto Inland Sea
Inoue Harima no Jō (1632–85), 109, 113
"Instructions on Nourishing Life." *See Yōjōkun*
Ippen Shōnin eden, 8
Ise Province, 42, 44, 46, 263
Ise Shrine (Grand Shrines of Ise), 39, 186, 196, 207
Ishikawa District (Kawachi Province), 251
Ishiyama Honganji, 9–11, 13, 15, 40–43, 261–62
Isoda Koryūsai (late eighteenth century), 148
Itachi Canal, 51, 201, 265; *map*, 51; *table*, 52
Itō Jinsai (1627–1705), 216, 221–22, 223
Itō Shinzō (1825–1880), 216
Iwashimazu Hachiman Shrine, 32–33, *map*, 35
Izumi Province, 11, 17, 31, 57, 85, 206, 243, 246, 248, *tables*, 205, 253, 255
Izumiya (Sumitomo) family, 69–71; Kichiemon, 84

Jenner, Edward (1749–1823), 231
Jesus Papers (*Yaso no shorui*), 209
Jeweled Market. *See* Sakai
jiin no chadokoro. See teahouses, "temple"

jikiso. See direct remonstration
jinaichō. See temple towns
jingikan. See Office of Shinto Worship
Jippu no Heibei ("True Father" Heibei), 134, 139
jisha bugyō. See commissioners, of temples and shrines
jōdai. See wardens, castle
jōban. See guards, regular
Jōdo Shinshū. *See* True Pure Land sect
Jōdoshū. *See* Pure Land sect
jōruri, 20, 104–13, 114, 116–19, 121, 122–24, 269. *See also* bunraku; theater, puppet
Jōruri Gozen monogatari (The Tale of Princess Jōruri), 105
Jōruri tōryū kohyakuban (Gidayū's Best One Hundred), 119

kabu nakama. See protective associations
kabuki, 105, 107, 109, 120–21, 123, 126, 130–31, 140, 142–43, 145–46, 148, 152, 159, 200, 269
kabukimono, 127–28, 130, 130n. 14
Kaeri Bunshichi utazaimon (ballad), 142
Kaga, domain and province, 42, 58, 61, 64, 96
Kaga no Jō (1635–1711), 109–13, 114, 117–19, 142
Kaguhashi Shrine. *See* shrines, Kashima Inari
kagura, 117, 183, 187, 189
Kaibara Ekken (Ekiken, 1630–1714), 222, 238
Kaifu Canal, *map*, 51, *table*, 52
Kaitai shinsho (A New Text on Human Anatomy), 225
Kaitate no Kichiemon ("Brand-New" Kichiemon, 1676?–1701), 133–37, 140
Kaitokudō, 217–18, 227, 240, 270
kakeya. See warehouses, controllers of
Kamakura and Kamakura shogunate, 28, 31–32, 144, 151–52
Kami Naniwa, 133, 141
Kamigata, 110
Kamigata gundai. See supervisors, of rural intendants
Kaminari Shōkurō ("Thunder" Shōkurō, 1671?–1702), 125, 133–37, 138–39, 143–44, 147–48, 156–57
Kanade Chūshingura (The Treasury of Loyal Retainers), 145
Kanazawa, 14, 127–28
kanjō bugyō. See commissioners, of finance
Kanō (school of painters), 50
Kansai region, 122, 149, 182n. 2
Kantō region, 12, 59, 64–65, 68, 72, 81, 182n. 2, 195–97, 266
Kanzaki (Mikuni) River, 29, 198, *map*, 35
Karakuri Rokubei ("Trickster" Rokubei, 1671?–1702), 133, 135–37, 138–39
Karigane Bunshichi (1674?–1702), 125, 126, 132–57 passim, 269. *See also* Seven's Gang

"Karigane Bunshichi: Dew of Autumn." See *Karigane Bunshichi aki no shimo*
Karigane Bunshichi aki no shimo (Karigane Bunshichi: Dew of Autumn, puppet play), 142–44
Karigane Bunshichi no isshūnen-ki (Commemorating the First Anniversry of Karigane Bunshichi's Death, puppet play), 142–44
Karigane Bunshichi Sennichi gonin otoko (ballad), 140, 142
Karigane Bunshichi utazaimon (Ballad of Karigane Bunshichi), 141–42
"Karigane Five in the Brothel Quarter, The." See *Seirō itsutsu Karigane*
Karigane gonin otoko (puppet play), 142
Karigane gonin otoko no kuruwa-nai sanpo (The Five Men of Karigane's Gang Strolling in the Licensed Quarter, print), 148
"Karigane's Five Gallant Stalwarts." See *Otokodate itsutsu no Karigane*
Kashima Inari Shrine (Kaguhashi Shrine), 195, 198, 202, 204
Kasuga (the deity), 206, *table*, 205
Katano District (Kawachi Province), 258
Katsukawa Shunshō (1726–92), 148
Katsuragawa Hoshū (1751–1809), 224
kawa bugyō, 244
Kawachi Province, 11, 17, 25–26, 30, 135, 186, 192, 206–7, 211, 243–44, 246, 248–49, 251–52, 255–56, 258, *tables*, 170, 205, 253, 255
Kawajiri (Amagasaki), 30, *map*, 35
Kawamura family (priests), 184–88
Kawamura Zuiken (1618–99), 60–61, 267
kawasemai. See mandatory rice purchases
Kawatake Mokuami (1816–93), 145
Kawate Bunjirō (1814–83), 210
Keichū (1640–1701), 270
Kenkaya Goroemon ("Goroemon the Brawler"), 134–36, 138–39
Kennyo Kōsa (1543–92), 10, 261–62
Kii Province, 11, 42, 56, 192, 263
Kinai region, 22, 34, 36, 56, 59, 67, 92, 245–47, 252, 255, 263, 266
Kinchū narabi ni kuge shohatto. See Regulations concerning the Imperial Household and the Aristocracy
kingoku-doiya (purchasing agents). See *under* middlemen
Kinpira Kaminari Shōkurō (The Swashbuckling Kaminari Shōkurō, puppet play), 144, 150
Kishimoto no Bō, 171–75, *table*, 170; Incident of Priest Kishimoto, 173–74
Kishin shirōto jōruri hyōbanki (Amateur Jōruri Critiques), 121–22
Kita Senba, 89, 90, 103
Kitagawa Utamaro (1753–1806), 148
Kitagumi. See Northern Precinct
Kiyokawa (Kiyotake, Kiyotaki, Kogiku), 142, 144, 147–48, 152

Kiyomizu Rihei (fl middle seventeenth century), 109, 114
Kiyotake. See Kiyokawa
Kiyotaki. See Kiyokawa
Kizu River, 28–30, 57, 67, 141, 200, 249, *maps*, 51, 66
Kobori Enshū (1579–1647), 49
Kōfukuji temple, 28–29, 32
Kogiku. See Kiyokawa
Koi goromo Bunshichi zome (1777 kabuki play), 140; 1852 play, 145
Kojiki, 180
Kokugaku (National Studies), 224, 239
Konishi Raizan (1654–1716), 268
Konkōkyō, 210
Konoe aristocratic family, 34; Konoe Motohiro (1648–1722), 118
Kōnoike family, 64–65; Shinroku, 65; Zen'emon, 64–65
Konpira (Daigongen), 164, 174, 176, 195, 207, 210, *table*, 205. See also Kotohira Shrine
Kōrai Bridge, 23, 67, 72–73, *map*, 66
Korea and Koreans, 1–2, 7, 17, 232, 252, 255, *tables*, 253, 255; Kōkuri (Koguryŏ), 3; Kudara (Paekche), 3; Shiragi (Silla), 3
Kōshin no Kanbei ("Three Worms" Kanbei, 1680?–?), 133, 135–37
Kōshin ritual observances, 133, 163–64, 176, 185
Kotake-shū (The Little Bamboo Collection), 113
Kotohira Shrine (Kotohiragū), 164, 174–75, 195, 210. See also Konpira (Daigongen)
kouta, 111
kōwaka-mai, 111, 116–18
Kubo Shunman (1757–1820), 150
Kulmus, Johann Adam (1689–1745), 224
kura yashiki. See daimyo warehouses
Kurainetama no Mikoto. See Uka no Mitama no Mikoto
Kuramadera (the temple Kurama), 158–61, 165, 169, 171, 173, 175, 177, 179
kuramoto. See warehouses, managers of
Kuroda Nagamasa (1568–1623), 49
Kurozumikyō, 193, 209–210
Kusaka Genki (1820–54), 215
Kusaka Genzui (1840–64), 215
Kyō Bridge, 17, 56, 60, *maps*, 16, 47
kyōdōtai. See self-governance
kyōgen, 111, 185
Kyōmachi Canal, 51–52, 57, 265; *map*, 51; *table*, 52
Kyōnyo Kōju (1558–1614), 11, 42
Kyoto (Heian, Heiankyō), 6–7, 12, 15, 18–20, 23–25, 28, 31, 34–37, 38, 40–41, 44–46, 48, 56, 65, 68–69, 96, 98, 109–10, 112, 114, 121–22, 140, 144, 148, 158–59, 167–68, 176, 180, 183–85, 191–96, 209, 222, 231–33, 245, 247, 252, 262, 264, 270, *map*, 35

Kyūshū, 1, 12, 26, 49, 51, 57, 59, 60, 67, 80, 181, 222

lacquer and lacquerware, 38, 61, 65, 72–73, *table*, 62–63
lamp oil, 59, 60–61, 68, 264, 264, *table*, 62–63
Latin, 225, 230
leather and leather goods, 71–72, 266, *table*, 62–63
licensed quarters, 124, 132–34, 139–40, 142–44, 146, 156, 270. *See also* prostitutes and prostitution
lineage groups (*uji*), 1, 4
"Little Bamboo Collection, The." See *Kotakeshū*
lords. *See* daimyo and daimyo domains
"Love Suicides at Sonezaki." See *Sonezaki shinjū*

machi. *See* residential quarters
machi bugyō. *See* city magistrates
machi yakko, 128–31
machidoshiyori. *See* neighborhood elders, Osaka; city elders, Edo
Maeda daimyo, 15, 58, 61
Maki kaesu mikari Soga (kabuki play), 146
Mamuta District (Kawachi Province), 258
mandatory rice purchases (*kawasemai*), 84–84, 87, 88–90, 92–100, 97n. 22, 103
marketing and distribution systems, 59, 65–67, 71, 79, 84, 243, 264; capital marketing sphere, 42
markets, in Osaka, 264–65; fish, 56–57; fruits and vegetables, 56; rice, 58; Three Great Markets, 56–58. *See also* Dōjima and Dōjima Shinchi
Masuya (Iwaki) family and dry goods store, 64, 73; Masuya Heiemon, 64
Matsudaira Sadanobu (1759–1829), 218
Matsudaira Tadaakira (1583–1644), 46–48, 51, 57, 60, 265
Matsumoto Ryōjun, 235, 237
Matsuyasu Shōemon, 86, 87–88, 97n. 22
Maeno Ryōtaku (1723–1803), 224
medicines and medicinal herbs, 61, 65, 195, 266, *table*, 62–63
Meiji Restoration and government, 213, 235, 239
merchant delegates (*yōkiki, yōtashi*), 247–52, 256–59, *map*, 258; Atarashiya Yahei, 250; Haya Ichirōbei, 250; Hinoya Shōsukei, 251; Iwataya Rizaemon, 257–58; Kohashi Chōbei, 257; Yorozuya Ihei, 251
merchants and merchant families, 8, 10–11, 14, 17–20, 22, 33–38, 39–40, 42–43, 45, 51–54, 72–75, 80–86, 87–95, 98–103, 113, 127–29, 139, 144, 146, 164, 167, 174–75, 184–85, 198, 200, 202–3, 213–14, 217, 227, 243–45, 247–49, 253–54, 257, 262–70

metal and metal workers, 8, 39, 73
middlemen, 59–61, 64, 65–67, 70, 72–73, 79; distributors, 59–61, 83; forwarding agents, 59; purchasing agents, 59–61; receiving agents, 59–60; wholesalers, 17, 36–37, 57, 59–60, 83
miko, 183, 190–94, 197, 204, 208–10, 212; "Ōhara maidens," 183. *See also* shamans, spiritualists
Mikuni River. *See* Kanzaki (Mikuni) River
Minami Horie, 133–35
Minamigumi. *See* Southern Precinct
Minamoto no Yorimasa (1104–80), 26
Minamoto no Yorimitsu (948-1021), 26
Minamoto no Yoritomo (1147–99; shogun 1192–99), 151–52
Minamoto no Yoshitsune (1159–89), 26, 105, 151–52, 158
Mippiki Jihei, 133, 136, 138, 157
Makrobiotik (*Macrobioticon, The Art of Prolonging Life*), 237–38
Mitsukuri Shūhei (1825–86), 216, 235
Miura Baien (1723–69), 227
Miyake Sekian (1665–1730), 270
Miyamoto Orie, 191, 194, 197
Mizuno Gunki (?–1825), 193, 209
Mon tsukushi gonin otoko (kabuki play), 145
money changers (*ryōgae*), 64–65, 67, 73, 84
monthly delegates (*gatsu gyōji, tsuki gyōgi*), 90, 93–94
monzen machi, 6, 8
Motoori Norinaga (1730–1801), 211, 270
Mount Kurama, 158–61, 163, 167, 169
mountain ascetics (*yamabushi*), 192, 194
"Mr. Fu's Advice to Physicians." *See* "Fushi ikai no ryaku"
Mutsu Province, 85, 200

Naga Canal, 51–52, 67, 69–70, 73, 265; *map*, 51; *table*, 52
Nagahori Yotsu Bridge, 133–34
Nagasaki, 65, 71, 209, 213, 215, 226–27, 231, 233–35
Nagasaki Haruma. See *Haruma wage*
Nagayo Sensai (1838–1902), 216, 228, 235
Naitō Nobumasa (1586–1626), 48
Naka no Shima, 67, *maps*, 66, 258; Kami Naka no Shima, 89
Naka Ten'yū (1783–1835), 226
nakagai (distributors). *See under* middlemen
Nakagawa Jun'an (1739–86), 224
Nakai Chikuzan (1730–1804), 218
Nakai Riken (1732–1817), 218–19, 227
nakama. *See* protective associations
Nakamura Tokuhei, 192, 194
Namikawa Kansen (1796–1878), 217
Nanba Shinchi, 72, 75, *map*, 66
Naniwa and Naniwakyō, 1–6, 15, 22–26, 34, 40, 54

Naniwa Bay. *See* Osaka Bay
Naniwa meibutsu-Jōruri zasshi (Osaka's Finest: The *Jōruri* Magazine), 122
Naniwa Ōtsu, 22–24
nanushi. See neighborhood elders
Nara (Heijō, Heijōkyō), 6, 22, 28, 31–34, 36–37, 38
national seclusion policy (*sakoku*), 45. *See also* foreign relations and trade
National Studies. *See* Kokugaku
neighborhood elders
 Edo, (*nanushi*), 83
 Osaka (*machidoshiyori*; also glossed as neighborhood chiefs), 53, 87, 89–91, 93–95, 99, 101, 103, 136–37, 139, 244, 267; Enamiya Gohei, 89
nenbutsu prayer formulas, 7–8, 163, 176, 178
Neo-Confucianism, 81–84, 208, 217
"new religions," 193, 209–12. *See also* Konkōkyō; Kurozumikyō; Tenrikyō
"New Text on Human Anatomy, A." *See Kaitai shinsho*
Nihon shoki, 1–2, 7, 180, 206
Nijō Castle, 18, 45, 252, *table*, 253
ningyō jōruri. See jōruri
Ninomiya Sontoku (1787–1856), 222
Ninshō (1217–1303), 8
Nishi Kōzu, 265
Nishi Nari District (Settsu Province), 40, 56, 256
Nishi no Bō, 163–64, 167, 171–72
Nishi Yoko Canal, 67–69, 136, 174, 265; *map*, 51; *table*, 52
Nishikibe District (Kawachi Province), 251
Nishinomiya, 191, 207–208
niuke-doiya (receiving agents). *See under* middlemen
nō. See noh
nobles and nobility. *See* aristocrats and aristocracy
Noda Kakuzaemon, 145, 147–48
noh, 107–8, 110–13, 116–18, 123, 146, 152; Okina, 111; Sanbasō, 111
Northern Precinct (Kitagumi), 53, 86, 89, 91, 92, 94, 98, 100–101
Notification of 1672, The, 162, 165–66, 176, 177–79
nuns. *See* clerics

Ō River, 23, 53, 67–68, 71, 249, *maps*, 16, 47, 66
ōban. See guards, great
Oda Nobunaga (1534–82), 11–12, 42, 261–62
Ogata Kōan (1810–63), 21, 213–42
Ōgetsu Hime no Mikoto. *See* Ukemochi no Kami
Ogyū Sorai (1666–1728), 217, 221, 223, 225
Office of Shinto Worship (*jingikan*), 184, 186, 196

Okudaira Nobumasa (1555–1615), 46
Ōmi Province, 56, 193, 246, 252, 263–64
Ōmu ga soma (Parrot Mountain), 119
Ōmura Masujirō (1824–69), 215
ongoku-doiya (purchasing agents). *See under* middlemen
Ōnin War, 10, 40
Ōoka Echizen no Kami (Tadasuke, 1677–1751), 85–86, 87–88, 92, 95–97
Opium War, 228; the Second Opium War (the "*Arrow* War"), 233, 239
Osaka Bay, 1, 8, 34, 49, 206, *maps*, 4, 35
Osaka Castle, 13–15, 44, 46–54, 243, 245, 248, 252, 254–55, 257, 262–65; *maps*, 16, 47, 51, 66, 258, 266, 268; *tables*, 253, 255; Octopus Stone, 50; Sakura Gate, 50; Sengan Turret, 53
Osaka Metropolitan Prefecture (*Ōsaka-fu*), 38, 204
"Osaka's Finest: The *Jōruri* Magazine." *See Naniwa meibutsu-Jōruri zasshi*
Ōsakaya Kuzaemon, 68–71
Ōshio Heihachirō (1793–1837), 208–209, 227
Ōtake-shū (The Great Bamboo Collection), 113
otokodate, 146–47, 147n. 46, 154
Otokodate itsutsu no Karigane (Karigane's Five Gallant Stalwarts), 145, 150
Ōtori District (Izumi Province), 248–49, 254
"Ōtsu pictures," 149–50
Ōtsuki Gentaku (1759–1827), 224–25, 226–27
outcasts, 8, 19, 71–72, 137; Taikoya Matabei, 71. *See also* village and villagers, Watanabe
outside lords (*tozama daimyō*), 45, 245
Oyaji no Saburō ("Old Man Saburō"). *See* Dōguya Yohei
Ōyamazaki, 32–33, 39, 41, 68, 264, *map*, 35

paper, 8, 36, 61, 67, *table*, 62–63
"Parrot Mountain." *See Ōmu ga soma*
patrolmen (*dōshin*), 50, 53, 267
peasants. *See* villages and villagers
persimmons, 38, 56
petitions and petition movements, 88–92, 94, 100, 102–3, 265
pharmaceuticals. *See* medicines and medicinal herbs
physicians, 17, 222, 224, 225–26, 229–31, 234–35, 237–38, 241–42
pilgrims and pilgrimage, 6–8, 38, 149, 164–65, 167, 173–76, 178, 195–96, 199n. 23, 203, 208; Great Western Circuit (*Saigoku junrei*), 196; Ise pilgrimage of 1830, 186–87
pleasure quarters. *See* licensed quarters
Pompe van Meerdervoot, Johannes Lydius Catherinus (1829–1908), 233–37
police and policing, 11, 50, 53–54, 72, 81, 125–27, 129n. 9, 131–38, 143, 208–9, 246, 269; Hazu Motoemon, 132, 137, 185; Sugiwara Yazaemon, 132, 137

popular culture and entertainments. *See* urban popular culture and entertainments
"Practical Instructions of Mr. Fu." *See Fushi keiken ikun*
priests, 8, 24, 42, 143, 158–76, 190, 192–93, 204, 252, *table*, 253; "dormitory" (*ryō-bōzu*), 169. *See also* clerics
"Procedures of the Engi Period, The." *See Engi shiki*
prostitutes and prostitution, 77, 138, 140, 142–44, 146–48, 192. *See also* licensed quarters; Shinmachi prostitution district
protective associations (*nakama, kabu nakama*), 64–65, 70, 103. *See also* guilds
public health, 215–16, 238–440
Pure Land sect (Jōdoshū), 8, 183

ramie, 37–38, 60, *table*, 62–63
Rangaku. *See* Dutch Studies
Rangaku kotohajime (The Beginnings of Rangaku), 225
rapeseed, 67–68, 264, *table*, 62–63
"Record of Some Outlaws of the Genroku Era." *See* "Genroku aburemono no ki"
"The Reed Cutter." *See Ashikari*
Regulations concerning the Imperial Household and the Aristocracy (*Kinchū narabi ni kuge shohatto*), 45
Regulations concerning Warrior Households (*Buke shohatto*), 45
religious districts (*shūshi kumiai*) and religious elders, 91, 92, 94–95, 98–101
Rennyo Kenju (1415–1499), 9–10, 40
renters (*shakuyanin, tanagarinin*), 138–39, 185, 189
residential quarters (*chō, machi*), 263–68; Andōji-chō, 72, 131; Awaji-machi, 92; Azuchi-machi, 263; Doshō-machi, 65, 94, *map*, 66; Furute-machi, 231; Gokō-machi, 132–35; Hama-machi, 89; Hinaya-machi, 136; Hon-machi, 53, 57, *map*, 66; Junkei-machi, 73, *map*, 66; Kami Uoya-machi, 57; Kita Kyūtarō-machi, 72–73; Kita Shin-machi, 188; Kyūhōji, 65, 134, 136–37, 263; Midōmae-chō, 72–73; Minami Kyūhōji-machi, 72–73; Obama, 132, 134; Owarisaka-chō, 68; Shin Kyōbashi-machi, 173; Shiraga-machi, 185; Tamatsukuri Ise-chō, 72; Tateuri Horihama, 132, 135, 156; Yamato-chō, 68
retailers. *See* merchants and merchant families
rice and rice prices, 8, 36, 58, 61, 64, 80, 81–86, 87, 88–90, 180, 266, *tables*, 62–63, 85. *See also* mandatory rice purchases
rice market. *See* markets
rivers and river transportation. *See* waterways and water transportation
Rokkaku warrior family, 264; Sadayori (1495–1552), 10, 41

rural intendants (rural magistrates, *daikan*), 243–45, 247–51, 253–59, *map*, 258; Ishiko Katsumasa, 253–54; Kuge Tōjūrō, 248–50; supervisor of, 252; Toshima Gonnojō, 256; Toshima Jūzaemon, 256
ryōgae. See money changers
Ryūkyū Islands, 252, *table*, 253

Saigō Takamori (1827–77), 215
Saikaku. *See* Ihara Saikaku
Sakai, 17, 33–34, 36, 38–40, 42, 65, 122, 261–62, 264; Jeweled Market, 38
saké and saké brewers, 8, 38–39, 59–60, 65, 71–73, 184, 188–89, 191–92, 266, *table*, 62–63; Inatsuka family, 188
sakoku. *See* national seclusion policy
salt, 8, 38, 59, 61, *table*, 62–63
samurai, 15–18, 45, 46–54, 57, 75, 81–84, 109–110, 113, 127–29, 139, 145–48, 181, 218, 228, 244, 247, 262, 267, 269
sankin kōtai. See alternate attendance and residence system
Sarashina nikki (As I Crossed a Bridge of Dreams), 24
Satsuma Canal, 51; *map*, 52; *table*, 52
Seirō itsutsu Karigane (The Karigane Five in the Brothel Quarter, *sharebon*), 147, 147n. 46
self-governance, 31–33, 39–43, 267; *egōshū*, 39; *kyōdōtai*, 37, 182
Sen no Rikyū (1522–91), 14
Senba, 17, 52, 67, 264, 265, 268, *maps*, 16, 47, 51, 66, 258
Sendai domain and castle town, 64, 127, 144n. 36
Sennichi Mae, 46, 75–77, 134, 137, 143, 152–53, *maps*, 47, 66
Seto Inland Sea, 8, 28, 38–39, 40, 56, 57, 60
Setsuyō kikan (The Wonders of Settsu Province), 152, 199, 204
Settsu meisho zue, 197
Settsu Province, 11, 17, 25–26, 29, 33, 36, 65, 135, 157, 183–84, 186, 191, 197, 206–7, 211, 243–44, 246, 248–49, 252, 254–56, 258, 264, *tables*, 205, 253, 255
Seven's Gang, 131–41, 147, 153–55, 269. *See also* Karigane Bunshichi
shakuyanin. See renters
shamans, 21, 190–94, 195, 197, 204, 208–10, 212, 270; Araki Naka (Sagami), 191, 194; Araki Sakura (Tonoe), 191; Kinu, 208; Sano, 208–209. *See also miko*, Toyoda Mitsugi, spiritualists
shamisen, 105–7, 109, 118, 120–21, 123
sharebon fiction, 146–47
Shibata Katsue (1522?–83), 264
Shichiku-shū (A Collection of Black Bamboo), 111, 119
Shikoku, 12, 57, 67, 164, 174, 186
Shima no Uchi, 67, 73, *maps*, 66, 258

Shima Shimo District (Settsu Province), 56
Shimokōbe Nagaru (Chōryū, 1627–86), 270
Shingon sect, 165, 167–68, 173, 178, 194, 198
Shinmachi prostitution district, 77, 139–40, 142–44
Shirakawa aristocratic family, 183, 194–97, 211
Shitennō (Four Heavenly Kings) and the temple Shitennōji, 6–9, 15, 17, 23, 36, 38, 72, 113, 151–52, *maps*, 16, 27, 35, 47
shōen, 24–29, 36, 38
shoguns and shogunates (*bakufu*). See *specific shoguns and shogunates*
Shōnyo Kōkyō (1516–1654), 10, 41
Shōtoku Taishi (574–622), 7, 113
shrines, 30, 38, 46, 111, 121, 173, 178, 181–88, 193, 196–97, 204, 205–7, 212, 233, 245, 262–63, *table*, 205; Asakayama, 199; Gionsha (Yasaka Shrine), 192; Hirota, 191; Kasa Inari, 198; Kasuga, 31–32; Kureha, 183–88, 197; Mitsuana Inari, 199; Morikawa Inari, 208; Sadakichi Inari, 208; Tamatsukuri (Toyotsu) Inari, 198, 202; Tsumagoi Inari, 195; Uho Inari, 186, 188. See also *specific shrines, ujigamisha*
Shugendō. See Way of Mountain Asceticism, The
Shunjō Chōgen, Abbot (1121–1206), 28–29, 32
shūshi kumiai. See religious districts (shūshi kumiai) and religious elders
Six-Six Incident, 136–38, 141, 144, 152–53
smallpox, 215, 230–31, 240
sōdoshiyori. See city elders
Soga brothers (Soga no Gorō Tokimune, Soga no Jūrō Sukenari), 145–46
Sonezaki (Shijimi) River, *map*, 51
Sonezaki Shinchi, 77, 265, *maps*, 66, 258
Sonezaki shinjū (Love Suicides at Sonezaki), 114, 142
Southern Precinct (Minamigumi), 53, 86, 91, 98, 100–101
soy sauce, 59, 72, 266, *table*, 62–63
spiritualists, 183, 194–97, 204, 212; Inari (Kōdaya) Kōhei, 191. See also diviners, *miko*, shamans
straw matting, 8, 36
street performers, 161, 164–65, 176. See also urban popular culture and entertainments
sugar, 61, 67, 169, *tables*, 62–63, 170
Sugi Kōji (1828–1917), 216
Sugita Genpaku (1733–1817), 224–25, 226
Sukeroku: Edo no hana (Sukeroku: Flower of Edo), 146
Sumitomo family. See Izumiya (Sumitomo) family
Sumiyoshi (the deity), 206, *table*, 205
Sumiyoshi Shrine, 6–8, 38, 154, 178, 261–62, *map*, 35

supervisors, of riparian matters (*tsutsumi bugyō*), 244, 246–47, 259; of rural intendants (*Kamigata gundai*), 252
Supreme Court of Justice (*hyōjōsho*), 208
"Swashbuckling Kaminari Shōkurō, The." See *Kinpira Kaminari Shōkurō*

Taika Reforms, 3–6
Takasago, 118
Takatsu Palace (Takatsu no Miya), 2
Takeda Izumo II (1691–1765), 145, 147
Takemoto Gidayū (1651–1714), and the Takemoto Theater, 105–6, 109, 113–22, 120, 123–24, 145, 269
Takemoto Masatayū (Harima no Shōjō, 1691–1744), 120
Takenoko-shū (A Collection of Bamboo Shoots), 111
Takizawa Bakin (1767–1848), 150–52
"The Tale of Heike." See *Heike monogatari*
"The Tale of Princess Jōruri." See *Jōruri Gozen monogatari*
Tamatsukuri, 15, 52; granary, 86
tanagarinin. See renters
Tanba Province, 152, 246, 252
Tanhoku District (Kawachi Province), 211
tatami-mat facing, 61, *table*, 62–63
tax commissioners (*bugashira*), 251–57, 259; Edoya Gen'emon, 256; Naraya Chōzaemon, 253–54
taxes and taxation, 11, 45, 80, 81–84, 87, 100–102, 129, 139, 202, 247–59, *tables*, 253, 255, 262, 264–65, 267
tea, 59, 266, *table*, 62–63
tea boats (*chabune*), 56
tea ceremony, 107
teahouses, 138, "temple teahouses" (*jiin no chadokoro*), 167–68
Tekijuku (Tekitekisaijuku), 21, 214–16, 219, 227–28, 230, 239–40, 270
temple towns (*jinaichō*), 11, 43, 264
temples and temple districts (*teramachi*), 15, 23–28, 30, 38, 46–48, 68, 121, 158–60, 164, 173, 178, 182, 185, 196, 198, 204, 206, 245, 262–63, 266, *map*, 16; Kannondō, 184–85; Kohanji, 167; Kōzu Shōhōji, 152; Senryūji temple, 92. See also *specific temples*
ten religious elders (*jūnin toshiyori*). See religious districts and religious elders
Tendai sect, 165, 167, 173, 178, 194, 198
Tenjin Bridge, 71–73, *maps*, 47, 66
Tenma (the deity), 206, *table*, 205
Tenma and Tenma Precinct (Tenmagumi), 68, 72, 86, 91, 99–101, *maps*, 51, 66, 258
Tenma Bridge, 53, 56, 71, *map*, 47
Tenma Canal, *maps*, 16, 47, 51, *table*, 52
Tenmagumi. See Tenma and Tenma Precinct
Tennōji, 8–9, 33–38, 39, 40, 113, 261–62, *map*, 35

Tenrikyō, 193, 209–210
Teshima District (Settsu Province), 56, 183–84, 191, 197, 206, table, 205
textiles, 8, 36–37, 59–61, 64, 73, 140, table, 62–63. See also cotton and cotton cloth
theater, 104–9, 113–22, 124, 126, 213, 269; Kado, 123; Morita, 146; puppet, 104–9, 124, 142–46, 150, 152, 159, 200, 269. See also bunraku, jōruri, Takemoto Gidayū; Nakamura, 145; National, 105, 123; Okamoto, 142. See also bunraku, jōruri, kabuki
tobacco and tobacconists, 61, 133, 141, table, 62–63
Tōdaiji, 23–29, 31
Tōdō Takatora (1556–1630), 44, 48–49
Tōhoku region, 80, 196–97
toiya (purchasing agents and wholesalers). See under middlemen
Tōkaidō Highway, 96, 149, 252
Tokugawa family and shogunate, 17–18, 22, 44–46, 50, 69–71, 75, 80–86, 87, 91, 92, 96, 99, 97, 110, 131, 159–60, 200, 207–9, 213, 218, 224, 227, 239–40, 243–48, 251, 252–57, 262–63, 267, 271, tables, 253, 255; Hidetada (1579–1632, shogun 1605–23), 44–45, 48, 265; Iemitsu (1604–51, shogun 1623–51), 45–46, 262, 265, 267, table, 253; Ieyasu (1543–1616, shogun 1603–1605), 17–18, 42–43, 44–46, 252, 265; Kazuko (1607–78), 45. (See also emperors and empresses, Meishō); Sen Hime (1597–1666), 18; Tsunayoshi (1646–1709, shogun 1680–1709), 129; Yoshimune (1684–1751; shogun 1716–45), 82
Tokyo. See Edo
toll stations (*sekisho*), 30–33
Tominaga Nakamoto (1715–46), 270
Tonbi Kan'emon ("Construction Worker" Kan'emon, 1678?–1702), 133, 135–37, 139, 156
Tondabayashi, 192, 194, 197, 251, 264
Tosa, domain and province, 61, 67
Tosabori River, 58, 67, 198, map, 51
Toyoda Mitsugi, 192–95, 204, 208–10
Toyotake Wakatayū (Echizen no Shōjō, 1681–1764) and the Toyotake Theater, 120
Toyotake Yamashiro no Shōjō (1878–1967), 123
Toyotomi Hideyori (1593–1615), 17–18, 44
Toyotomi Hideyoshi (1537–98), 12–17, 42–43, 262–66
Toyotsu Inari Shrine. See shrines, Tamatsukuri Inari
Toyouke Ōkami, 180, 206–207, table, 205
Toyozawa Danpei (1827–98), 123
tozama daimyō. See outside lords
"The Treasury of Loyal Retainers." See *Kanadehon Chūshingura*

True Pure Land sect (Jōdo Shinshū), 9–11, 40, 198, 261; Ikkō sect, 9, 11, 46, 189
Tsuboi Shindō (1795–1848), 227
Tsuchimikado aristocratic family, 167, 191, 194
Tsumagoi Inari Shrine, 195
Tsuruya Nanboku (1755–1829), 145
Tsuruzawa Dōhachi (1874–1951), 123n. 24
Tsutsui Junkei (1549–84), 15. See also residential quarters, Junkei-machi
tsutsumi bugyō. See supervisors of riparian matters

Udagawa Shinsai (1769–1834), 227, 229
Ueda Akinari (1734–1809), 270
Uemachi Plateau, 5–6, 9, 22, 25, 43, 48–49, 51, 201, 261–63, maps, 4, 16
Uemura Bunrakuken (1737–1810), 106. See also bunraku; jōruri; theater, puppet
Uhara District (Settsu Province), 211
Uji (city and river), 39, 247, 248, map, 35
Uji Kaga no Jō. See Kaga no Jō
ujigamisha, 181–83, 182n. 2, 188, 198, 204, 212
Uka no Mitama no Mikoto (Kurainetama no Mikoto), 180, 206, table, 205
Ukemochi no Kami (Ōgetsu Hime no Mikoto), 180, 206, table, 205
ukiyo-e. See wood-block prints
umbrellas and umbrella makers, 61, 72–73, 210, table, 62–63
Unagidani, 69, map, 66
urban popular culture and entertainments, 75–79, 107–8, 109, 122, 124, 125–27, 130, 142–50, 152, 159–62, 164–65, 176, 199–200, 207, 270. See also festivals
Utagawa Kunimasa (1773–1810), 148
utazaimon. See ballads
uwani boats, 56

villages and villagers (farmers and farm families), 41, 64–65, 68, 81–84, 85, 97n. 22, 180, 183, 186, 191–92, 196–97, 199, 201–2, 204, 208, 211, 244–56, 264–65; Fukae, 33, 36; Hama, 46, map, 47; Jūhachijō, 256; Komagatani, 246, 256; Jūsō, 202; Kōzu, 46, map, 47; Kyūhōji, 263; Miyake, 211; Noda, 46, map, 47; Obase, 46, 199, map, 47; Ozone, 197; Shindō, 192, 197; Shinke, 25; Tenma, 46, map, 47; Tobita, 46, 72, map, 47; Umeda, 46, map, 47; Watanabe, 71–72 (see also outcasts); Yoshihara, 46, map, 47
waka, 7, 107–8, 116
Wakae District (Kawachi Province), 258
wardens, castle (*jōdai*), 48, 50, 53–54, 129n. 9, 267; river (*kawa bugyō*), 244
warehouses, controllers of (*kakeya*), 64–65; managers of (*kuramoto*), 64

warriors. *See* samurai
Watanabe Masaka (1776–1840), 211
Watanabe Port (*Watanabe no tsu*), 6–7, 25–33, 40–42, *maps*, 27, 35
Watanabe warrior family, 6, 26–28, 261; Watanabe no Tsuna, 26
waterways and water transportation, 6, 50–53, 56–57, 60–61, 65–67, 268. See also *specific rivers*
Way of Mountain Asceticism, The (Shugendō), 173–75, 183, 192; Honzan and Tōzan factions, 194
West and Westerners, 122, 215, 233, 240; Western medicine and sciences, 209, 215, 216, 222, 227–28, 231–40
wholesalers. *See under* middlemen
"Wonders of Settsu Province, The." See *Setsuyō kikan*
wood and woodworkers, 8, 10, 36
wood-block prints (*ukiyo-e*), 126–27, 131, 147–48
Woordenboek de Nederduitsche en Fransche Taalen, 225–26. See also *Haruma wage*

yamabushi. *See* mountain ascetics
Yamagata Bantō (1748–1821), 217, 227
Yamanoi aristocratic family, 195
Yamashina, 9, 41, *map*, 35
Yamashiro Province, 26, 199, 206, 249, 255, 264
Yamato lineage and court, 1–7

Yamato Province, 29, 36, 186, 192, 198, 255
Yamato River, 48, 56, 60, 67, 199, 204, 261, *maps*, 16, 27, 47, 51, 66
Yamatoya Zenbei (?–1860), 231
yamori, 139
Yaso no shorui. *See* Jesus Papers
Yasui (Nariyasu) Dōton, 51, 263
Yasui Kuhei, 51
Yodo River, 1, 5–7, 9–10, 17, 40, 48, 56, 60, 67, 141, 208, 249, 261, 263–64, 266, *maps*, 4, 16, 27, 35, 47, 51, 66
Yodoya Bridge, 58, *map*, 66
Yodoya merchant family 58, 61, 64–65; Koan, 56, 58; Saburōemon (Hiromasa), 58
Yōjōkun (Instructions on Nourishing Life), 238
yōkiki. *See* merchant delegates
yoriki. *See* constables
Yoshida aristocratic family, 183, 194–96
Yoshida Kanemi (1535–1610), 15
yōtashi. *See* merchant delegates
Yume no shiro (In Place of Dreams), 217

za. *See* guilds
Zakoba-chō (Sagishima), 57. See also markets
Zeami (Seami, Kanze Motokiyo; 1363–1443), 33
zoku (vulgar, common, contemporary), 108
Zūfu Haruma. *See* Henkrik Doeff, *Haruma wage*